4

IKIGAMI

ATE LIMIT

STORY & ART BY MOTORO MASE

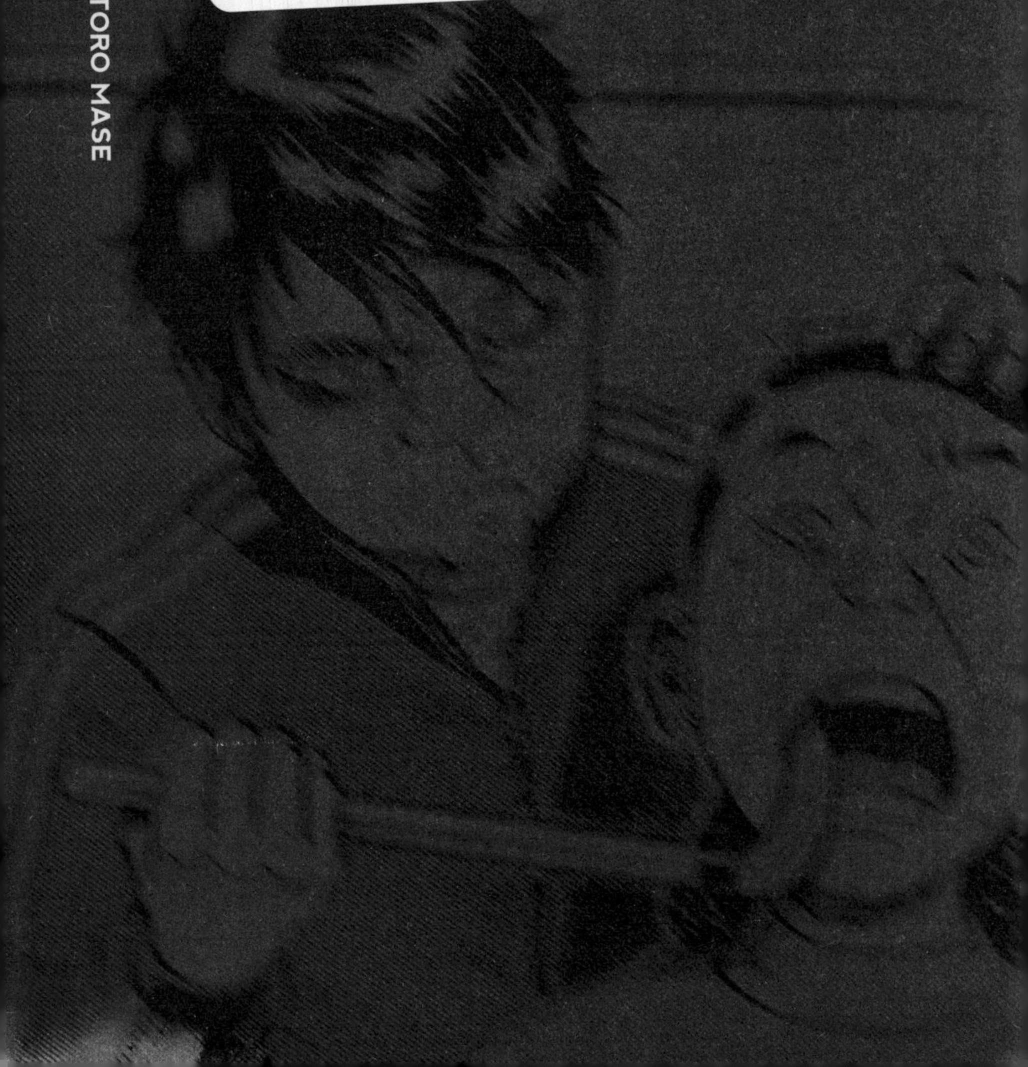

IKIGAMI: THE ULTIMATE LIMIT
Volume 4
VIZ Signature Edition

Story and Art by Motoro MASE

© 2005 Motoro MASE/Shogakukan
All rights reserved.
Original Japanese edition "IKIGAMI"
published by SHOGAKUKAN Inc.

Translation/John Werry
English Adaptation/Kristina Blachere
Touch-up Art & Lettering/Freeman Wong
Design/Amy Martin
Editor/Rich Amtower

VP, Production/Alvin Lu
VP, Sales & Product Marketing/Gonzalo Ferreyra
VP, Creative/Linda Espinosa
Publisher/Hyoe Narita

Printed in the U.S.A.

Published by VIZ Media, LLC
P.O. Box 77010
San Francisco, CA 94107

10 9 8 7 6 5 4 3 2 1
First printing, February 2010

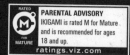

PARENTAL ADVISORY
IKIGAMI is rated M for Mature
and is recommended for ages
18 and up.
ratings.viz.com

VIZ
MEDIA
www.viz.com

VIZ SIGNATURE
www.vizsignature.com

IKIGAMI

THE ULTIMATE LIMIT

VOL. 4 STORY & ART BY MOTORO MASE

THE ULTIMATE LIMIT

CONTENTS

Episode 7 The Last Lesson Act 1

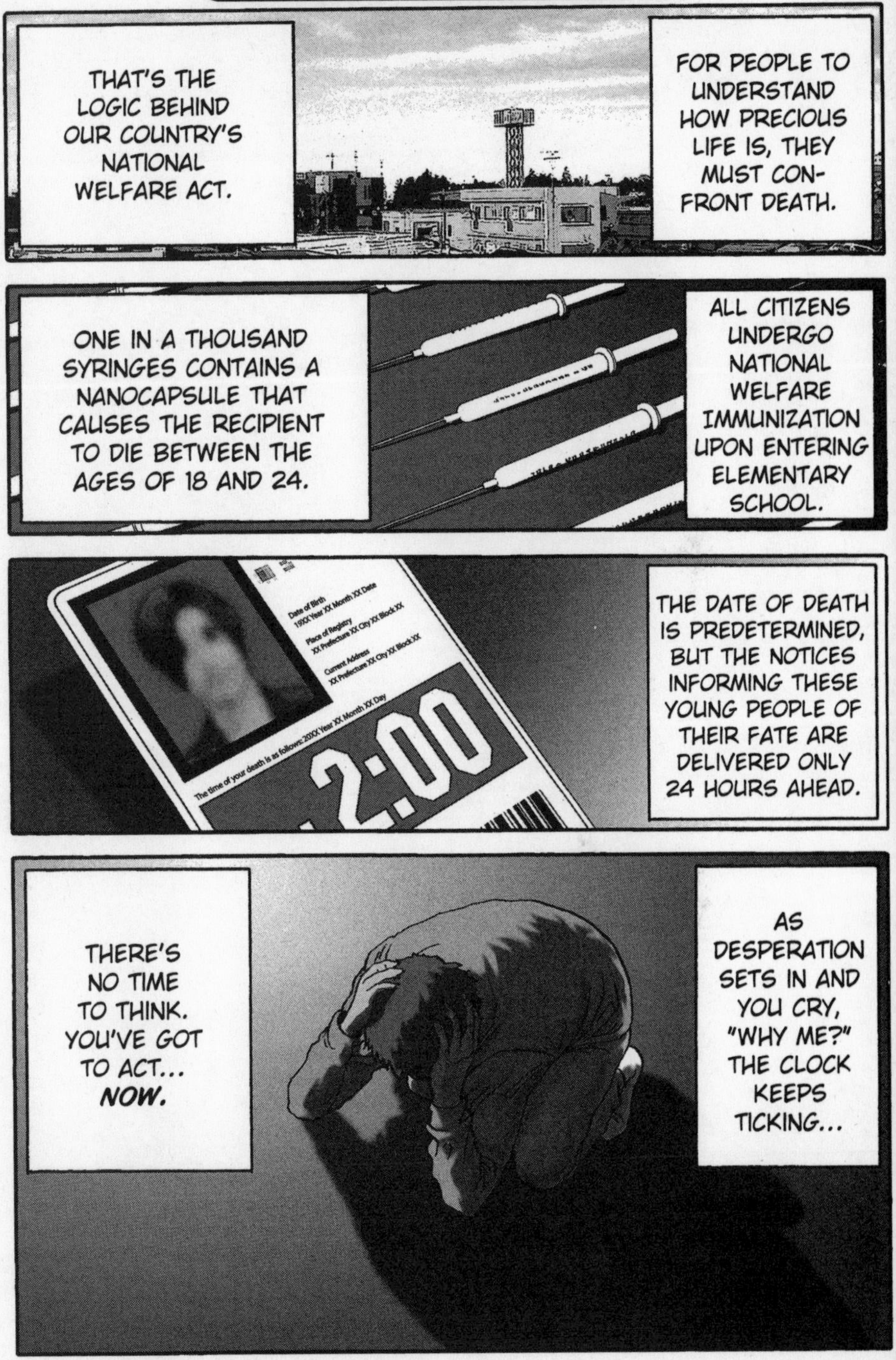

FOR PEOPLE TO UNDERSTAND HOW PRECIOUS LIFE IS, THEY MUST CONFRONT DEATH.
THAT'S THE LOGIC BEHIND OUR COUNTRY'S NATIONAL WELFARE ACT.
ALL CITIZENS UNDERGO NATIONAL WELFARE IMMUNIZATION UPON ENTERING ELEMENTARY SCHOOL.
ONE IN A THOUSAND SYRINGES CONTAINS A NANOCAPSULE THAT CAUSES THE RECIPIENT TO DIE BETWEEN THE AGES OF 18 AND 24.
THE DATE OF DEATH IS PREDETERMINED, BUT THE NOTICES INFORMING THESE YOUNG PEOPLE OF THEIR FATE ARE DELIVERED ONLY 24 HOURS AHEAD.
Date of Birth
19XX Year XX Month XX Date
Place of Registry
XX Prefecture XX City XX Block XX
Current Address
XX Prefecture XX City XX Block XX
The time of your death is as follows: 20XX Year XX Month XX Day
12:00
AS DESPERATION SETS IN AND YOU CRY, "WHY ME?" THE CLOCK KEEPS TICKING...
THERE'S NO TIME TO THINK. YOU'VE GOT TO ACT... *NOW.*

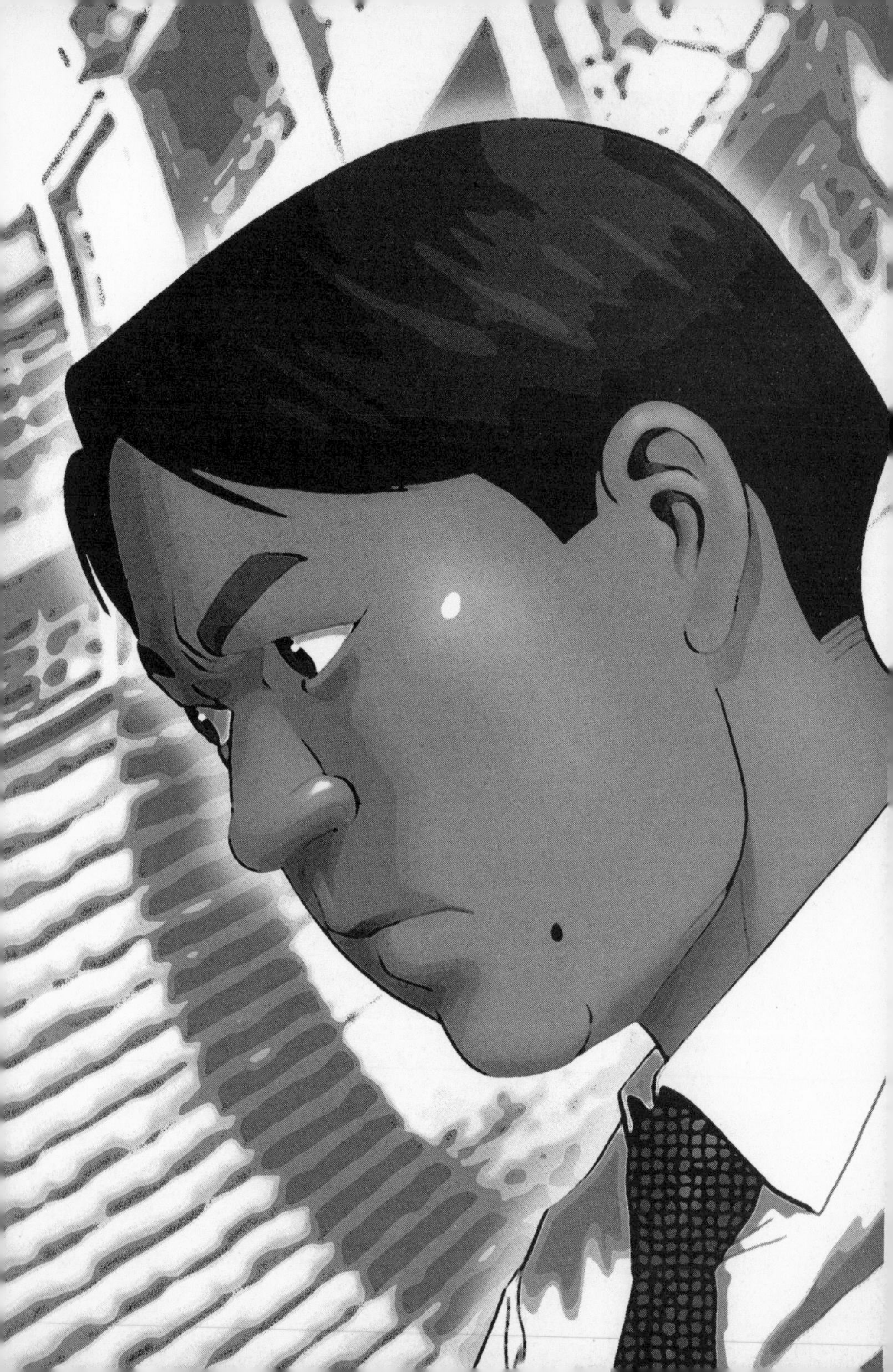

Episode 7 The Last Lesson Act1

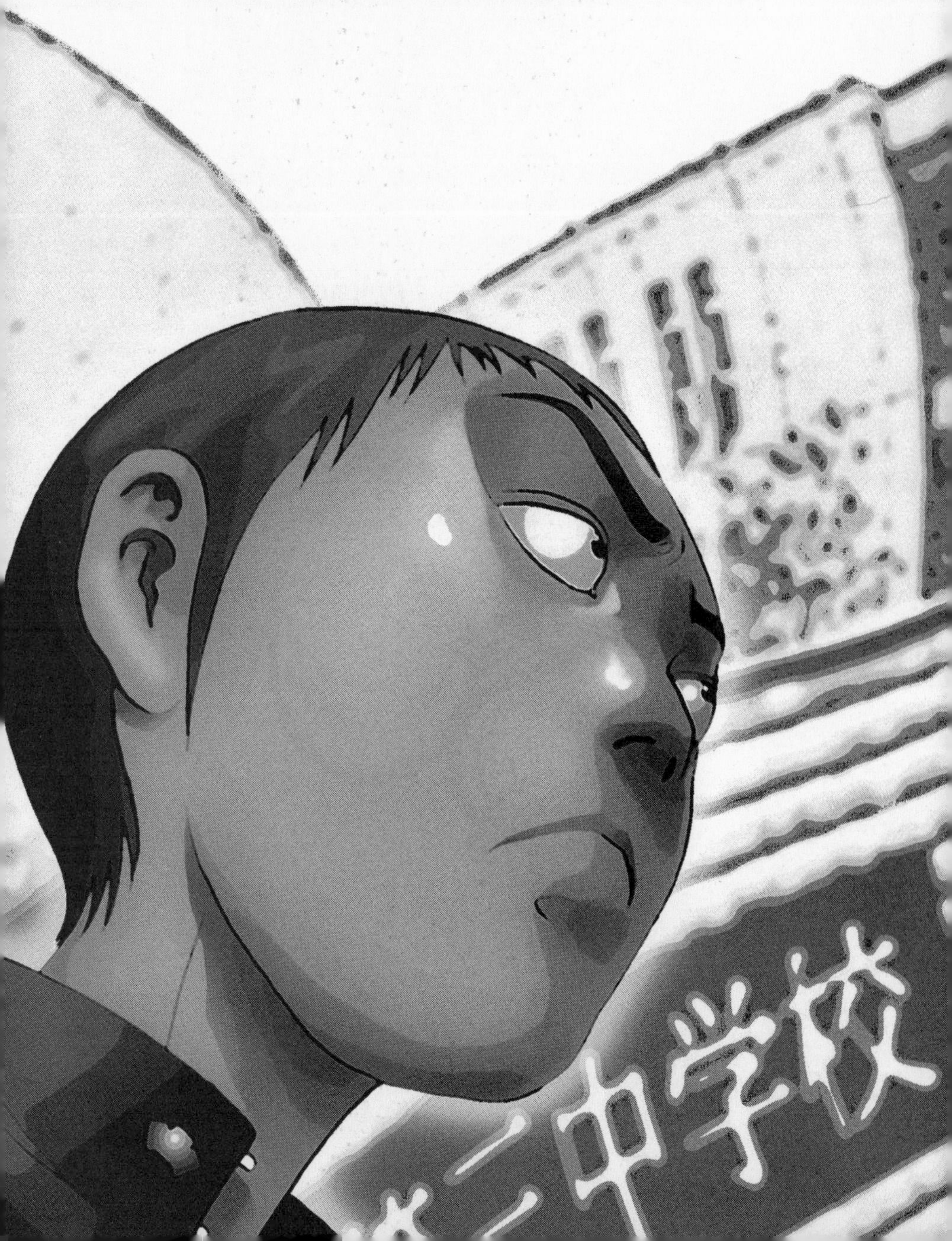
中学校

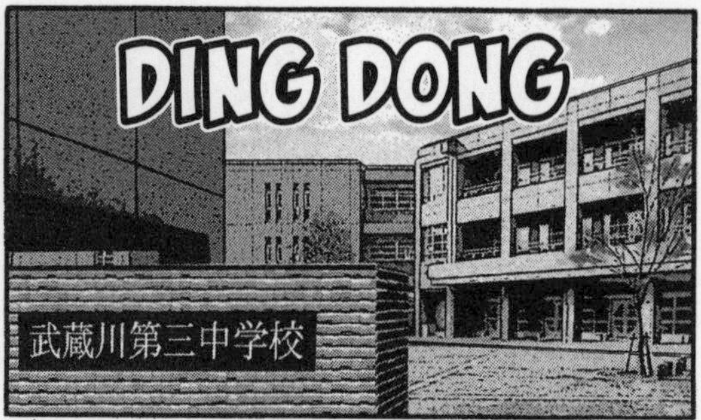
DING DONG
武蔵川第三中学校

*Musashigawa Third Junior High School

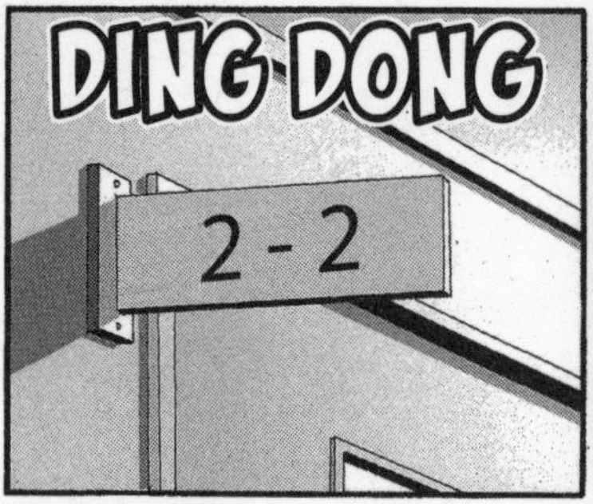
DING DONG
2-2

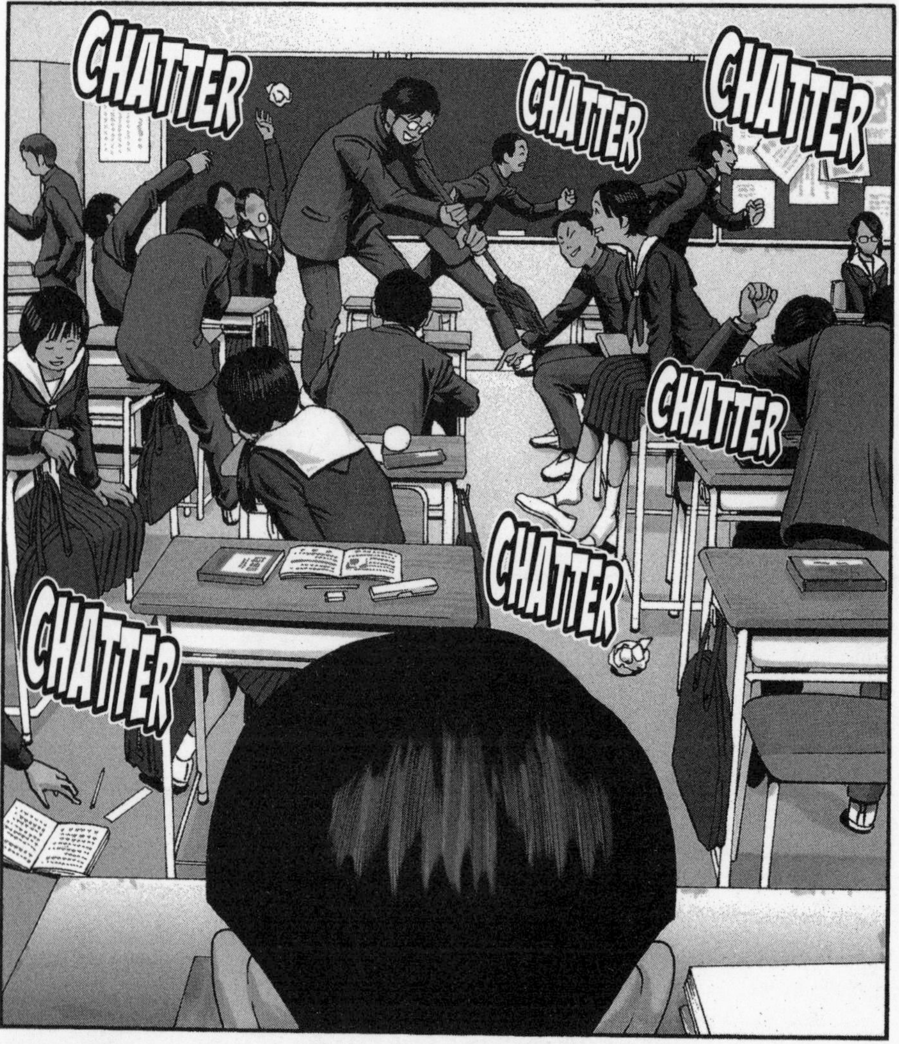
CHATTER
CHATTER
CHATTER
CHATTER
CHATTER
CHATTER

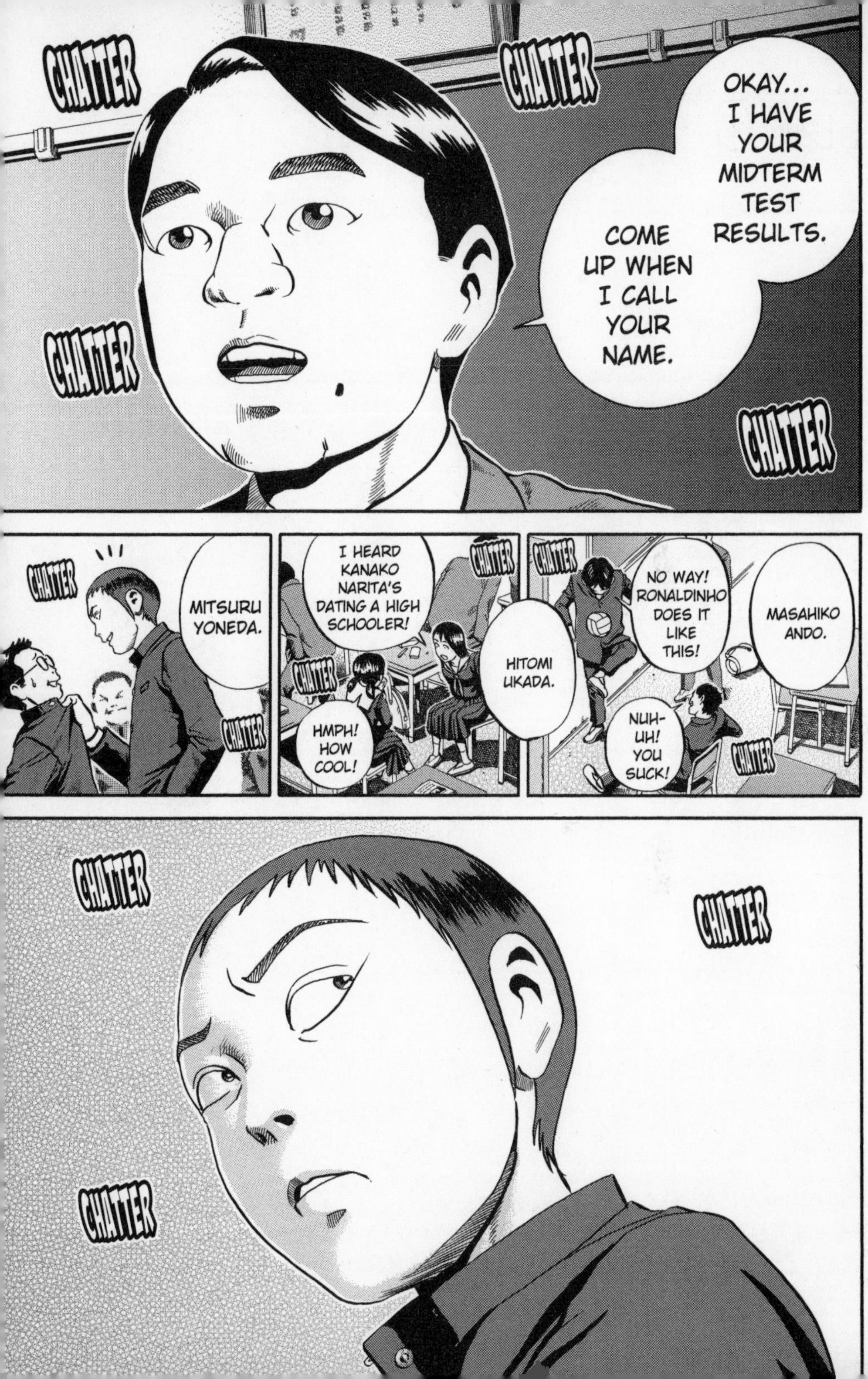
CHATTER
CHATTER
OKAY... I HAVE YOUR MIDTERM TEST RESULTS.
COME UP WHEN I CALL YOUR NAME.
CHATTER
CHATTER
MASAHIKO ANDO.
CHATTER
NO WAY! RONALDINHO DOES IT LIKE THIS!
NUH-UH! YOU SUCK!
CHATTER
CHATTER
I HEARD KANAKO NARITA'S DATING A HIGH SCHOOLER!
HITOMI UKADA.
CHATTER
HMPH! HOW COOL!
MITSURU YONEDA.
CHATTER
CHATTER
CHATTER
CHATTER
CHATTER

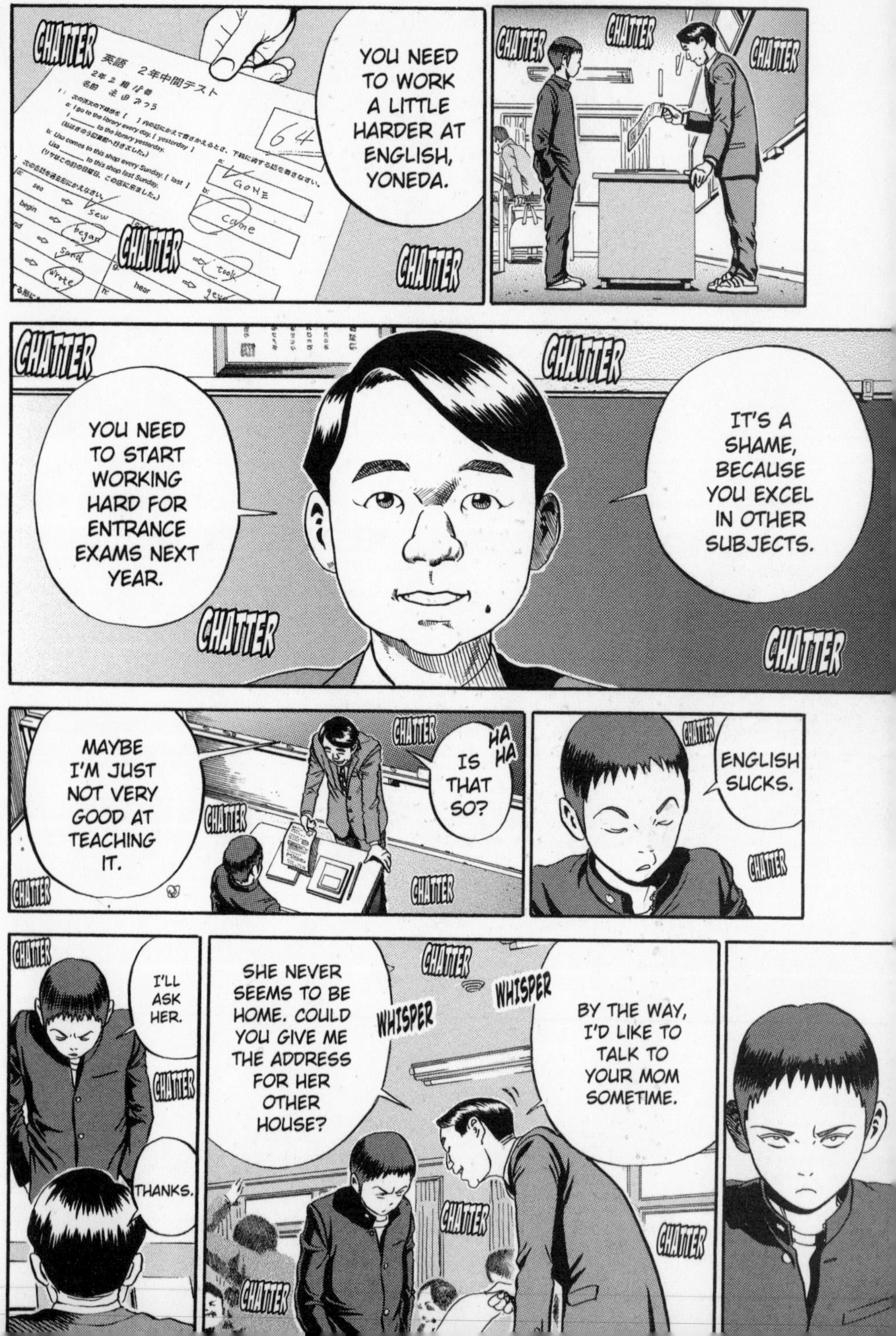

CHATTER
CHATTER
CHATTER
CHATTER
YOU NEED TO WORK A LITTLE HARDER AT ENGLISH, YONEDA.
CHATTER
CHATTER
CHATTER
IT'S A SHAME, BECAUSE YOU EXCEL IN OTHER SUBJECTS.
YOU NEED TO START WORKING HARD FOR ENTRANCE EXAMS NEXT YEAR.
CHATTER
CHATTER
CHATTER
ENGLISH SUCKS.
CHATTER
CHATTER
HA HA
IS THAT SO?
CHATTER
MAYBE I'M JUST NOT VERY GOOD AT TEACHING IT.
CHATTER
CHATTER
BY THE WAY, I'D LIKE TO TALK TO YOUR MOM SOMETIME.
CHATTER
WHISPER
CHATTER
WHISPER
SHE NEVER SEEMS TO BE HOME. COULD YOU GIVE ME THE ADDRESS FOR HER OTHER HOUSE?
CHATTER
CHATTER
CHATTER
I'LL ASK HER.
CHATTER
THANKS.

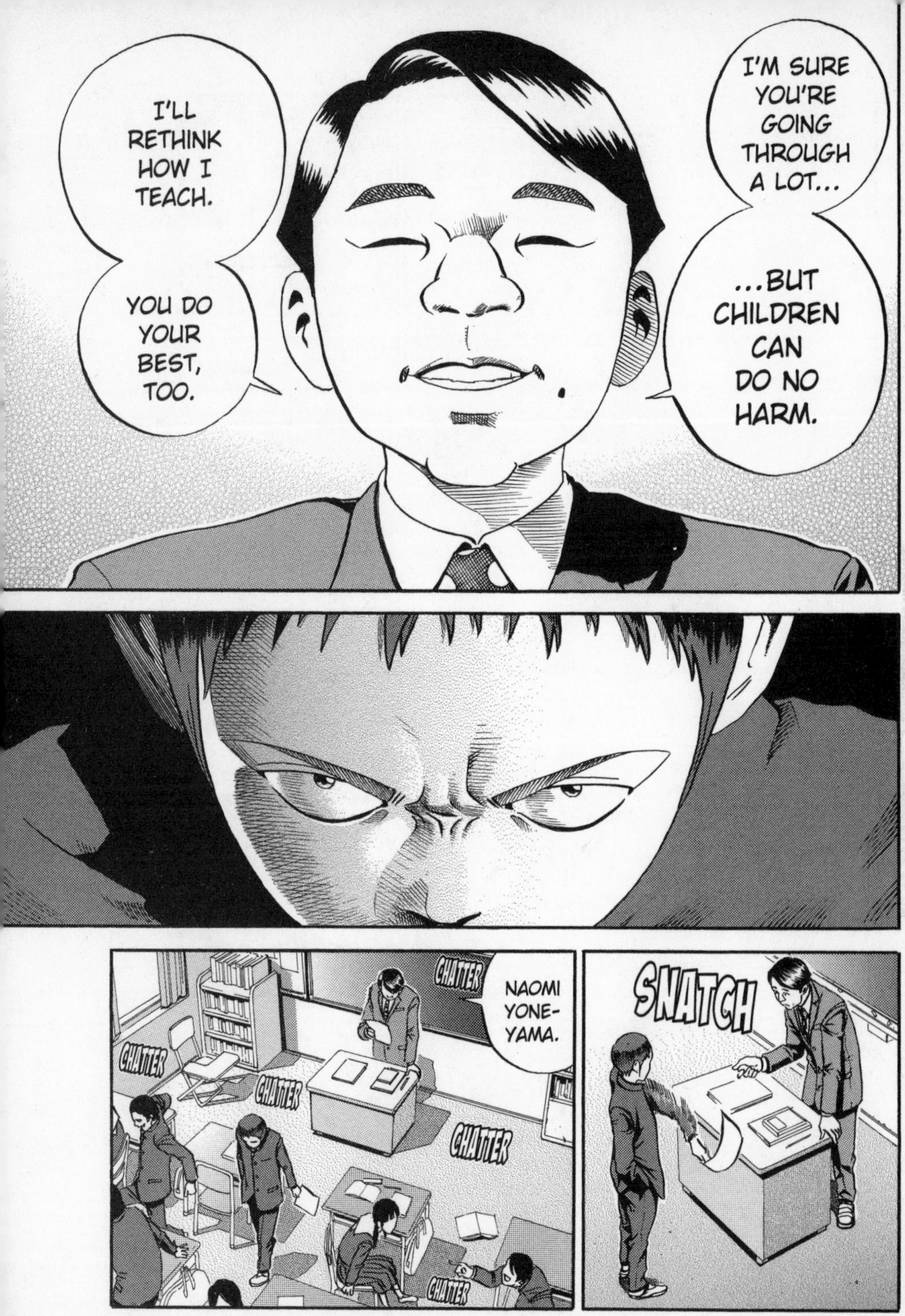
I'M SURE YOU'RE GOING THROUGH A LOT...
...BUT CHILDREN CAN DO NO HARM.
I'LL RETHINK HOW I TEACH.
YOU DO YOUR BEST, TOO.
SNATCH
NAOMI YONE-YAMA.
CHATTER
CHATTER
CHATTER
CHATTER
CHATTER

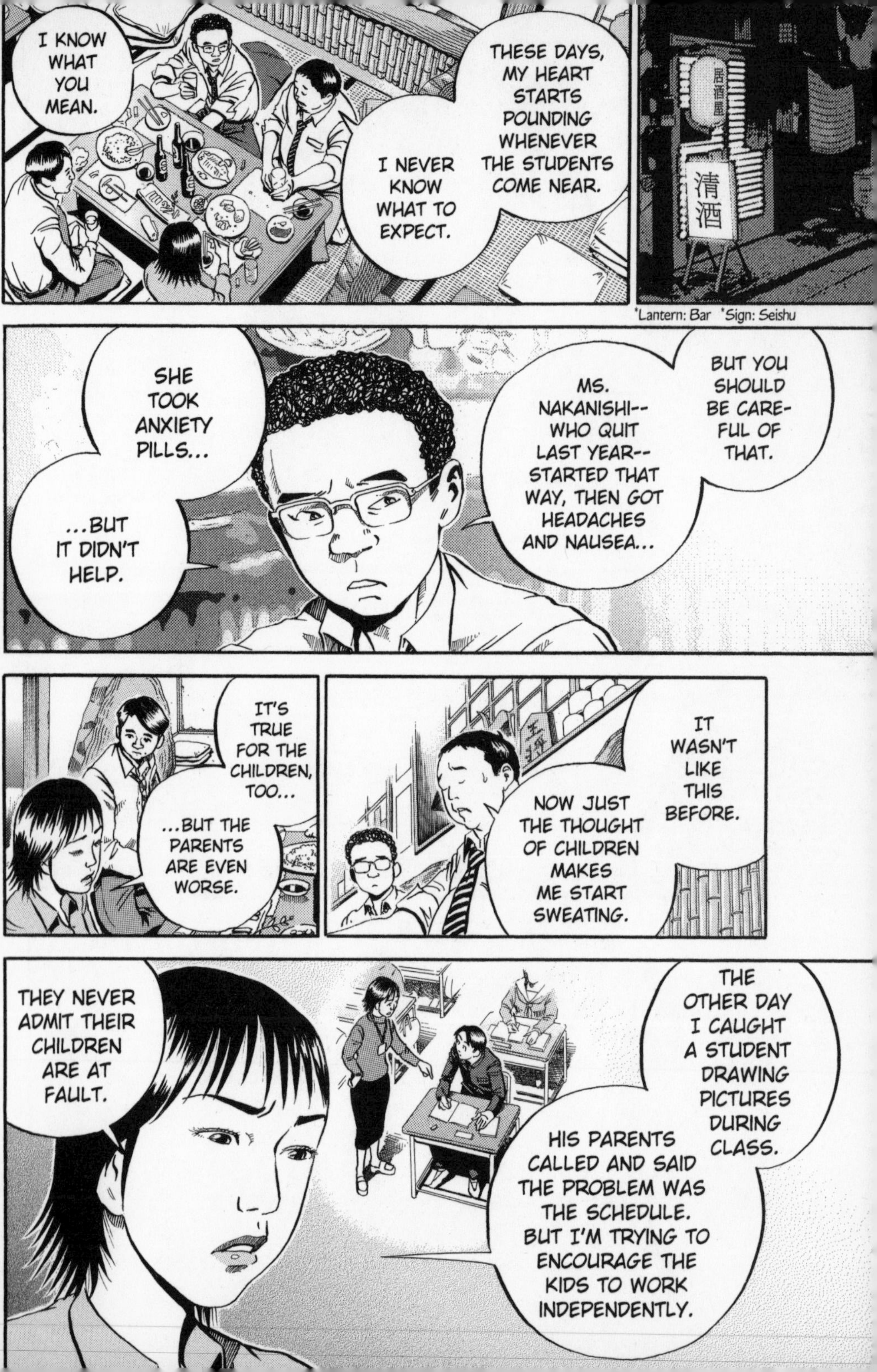
居酒屋
清酒
THESE DAYS, MY HEART STARTS POUNDING WHENEVER THE STUDENTS COME NEAR.
I NEVER KNOW WHAT TO EXPECT.
I KNOW WHAT YOU MEAN.
BUT YOU SHOULD BE CARE-FUL OF THAT.
MS. NAKANISHI--WHO QUIT LAST YEAR--STARTED THAT WAY, THEN GOT HEADACHES AND NAUSEA...
SHE TOOK ANXIETY PILLS...
...BUT IT DIDN'T HELP.
IT WASN'T LIKE THIS BEFORE.
NOW JUST THE THOUGHT OF CHILDREN MAKES ME START SWEATING.
IT'S TRUE FOR THE CHILDREN, TOO...
...BUT THE PARENTS ARE EVEN WORSE.
THE OTHER DAY I CAUGHT A STUDENT DRAWING PICTURES DURING CLASS.
HIS PARENTS CALLED AND SAID THE PROBLEM WAS THE SCHEDULE. BUT I'M TRYING TO ENCOURAGE THE KIDS TO WORK INDEPENDENTLY.
THEY NEVER ADMIT THEIR CHILDREN ARE AT FAULT.

*Lantern: Bar *Sign: Seishu

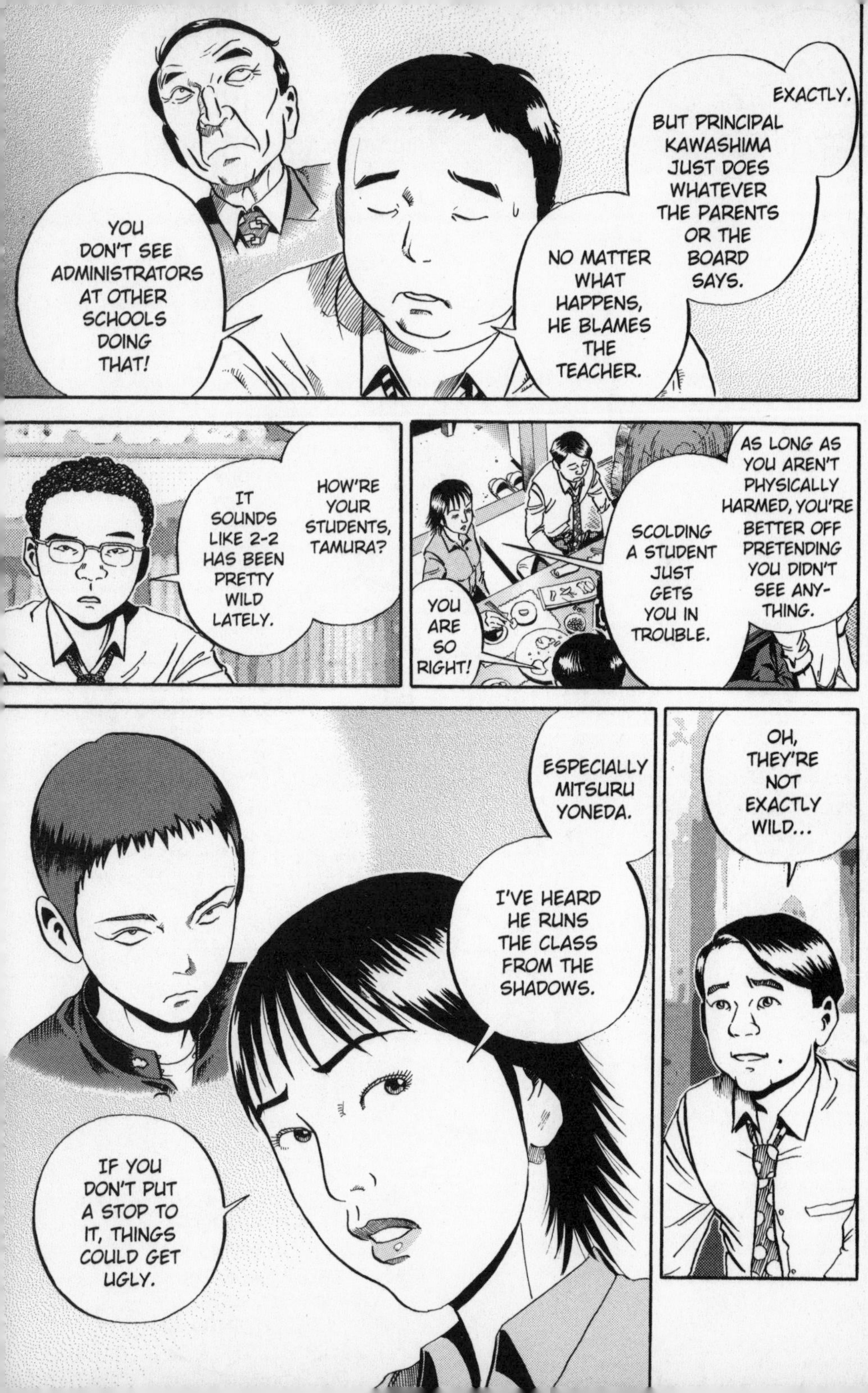
EXACTLY.
BUT PRINCIPAL KAWASHIMA JUST DOES WHATEVER THE PARENTS OR THE BOARD SAYS.
NO MATTER WHAT HAPPENS, HE BLAMES THE TEACHER.
YOU DON'T SEE ADMINISTRATORS AT OTHER SCHOOLS DOING THAT!
AS LONG AS YOU AREN'T PHYSICALLY HARMED, YOU'RE BETTER OFF PRETENDING YOU DIDN'T SEE ANY-THING.
SCOLDING A STUDENT JUST GETS YOU IN TROUBLE.
YOU ARE SO RIGHT!
HOW'RE YOUR STUDENTS, TAMURA?
IT SOUNDS LIKE 2-2 HAS BEEN PRETTY WILD LATELY.
OH, THEY'RE NOT EXACTLY WILD...
ESPECIALLY MITSURU YONEDA.
I'VE HEARD HE RUNS THE CLASS FROM THE SHADOWS.
IF YOU DON'T PUT A STOP TO IT, THINGS COULD GET UGLY.

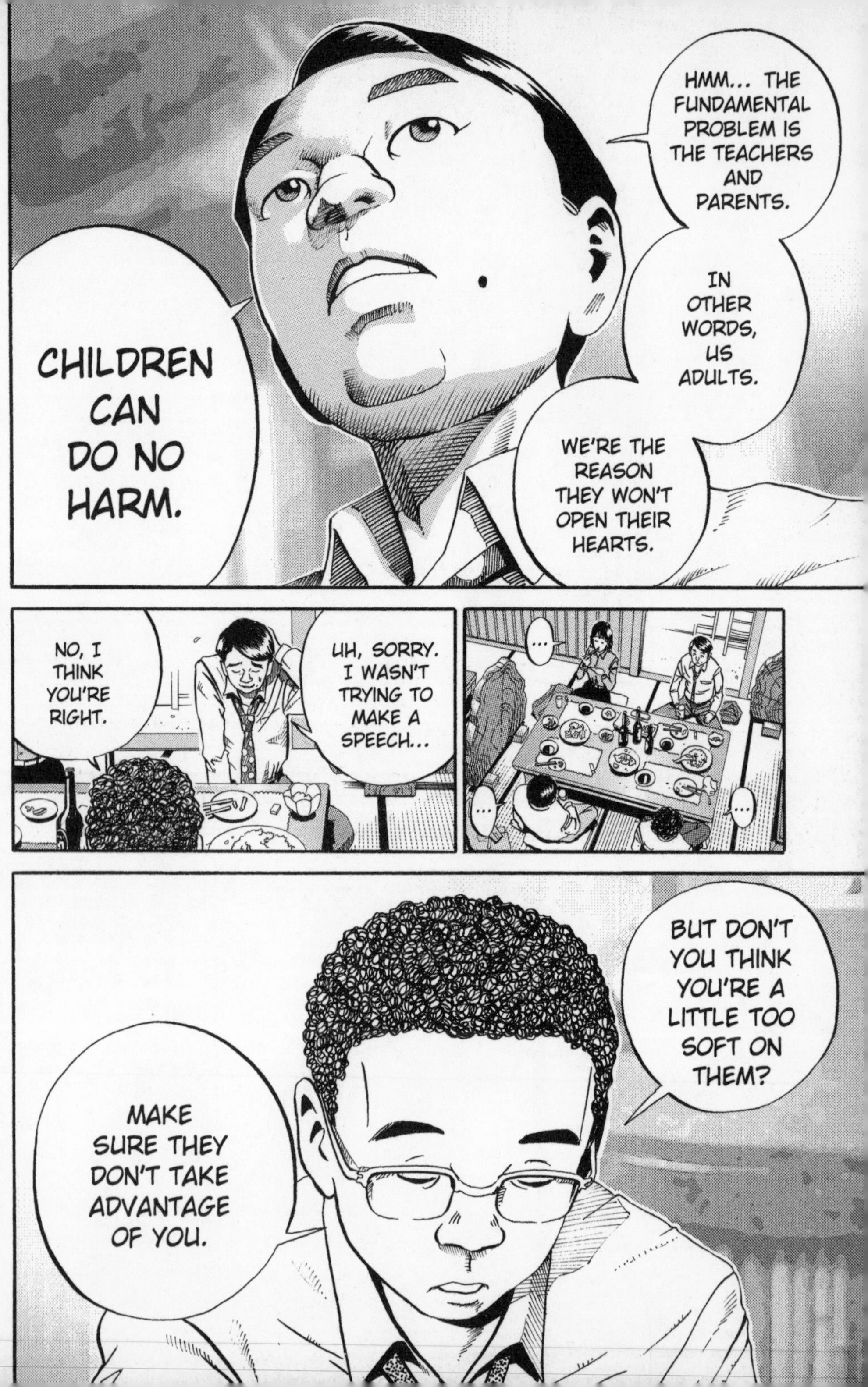
HMM... THE FUNDAMENTAL PROBLEM IS THE TEACHERS AND PARENTS.
IN OTHER WORDS, US ADULTS.
WE'RE THE REASON THEY WON'T OPEN THEIR HEARTS.
CHILDREN CAN DO NO HARM.
...
...
...
UH, SORRY. I WASN'T TRYING TO MAKE A SPEECH...
NO, I THINK YOU'RE RIGHT.
BUT DON'T YOU THINK YOU'RE A LITTLE TOO SOFT ON THEM?
MAKE SURE THEY DON'T TAKE ADVANTAGE OF YOU.

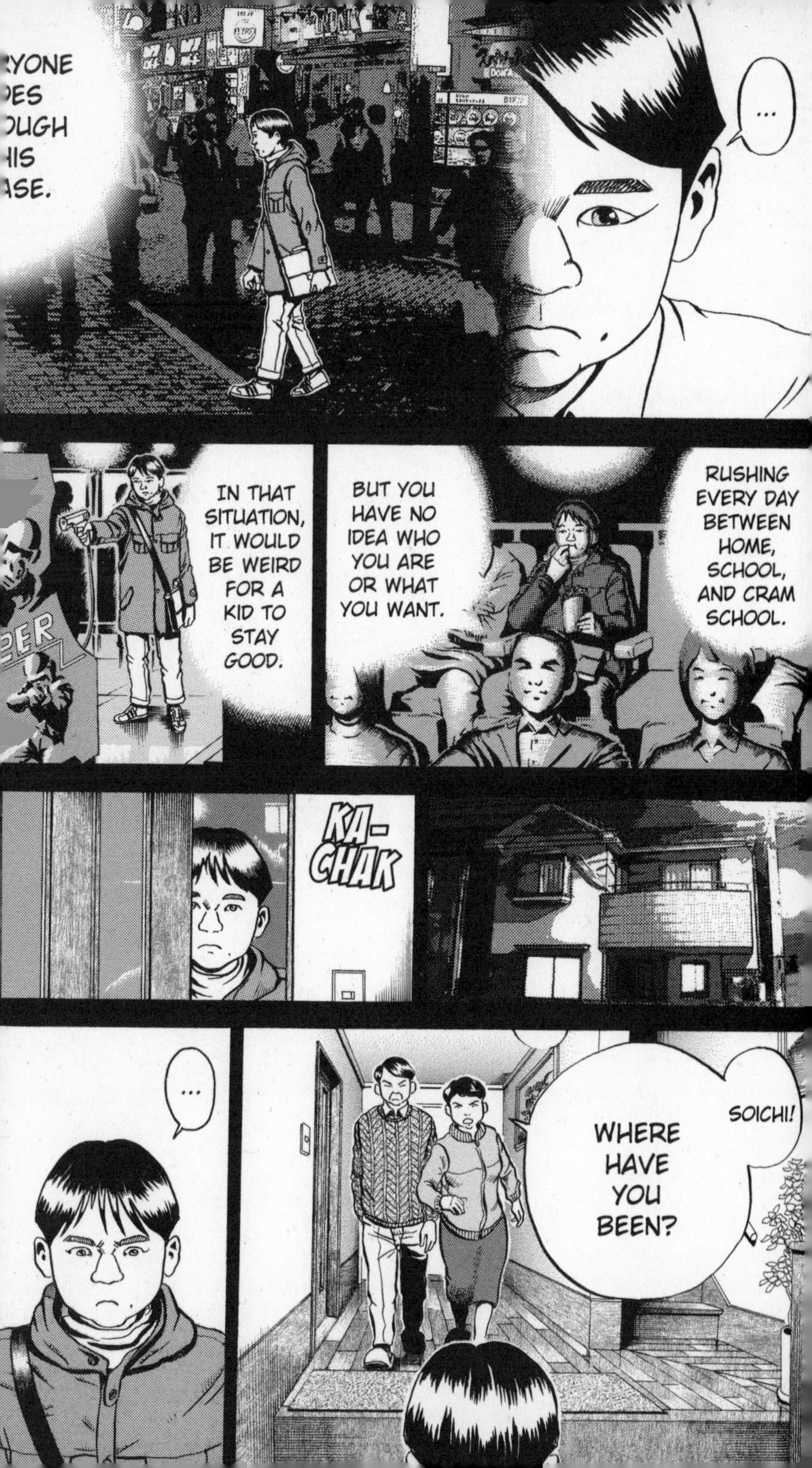
...
RYONE
ES
OUGH
HIS
ASE.
RUSHING EVERY DAY BETWEEN HOME, SCHOOL, AND CRAM SCHOOL.
BUT YOU HAVE NO IDEA WHO YOU ARE OR WHAT YOU WANT.
IN THAT SITUATION, IT WOULD BE WEIRD FOR A KID TO STAY GOOD.
KA-CHAK
SOICHI!
WHERE HAVE YOU BEEN?
...

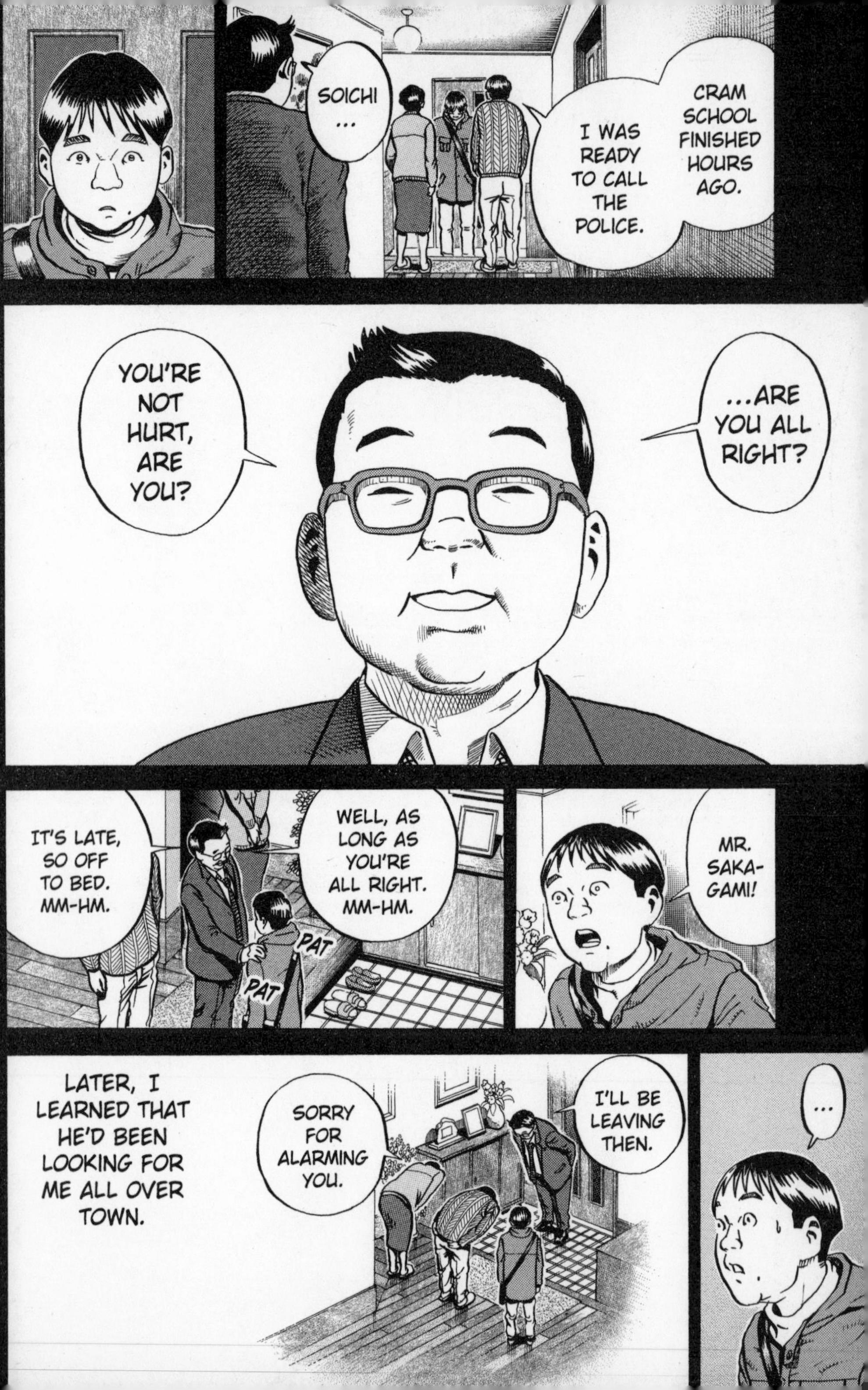
CRAM SCHOOL FINISHED HOURS AGO.
I WAS READY TO CALL THE POLICE.
SOICHI ...
...ARE YOU ALL RIGHT?
YOU'RE NOT HURT, ARE YOU?
MR. SAKA-GAMI!
WELL, AS LONG AS YOU'RE ALL RIGHT. MM-HM.
IT'S LATE, SO OFF TO BED. MM-HM.
PAT
PAT
...
I'LL BE LEAVING THEN.
SORRY FOR ALARMING YOU.
LATER, I LEARNED THAT HE'D BEEN LOOKING FOR ME ALL OVER TOWN.

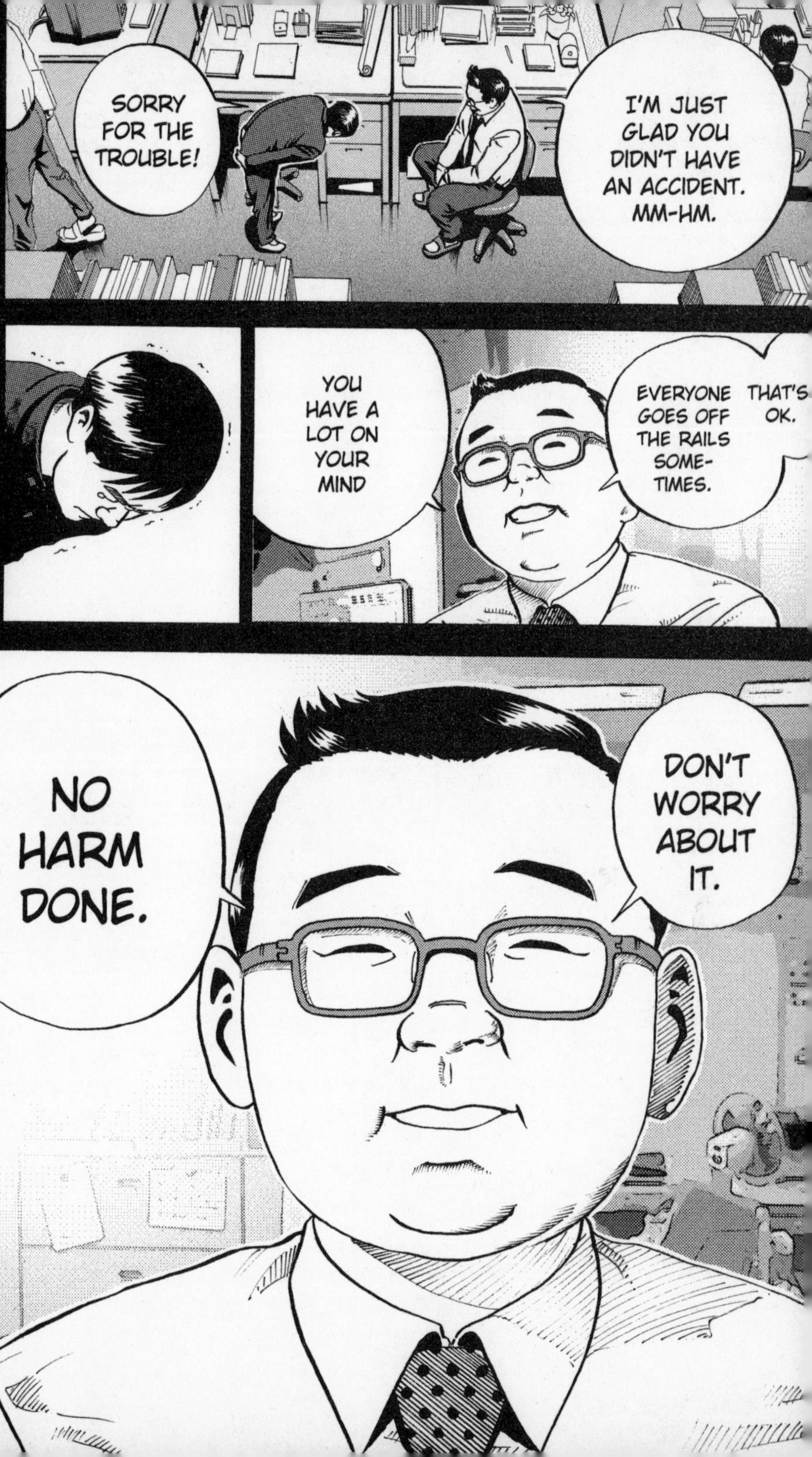
I'M JUST GLAD YOU DIDN'T HAVE AN ACCIDENT. MM-HM.
SORRY FOR THE TROUBLE!
THAT'S OK.
EVERYONE GOES OFF THE RAILS SOME-TIMES.
YOU HAVE A LOT ON YOUR MIND
DON'T WORRY ABOUT IT.
NO HARM DONE.

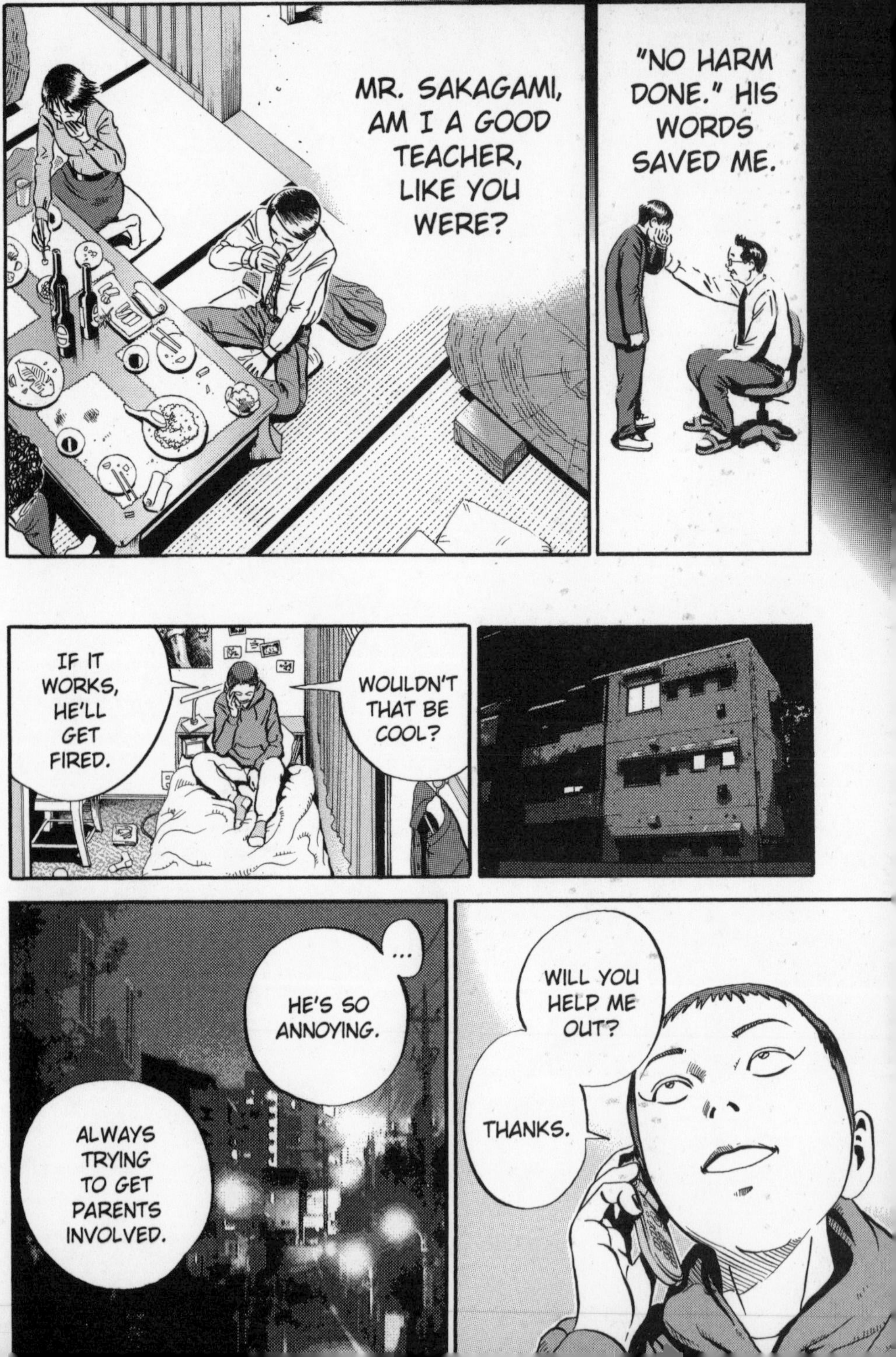
"NO HARM DONE." HIS WORDS SAVED ME.
MR. SAKAGAMI, AM I A GOOD TEACHER, LIKE YOU WERE?
WOULDN'T THAT BE COOL?
IF IT WORKS, HE'LL GET FIRED.
WILL YOU HELP ME OUT?
THANKS.
...
HE'S SO ANNOYING.
ALWAYS TRYING TO GET PARENTS INVOLVED.

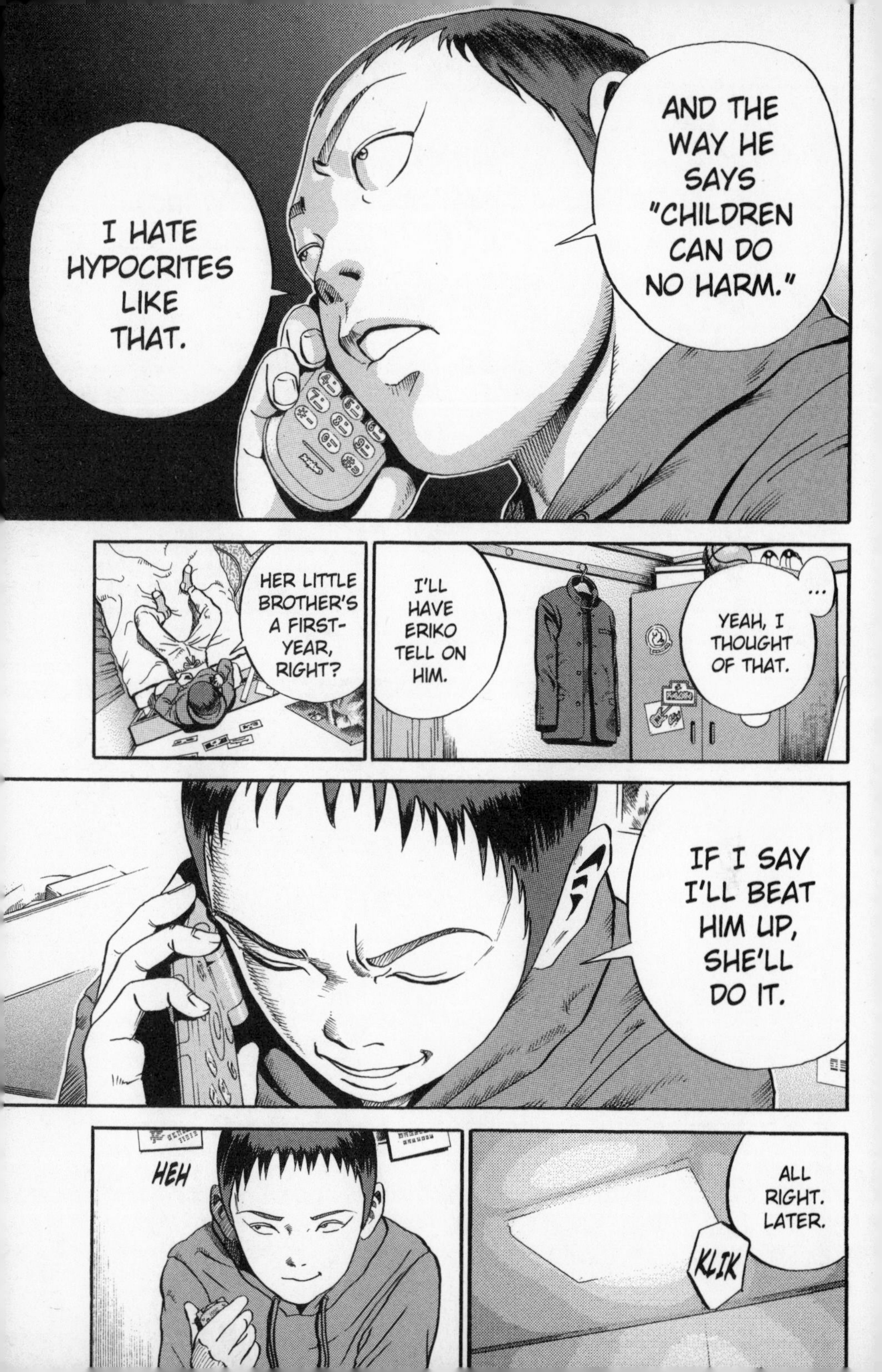
AND THE WAY HE SAYS "CHILDREN CAN DO NO HARM."
I HATE HYPOCRITES LIKE THAT.
...
YEAH, I THOUGHT OF THAT.
I'LL HAVE ERIKO TELL ON HIM.
HER LITTLE BROTHER'S A FIRST-YEAR, RIGHT?
IF I SAY I'LL BEAT HIM UP, SHE'LL DO IT.
ALL RIGHT. LATER.
KLIK
HEH

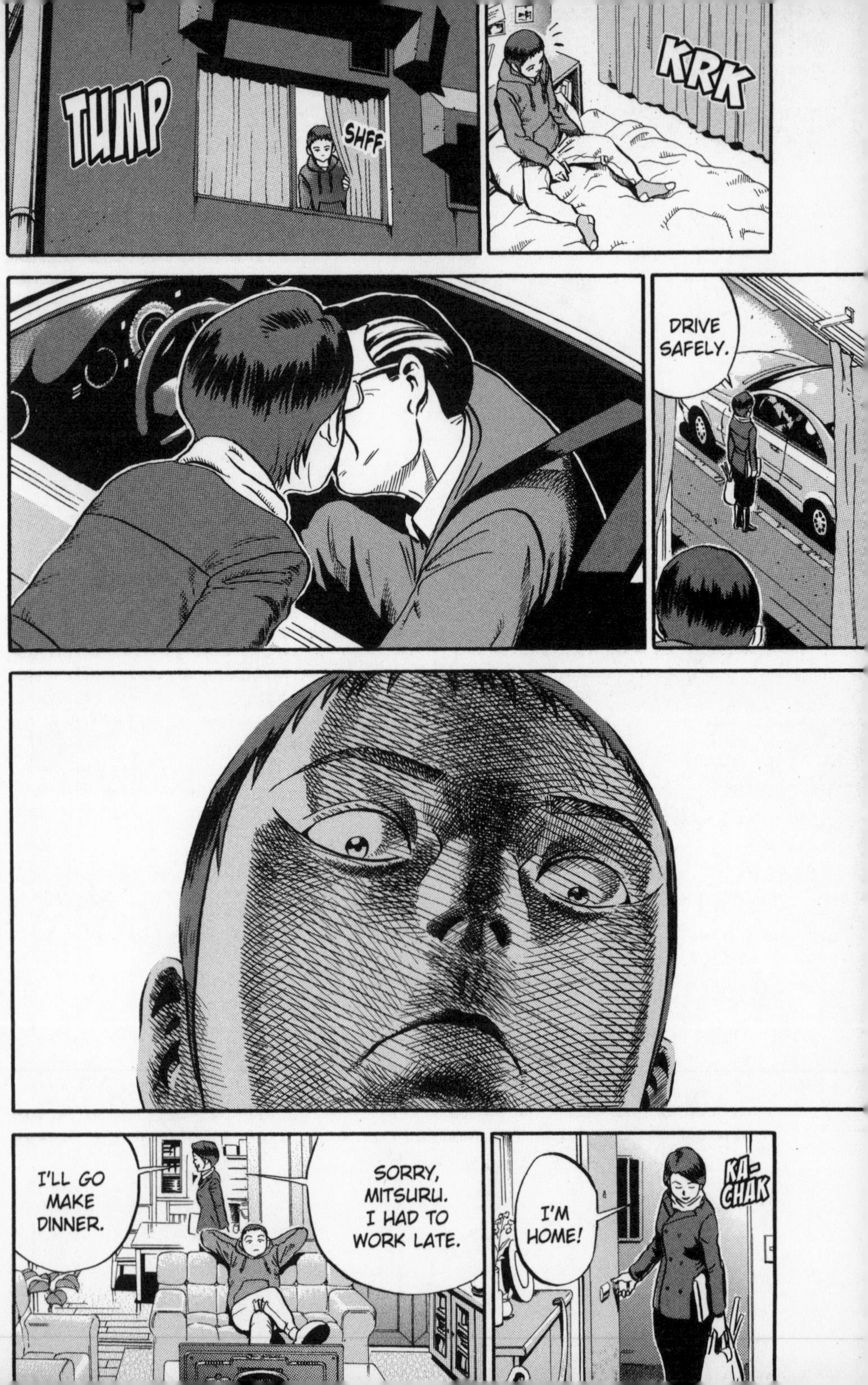
KRK
TUMP
SHFF
DRIVE SAFELY.
KA-CHAK
I'M HOME!
SORRY, MITSURU. I HAD TO WORK LATE.
I'LL GO MAKE DINNER.

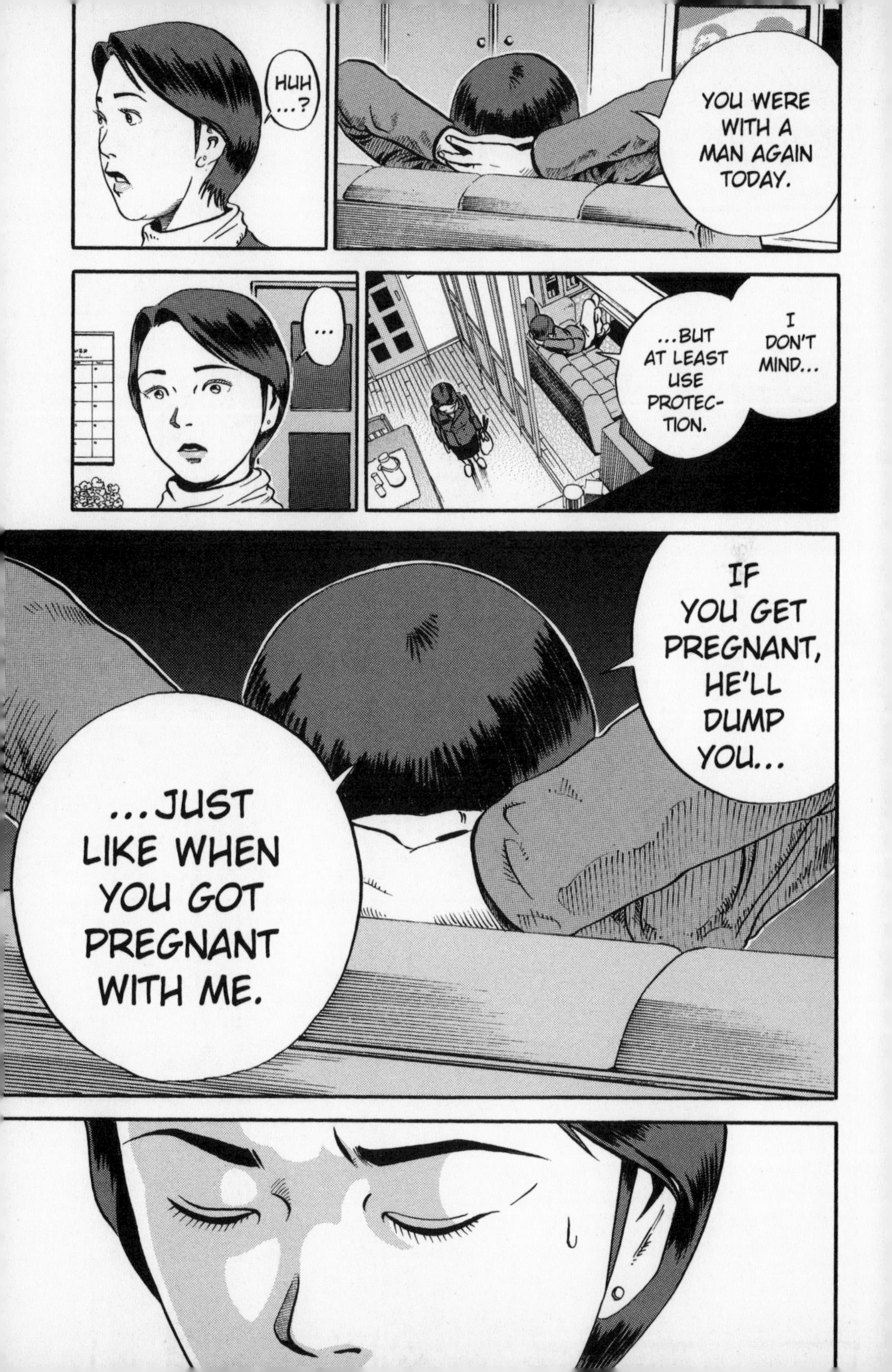
YOU WERE WITH A MAN AGAIN TODAY.
HUH ...?
I DON'T MIND...
...BUT AT LEAST USE PROTECTION.
...
IF YOU GET PREGNANT, HE'LL DUMP YOU...
...JUST LIKE WHEN YOU GOT PREGNANT WITH ME.

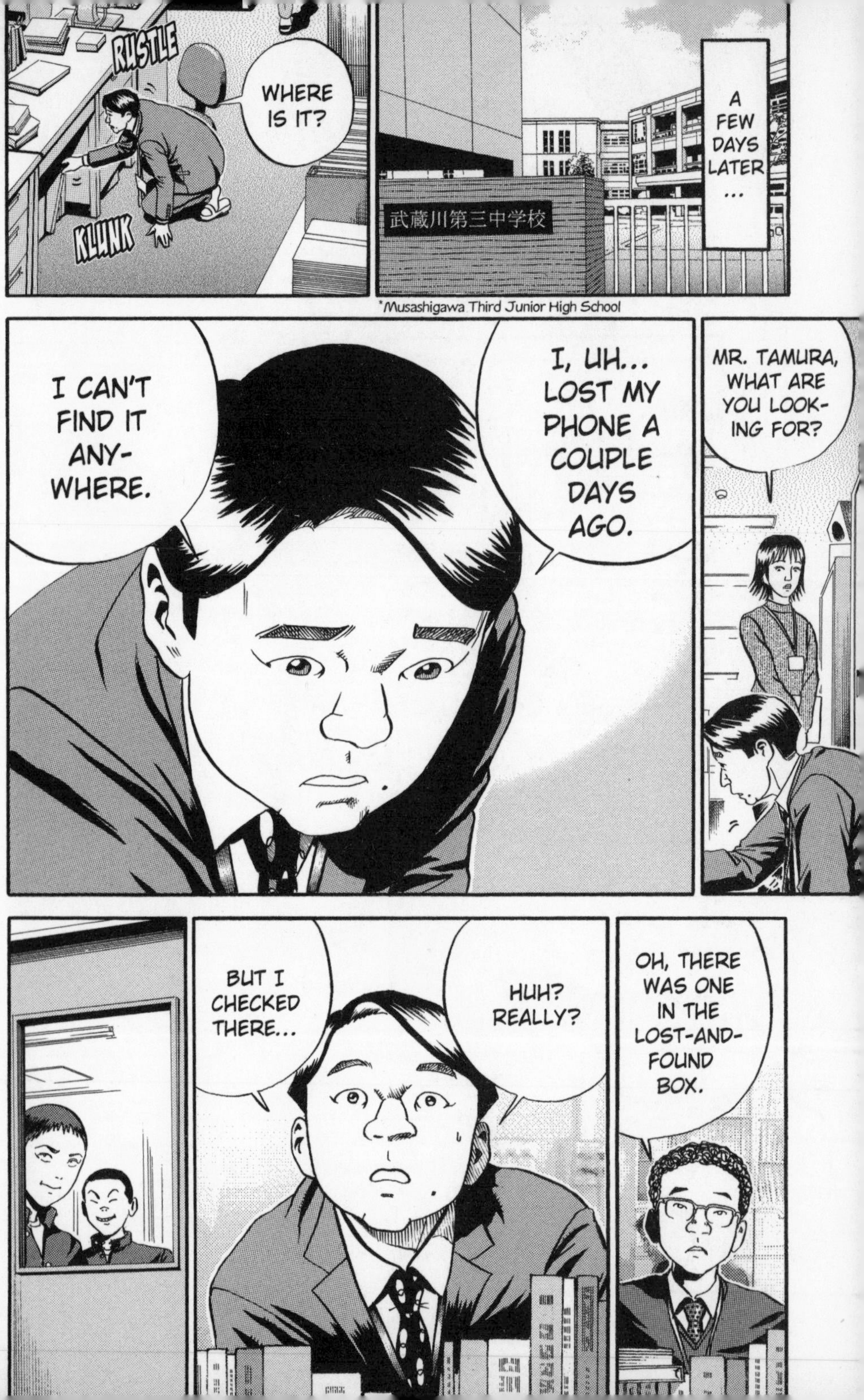
A FEW DAYS LATER...
武蔵川第三中学校
RUSTLE
WHERE IS IT?
KLUNK
*Musashigawa Third Junior High School
MR. TAMURA, WHAT ARE YOU LOOK-ING FOR?
I, UH... LOST MY PHONE A COUPLE DAYS AGO.
I CAN'T FIND IT ANY-WHERE.
OH, THERE WAS ONE IN THE LOST-AND-FOUND BOX.
HUH? REALLY?
BUT I CHECKED THERE...

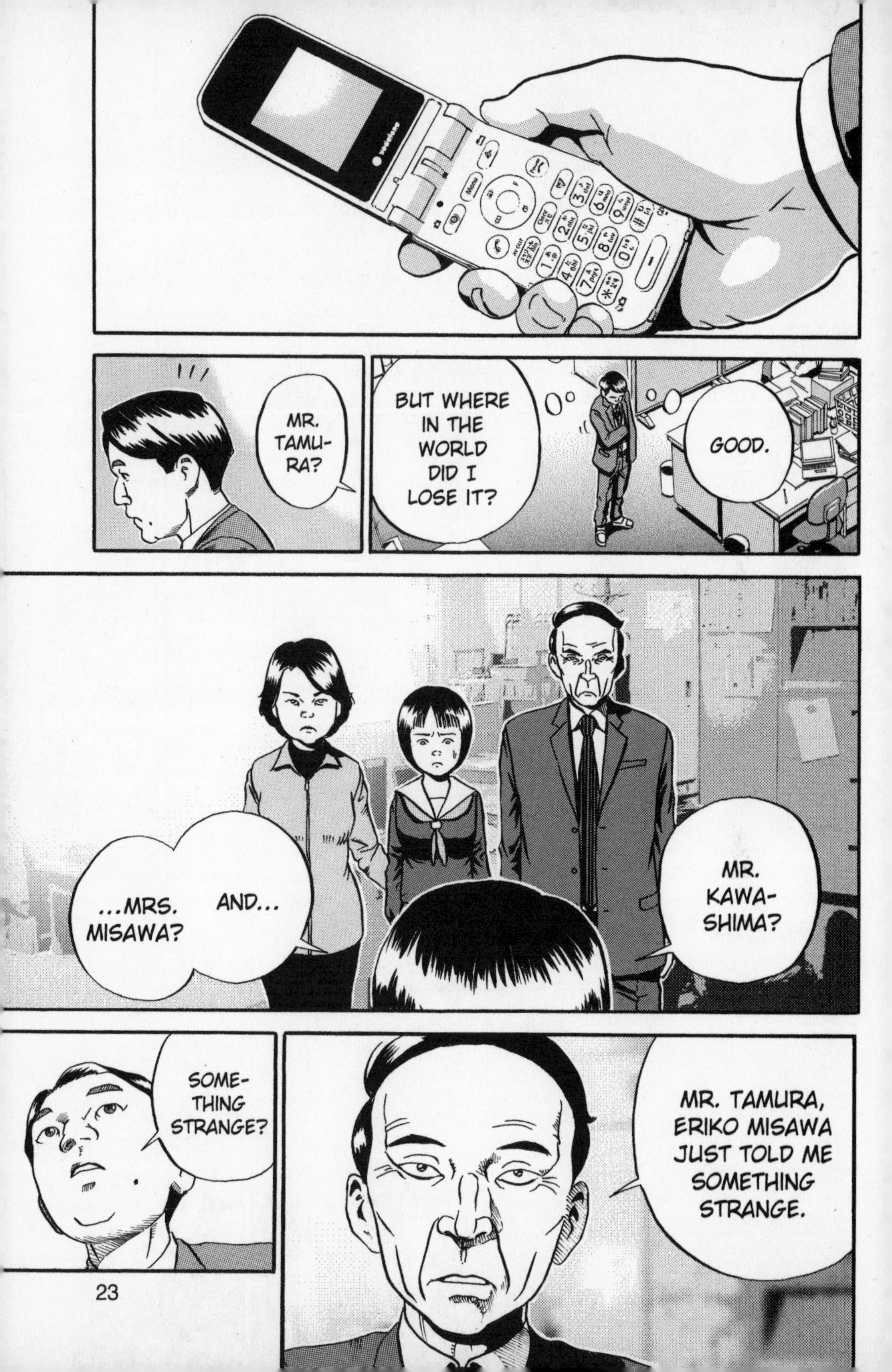
GOOD.
BUT WHERE IN THE WORLD DID I LOSE IT?
MR. TAMU-RA?
MR. KAWA-SHIMA?
AND...
...MRS. MISAWA?
MR. TAMURA, ERIKO MISAWA JUST TOLD ME SOMETHING STRANGE.
SOME-THING STRANGE?

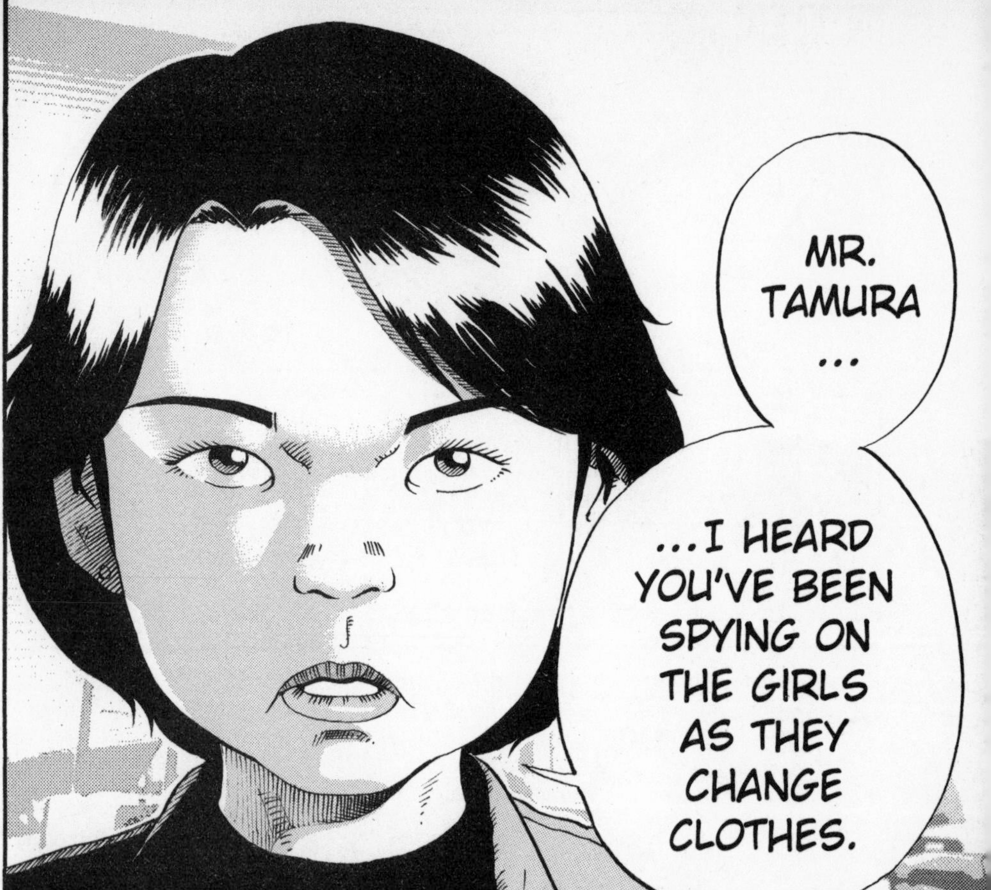
MR. TAMURA ...
...I HEARD YOU'VE BEEN SPYING ON THE GIRLS AS THEY CHANGE CLOTHES.
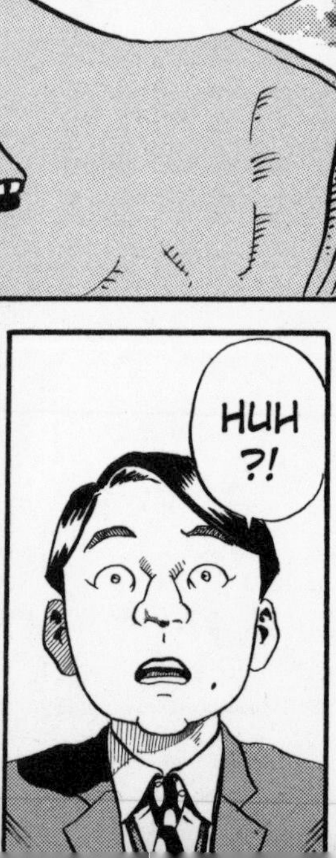
HUH ?!
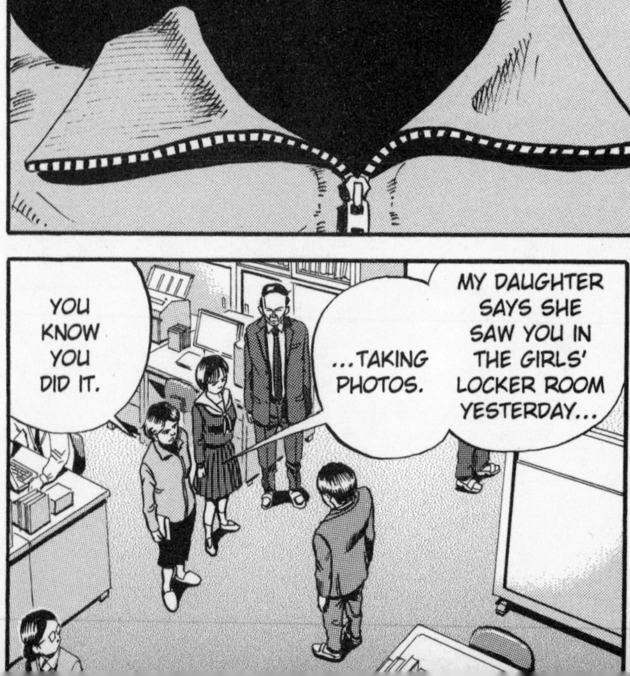
MY DAUGHTER SAYS SHE SAW YOU IN THE GIRLS' LOCKER ROOM YESTERDAY...
...TAKING PHOTOS.
YOU KNOW YOU DID IT.

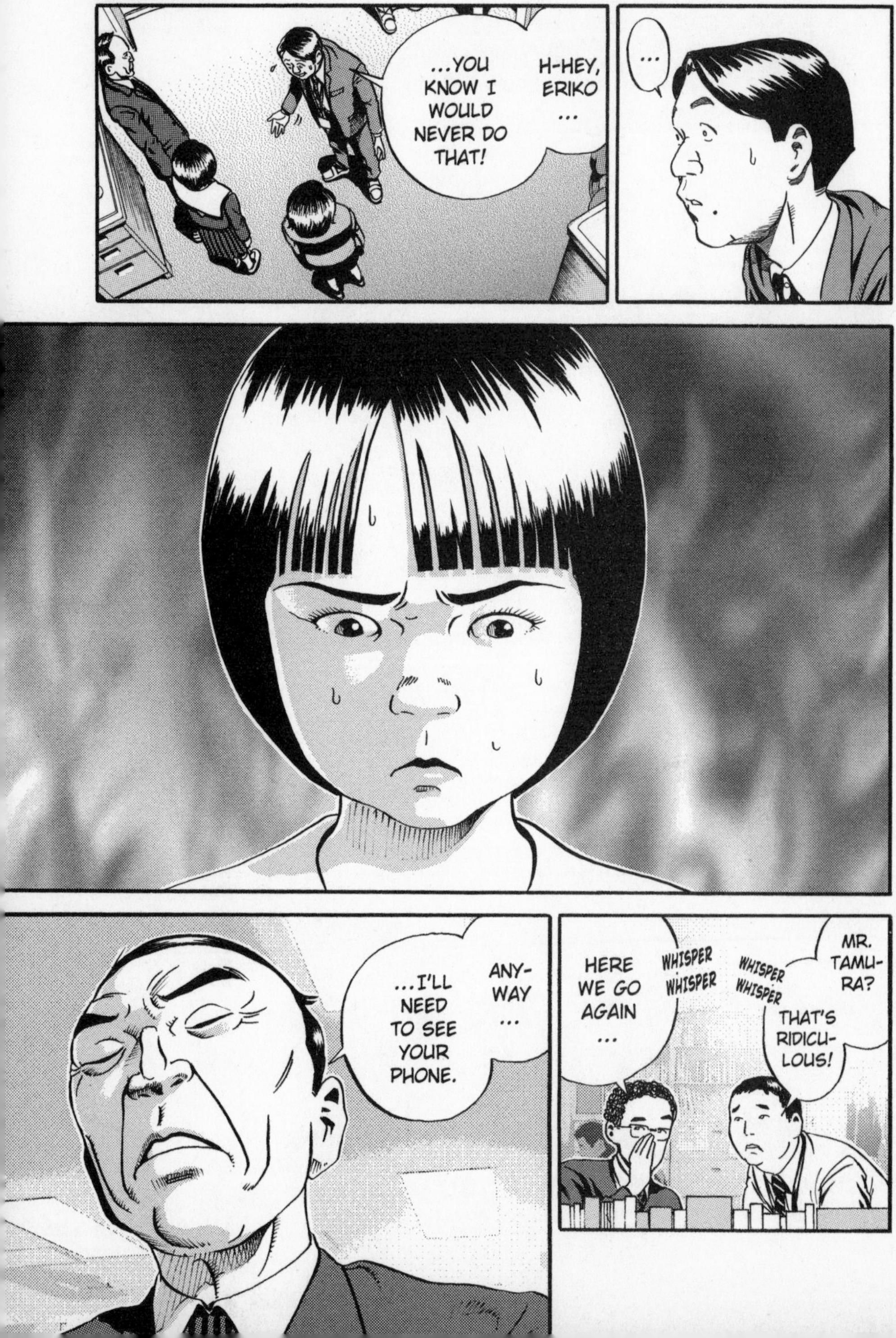
...
H-HEY, ERIKO ...
...YOU KNOW I WOULD NEVER DO THAT!
MR. TAMU-RA?
THAT'S RIDICU-LOUS!
WHISPER WHISPER
WHISPER WHISPER
HERE WE GO AGAIN ...
ANY-WAY ...
...I'LL NEED TO SEE YOUR PHONE.

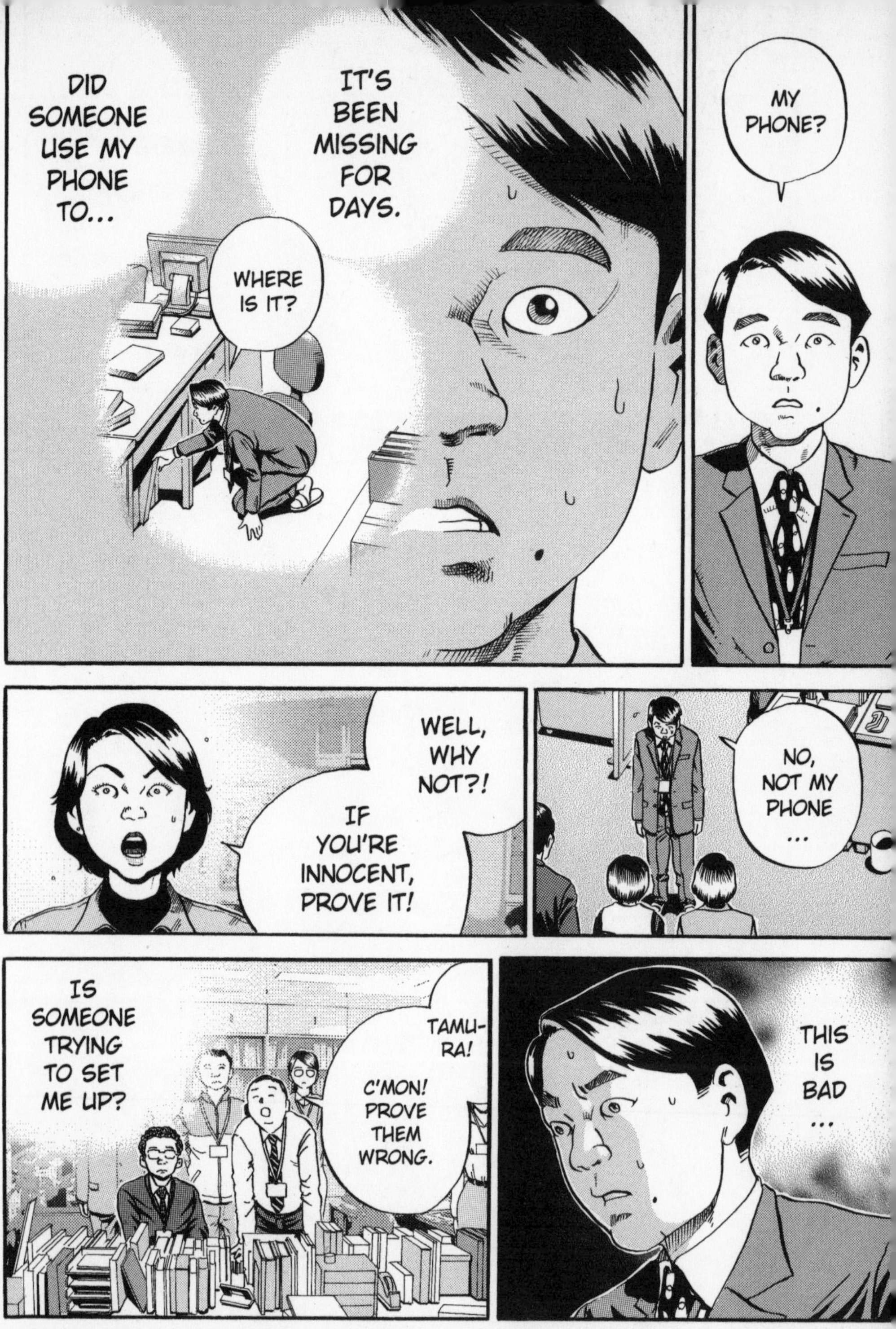
MY PHONE?
IT'S BEEN MISSING FOR DAYS.
DID SOMEONE USE MY PHONE TO...
WHERE IS IT?
NO, NOT MY PHONE ...
WELL, WHY NOT?!
IF YOU'RE INNOCENT, PROVE IT!
THIS IS BAD ...
TAMU-RA!
C'MON! PROVE THEM WRONG.
IS SOMEONE TRYING TO SET ME UP?

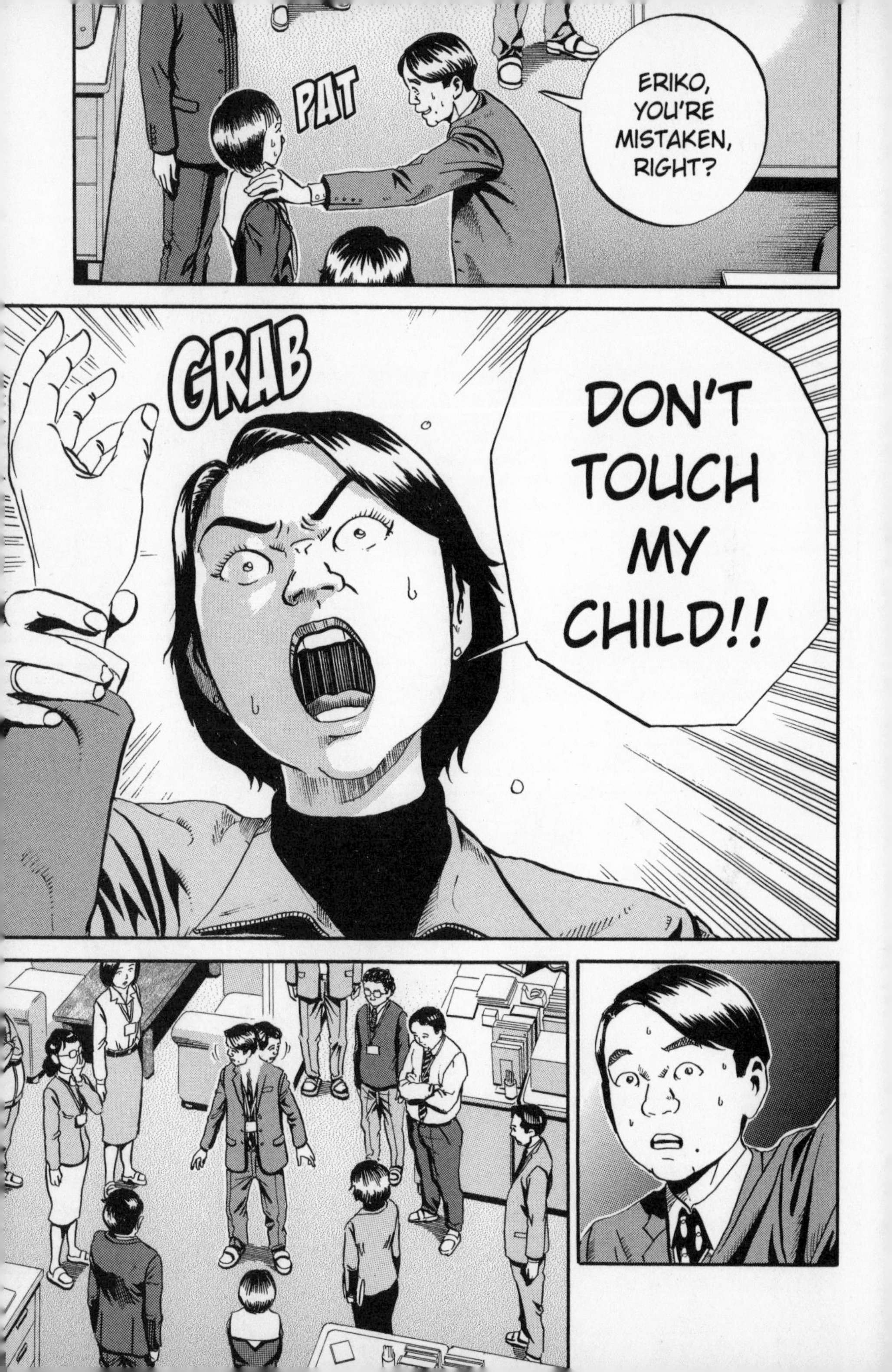
ERIKO, YOU'RE MISTAKEN, RIGHT?
PAT
DON'T TOUCH MY CHILD!!
GRAB

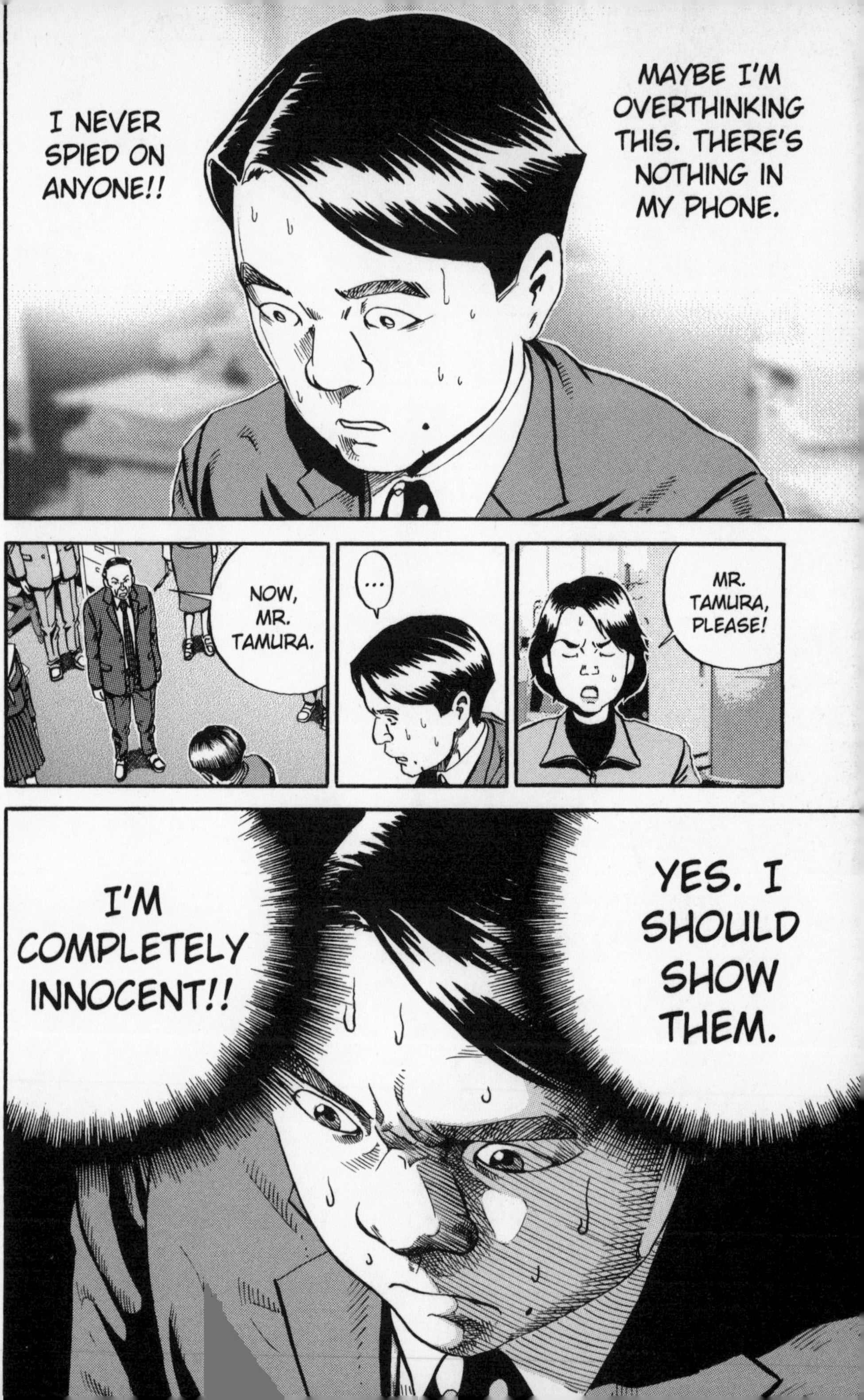
MAYBE I'M OVERTHINKING THIS. THERE'S NOTHING IN MY PHONE.
I NEVER SPIED ON ANYONE!!
MR. TAMURA, PLEASE!
...
NOW, MR. TAMURA.
YES. I SHOULD SHOW THEM.
I'M COMPLETELY INNOCENT!!

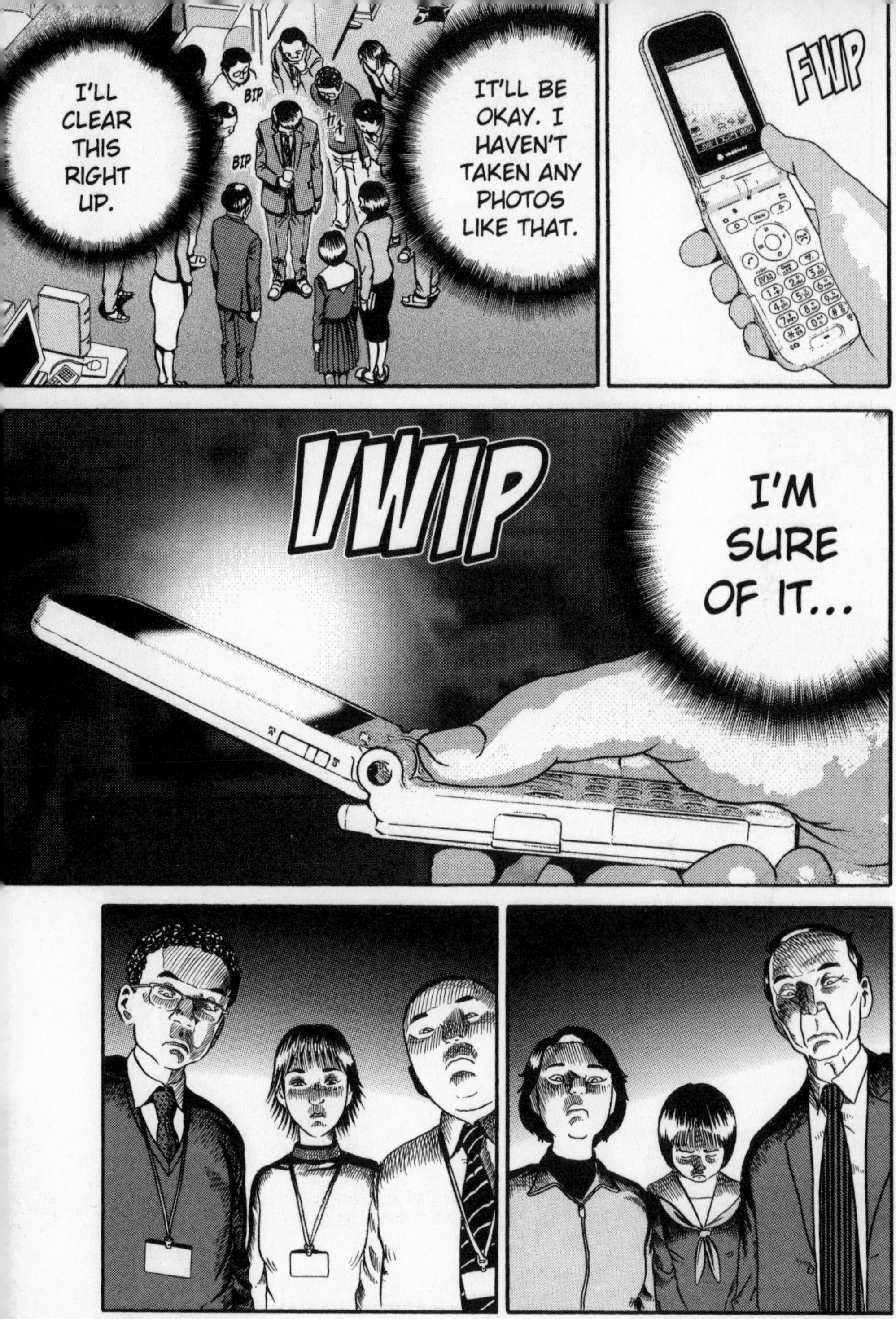
FWP
IT'LL BE OKAY. I HAVEN'T TAKEN ANY PHOTOS LIKE THAT.
BIP
BIP
I'LL CLEAR THIS RIGHT UP.
I'M SURE OF IT...
VWIP

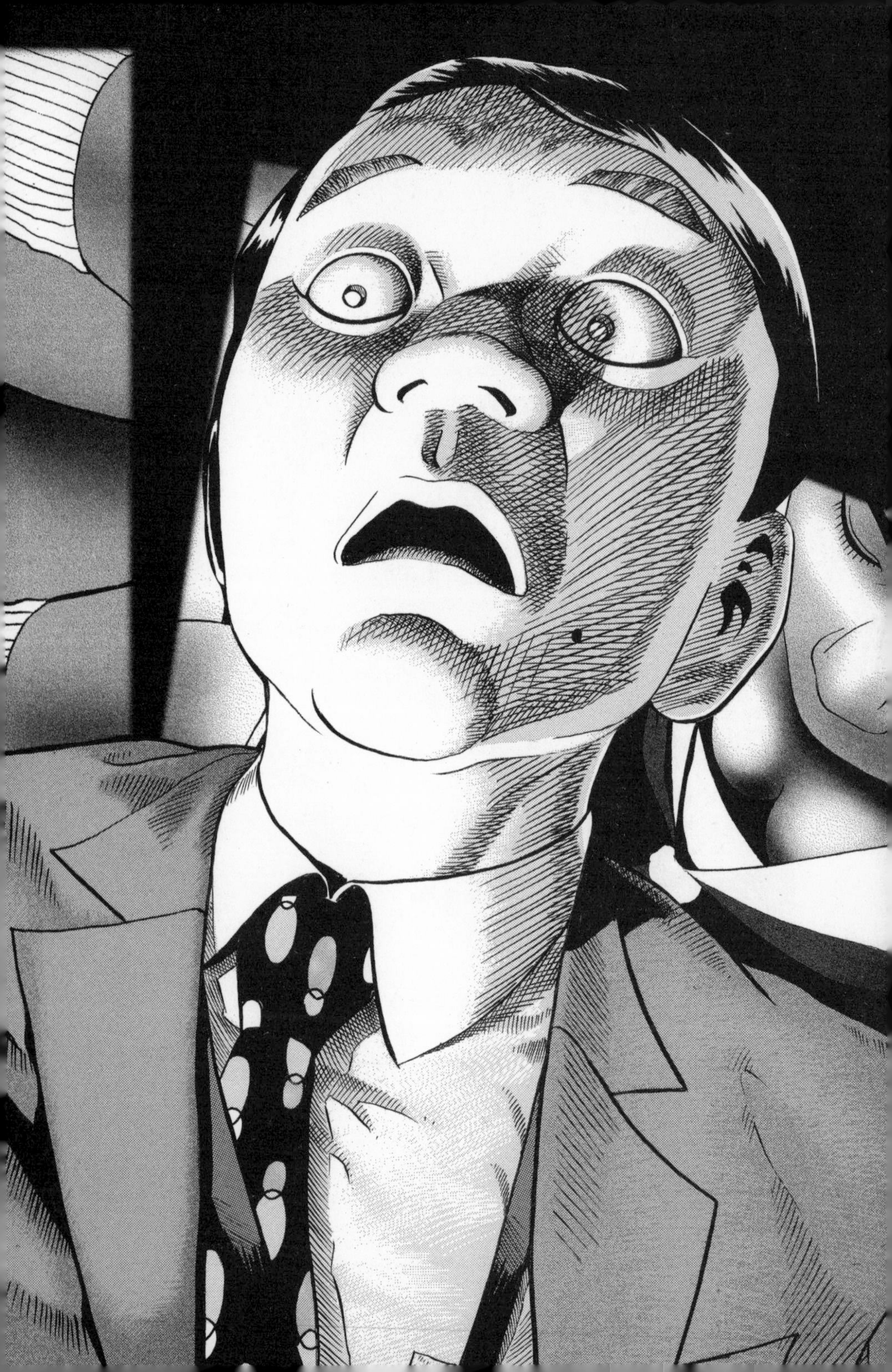

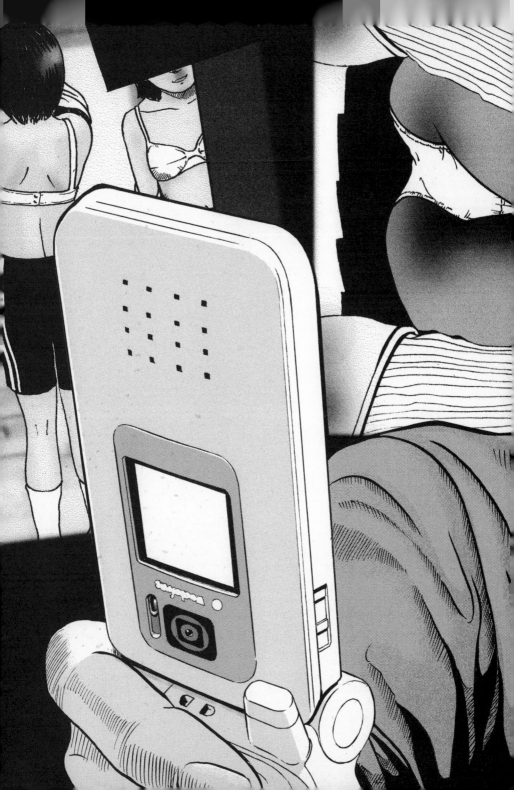

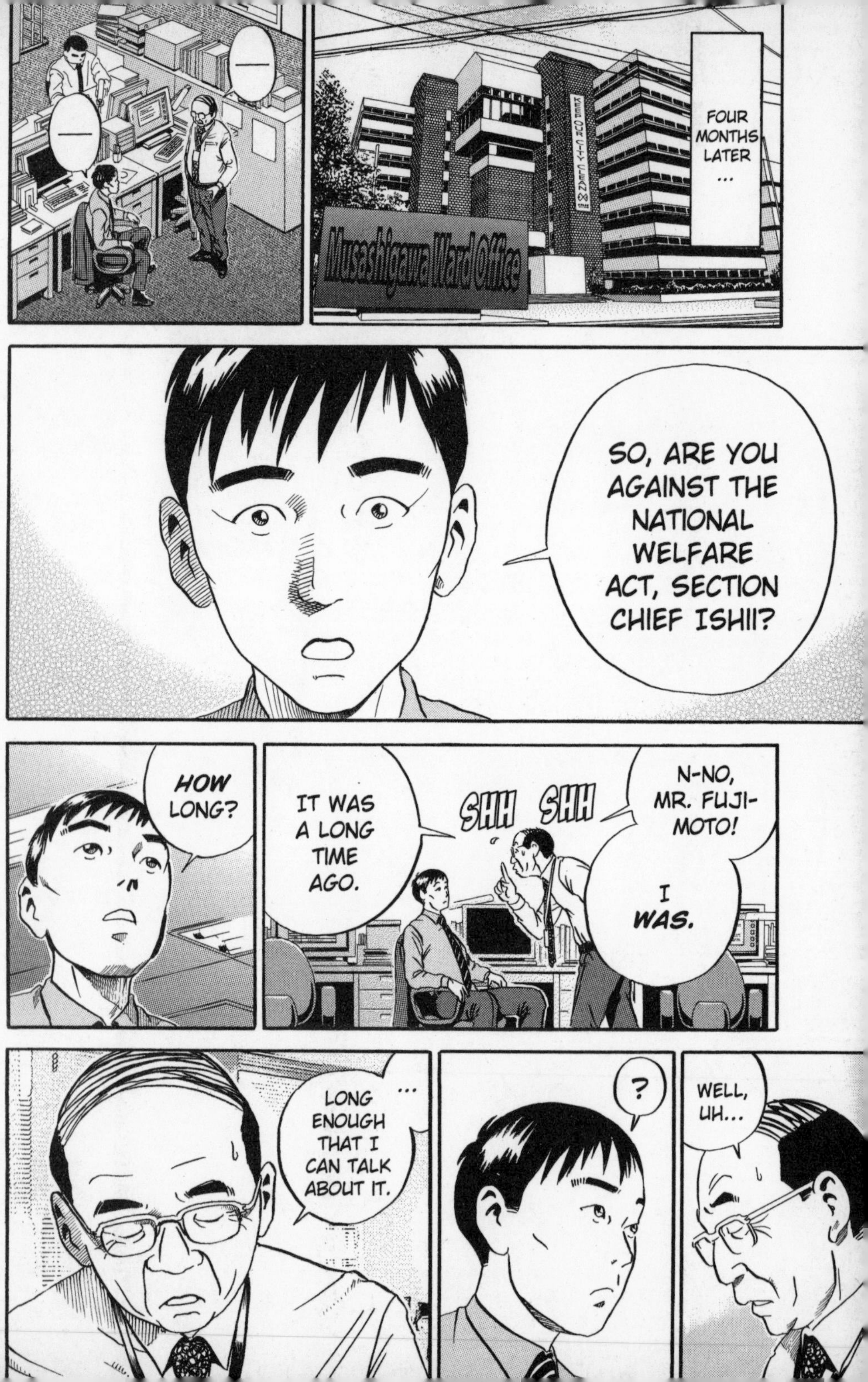
FOUR MONTHS LATER ...
KEEP OUR CITY CLEAN
Musashigawa Ward Office
—
—
SO, ARE YOU AGAINST THE NATIONAL WELFARE ACT, SECTION CHIEF ISHII?
N-NO, MR. FUJI-MOTO!
SHH SHH
I WAS.
IT WAS A LONG TIME AGO.
HOW LONG?
WELL, UH...
?
...
LONG ENOUGH THAT I CAN TALK ABOUT IT.

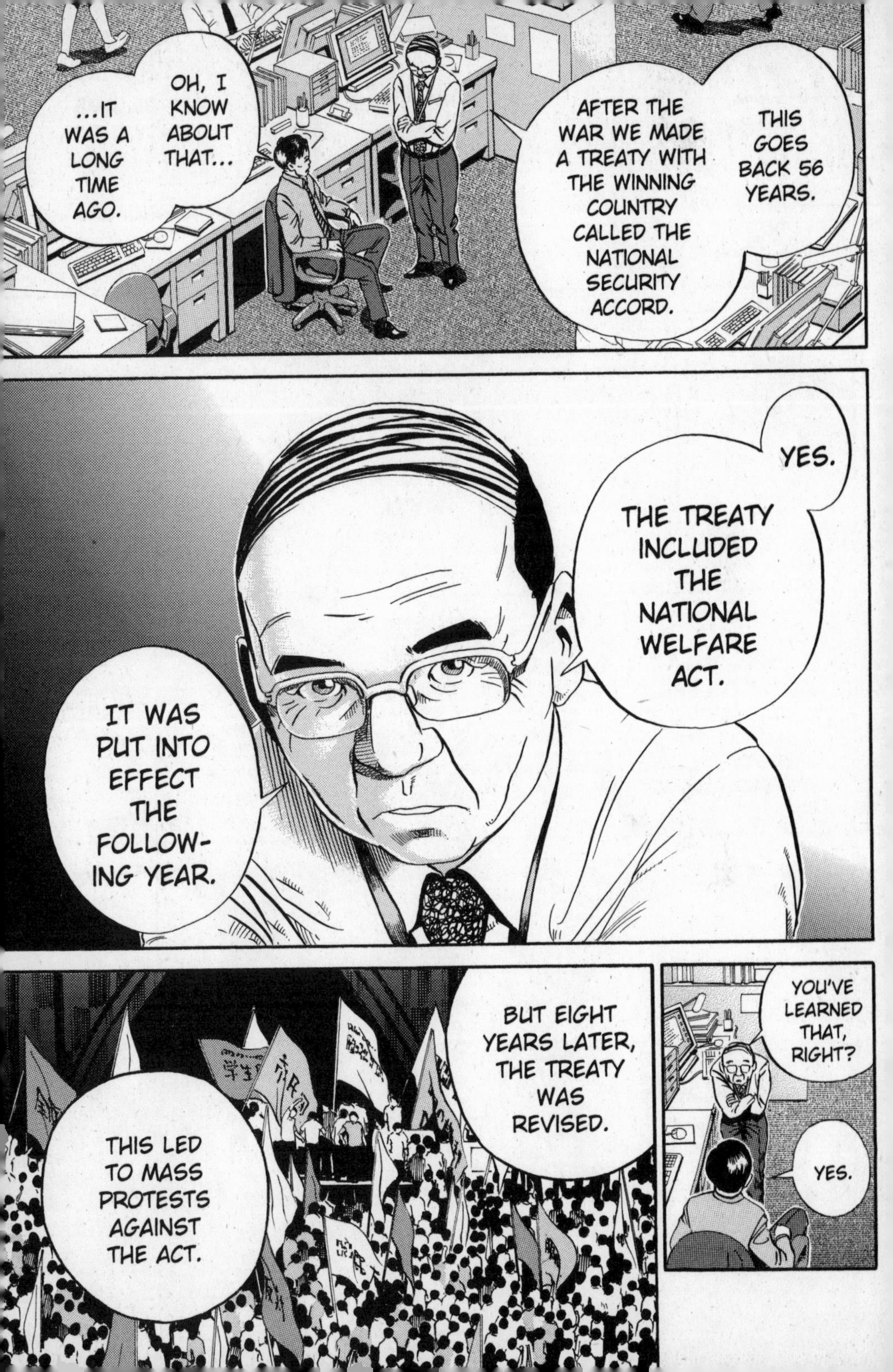
THIS GOES BACK 56 YEARS.
AFTER THE WAR WE MADE A TREATY WITH THE WINNING COUNTRY CALLED THE NATIONAL SECURITY ACCORD.
OH, I KNOW ABOUT THAT...
...IT WAS A LONG TIME AGO.
YES.
THE TREATY INCLUDED THE NATIONAL WELFARE ACT.
IT WAS PUT INTO EFFECT THE FOLLOWING YEAR.
YOU'VE LEARNED THAT, RIGHT?
YES.
BUT EIGHT YEARS LATER, THE TREATY WAS REVISED.
THIS LED TO MASS PROTESTS AGAINST THE ACT.

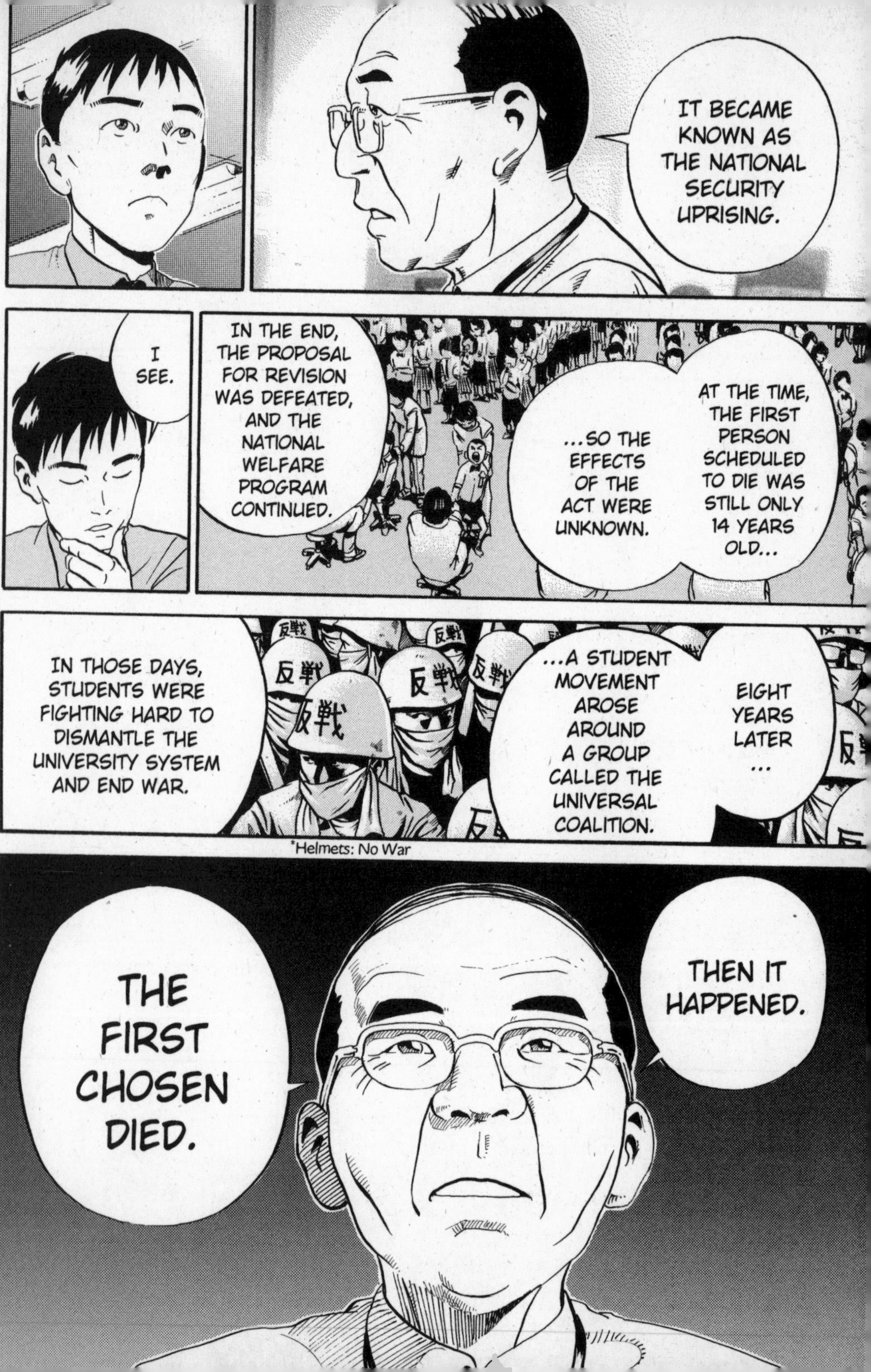
IT BECAME KNOWN AS THE NATIONAL SECURITY UPRISING.
AT THE TIME, THE FIRST PERSON SCHEDULED TO DIE WAS STILL ONLY 14 YEARS OLD...
...SO THE EFFECTS OF THE ACT WERE UNKNOWN.
IN THE END, THE PROPOSAL FOR REVISION WAS DEFEATED, AND THE NATIONAL WELFARE PROGRAM CONTINUED.
I SEE.
EIGHT YEARS LATER...
...A STUDENT MOVEMENT AROSE AROUND A GROUP CALLED THE UNIVERSAL COALITION.
反戦
IN THOSE DAYS, STUDENTS WERE FIGHTING HARD TO DISMANTLE THE UNIVERSITY SYSTEM AND END WAR.
*Helmets: No War
THEN IT HAPPENED.
THE FIRST CHOSEN DIED.

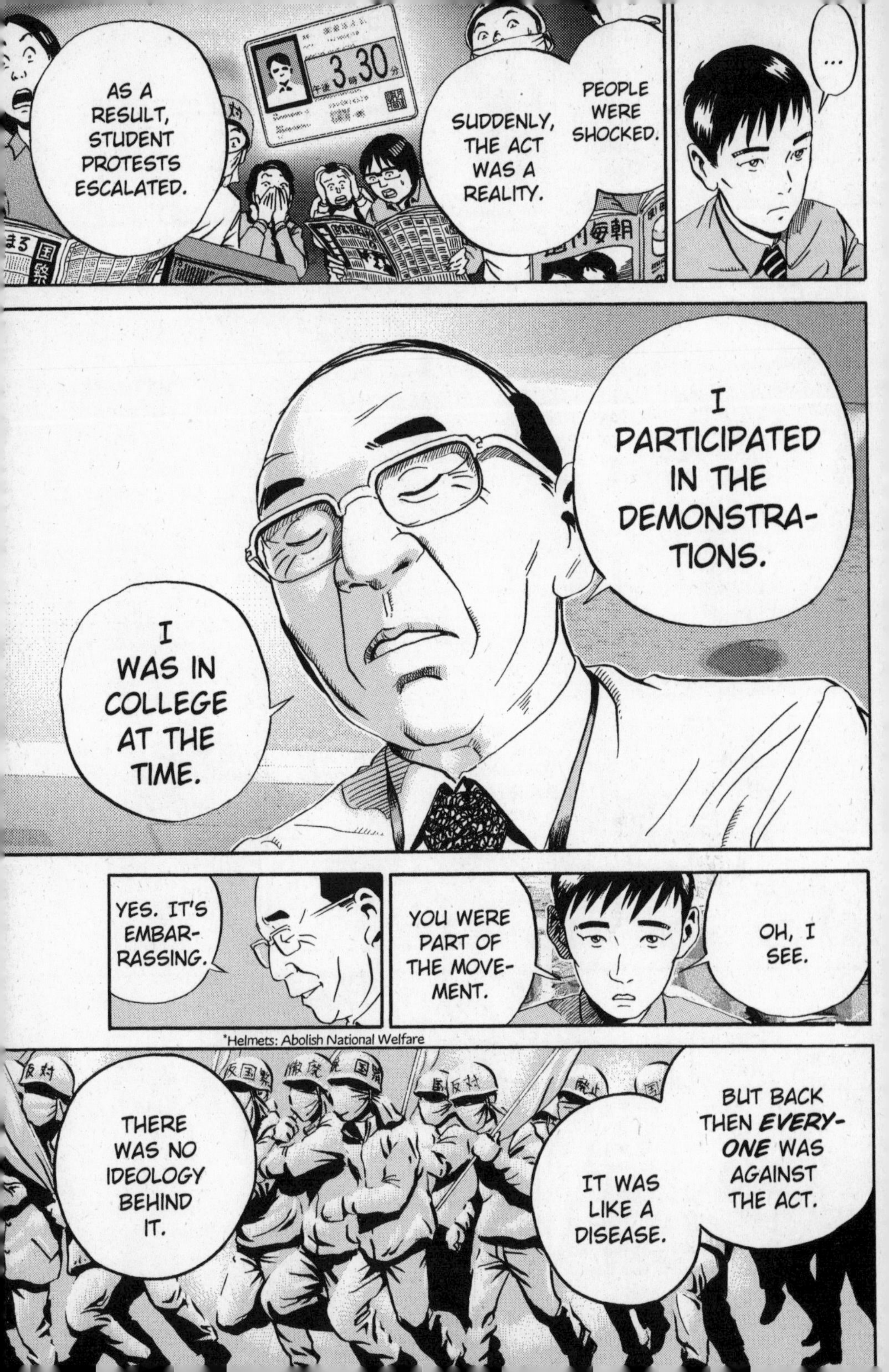
...
PEOPLE WERE SHOCKED.
SUDDENLY, THE ACT WAS A REALITY.
AS A RESULT, STUDENT PROTESTS ESCALATED.
I PARTICIPATED IN THE DEMONSTRATIONS.
I WAS IN COLLEGE AT THE TIME.
OH, I SEE.
YOU WERE PART OF THE MOVEMENT.
YES. IT'S EMBARRASSING.
*Helmets: Abolish National Welfare
BUT BACK THEN *EVERYONE* WAS AGAINST THE ACT.
IT WAS LIKE A DISEASE.
THERE WAS NO IDEOLOGY BEHIND IT.

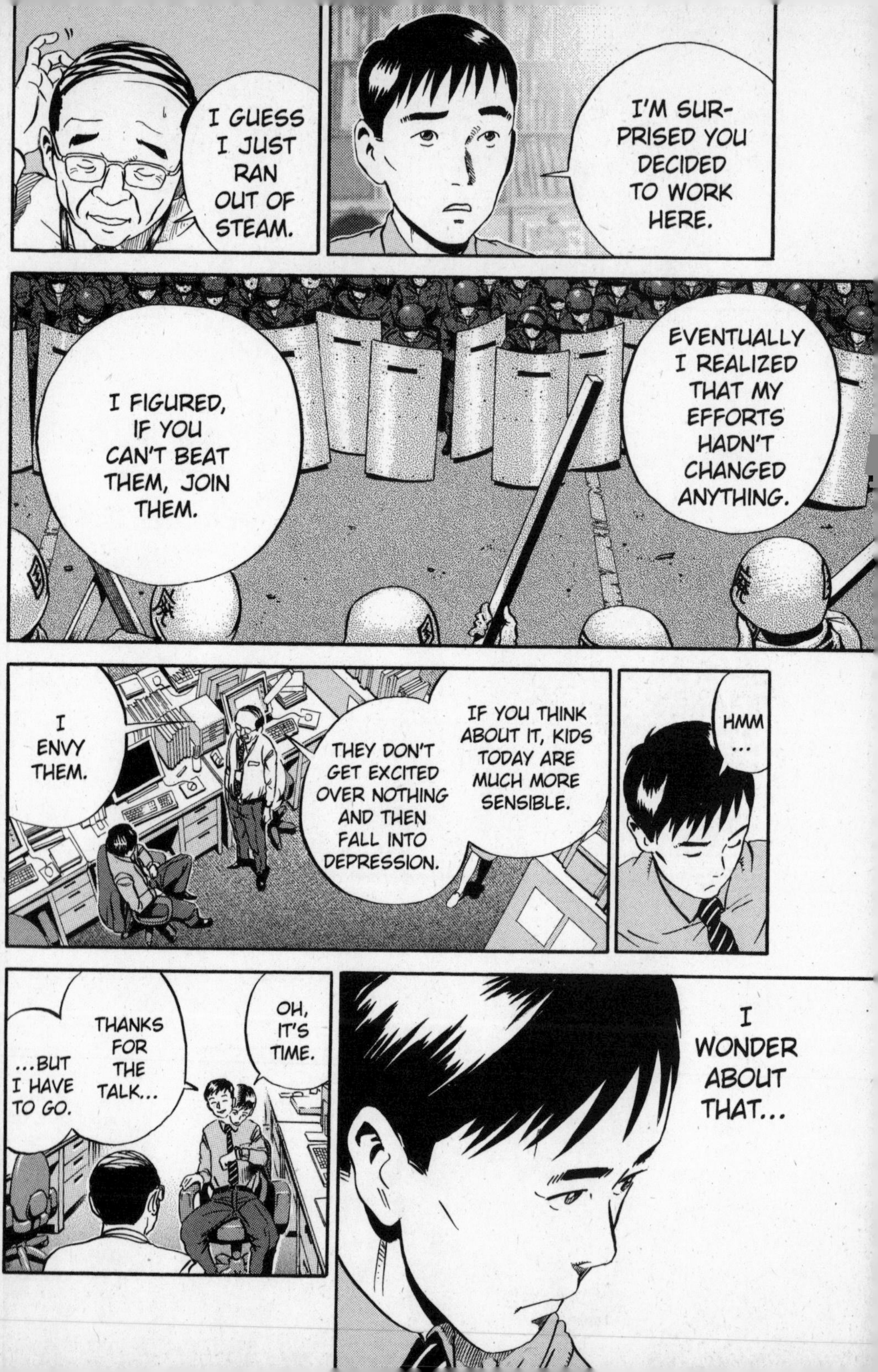
I'M SUR-PRISED YOU DECIDED TO WORK HERE.
I GUESS I JUST RAN OUT OF STEAM.
EVENTUALLY I REALIZED THAT MY EFFORTS HADN'T CHANGED ANYTHING.
I FIGURED, IF YOU CAN'T BEAT THEM, JOIN THEM.
HMM...
IF YOU THINK ABOUT IT, KIDS TODAY ARE MUCH MORE SENSIBLE.
THEY DON'T GET EXCITED OVER NOTHING AND THEN FALL INTO DEPRESSION.
I ENVY THEM.
I WONDER ABOUT THAT...
OH, IT'S TIME.
THANKS FOR THE TALK...
...BUT I HAVE TO GO.

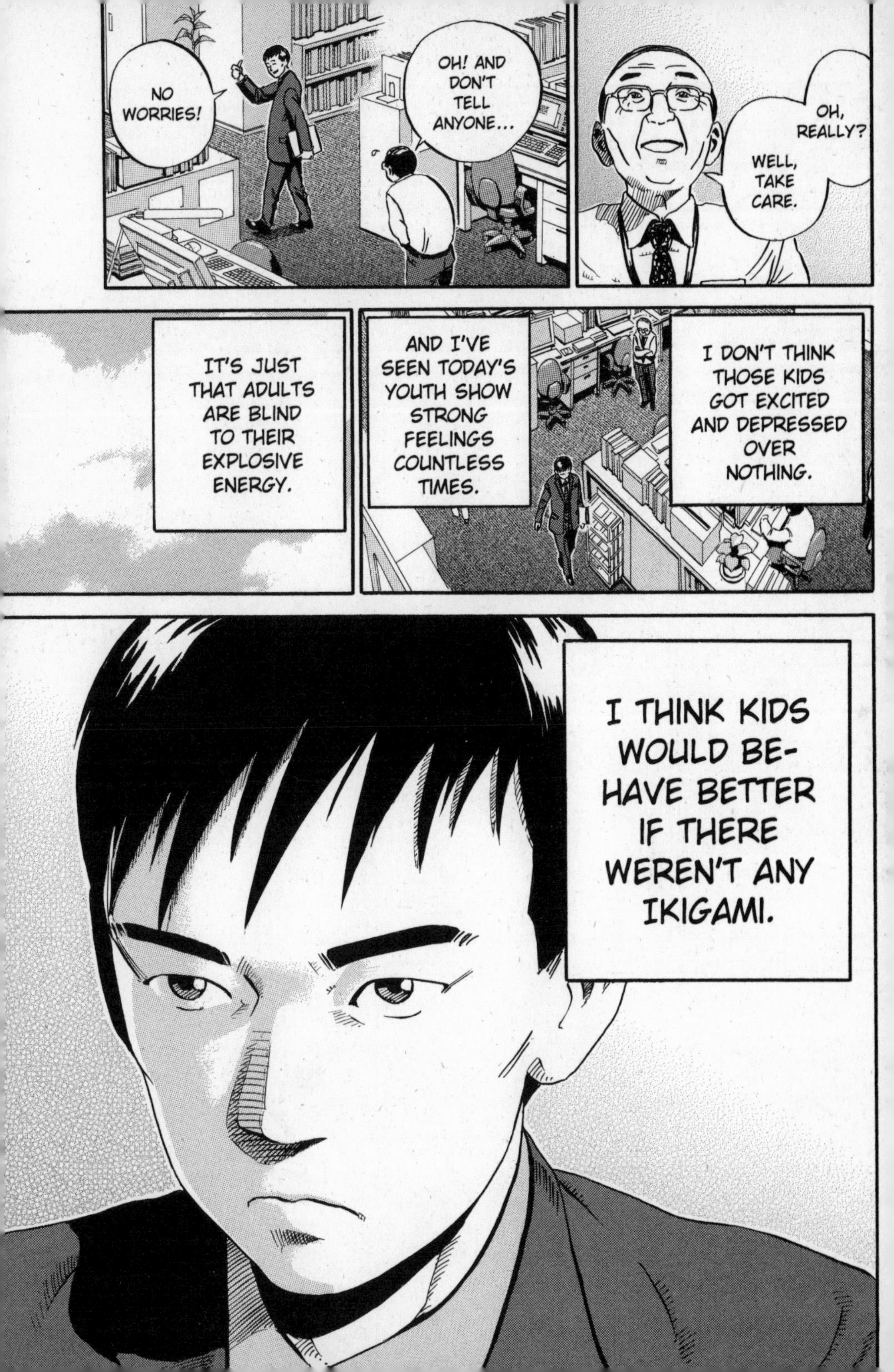
OH, REALLY?
WELL, TAKE CARE.
OH! AND DON'T TELL ANYONE...
NO WORRIES!
I DON'T THINK THOSE KIDS GOT EXCITED AND DEPRESSED OVER NOTHING.
AND I'VE SEEN TODAY'S YOUTH SHOW STRONG FEELINGS COUNTLESS TIMES.
IT'S JUST THAT ADULTS ARE BLIND TO THEIR EXPLOSIVE ENERGY.
I THINK KIDS WOULD BE-HAVE BETTER IF THERE WEREN'T ANY IKIGAMI.

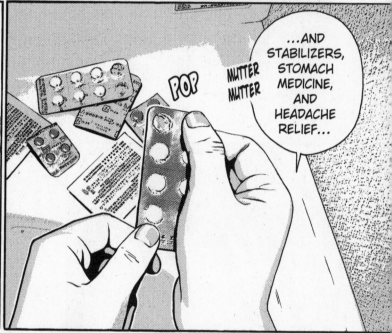

...AND STABILIZERS, STOMACH MEDICINE, AND HEADACHE RELIEF...

MUTTER MUTTER

POP

MUTTER
MUTTER
MUTTER

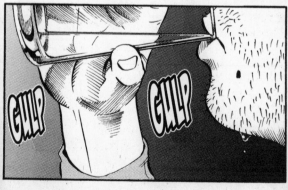

GULP

GULP

MEOW~

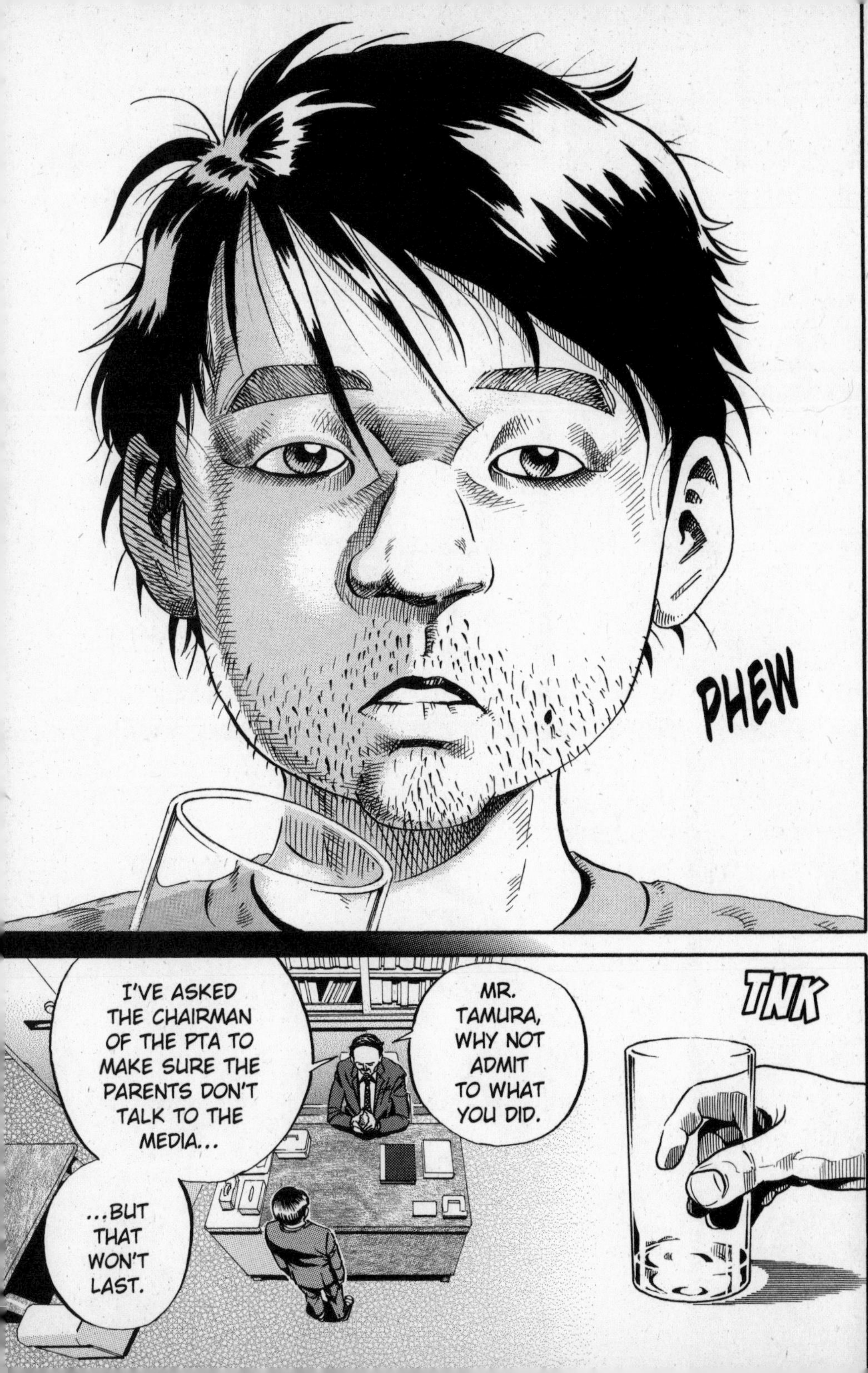
PHEW
TNK
MR. TAMURA, WHY NOT ADMIT TO WHAT YOU DID.
I'VE ASKED THE CHAIRMAN OF THE PTA TO MAKE SURE THE PARENTS DON'T TALK TO THE MEDIA...
...BUT THAT WON'T LAST.

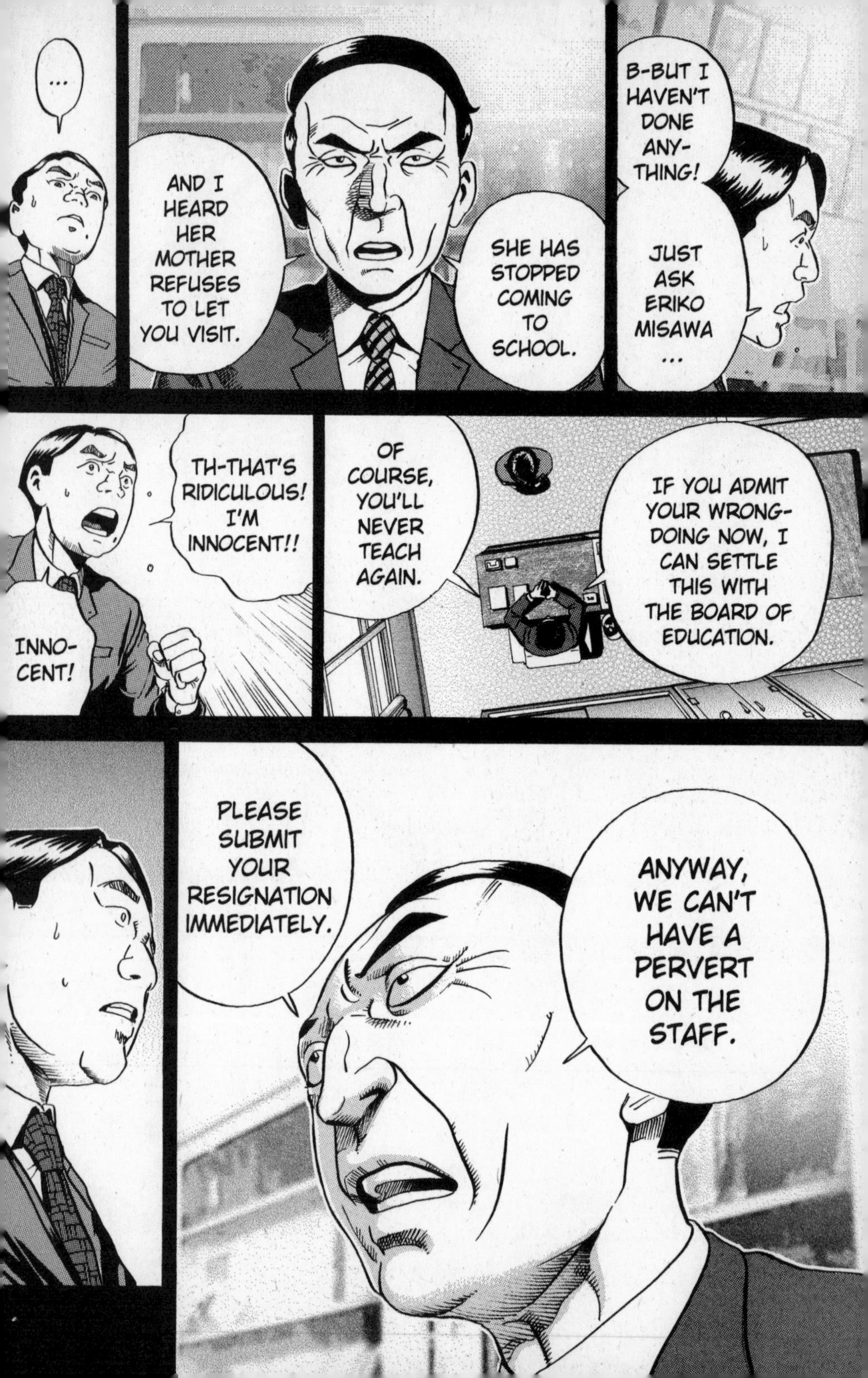
B-BUT I HAVEN'T DONE ANYTHING!
JUST ASK ERIKO MISAWA ...
SHE HAS STOPPED COMING TO SCHOOL.
AND I HEARD HER MOTHER REFUSES TO LET YOU VISIT.
...
IF YOU ADMIT YOUR WRONGDOING NOW, I CAN SETTLE THIS WITH THE BOARD OF EDUCATION.
OF COURSE, YOU'LL NEVER TEACH AGAIN.
TH-THAT'S RIDICULOUS! I'M INNOCENT!!
INNOCENT!
ANYWAY, WE CAN'T HAVE A PERVERT ON THE STAFF.
PLEASE SUBMIT YOUR RESIGNATION IMMEDIATELY.

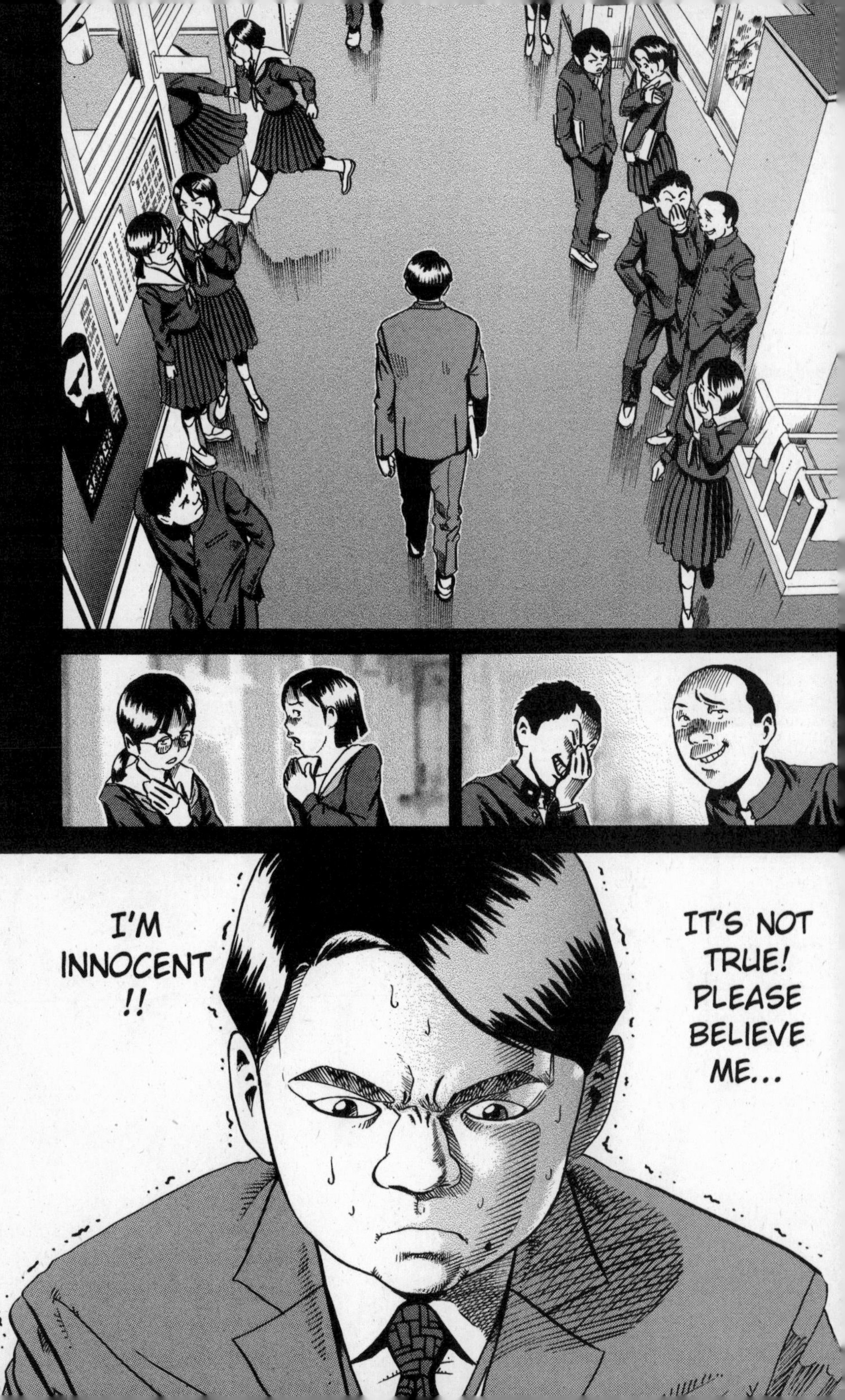
IT'S NOT TRUE! PLEASE BELIEVE ME...
I'M INNOCENT!!

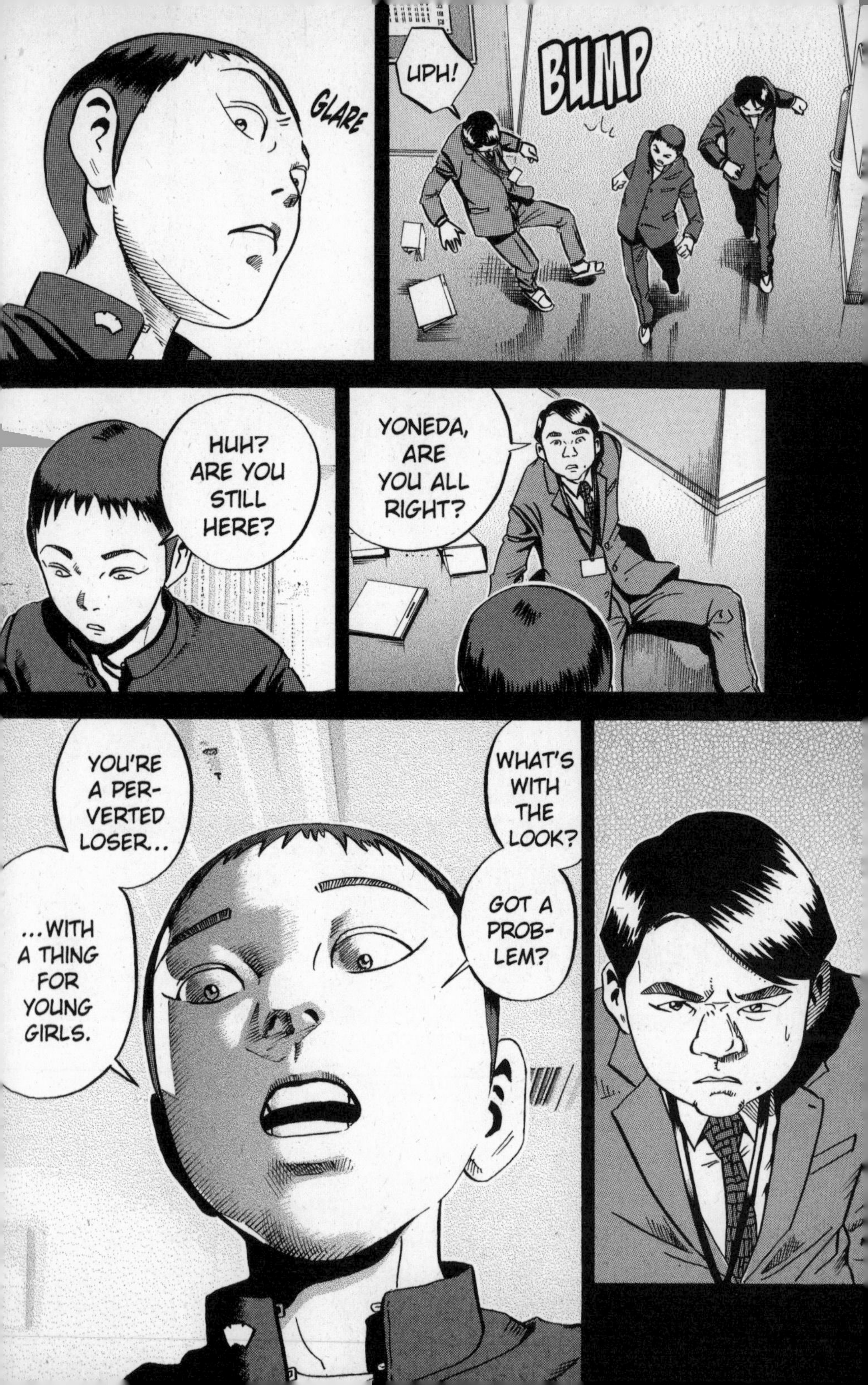
UPH!
BUMP
GLARE
YONEDA, ARE YOU ALL RIGHT?
HUH? ARE YOU STILL HERE?
WHAT'S WITH THE LOOK?
GOT A PROB-LEM?
YOU'RE A PER-VERTED LOSER...
...WITH A THING FOR YOUNG GIRLS.

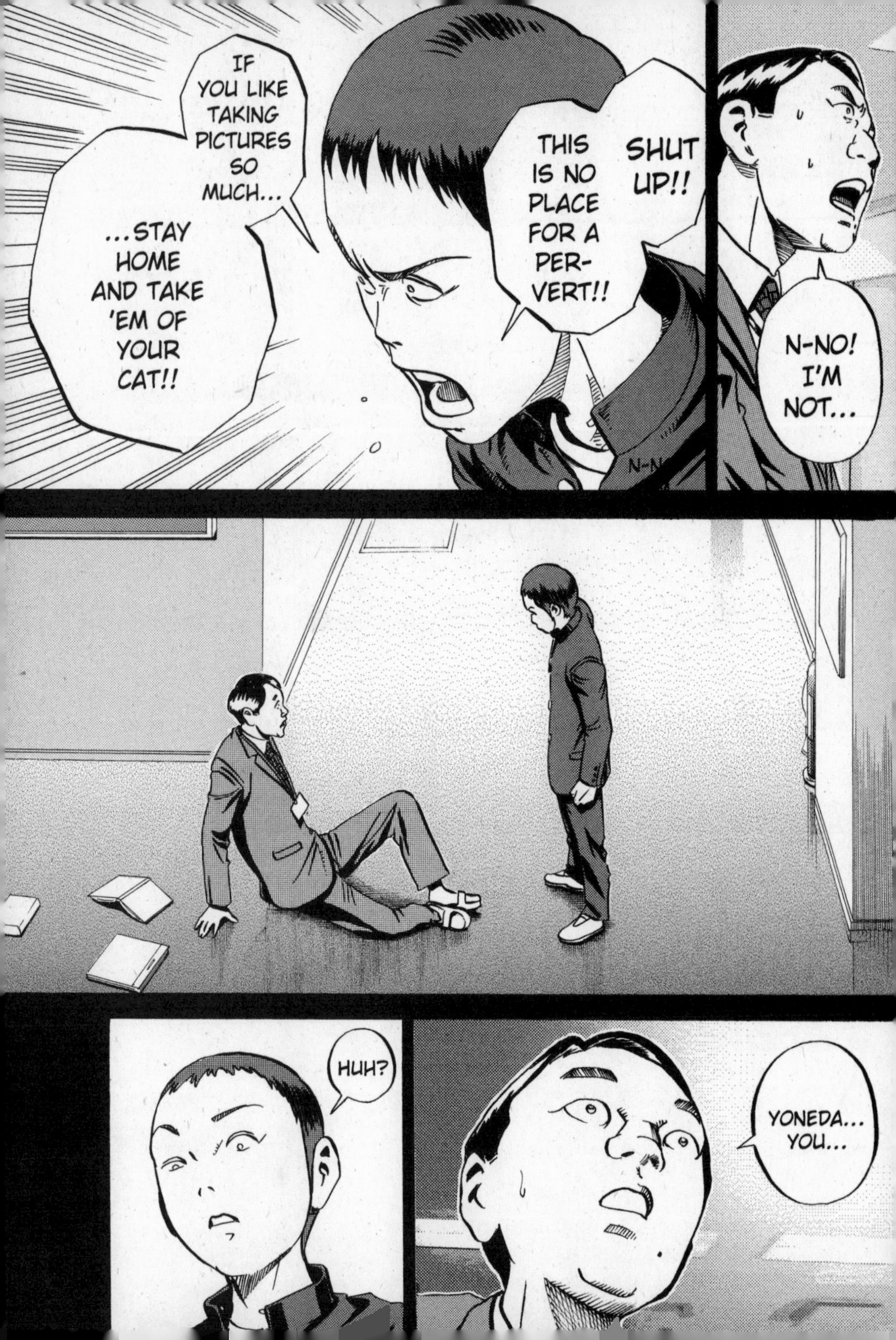
N-NO! I'M NOT...
SHUT UP!!
THIS IS NO PLACE FOR A PER-VERT!!
IF YOU LIKE TAKING PICTURES SO MUCH...
...STAY HOME AND TAKE 'EM OF YOUR CAT!!
N-N
YONEDA... YOU...
HUH?

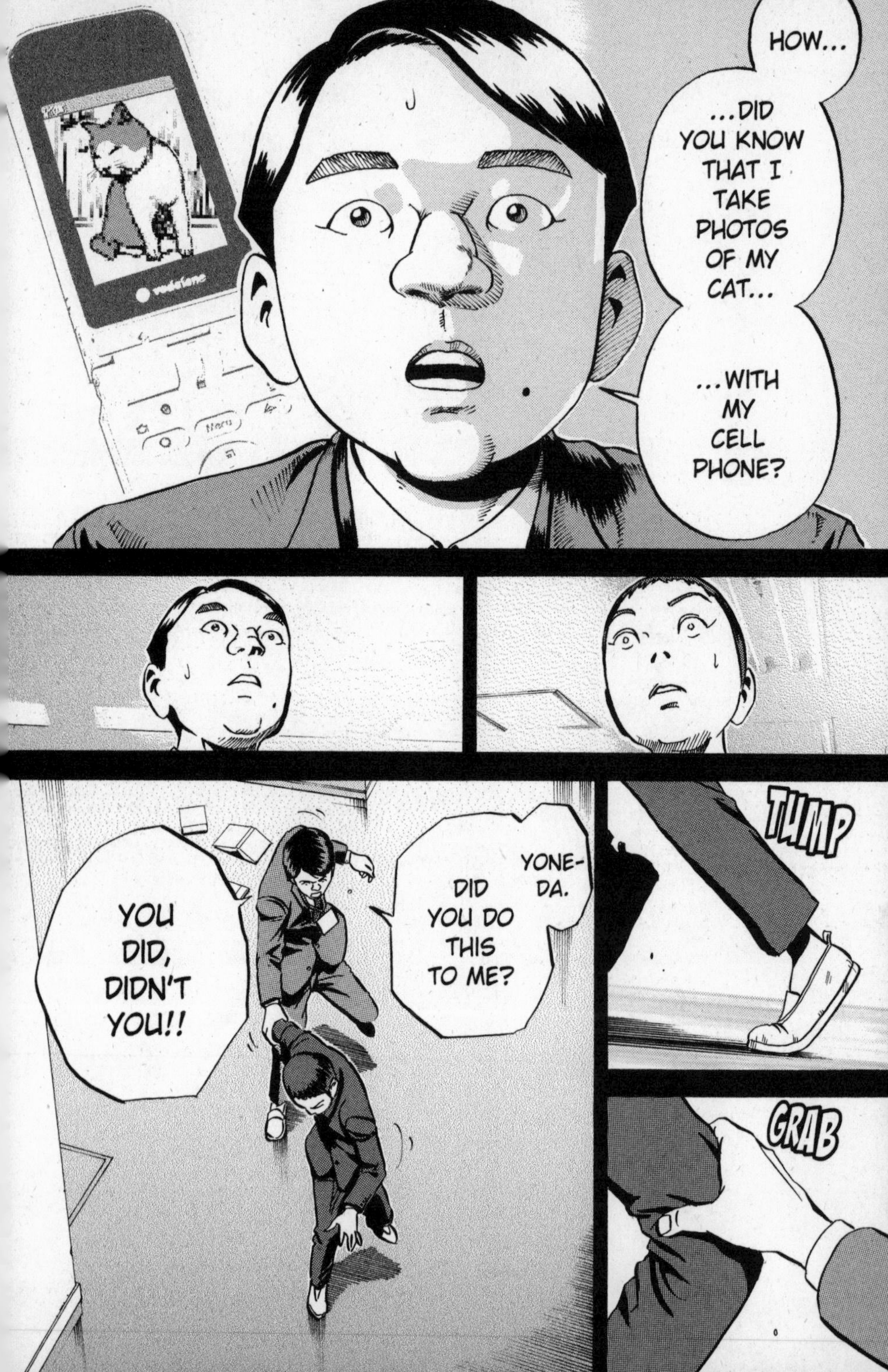
HOW...
...DID YOU KNOW THAT I TAKE PHOTOS OF MY CAT...
...WITH MY CELL PHONE?
TUMP
GRAB
YONE-DA.
DID YOU DO THIS TO ME?
YOU DID, DIDN'T YOU!!

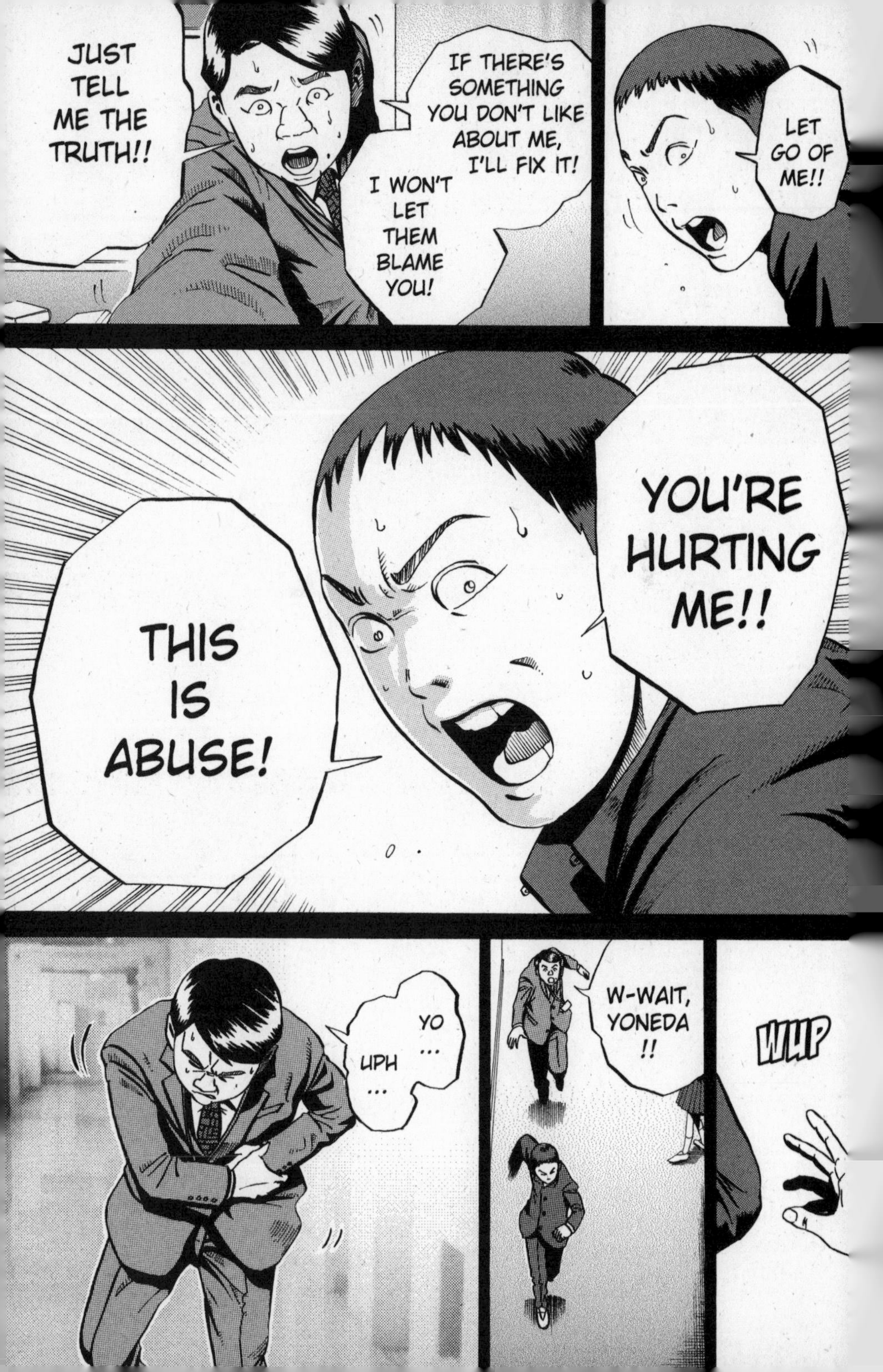
LET GO OF ME!!
IF THERE'S SOMETHING YOU DON'T LIKE ABOUT ME, I'LL FIX IT!
I WON'T LET THEM BLAME YOU!
JUST TELL ME THE TRUTH!!
YOU'RE HURTING ME!!
THIS IS ABUSE!
WUP
W-WAIT, YONEDA!!
YO...
UPH...

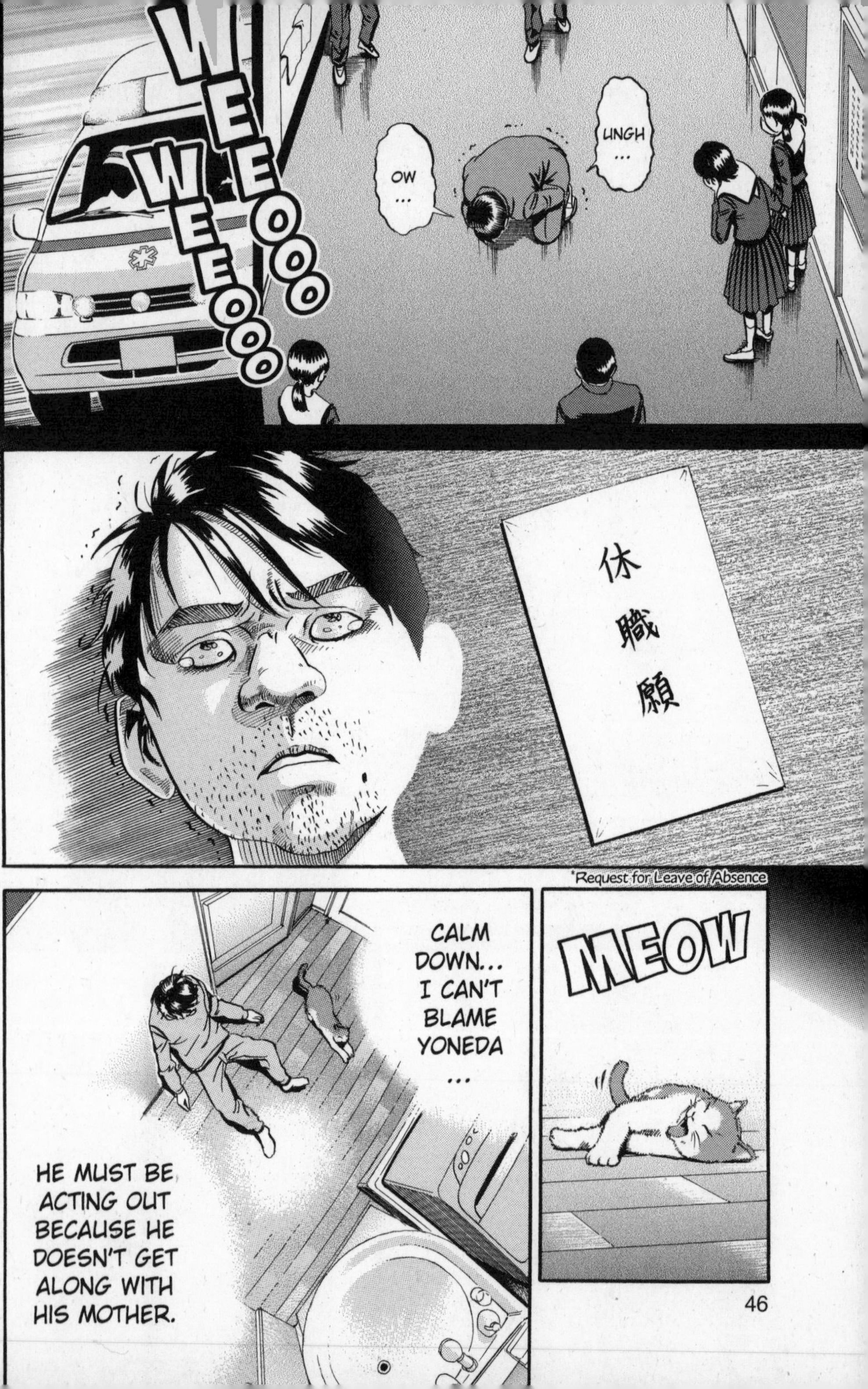
UNGH ...
OW ...
WEEOOO
WEEOOO
休職願
*Request for Leave of Absence
MEOW
CALM DOWN... I CAN'T BLAME YONEDA ...
HE MUST BE ACTING OUT BECAUSE HE DOESN'T GET ALONG WITH HIS MOTHER.

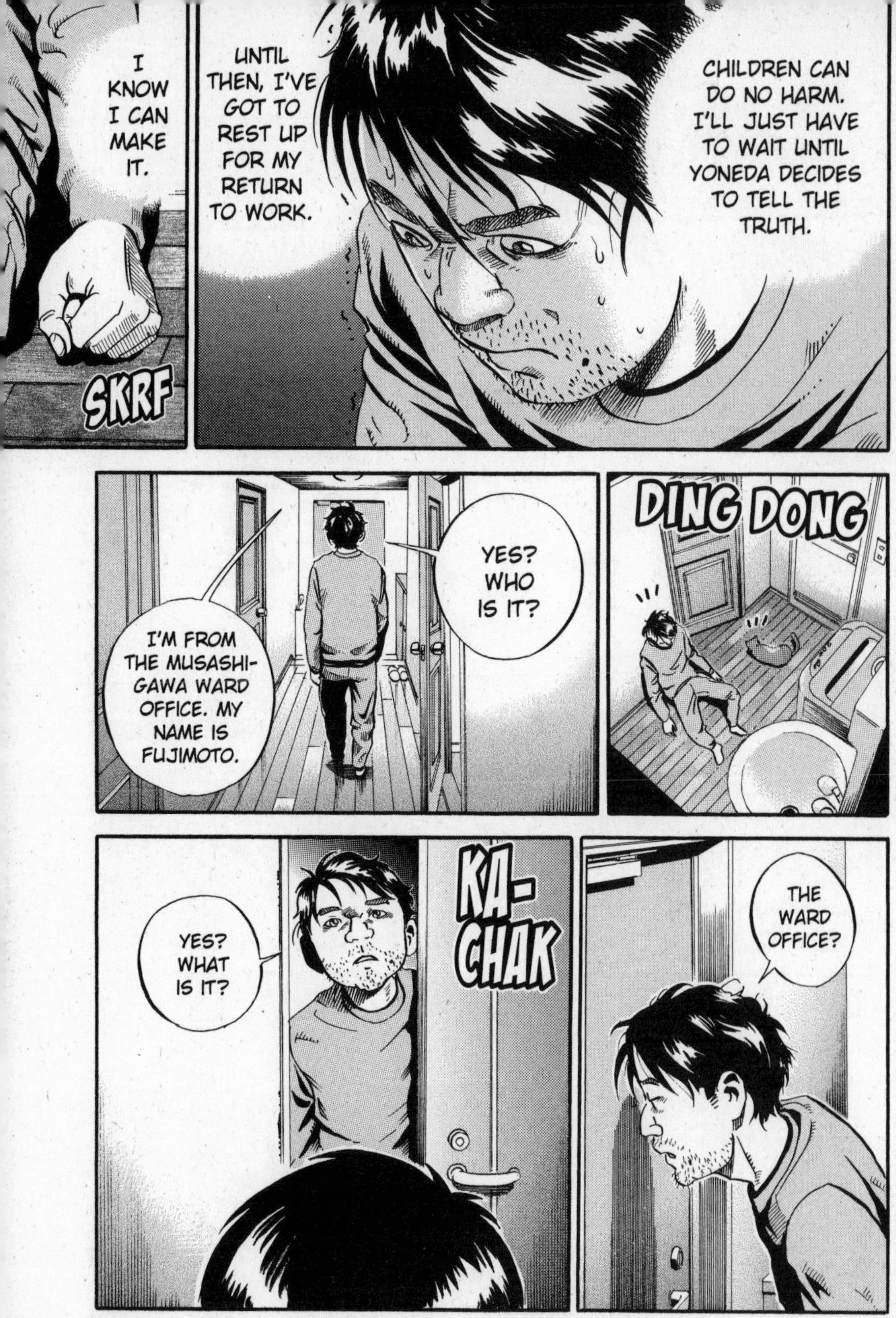
CHILDREN CAN DO NO HARM. I'LL JUST HAVE TO WAIT UNTIL YONEDA DECIDES TO TELL THE TRUTH.
UNTIL THEN, I'VE GOT TO REST UP FOR MY RETURN TO WORK.
I KNOW I CAN MAKE IT.
SKRF
DING DONG
YES? WHO IS IT?
I'M FROM THE MUSASHI-GAWA WARD OFFICE. MY NAME IS FUJIMOTO.
THE WARD OFFICE?
KA-CHAK
YES? WHAT IS IT?

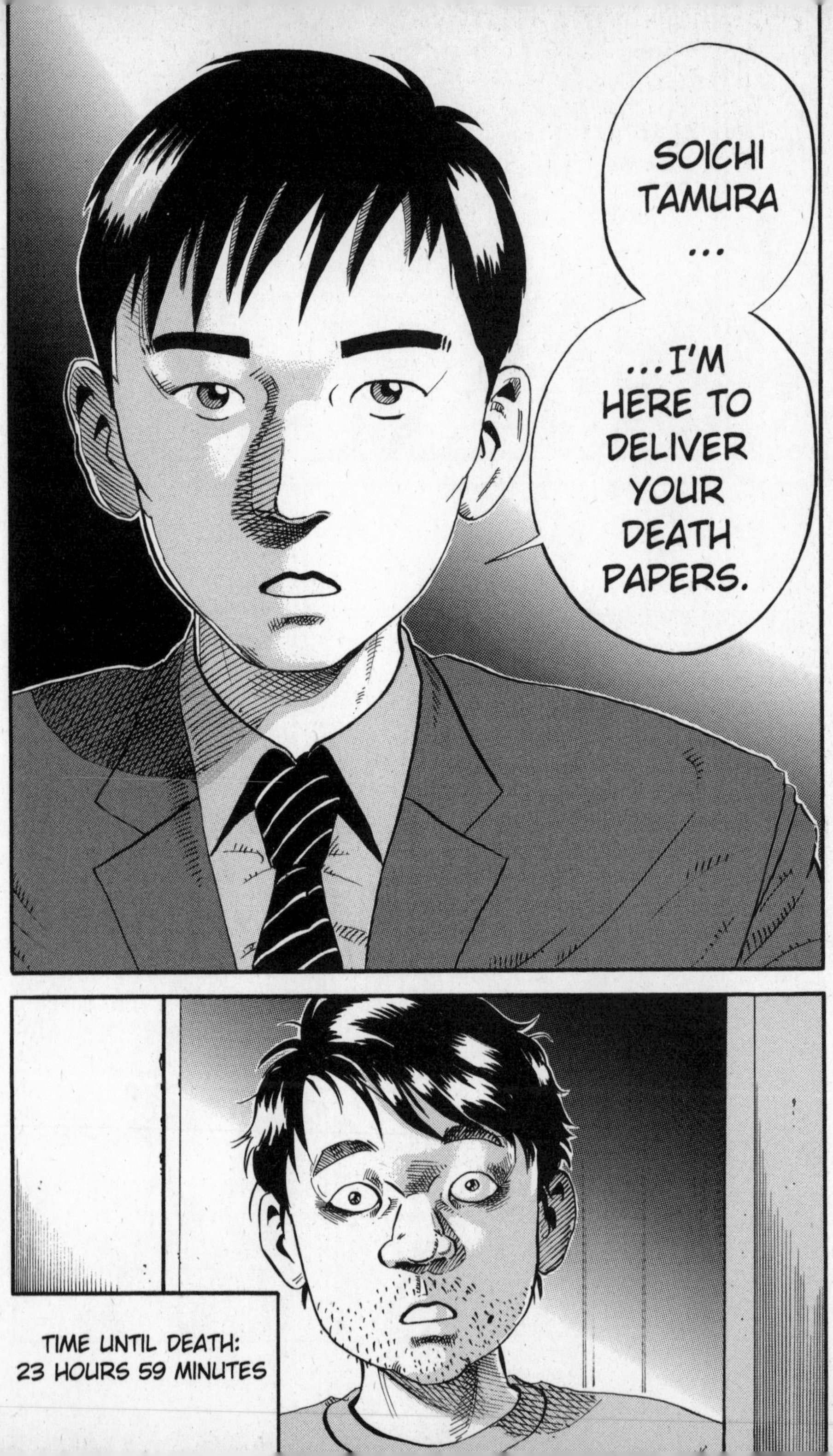
SOICHI TAMURA ...
...I'M HERE TO DELIVER YOUR DEATH PAPERS.
TIME UNTIL DEATH: 23 HOURS 59 MINUTES

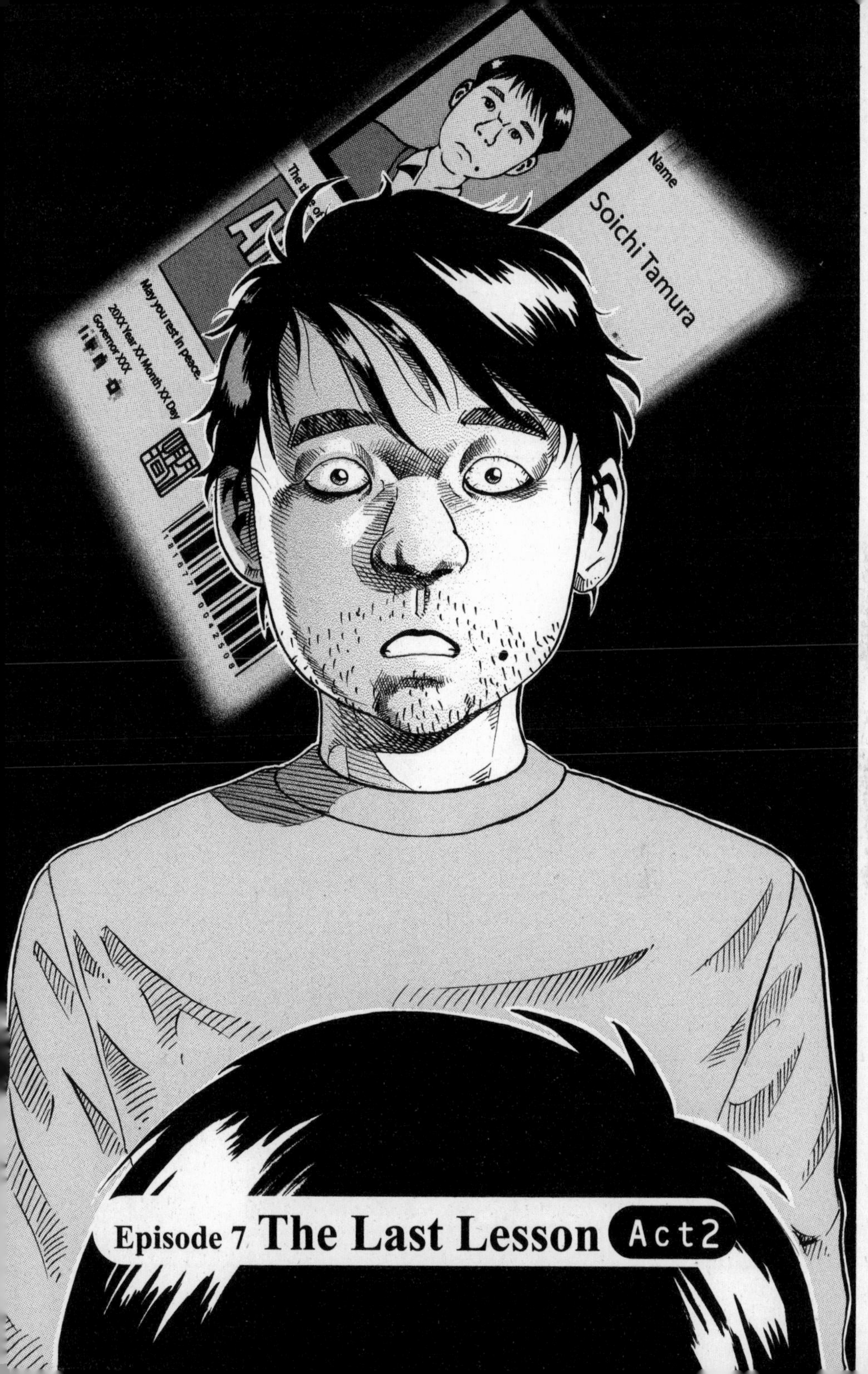
Name
Soichi Tamura
May you rest in peace.
20XX Year XX Month XX Day
Governor XXX
Episode 7 The Last Lesson Act2

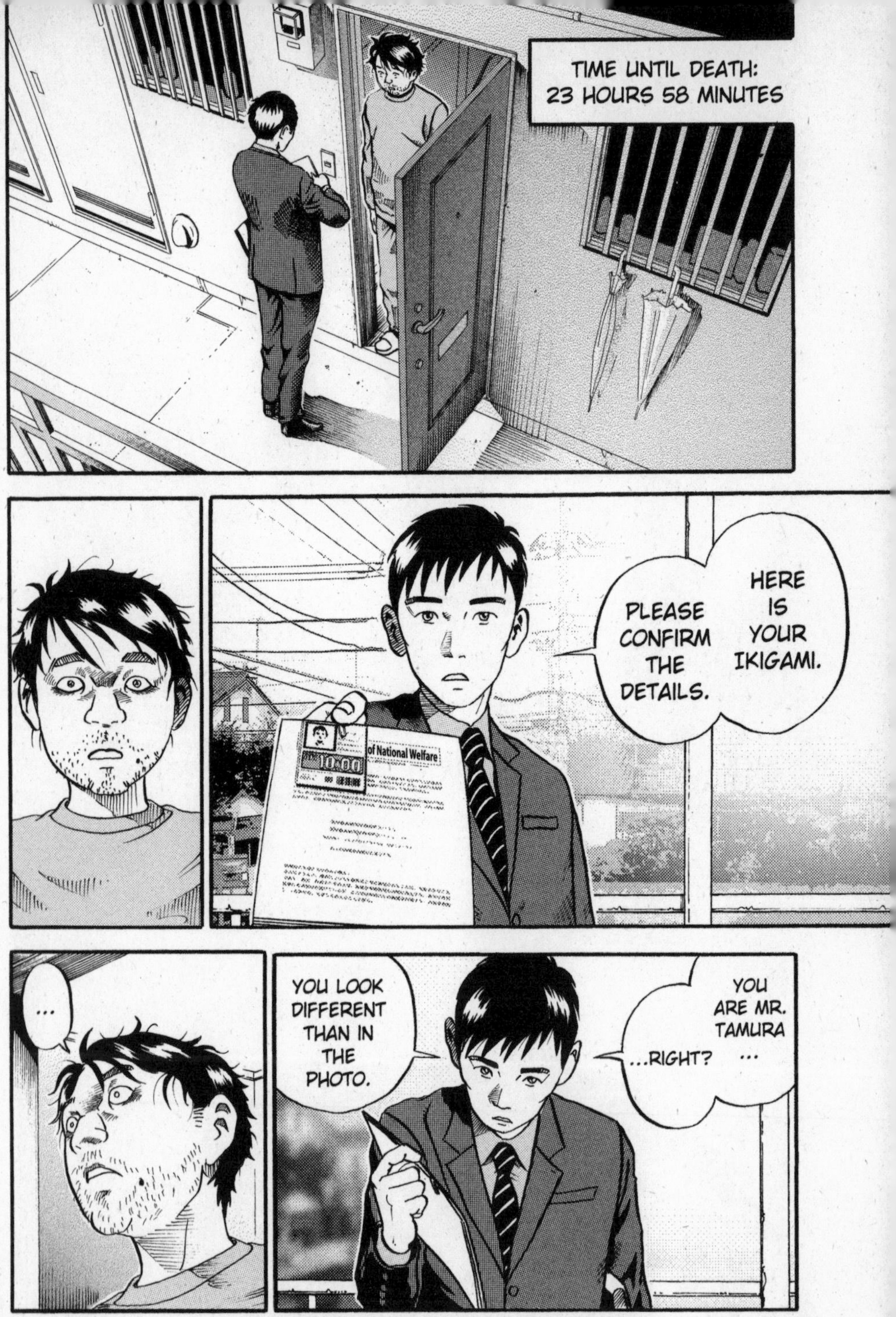
TIME UNTIL DEATH: 23 HOURS 58 MINUTES
HERE IS YOUR IKIGAMI.
PLEASE CONFIRM THE DETAILS.
of National Welfare
10:00
YOU ARE MR. TAMURA ...
...RIGHT?
YOU LOOK DIFFERENT THAN IN THE PHOTO.
...

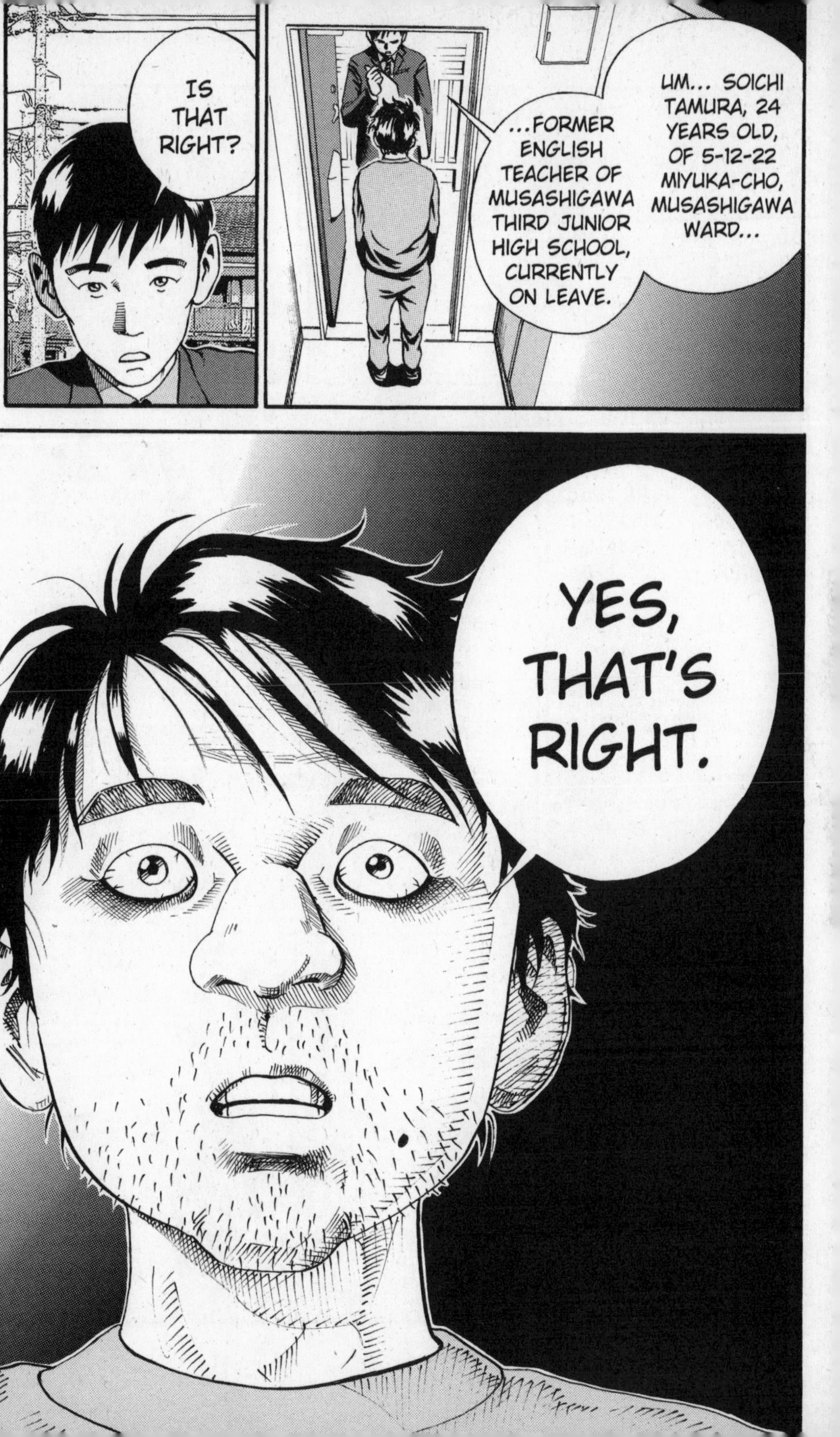
UM... SOICHI TAMURA, 24 YEARS OLD, OF 5-12-22 MIYUKA-CHO, MUSASHIGAWA WARD...
...FORMER ENGLISH TEACHER OF MUSASHIGAWA THIRD JUNIOR HIGH SCHOOL, CURRENTLY ON LEAVE.
IS THAT RIGHT?
YES, THAT'S RIGHT.

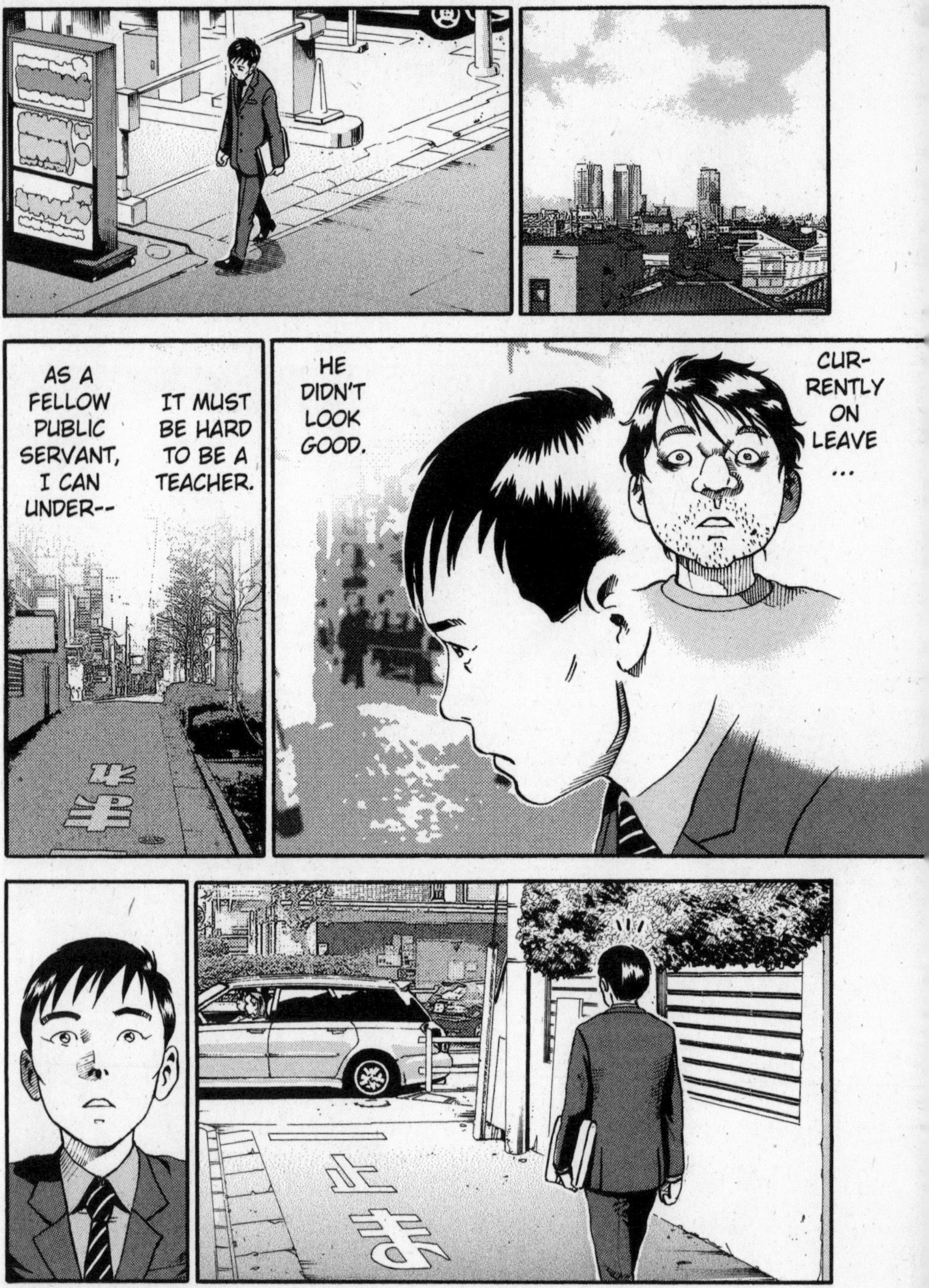
CUR-RENTLY ON LEAVE ...
HE DIDN'T LOOK GOOD.
IT MUST BE HARD TO BE A TEACHER.
AS A FELLOW PUBLIC SERVANT, I CAN UNDER--

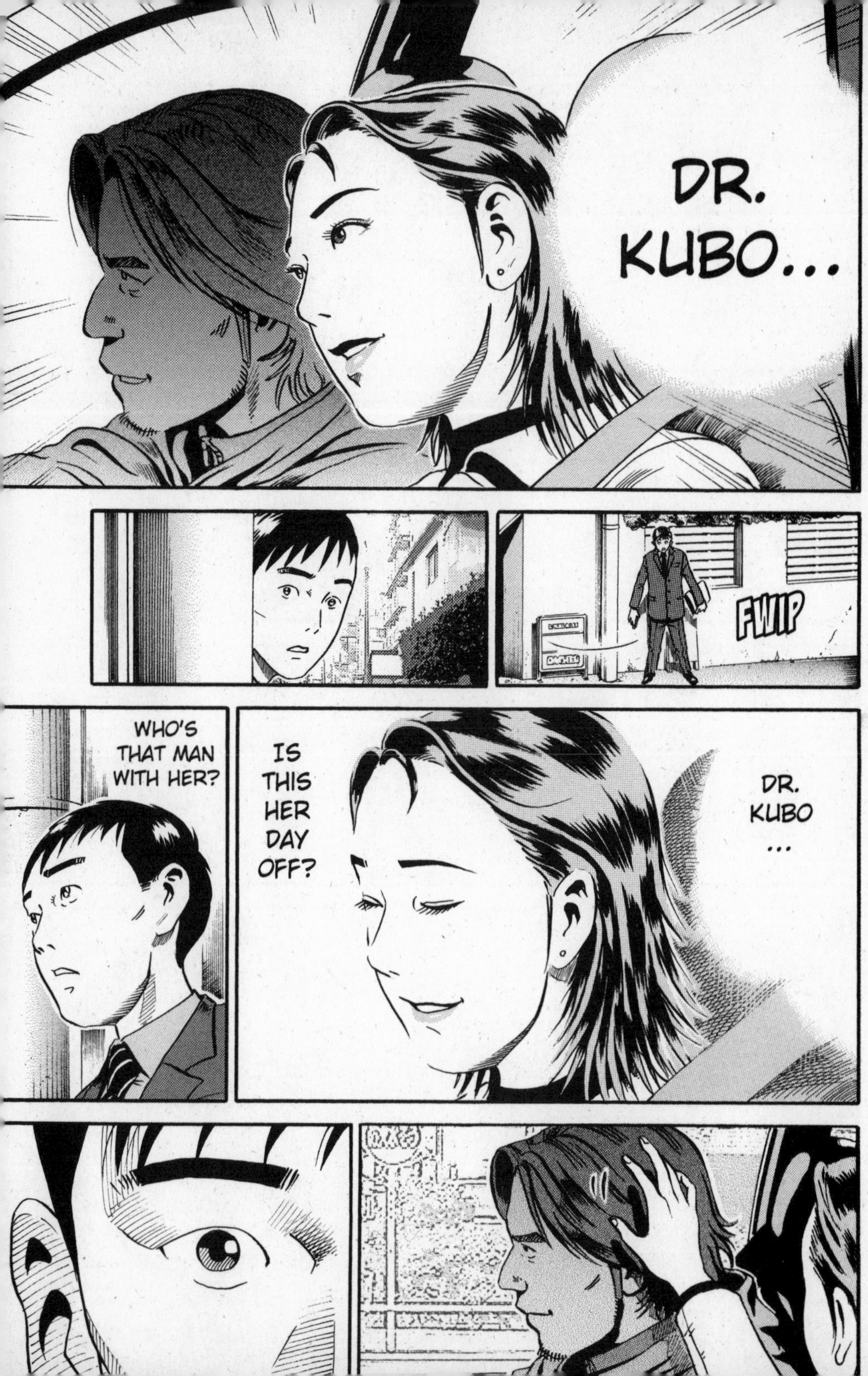
DR. KUBO...
FWIP
DR. KUBO ...
IS THIS HER DAY OFF?
WHO'S THAT MAN WITH HER?

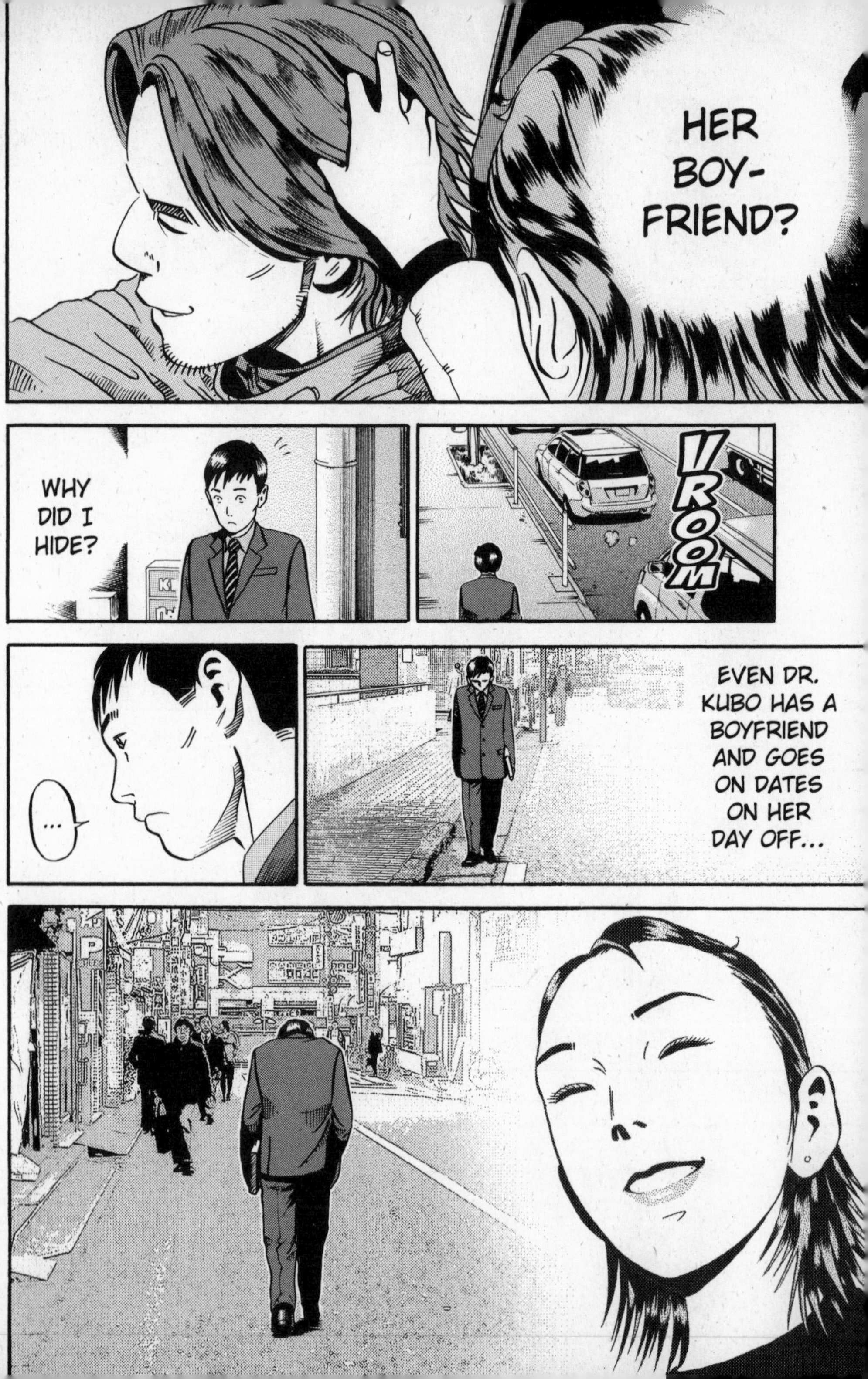
HER BOY-FRIEND?
VROOM
WHY DID I HIDE?
EVEN DR. KUBO HAS A BOYFRIEND AND GOES ON DATES ON HER DAY OFF...
...

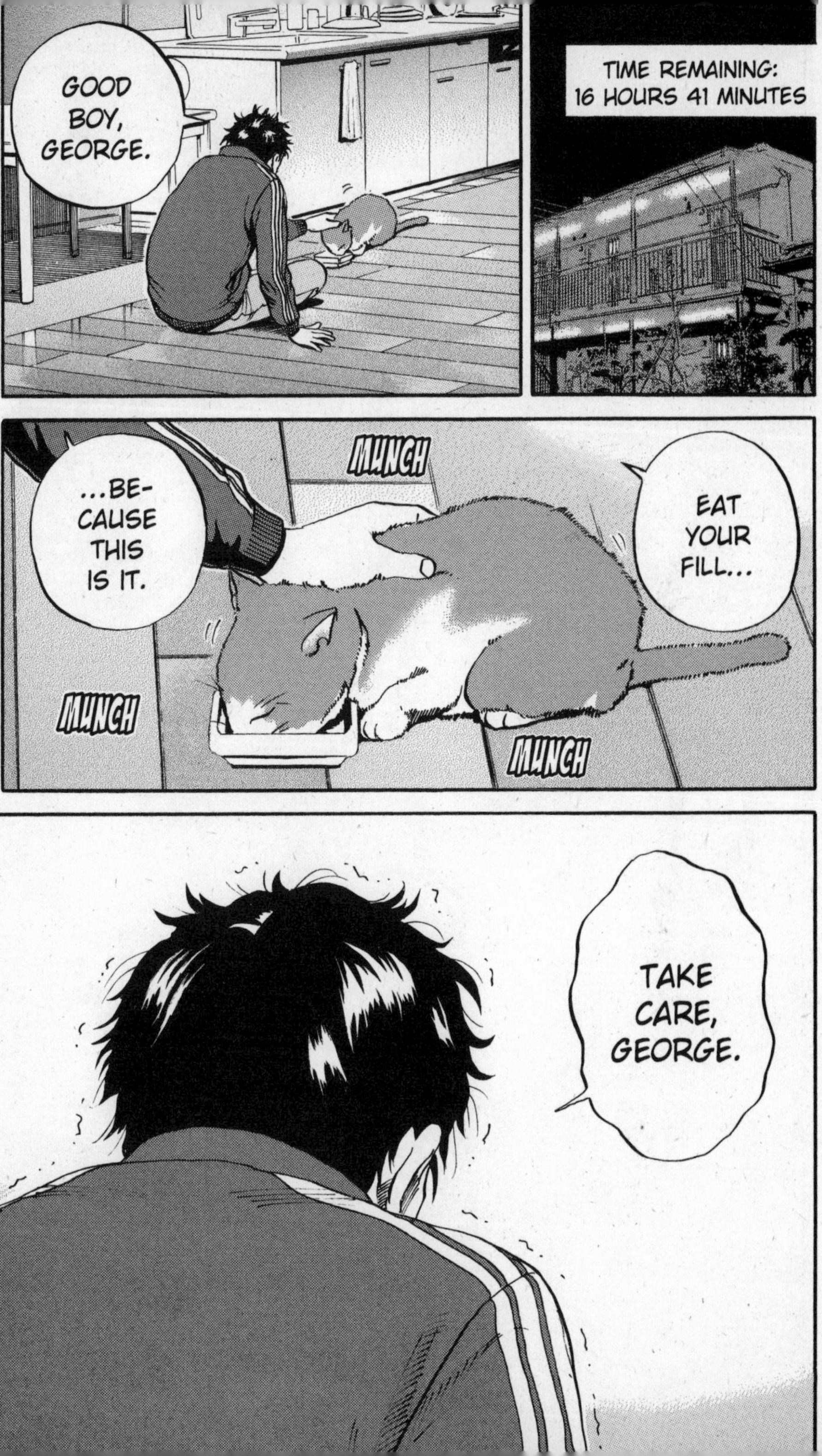
TIME REMAINING: 16 HOURS 41 MINUTES
GOOD BOY, GEORGE.
EAT YOUR FILL...
MUNCH
...BE-CAUSE THIS IS IT.
MUNCH
MUNCH
TAKE CARE, GEORGE.

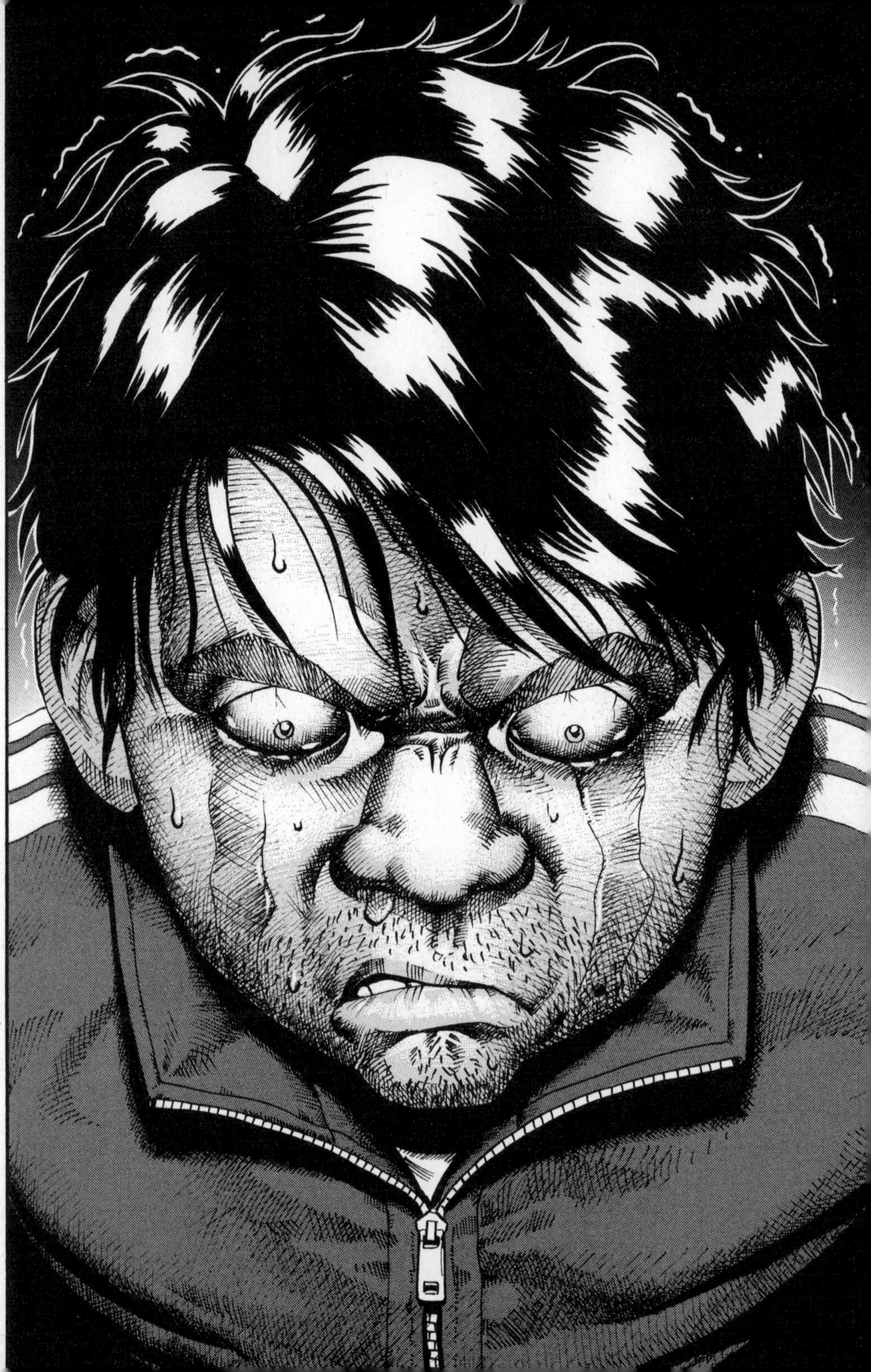

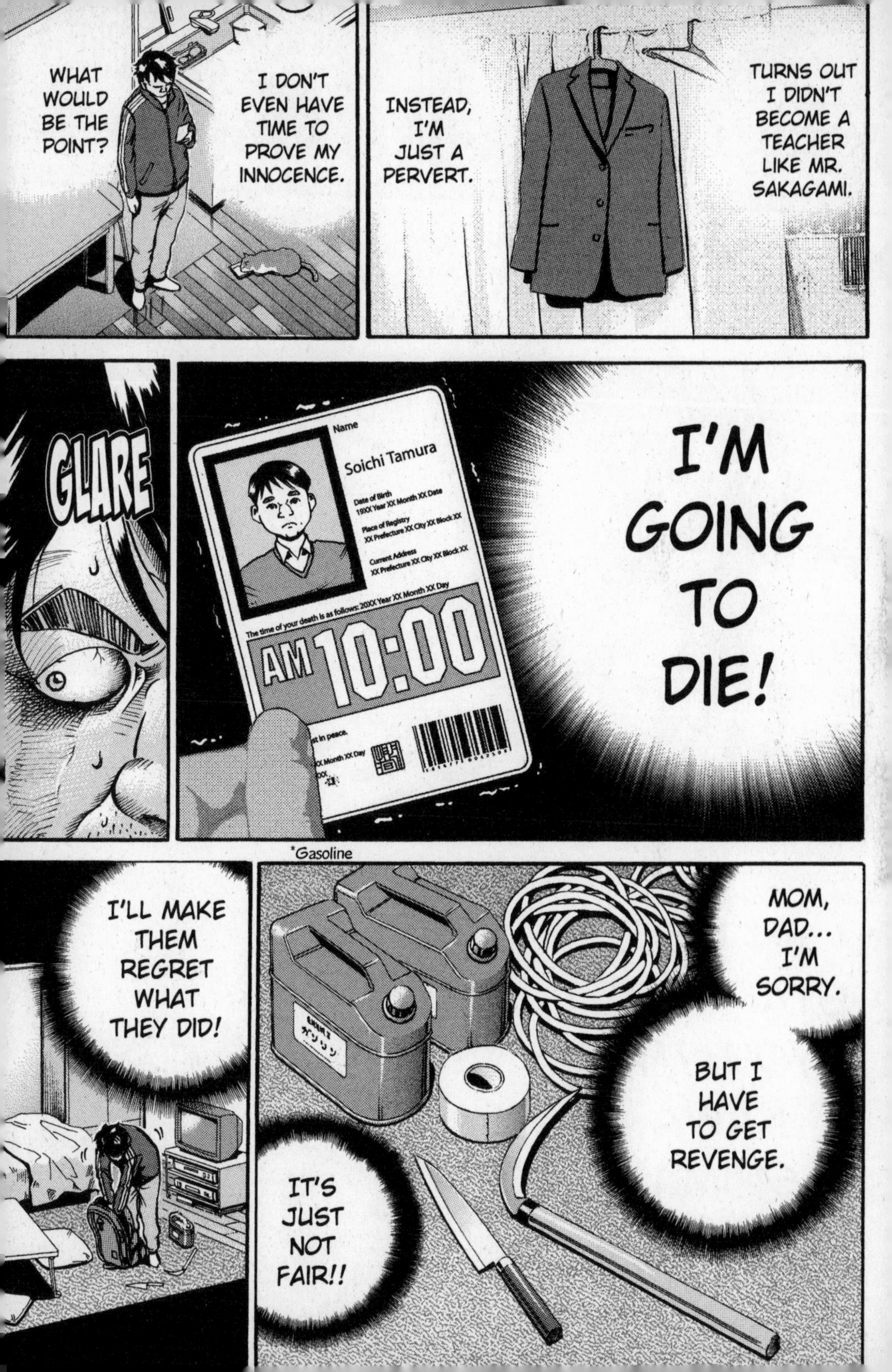
TURNS OUT I DIDN'T BECOME A TEACHER LIKE MR. SAKAGAMI.
INSTEAD, I'M JUST A PERVERT.
I DON'T EVEN HAVE TIME TO PROVE MY INNOCENCE.
WHAT WOULD BE THE POINT?
Name
Soichi Tamura
Date of Birth
19XX Year XX Month XX Date
Place of Registry
XX Prefecture XX City XX Block XX
Current Address
XX Prefecture XX City XX Block XX
The time of your death is as follows: 20XX Year XX Month XX Day
AM 10:00
I'M GOING TO DIE!
GLARE
*Gasoline
MOM, DAD... I'M SORRY.
BUT I HAVE TO GET REVENGE.
IT'S JUST NOT FAIR!!
I'LL MAKE THEM REGRET WHAT THEY DID!

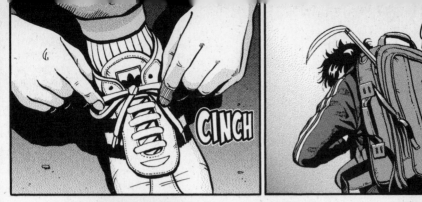

CINCH

SHUMP

ANYWAY, WE CAN'T HAVE A PERVERT ON THE STAFF.

AND I'LL START WITH YOU, MR. KAWA-SHIMA...

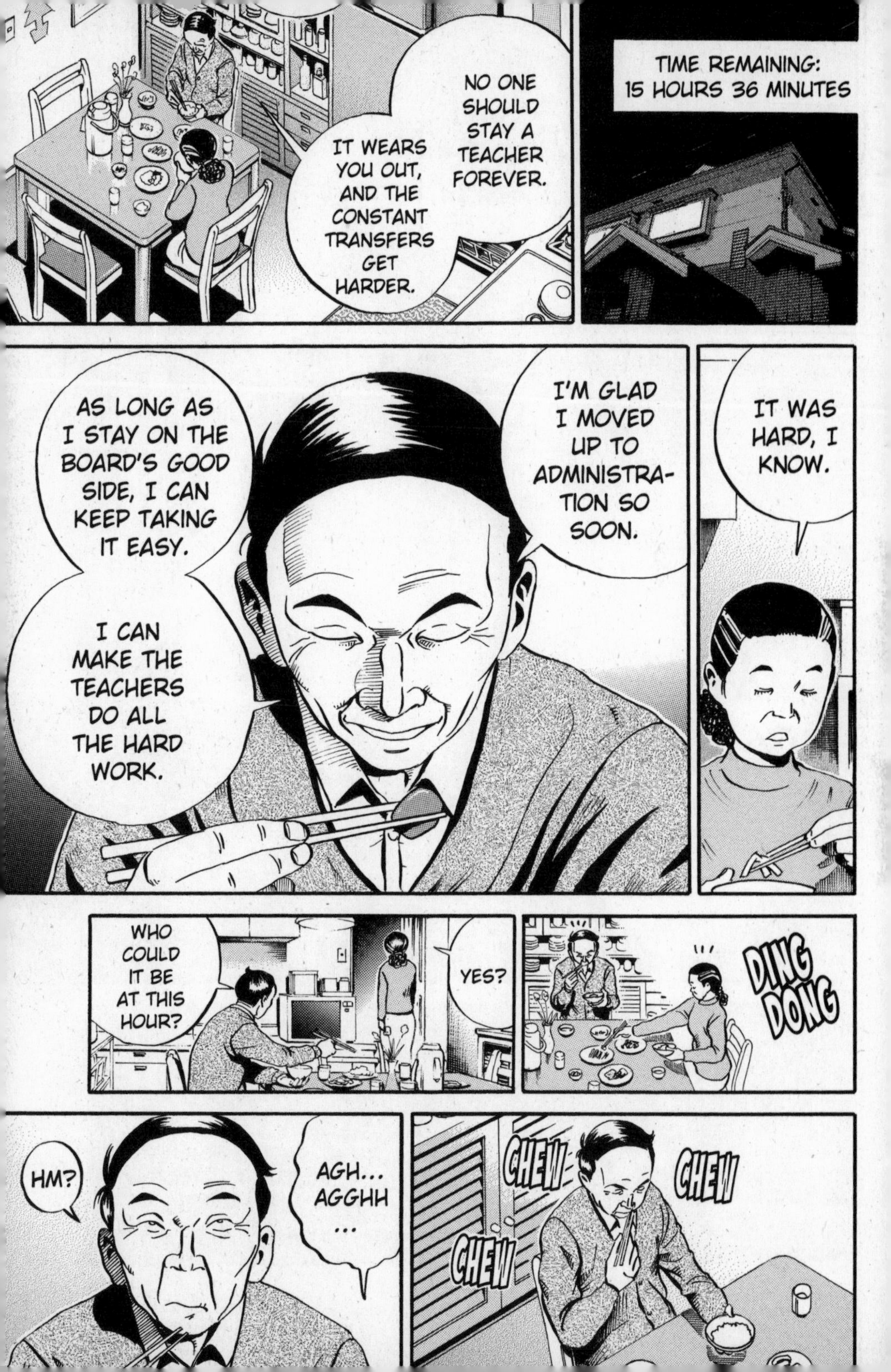
TIME REMAINING:
15 HOURS 36 MINUTES
NO ONE SHOULD STAY A TEACHER FOREVER.
IT WEARS YOU OUT, AND THE CONSTANT TRANSFERS GET HARDER.
IT WAS HARD, I KNOW.
I'M GLAD I MOVED UP TO ADMINISTRA-TION SO SOON.
AS LONG AS I STAY ON THE BOARD'S GOOD SIDE, I CAN KEEP TAKING IT EASY.
I CAN MAKE THE TEACHERS DO ALL THE HARD WORK.
DING DONG
YES?
WHO COULD IT BE AT THIS HOUR?
CHEW
CHEW
CHEW
AGH... AGGHH ...
HM?

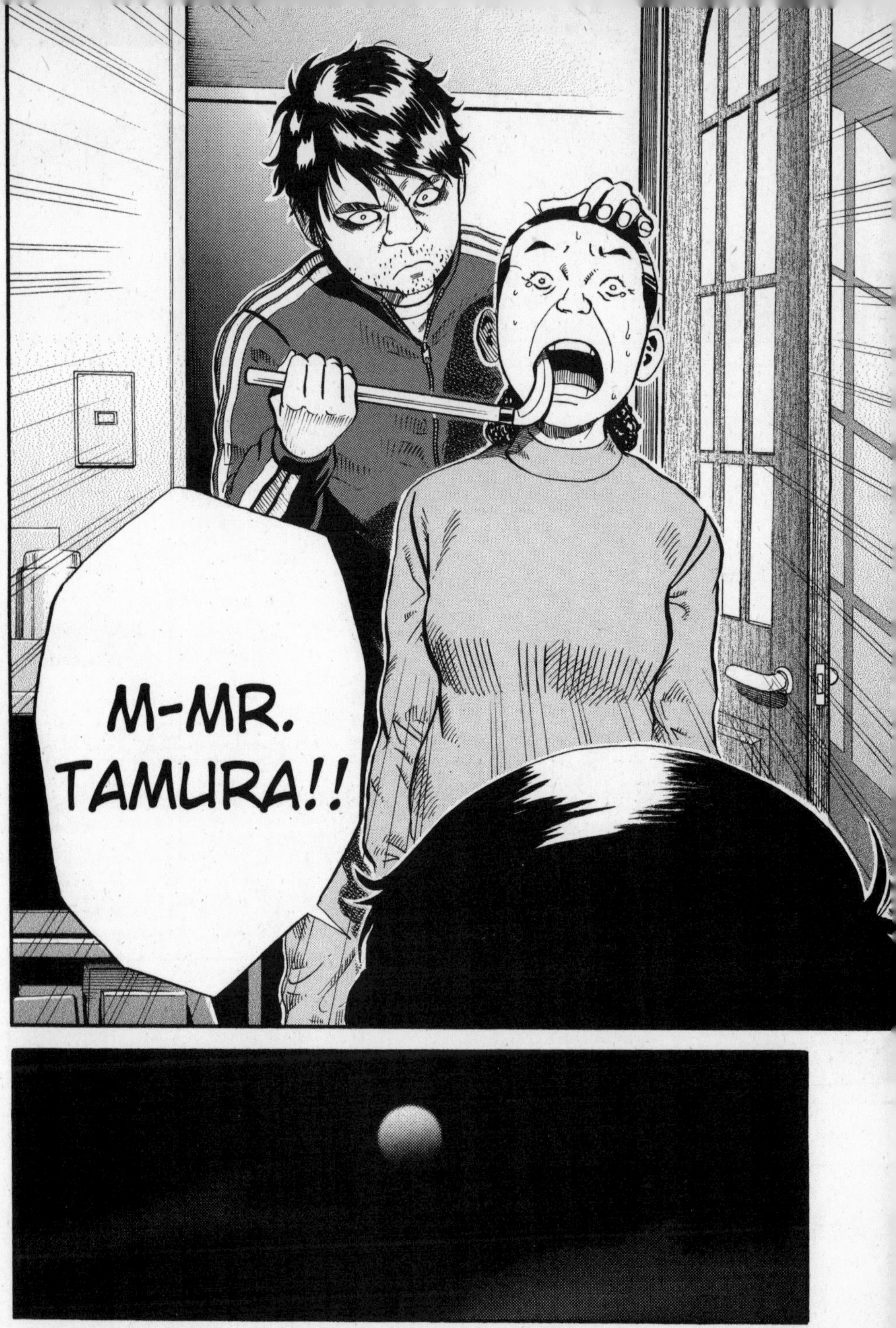
M-MR. TAMURA!!

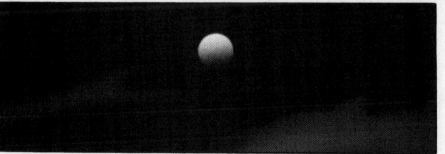

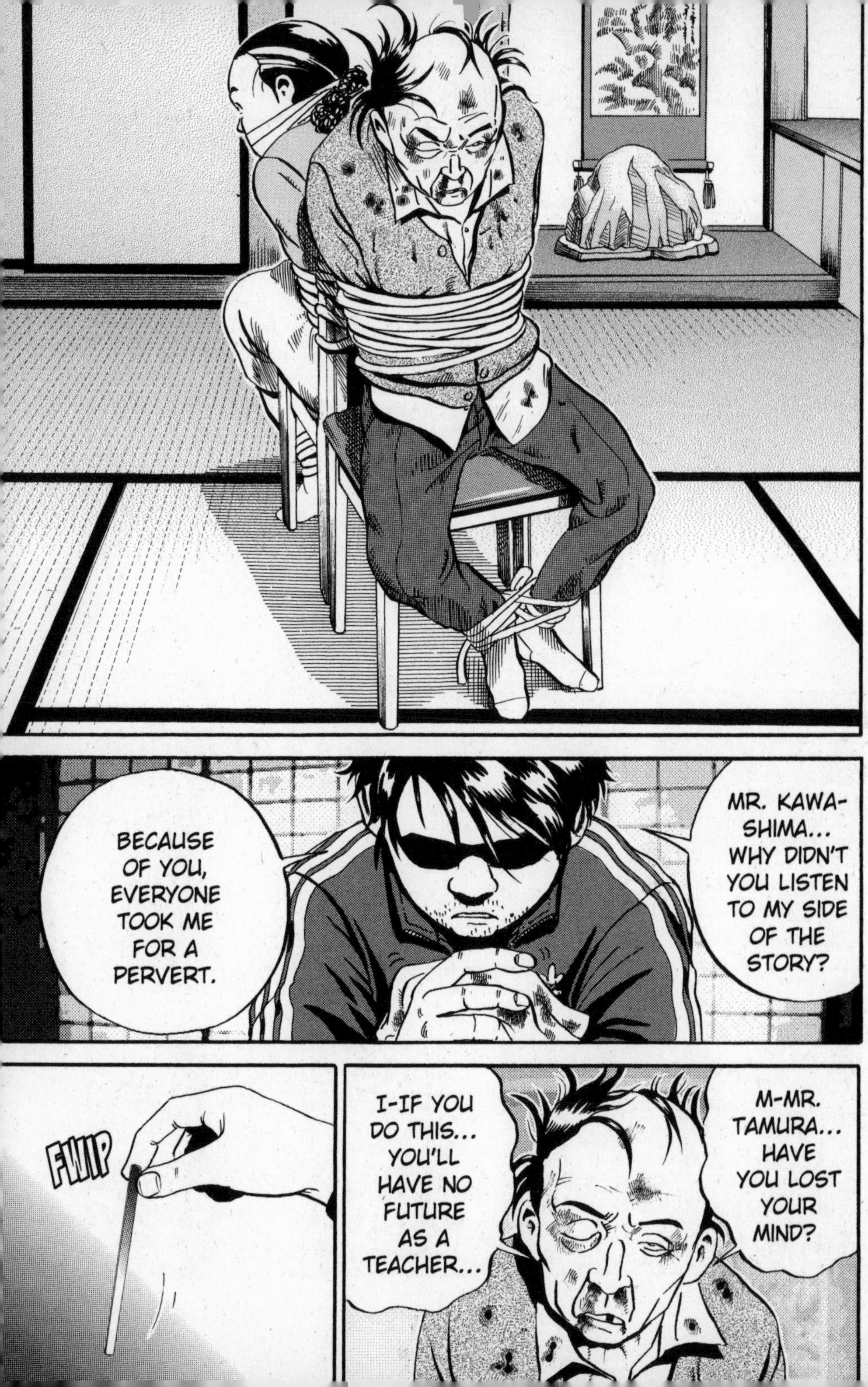
MR. KAWA-SHIMA... WHY DIDN'T YOU LISTEN TO MY SIDE OF THE STORY?
BECAUSE OF YOU, EVERYONE TOOK ME FOR A PERVERT.
M-MR. TAMURA... HAVE YOU LOST YOUR MIND?
I-IF YOU DO THIS... YOU'LL HAVE NO FUTURE AS A TEACHER...
FWIP

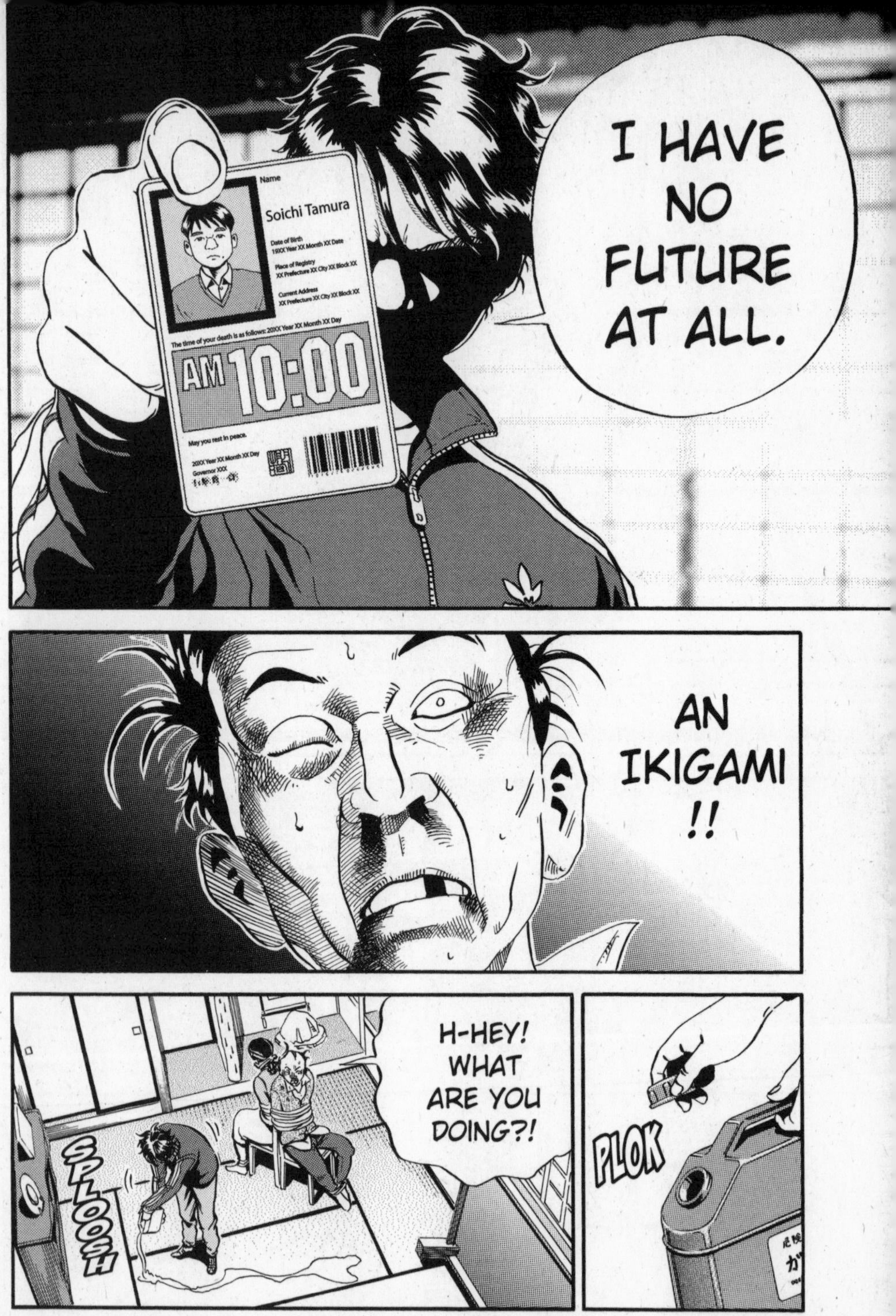
Name
Soichi Tamura
Date of Birth
19XX Year XX Month XX Date
Place of Registry
XX Prefecture XX City XX Block XX
Current Address
XX Prefecture XX City XX Block XX
The time of your death is as follows: 20XX Year XX Month XX Day
AM 10:00
May you rest in peace.
20XX Year XX Month XX Day
Governor XXX
I HAVE NO FUTURE AT ALL.
AN IKIGAMI !!
PLOK
H-HEY! WHAT ARE YOU DOING?!
SPLOOSH

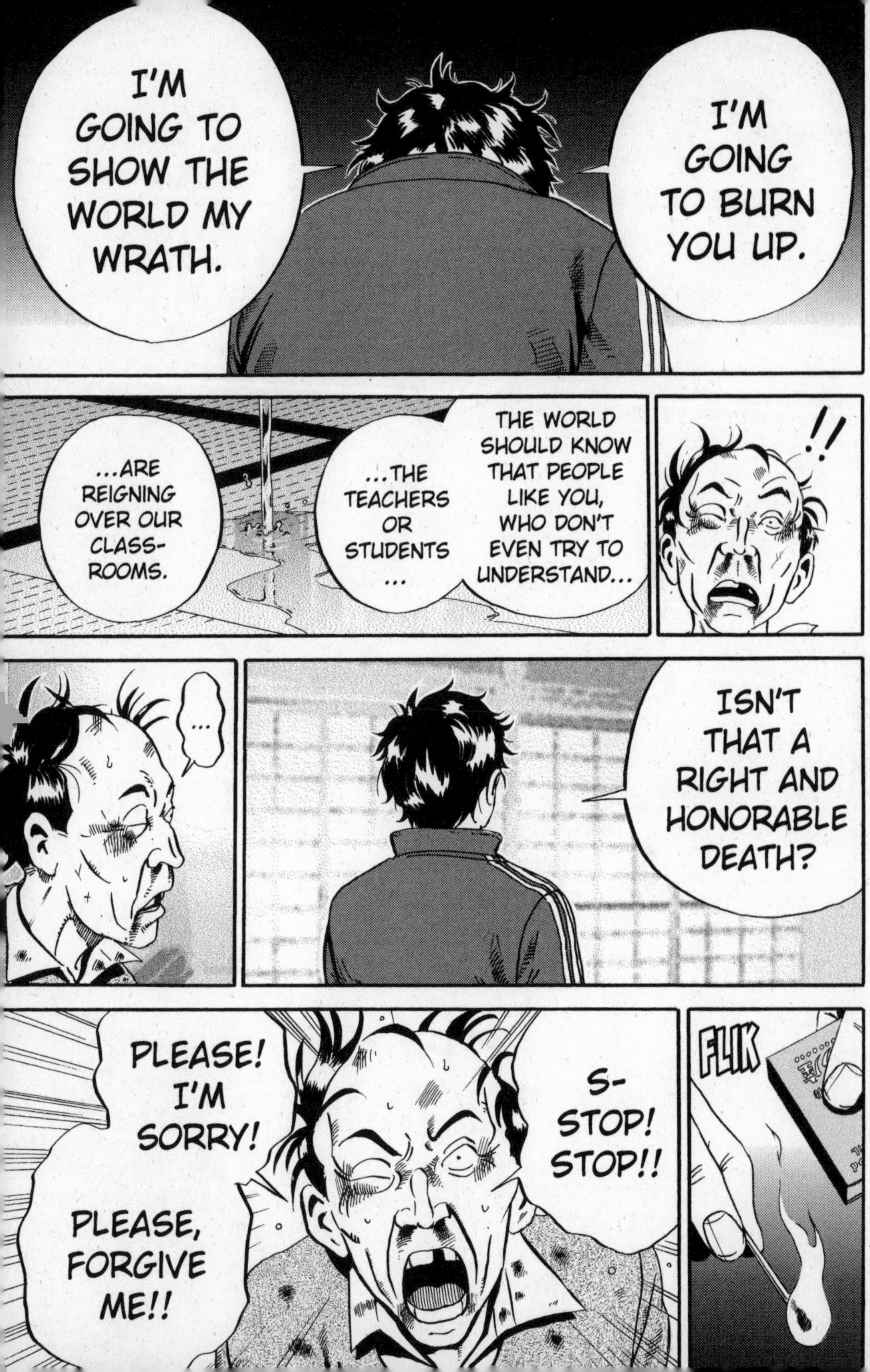
I'M GOING TO BURN YOU UP.
I'M GOING TO SHOW THE WORLD MY WRATH.
!!
THE WORLD SHOULD KNOW THAT PEOPLE LIKE YOU, WHO DON'T EVEN TRY TO UNDERSTAND...
...THE TEACHERS OR STUDENTS...
...ARE REIGNING OVER OUR CLASS-ROOMS.
ISN'T THAT A RIGHT AND HONORABLE DEATH?
...
FLIK
S-STOP! STOP!!
PLEASE! I'M SORRY!
PLEASE, FORGIVE ME!!

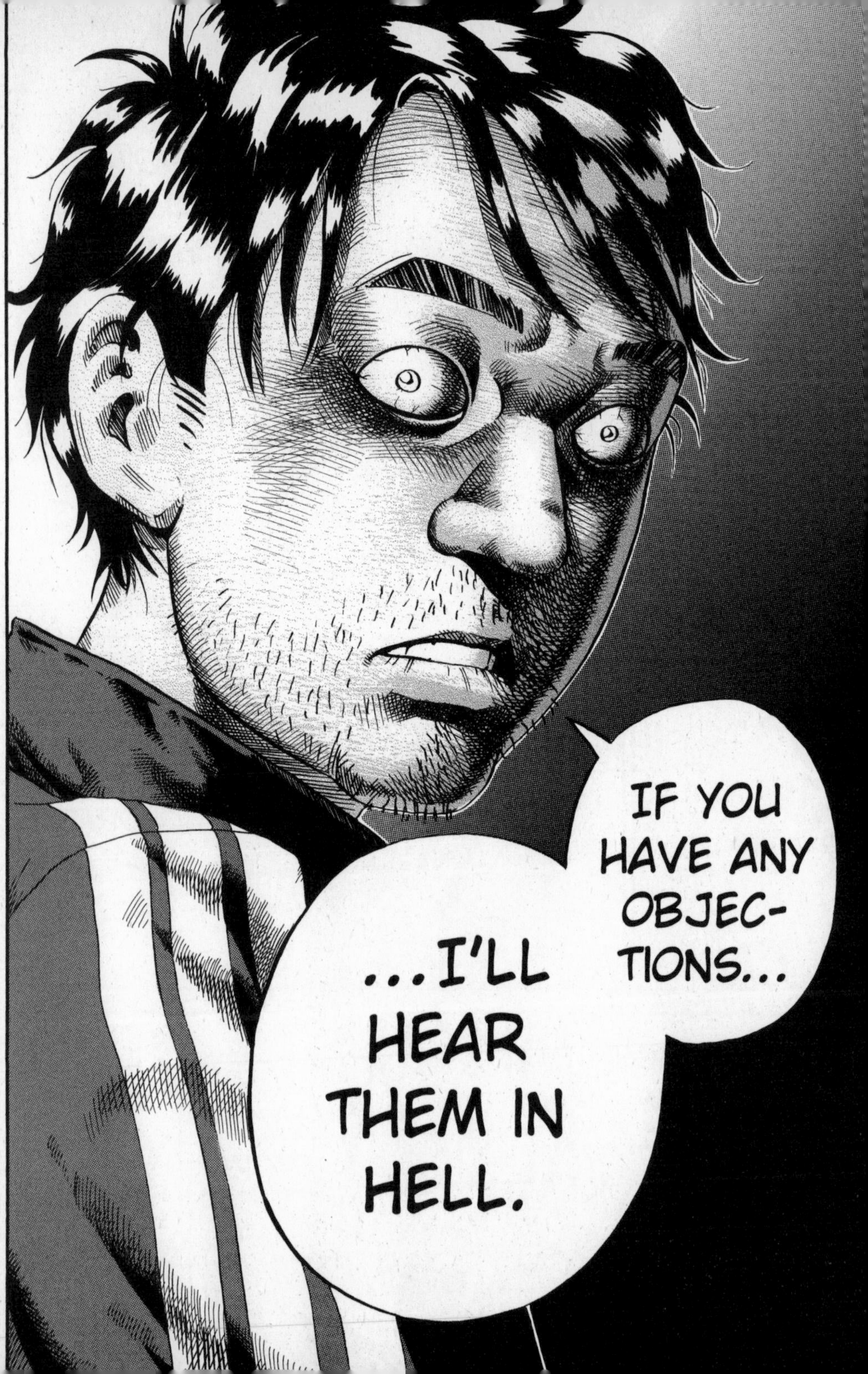
IF YOU HAVE ANY OBJECTIONS...
...I'LL HEAR THEM IN HELL.

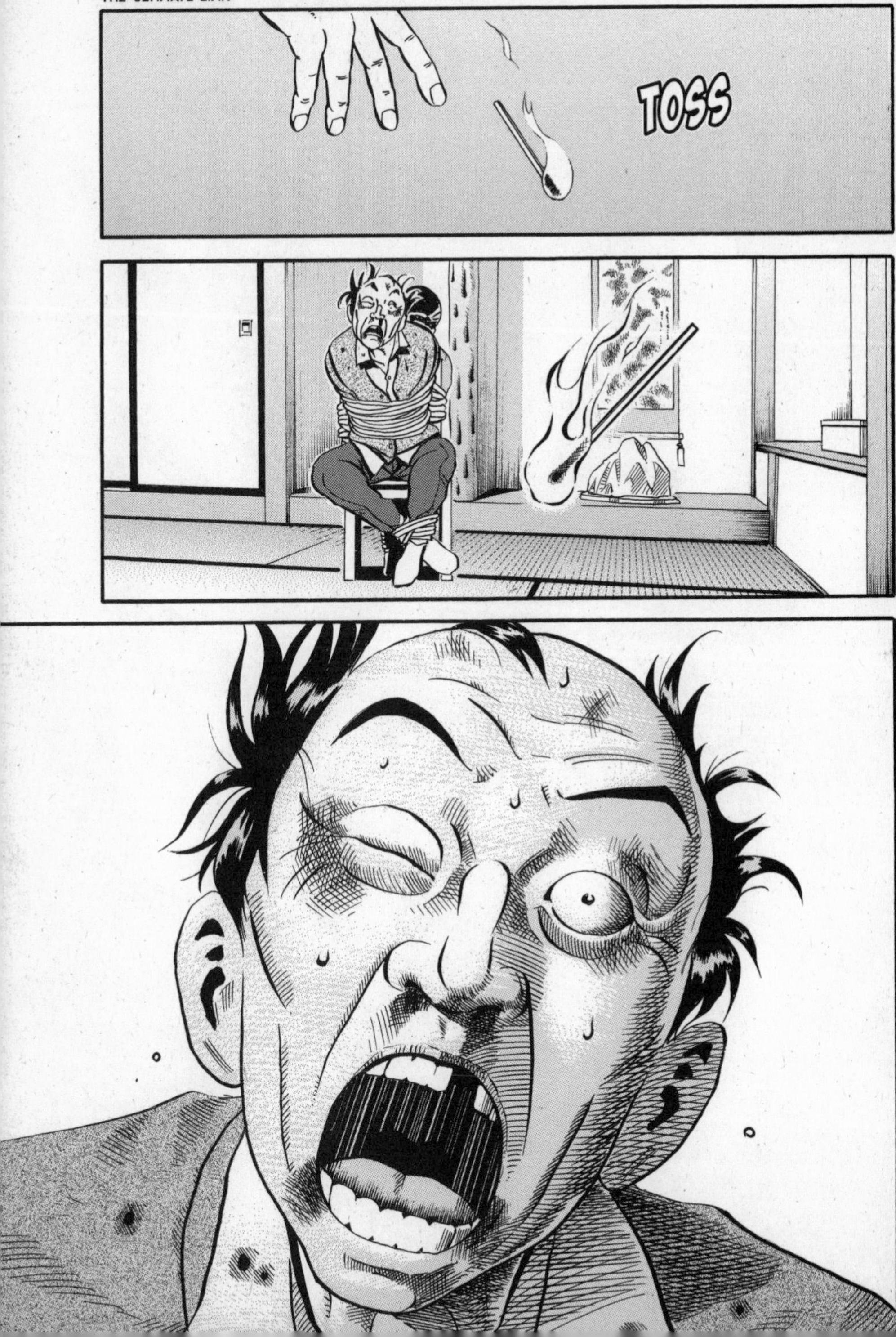
TOSS

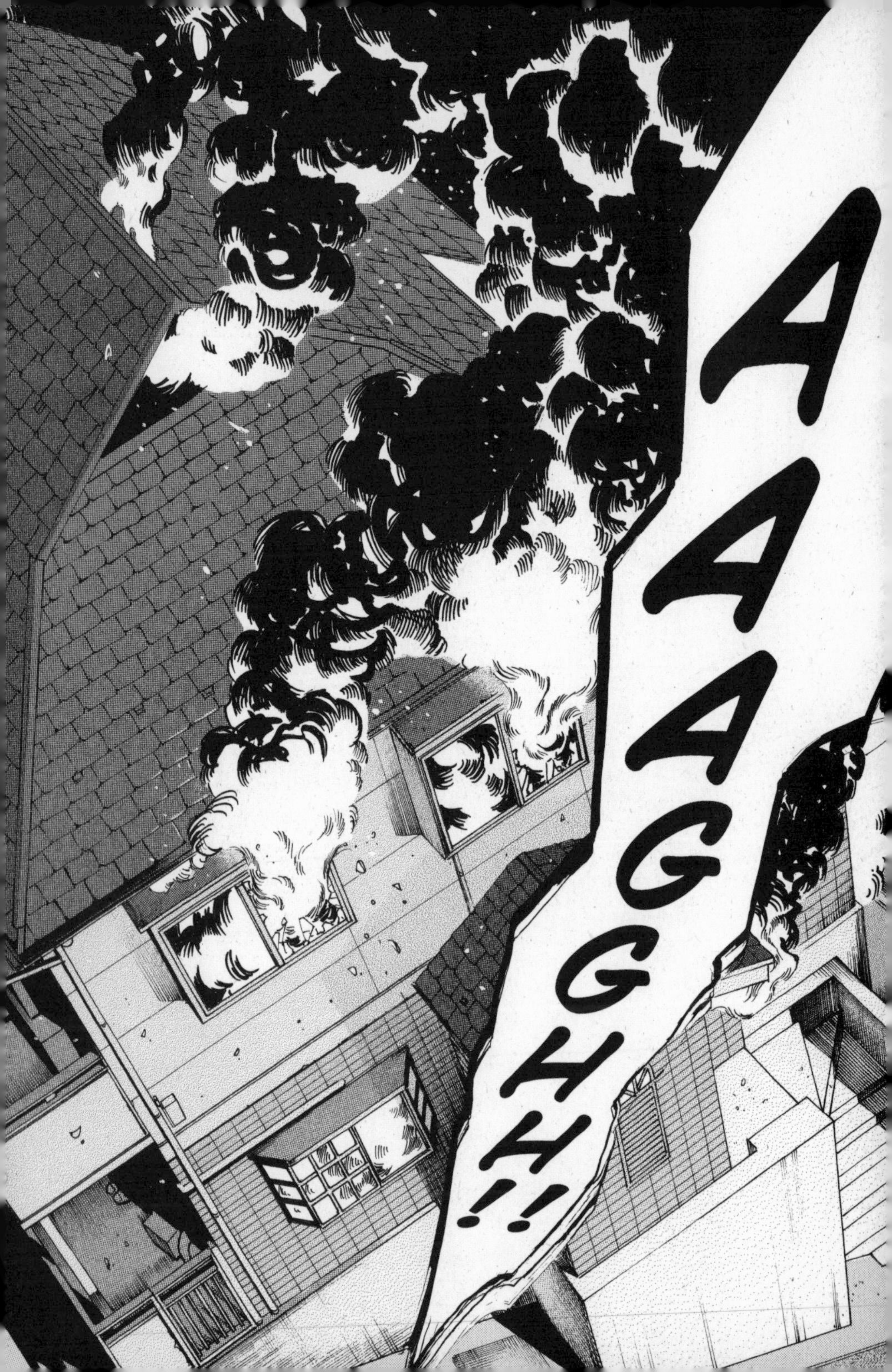
AAAAGGGHHH!!

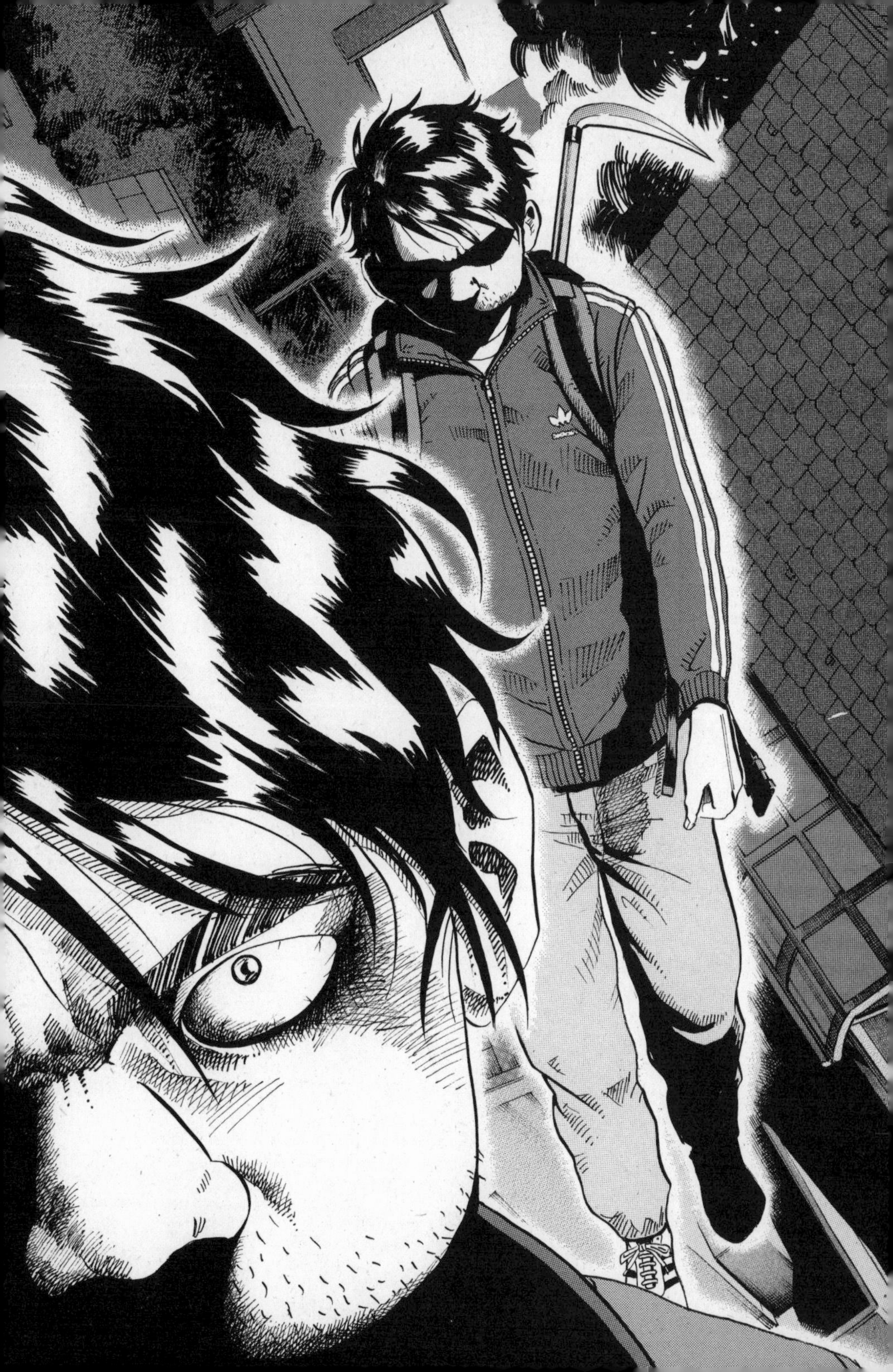

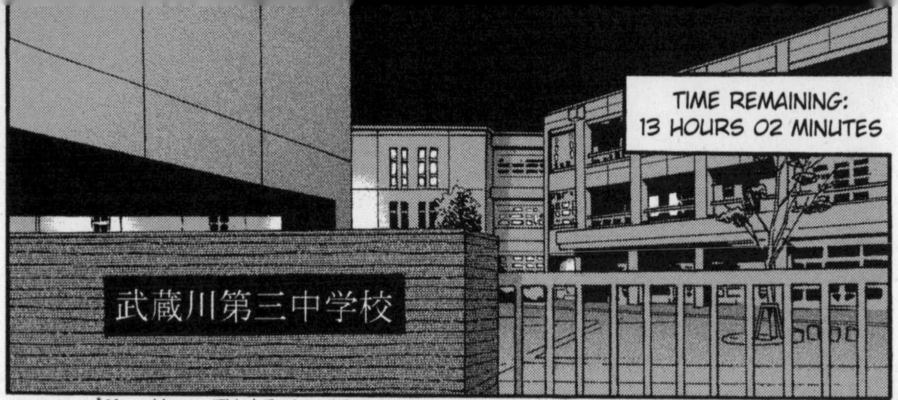
TIME REMAINING:
13 HOURS 02 MINUTES
武蔵川第三中学校
*Musashigawa Third Junior High School

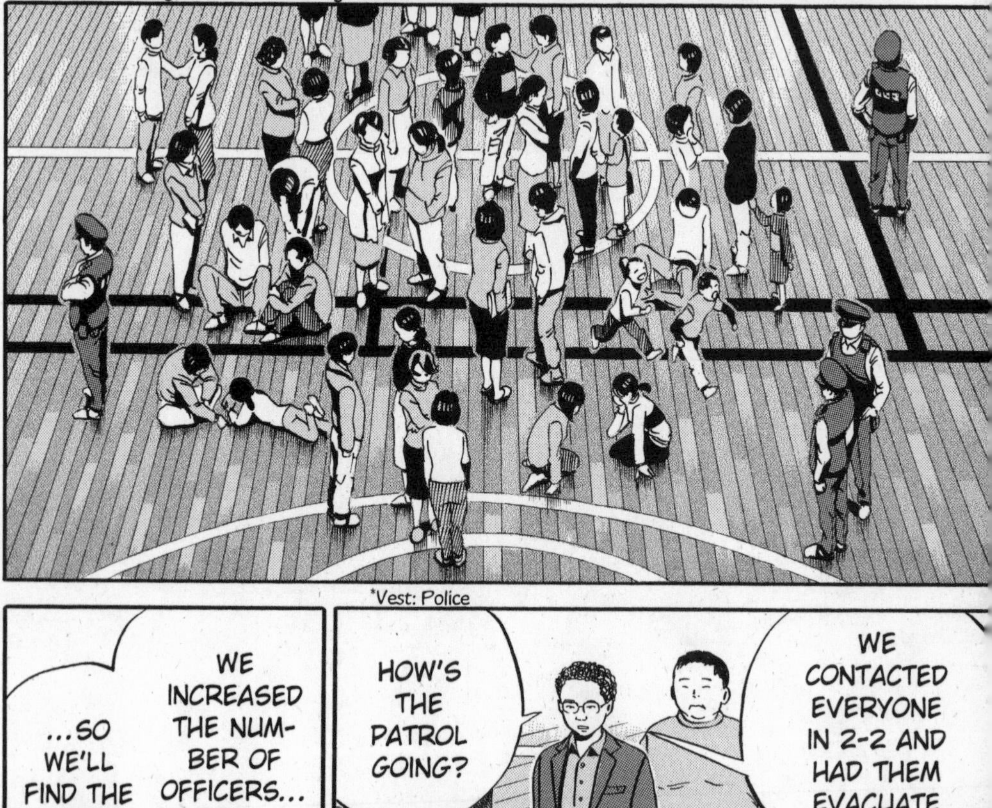
*Vest: Police

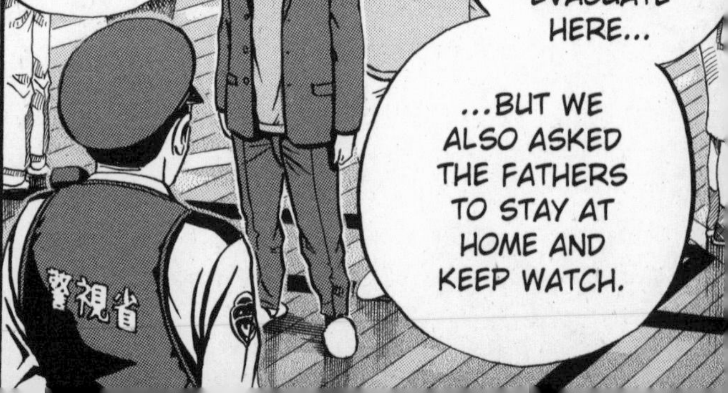
WE CONTACTED EVERYONE IN 2-2 AND HAD THEM EVACUATE HERE...
...BUT WE ALSO ASKED THE FATHERS TO STAY AT HOME AND KEEP WATCH.
HOW'S THE PATROL GOING?
警視省

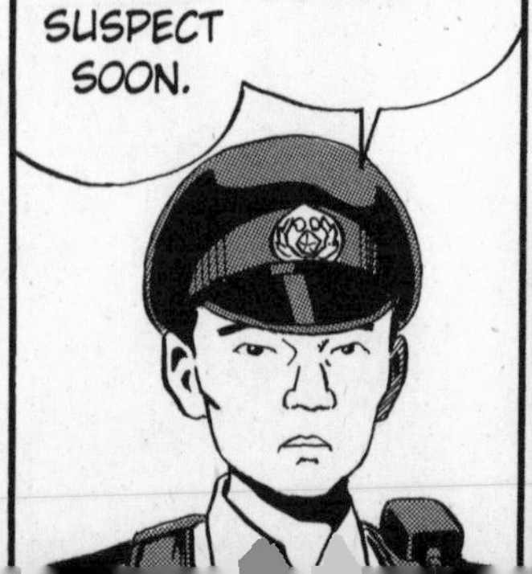
WE INCREASED THE NUM-BER OF OFFICERS...
...SO WE'LL FIND THE SUSPECT SOON.

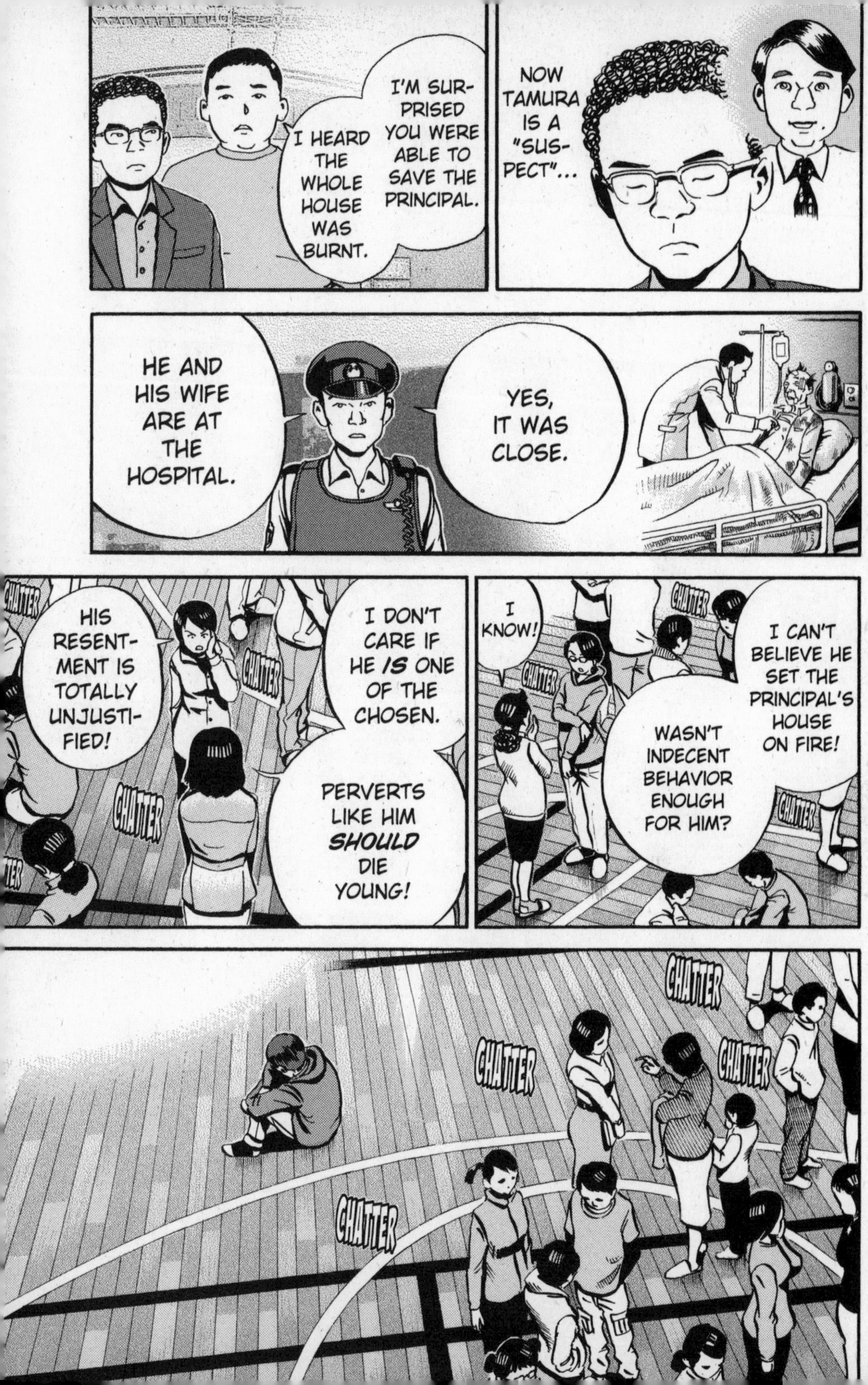
NOW TAMURA IS A "SUS-PECT"...
I'M SUR-PRISED YOU WERE ABLE TO SAVE THE PRINCIPAL.
I HEARD THE WHOLE HOUSE WAS BURNT.
YES, IT WAS CLOSE.
HE AND HIS WIFE ARE AT THE HOSPITAL.
CHATTER
I CAN'T BELIEVE HE SET THE PRINCIPAL'S HOUSE ON FIRE!
I KNOW!
CHATTER
WASN'T INDECENT BEHAVIOR ENOUGH FOR HIM?
CHATTER
I DON'T CARE IF HE *IS* ONE OF THE CHOSEN.
CHATTER
HIS RESENT-MENT IS TOTALLY UNJUSTI-FIED!
CHATTER
PERVERTS LIKE HIM ***SHOULD*** DIE YOUNG!
CHATTER
CHATTER
CHATTER
CHATTER
CHATTER

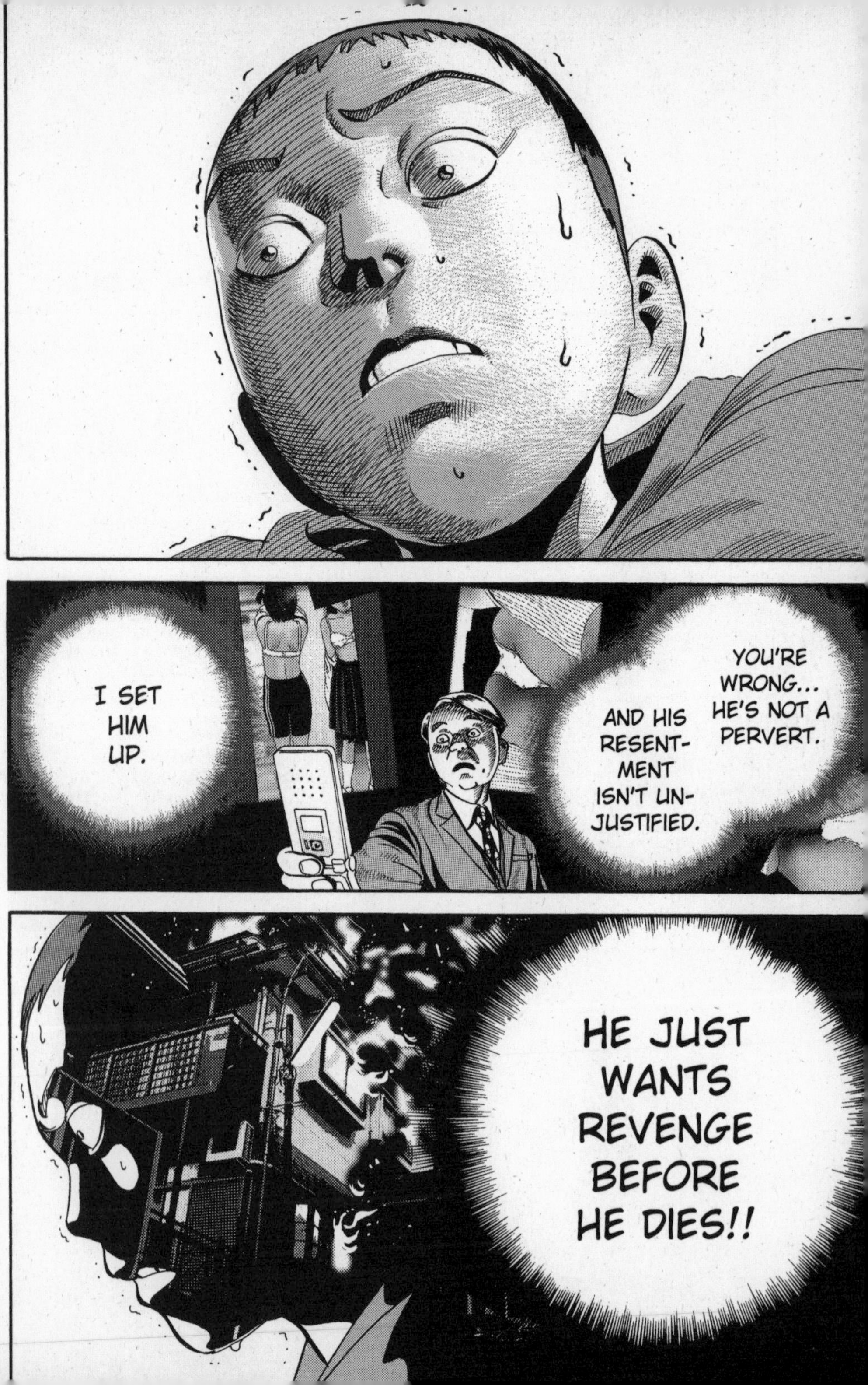
YOU'RE WRONG... HE'S NOT A PERVERT.
AND HIS RESENT-MENT ISN'T UN-JUSTIFIED.
I SET HIM UP.
HE JUST WANTS REVENGE BEFORE HE DIES!!

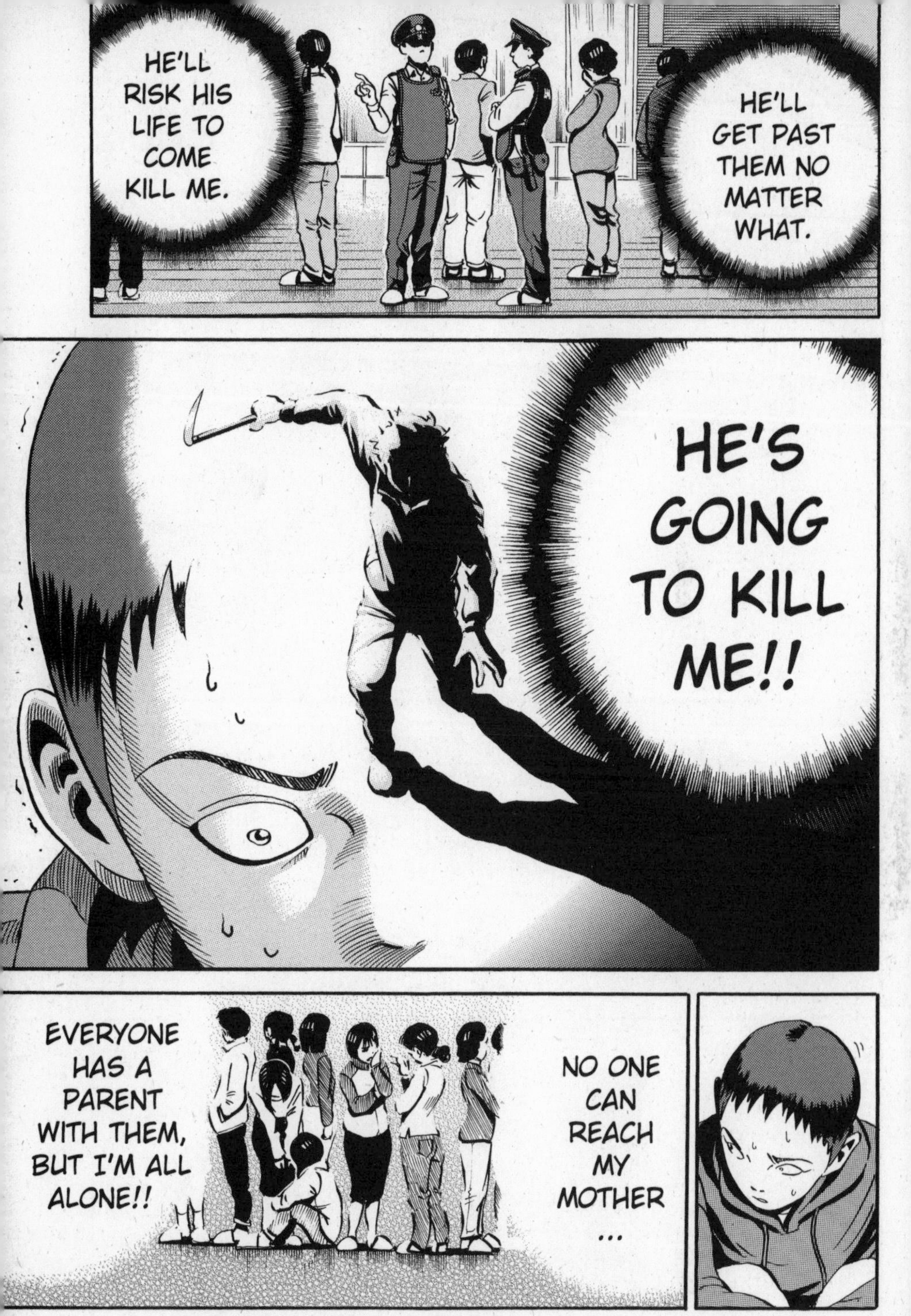
HE'LL GET PAST THEM NO MATTER WHAT.
HE'LL RISK HIS LIFE TO COME KILL ME.
HE'S GOING TO KILL ME!!
NO ONE CAN REACH MY MOTHER ...
EVERYONE HAS A PARENT WITH THEM, BUT I'M ALL ALONE!!

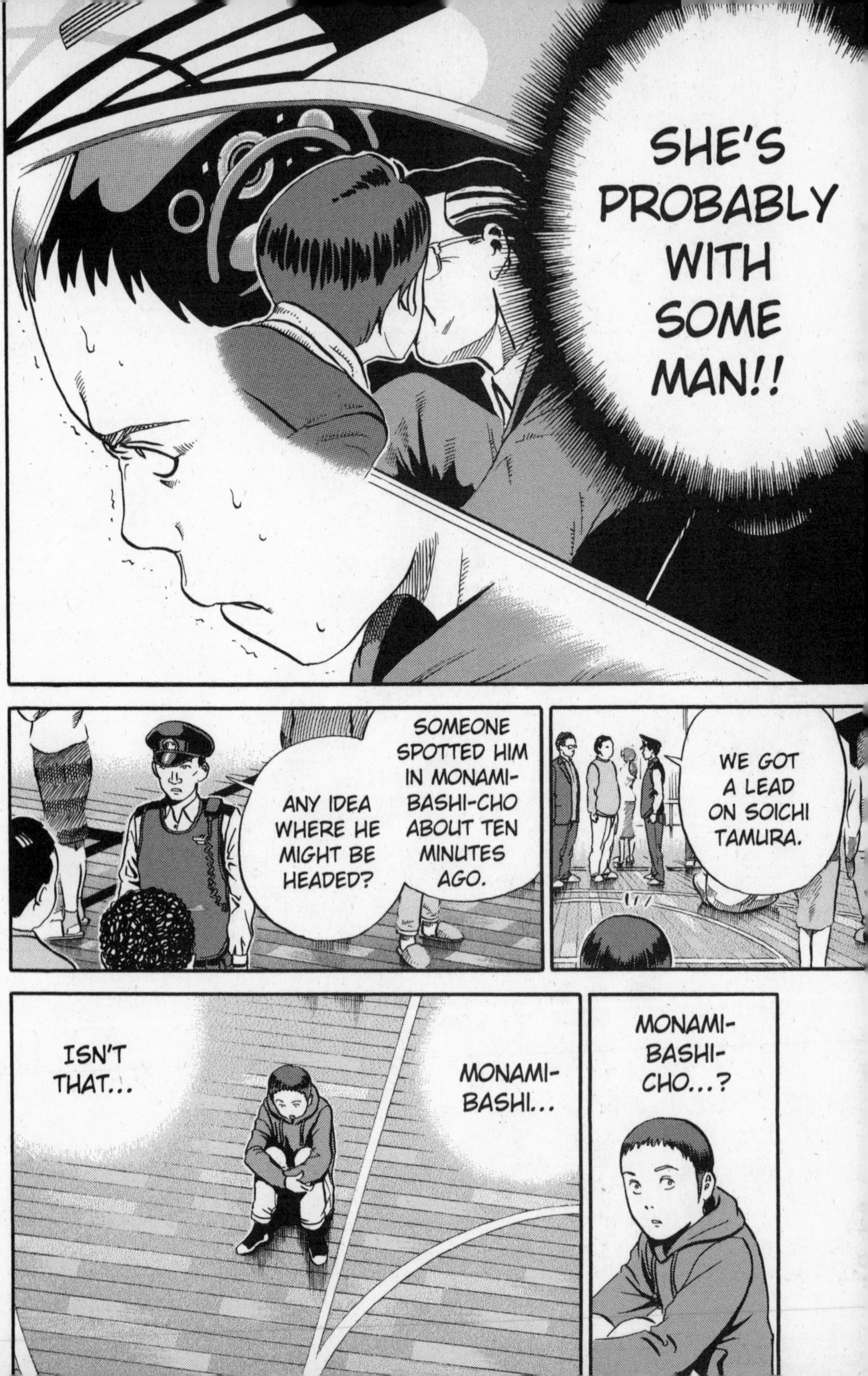
SHE'S PROBABLY WITH SOME MAN!!
WE GOT A LEAD ON SOICHI TAMURA.
SOMEONE SPOTTED HIM IN MONAMI-BASHI-CHO ABOUT TEN MINUTES AGO.
ANY IDEA WHERE HE MIGHT BE HEADED?
MONAMI-BASHI-CHO...?
MONAMI-BASHI...
ISN'T THAT...

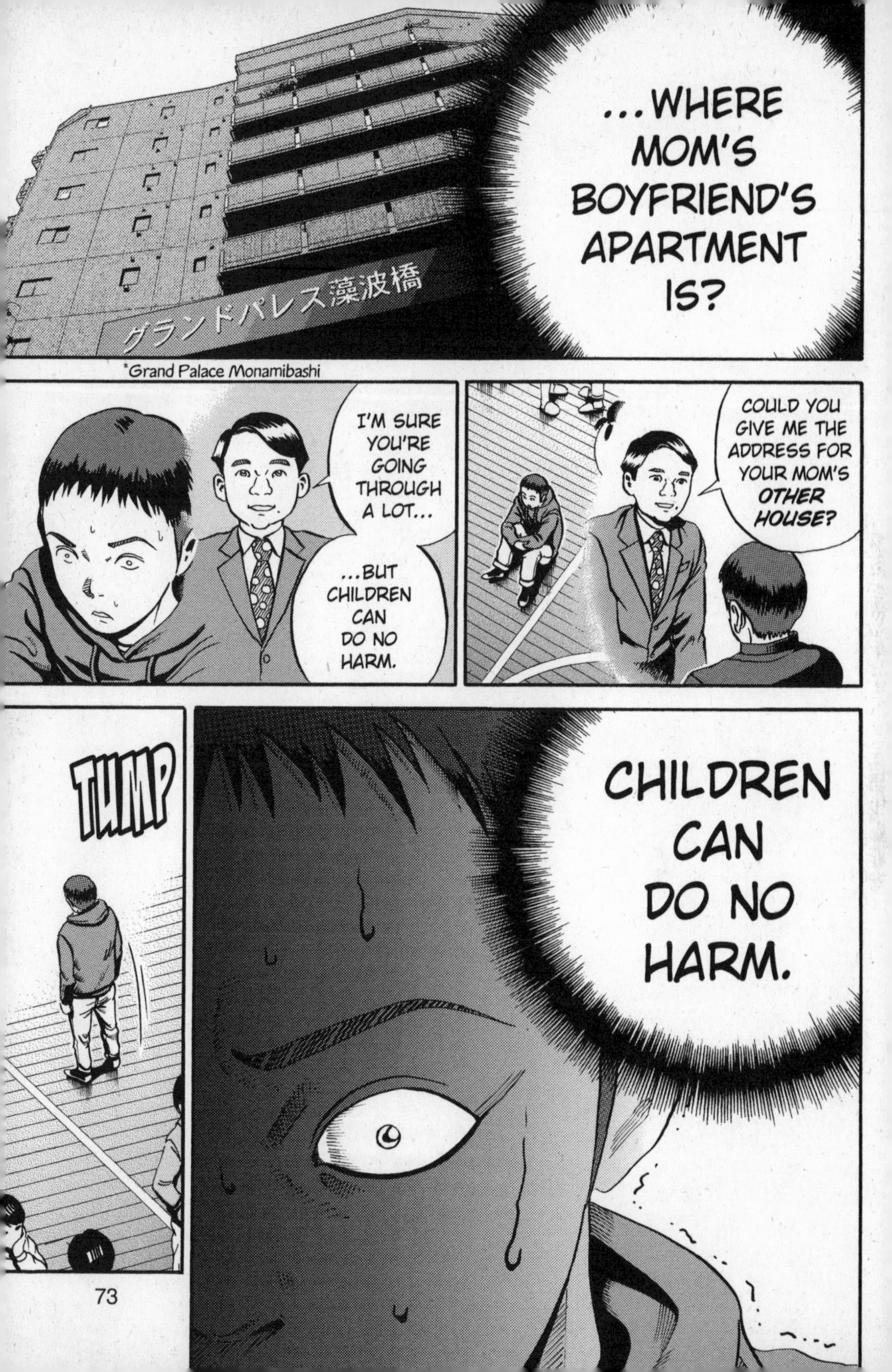
グランドパレス藻波橋
...WHERE MOM'S BOYFRIEND'S APARTMENT IS?
*Grand Palace Monamibashi
COULD YOU GIVE ME THE ADDRESS FOR YOUR MOM'S *OTHER HOUSE*?
I'M SURE YOU'RE GOING THROUGH A LOT...
...BUT CHILDREN CAN DO NO HARM.
CHILDREN CAN DO NO HARM.
THUMP

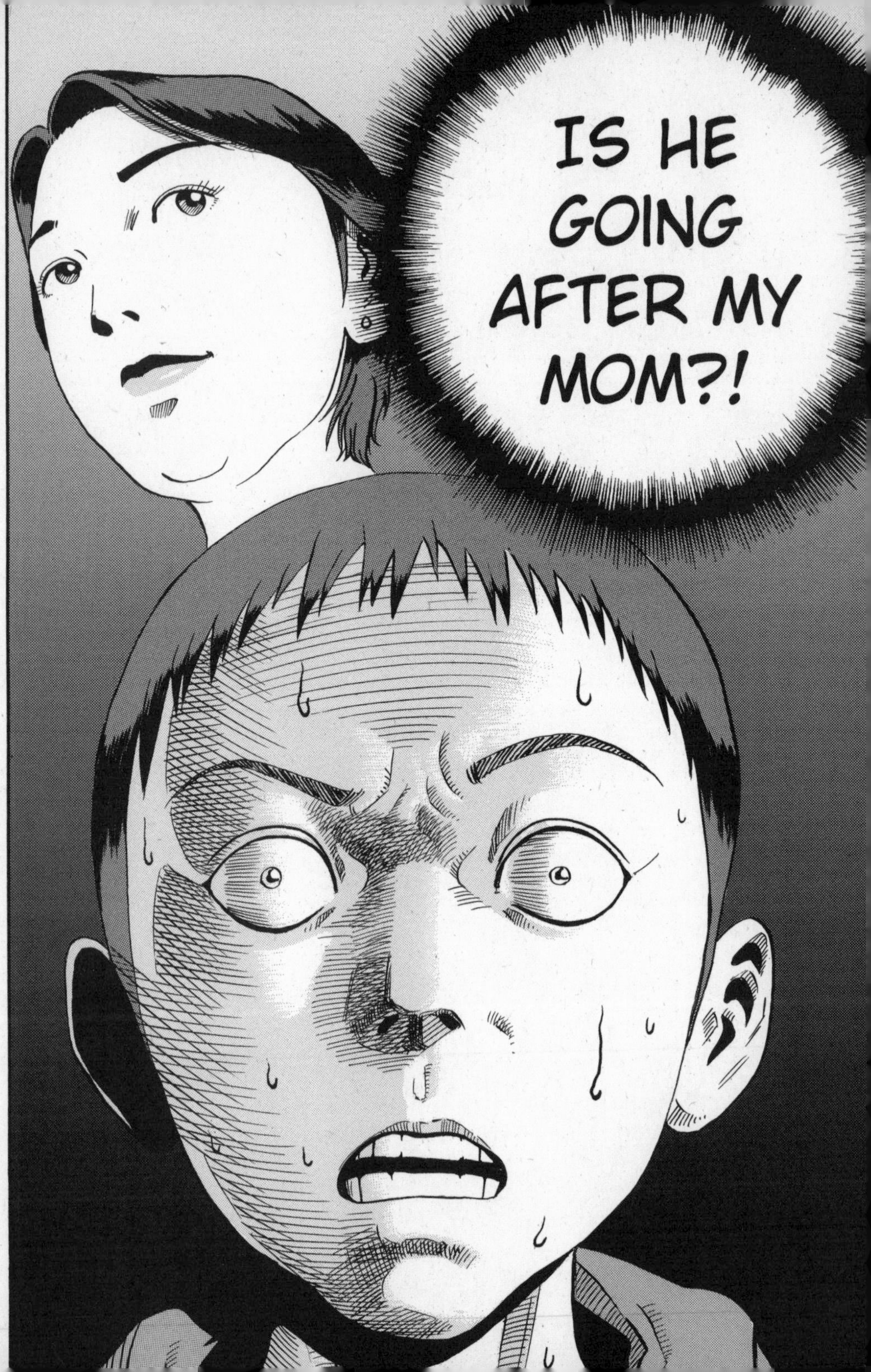
IS HE GOING AFTER MY MOM?!

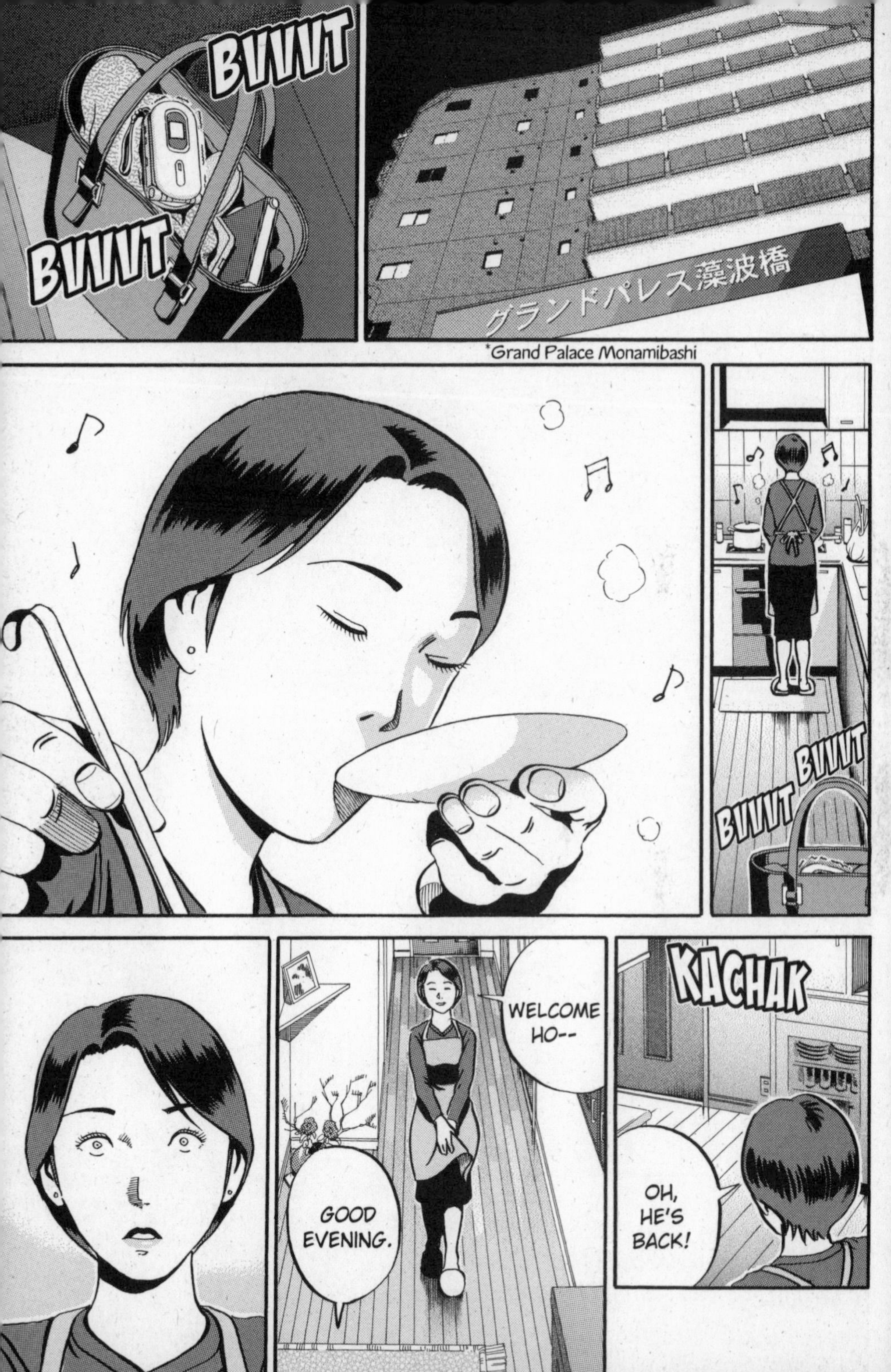
グランドパレス藻波橋
*Grand Palace Monamibashi
BVVVT
BVVVT
BVVVT
BVVVT
KACHAK
OH, HE'S BACK!
WELCOME HO--
GOOD EVENING.

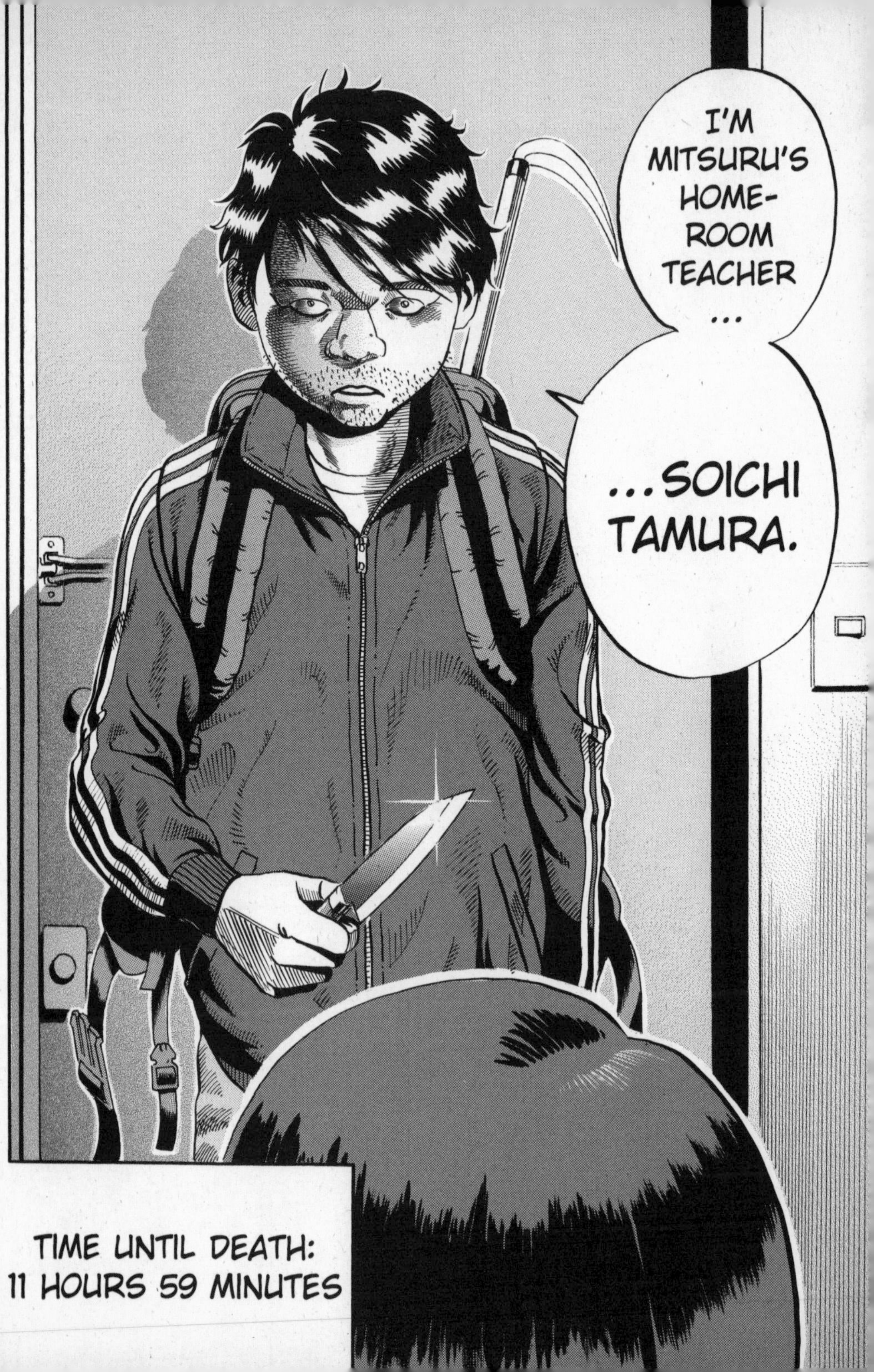
I'M MITSURU'S HOME-ROOM TEACHER ...
...SOICHI TAMURA.
TIME UNTIL DEATH: 11 HOURS 59 MINUTES

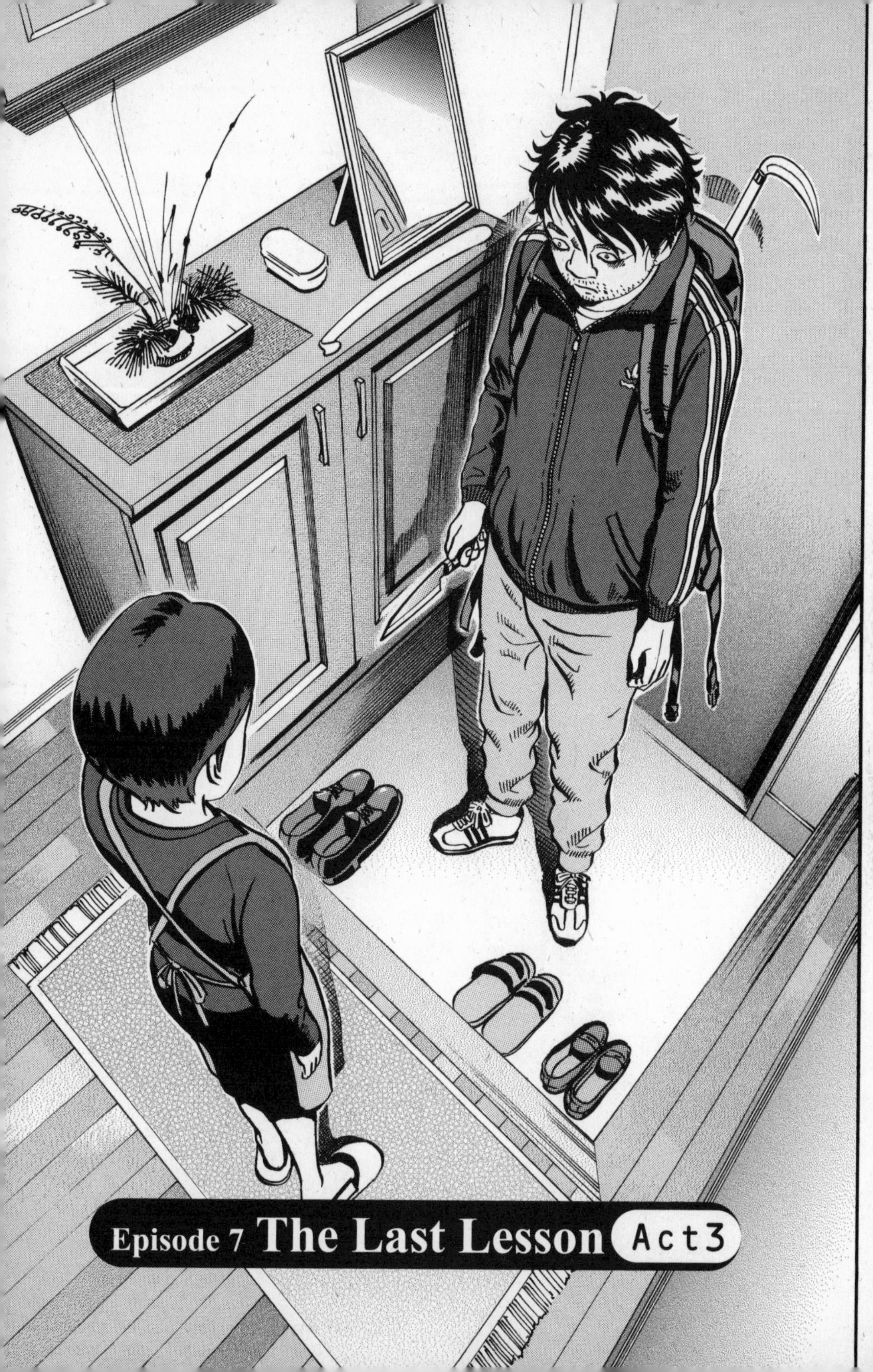
Episode 7 The Last Lesson Act 3

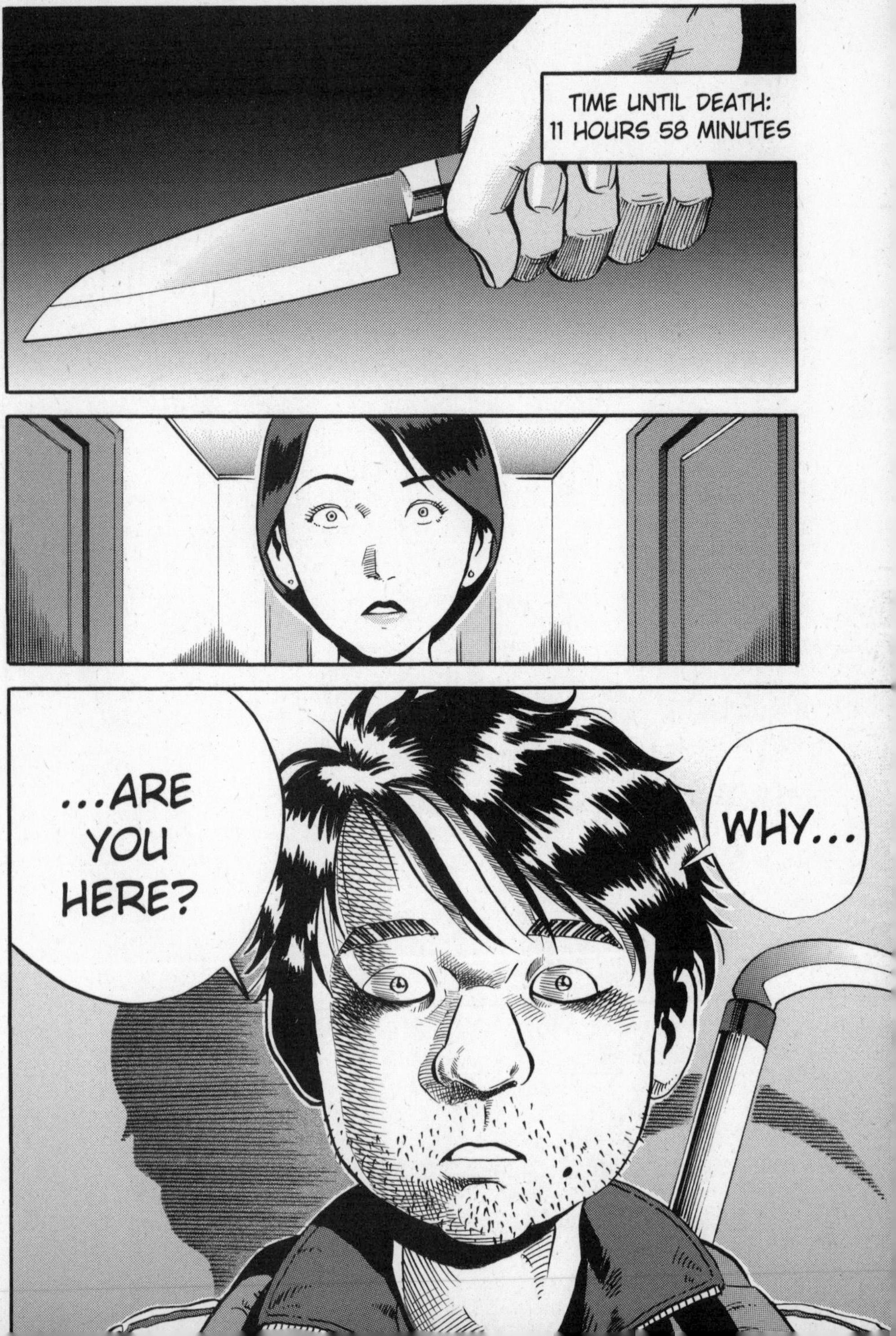
TIME UNTIL DEATH:
11 HOURS 58 MINUTES
WHY...
...ARE YOU HERE?

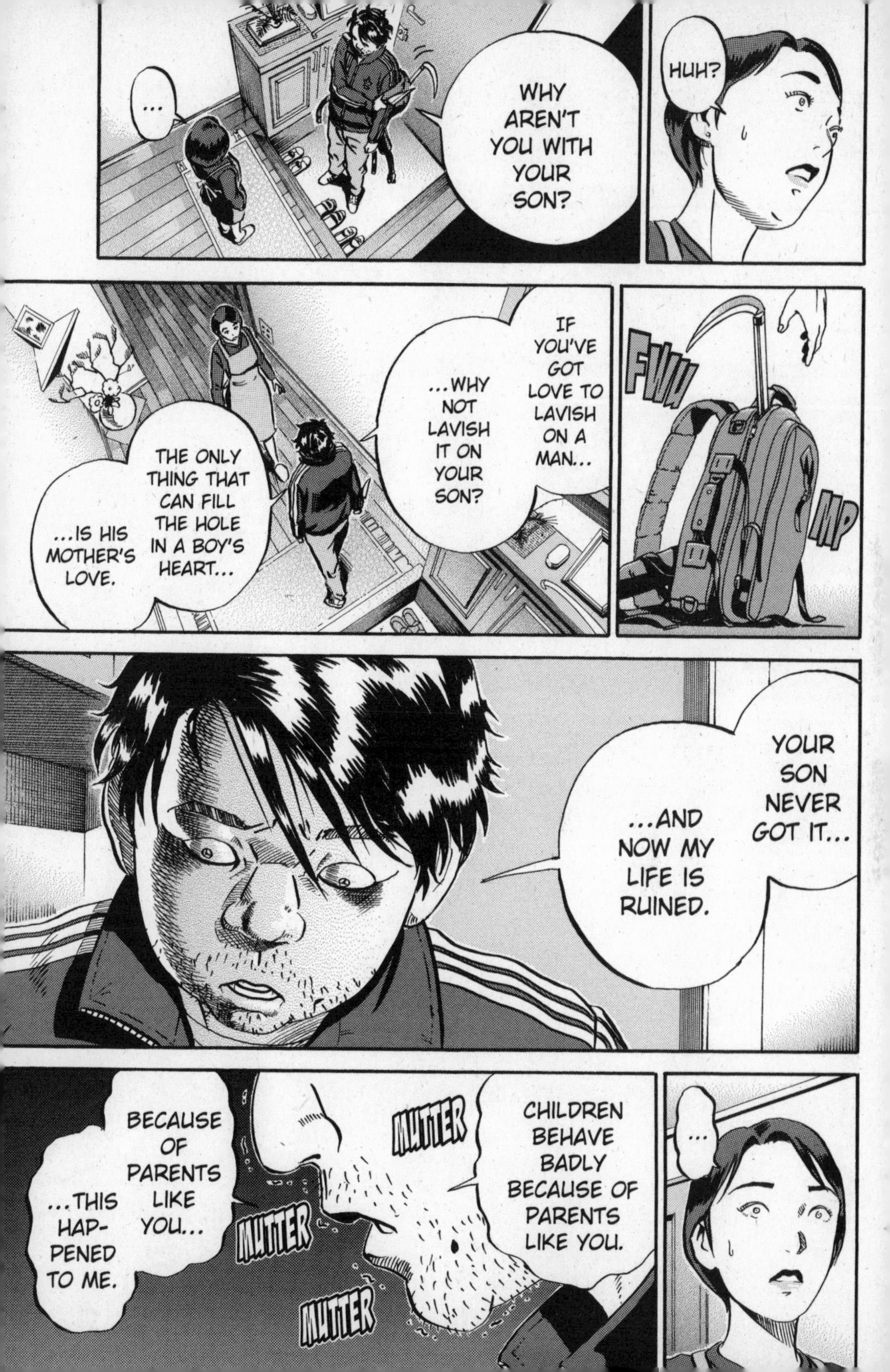
HUH?
...
WHY AREN'T YOU WITH YOUR SON?
FWU
MP
IF YOU'VE GOT LOVE TO LAVISH ON A MAN...
...WHY NOT LAVISH IT ON YOUR SON?
THE ONLY THING THAT CAN FILL THE HOLE IN A BOY'S HEART...
...IS HIS MOTHER'S LOVE.
YOUR SON NEVER GOT IT...
...AND NOW MY LIFE IS RUINED.
...
CHILDREN BEHAVE BADLY BECAUSE OF PARENTS LIKE YOU.
MUTTER
BECAUSE OF PARENTS LIKE YOU...
...THIS HAP-PENED TO ME.
MUTTER
MUTTER

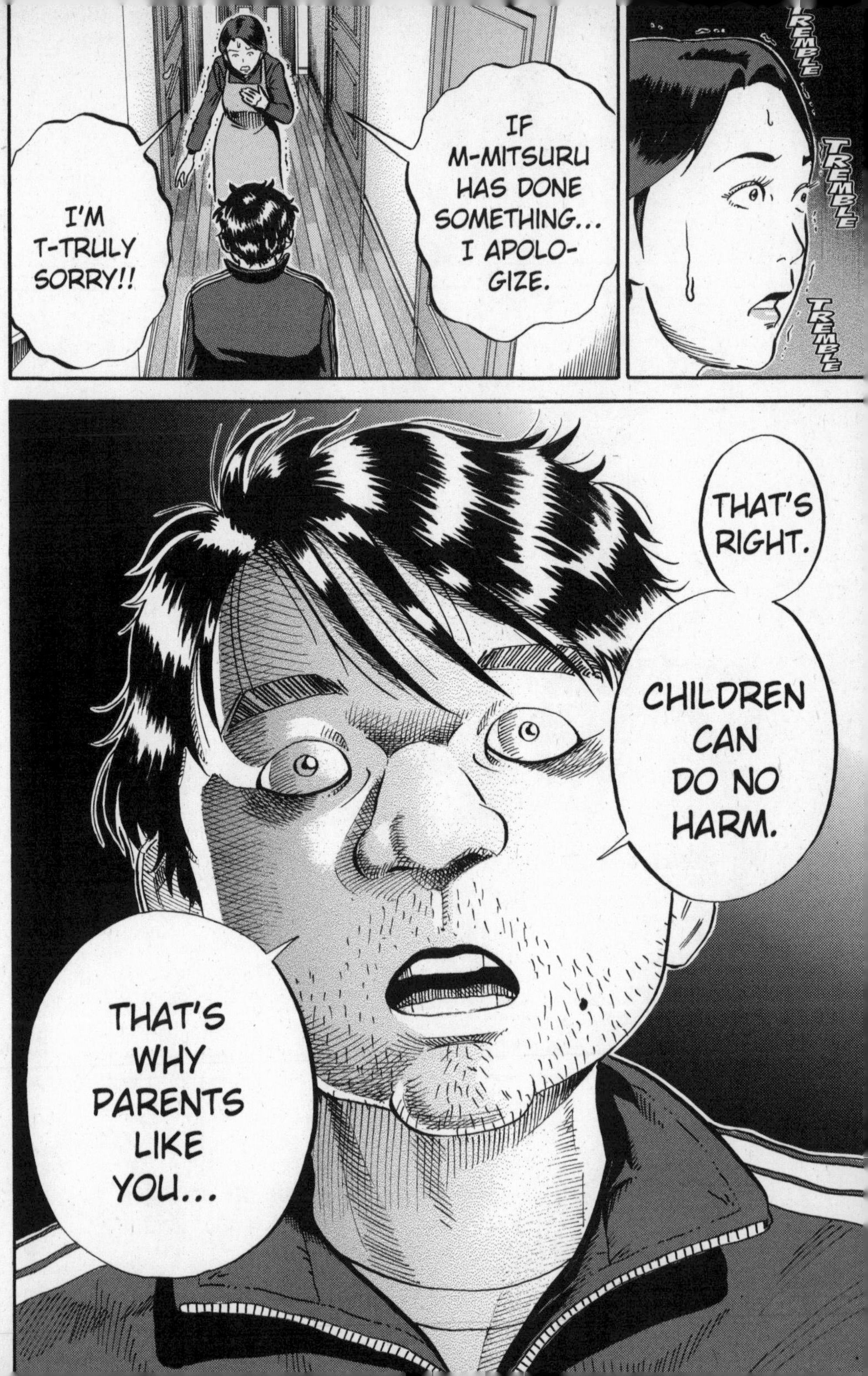
TREMBLE
TREMBLE
TREMBLE
IF M-MITSURU HAS DONE SOMETHING... I APOLOGIZE.
I'M T-TRULY SORRY!!
THAT'S RIGHT.
CHILDREN CAN DO NO HARM.
THAT'S WHY PARENTS LIKE YOU...

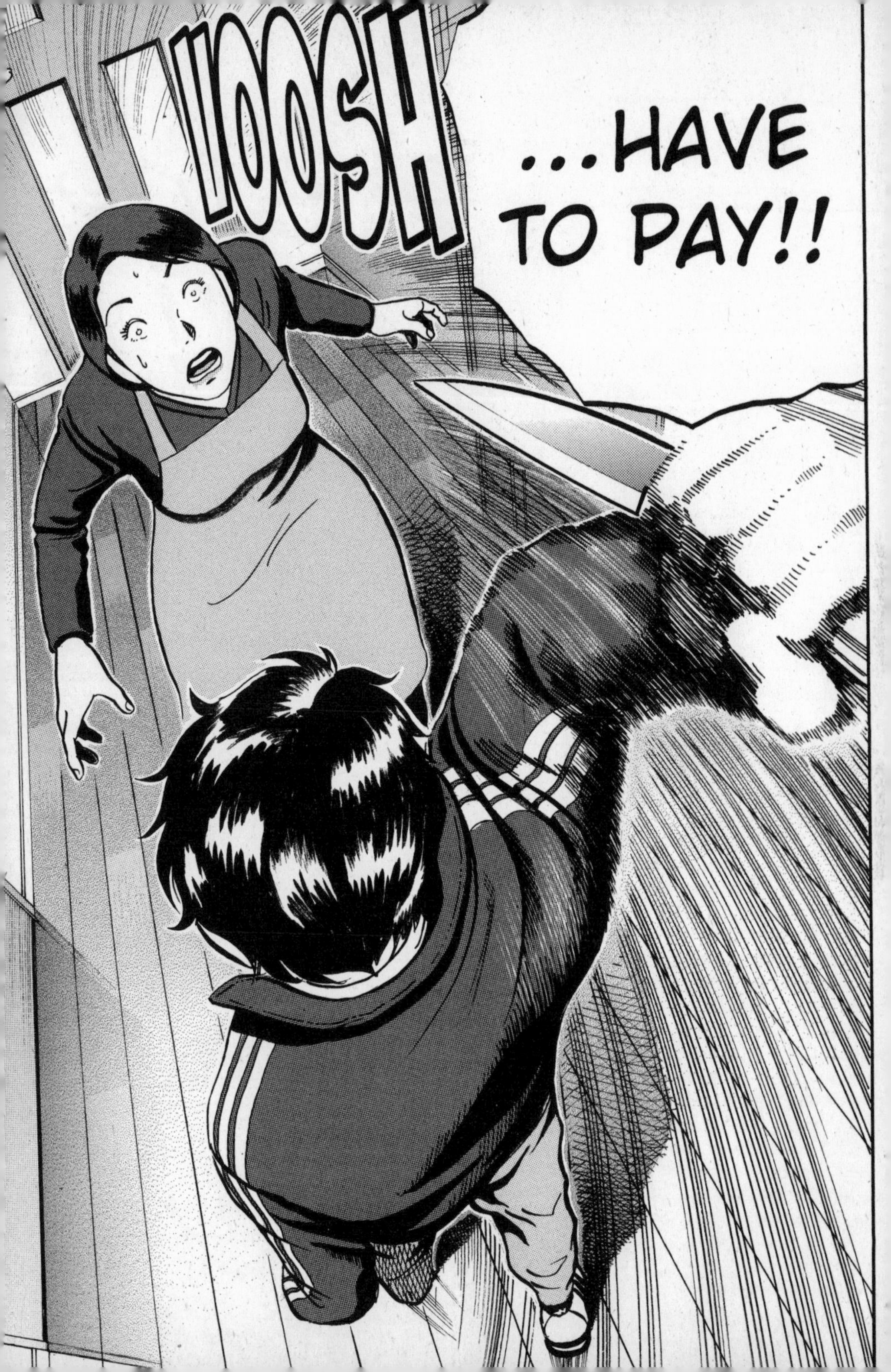
VOOSH
...HAVE TO PAY!!

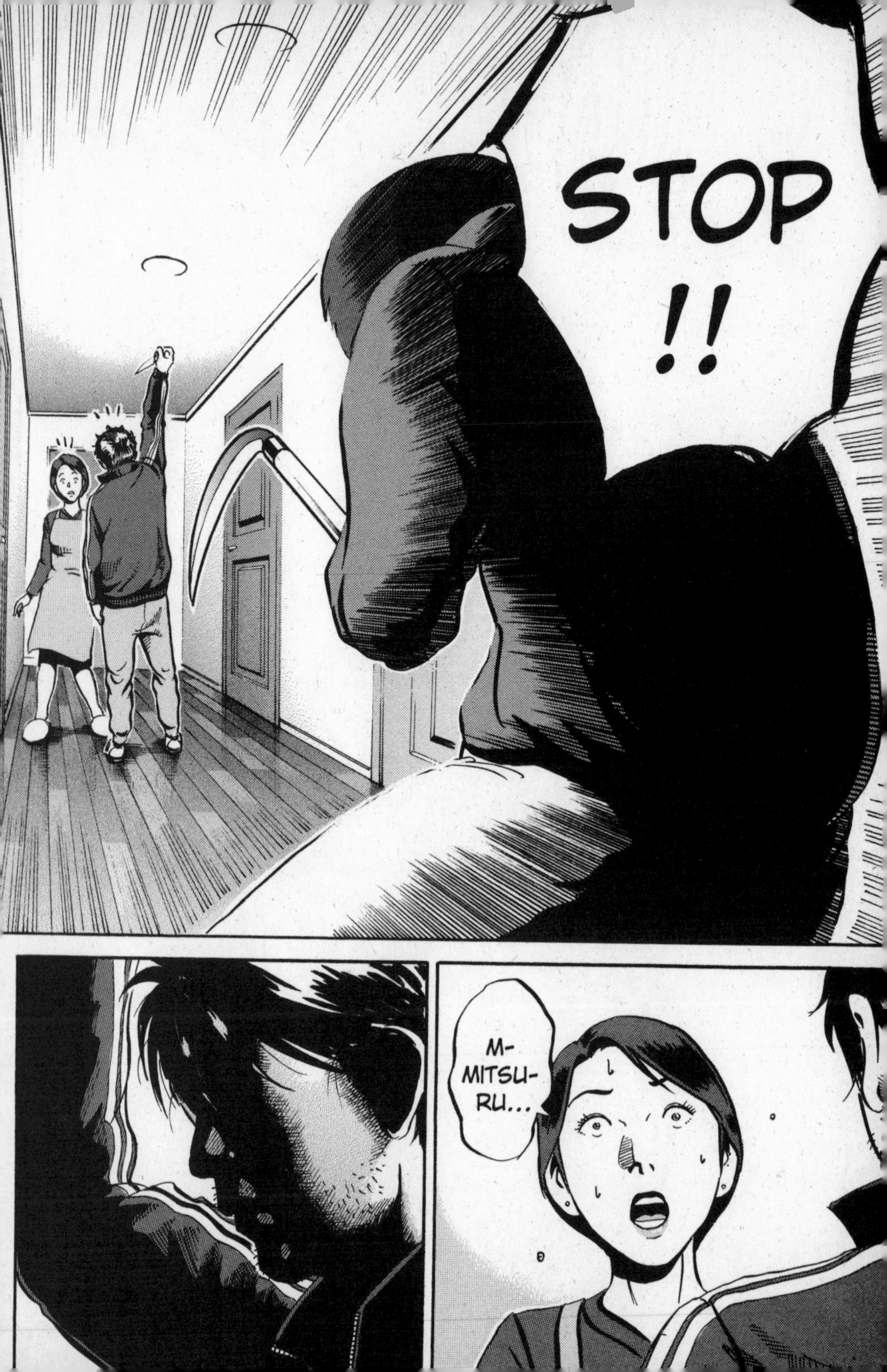
STOP!!
M-MITSU-RU...

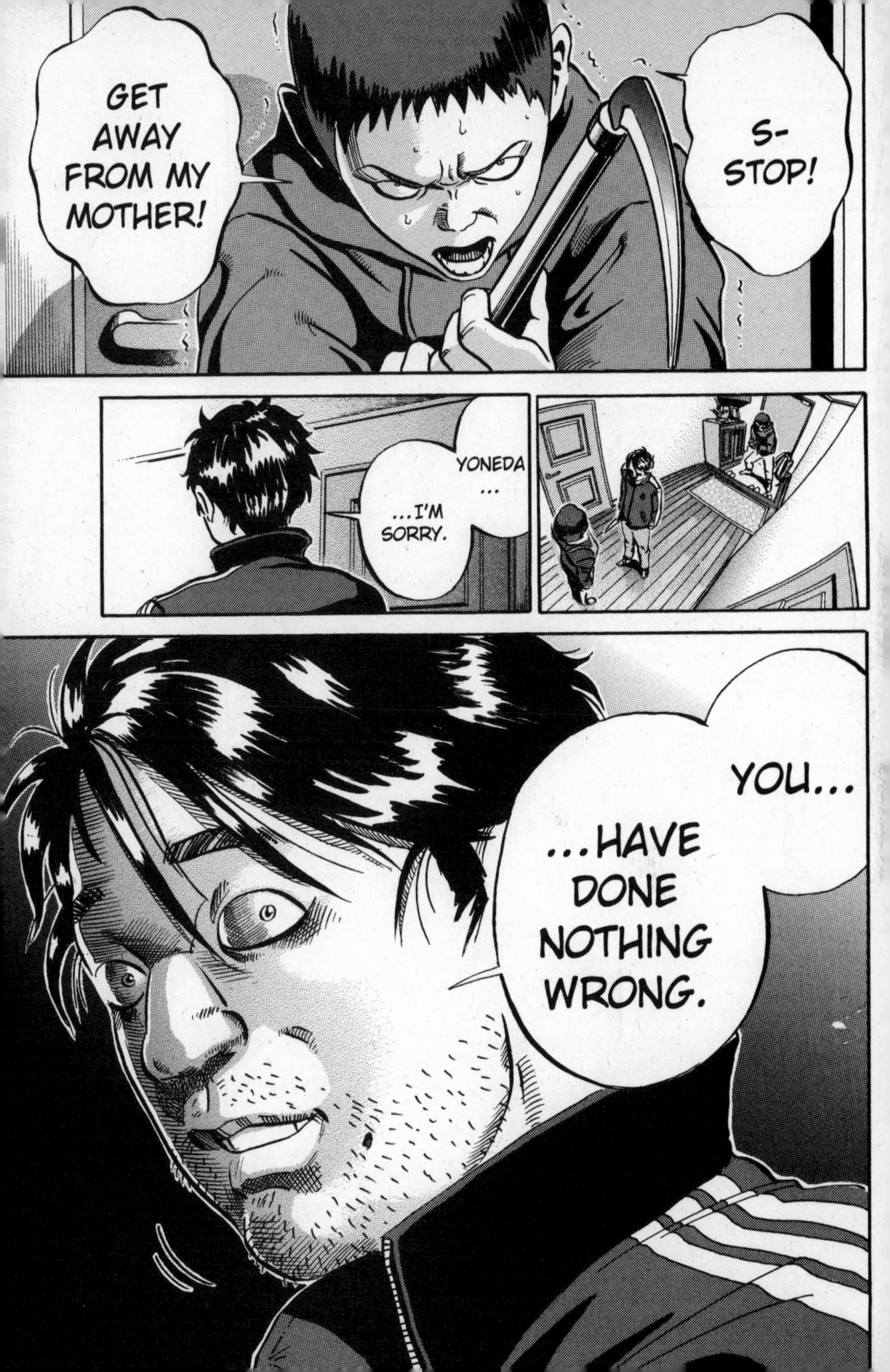
S-STOP!
GET AWAY FROM MY MOTHER!
YONEDA...
...I'M SORRY.
YOU...
...HAVE DONE NOTHING WRONG.

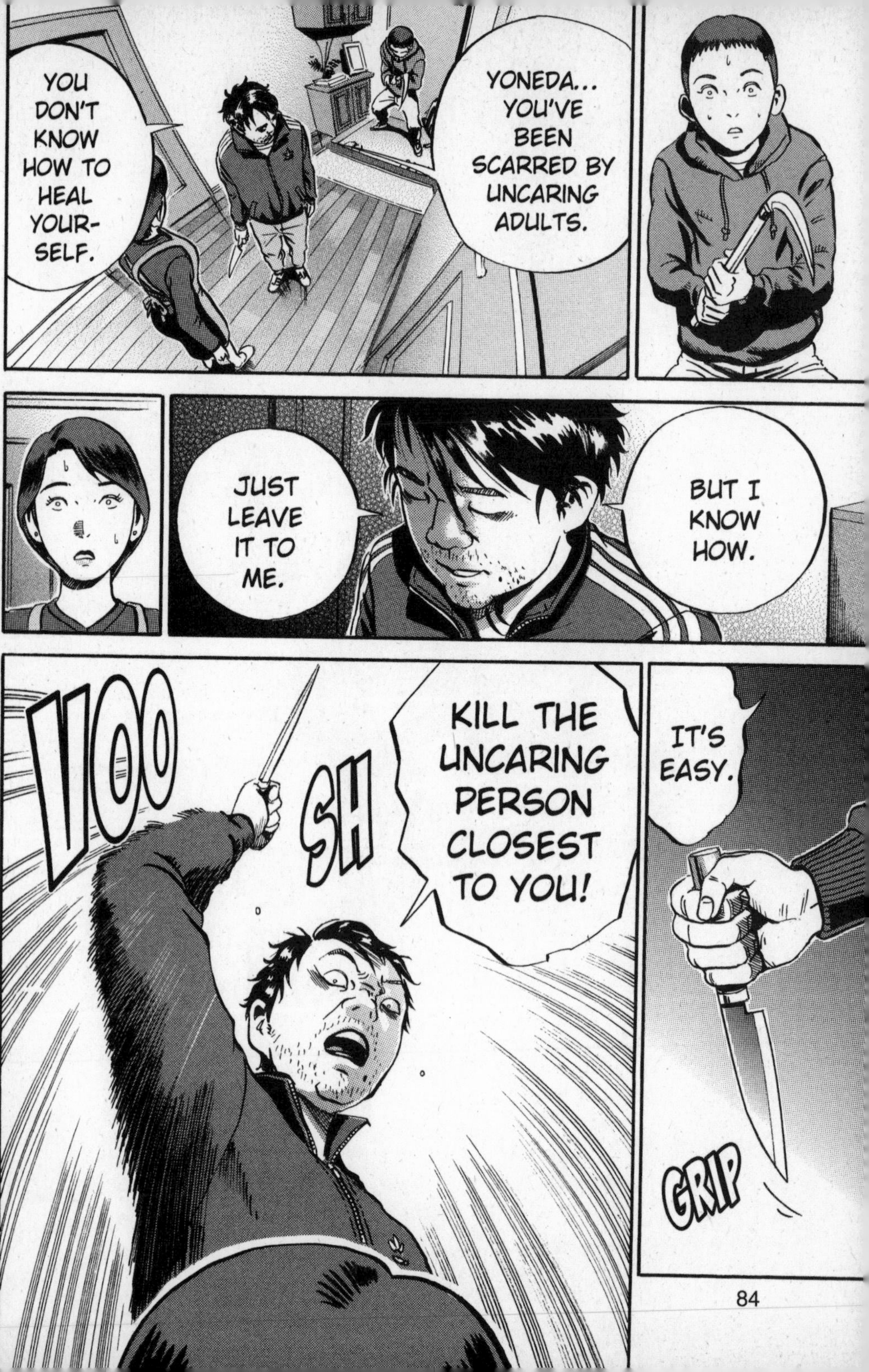
YONEDA... YOU'VE BEEN SCARRED BY UNCARING ADULTS.
YOU DON'T KNOW HOW TO HEAL YOUR-SELF.
BUT I KNOW HOW.
JUST LEAVE IT TO ME.
IT'S EASY.
GRIP
KILL THE UNCARING PERSON CLOSEST TO YOU!
VOOSH

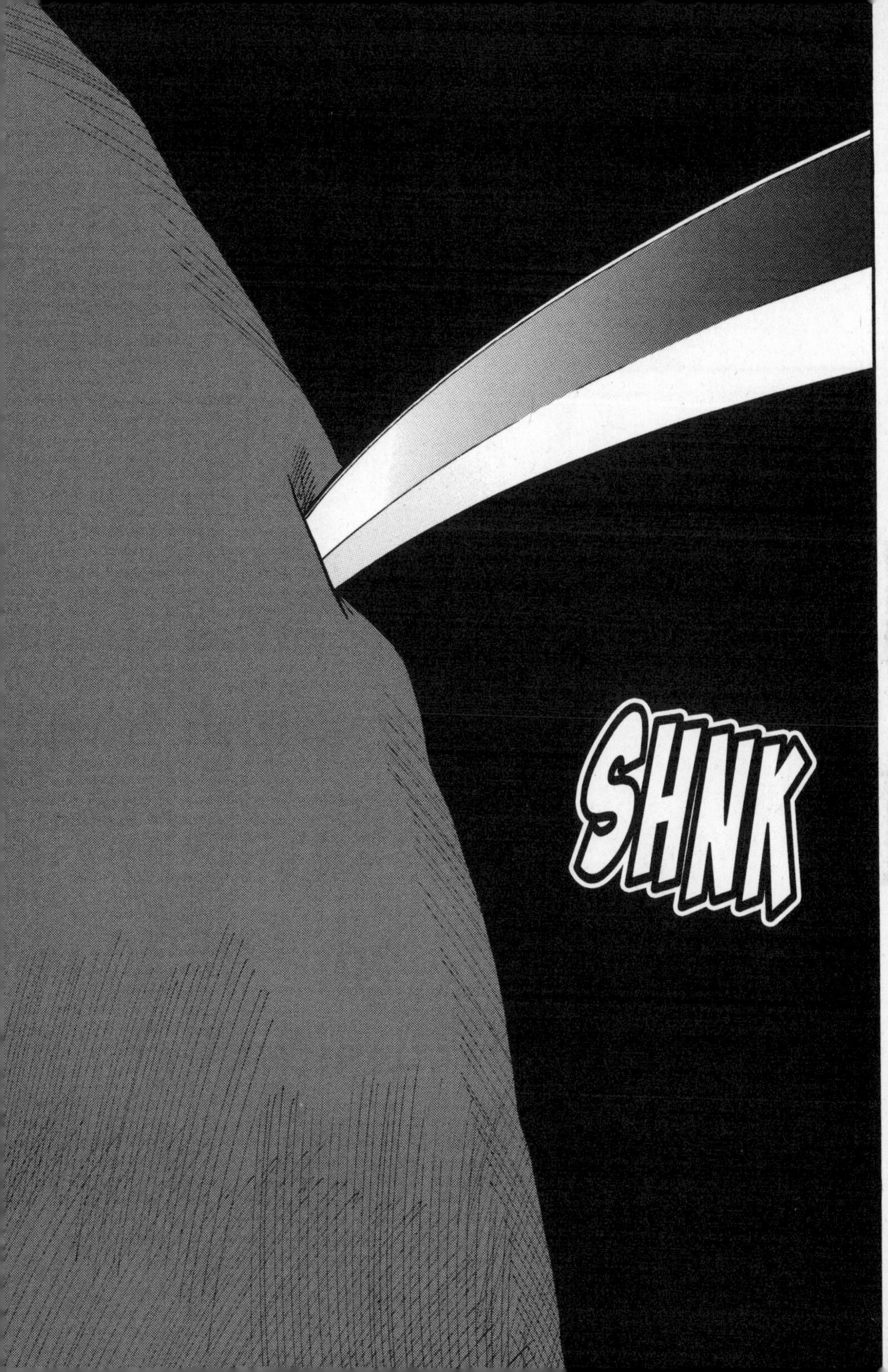
SHNK

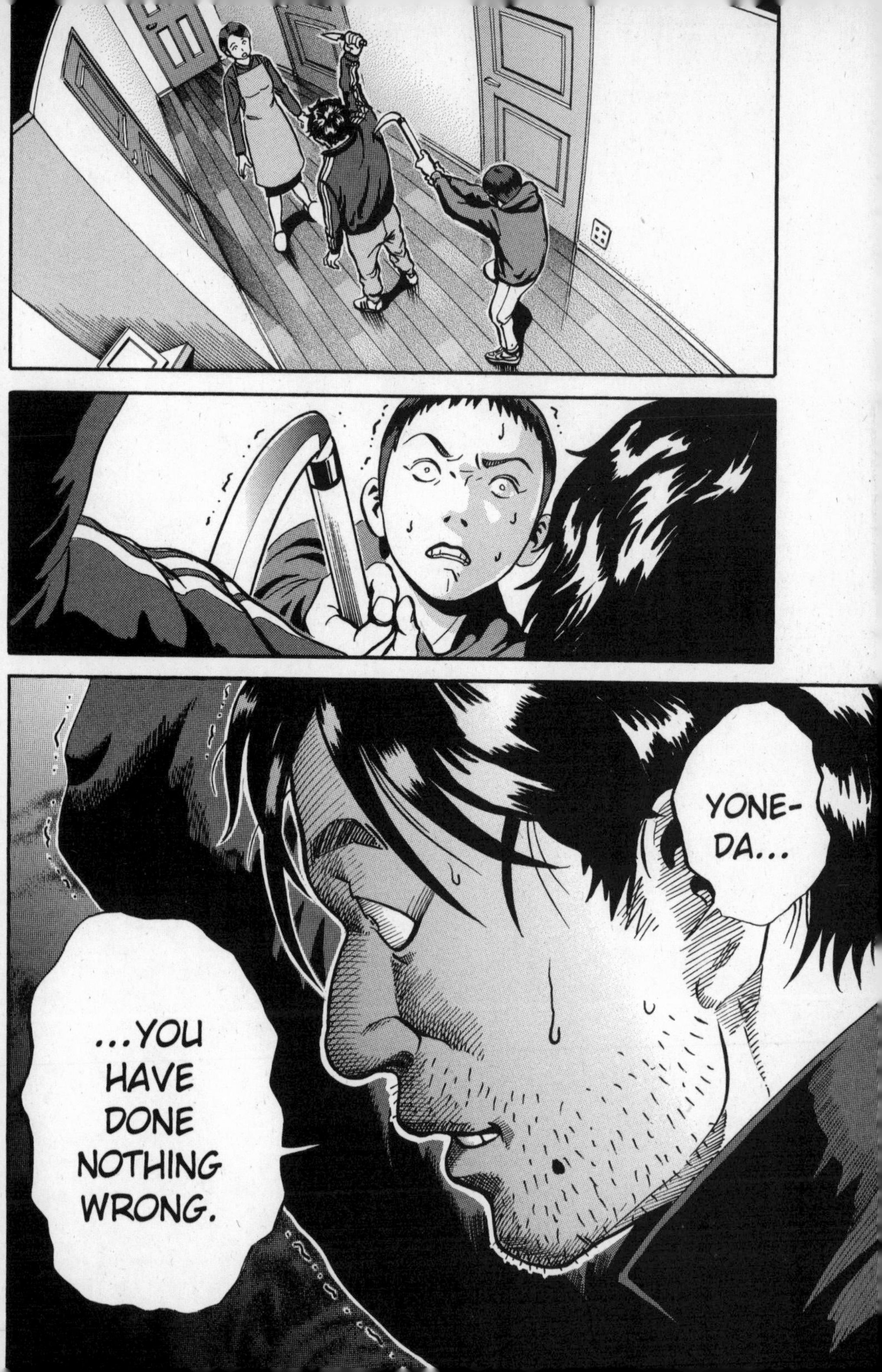
YONE-DA...
...YOU HAVE DONE NOTHING WRONG.

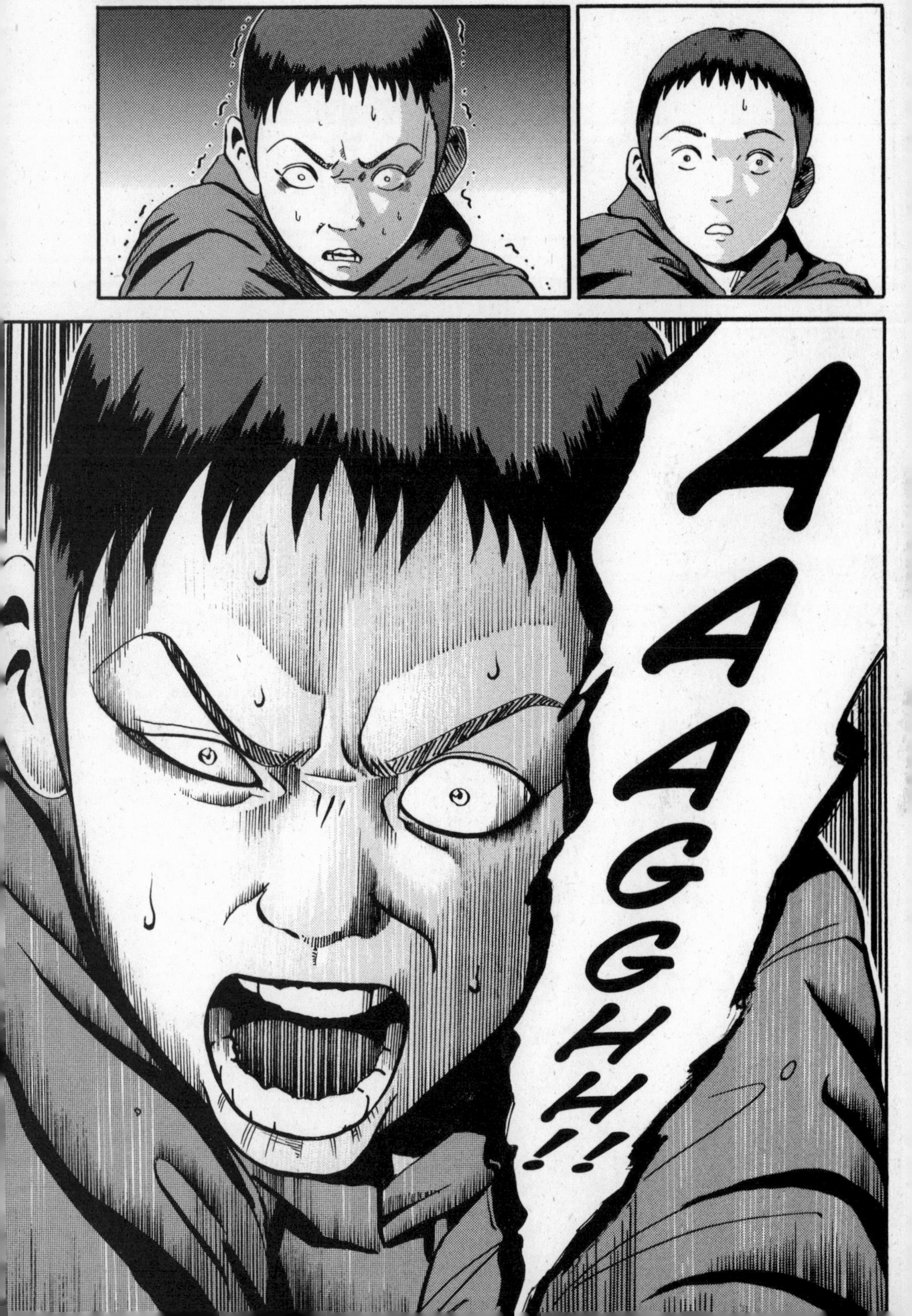
AAAGGHH!!

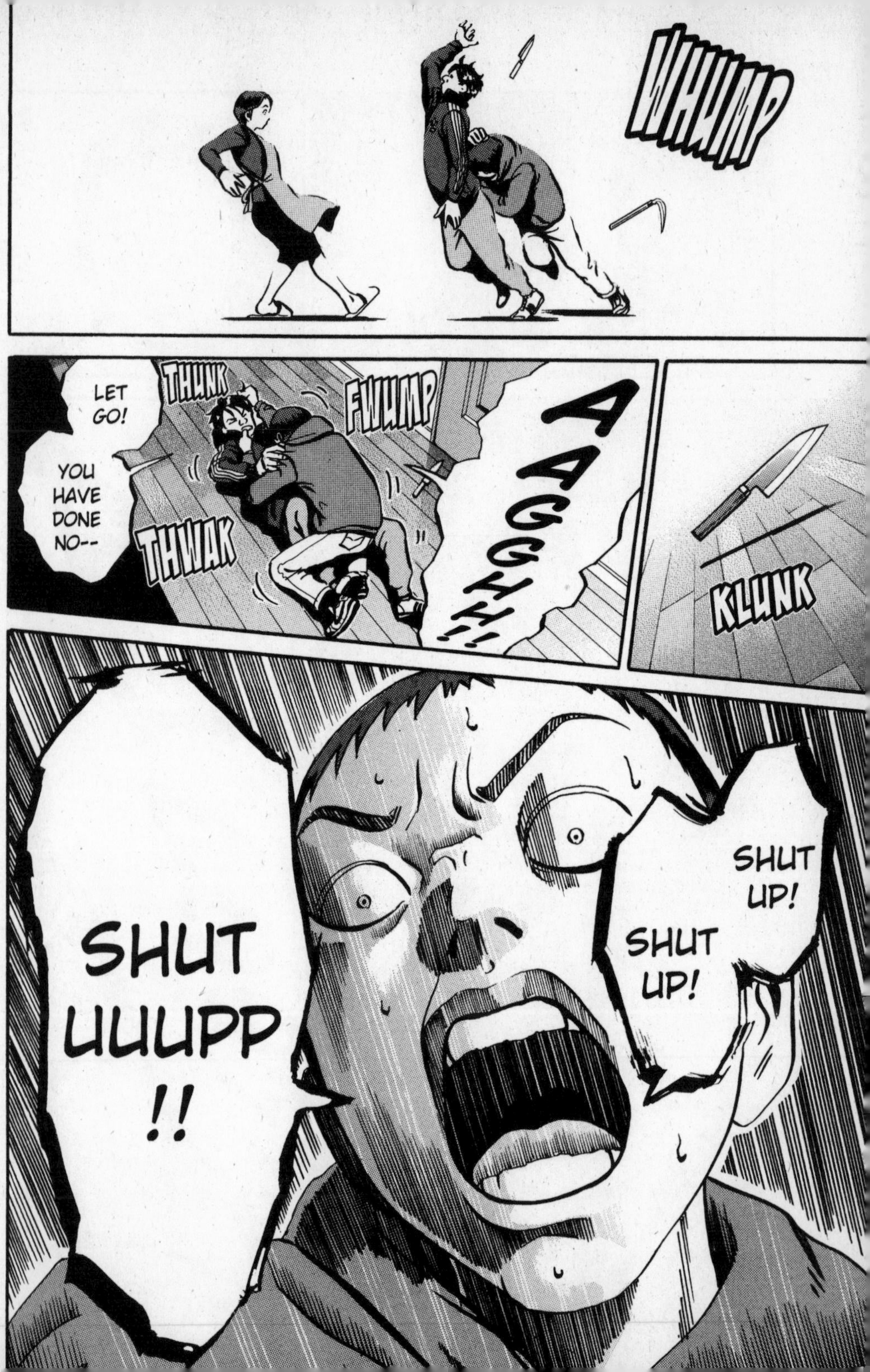
WHUMP
KLUNK
AAGGHH!!
FWUMP
THUNK
LET GO!
YOU HAVE DONE NO--
THWAK
SHUT UP!
SHUT UP!
SHUT UUUPP!!

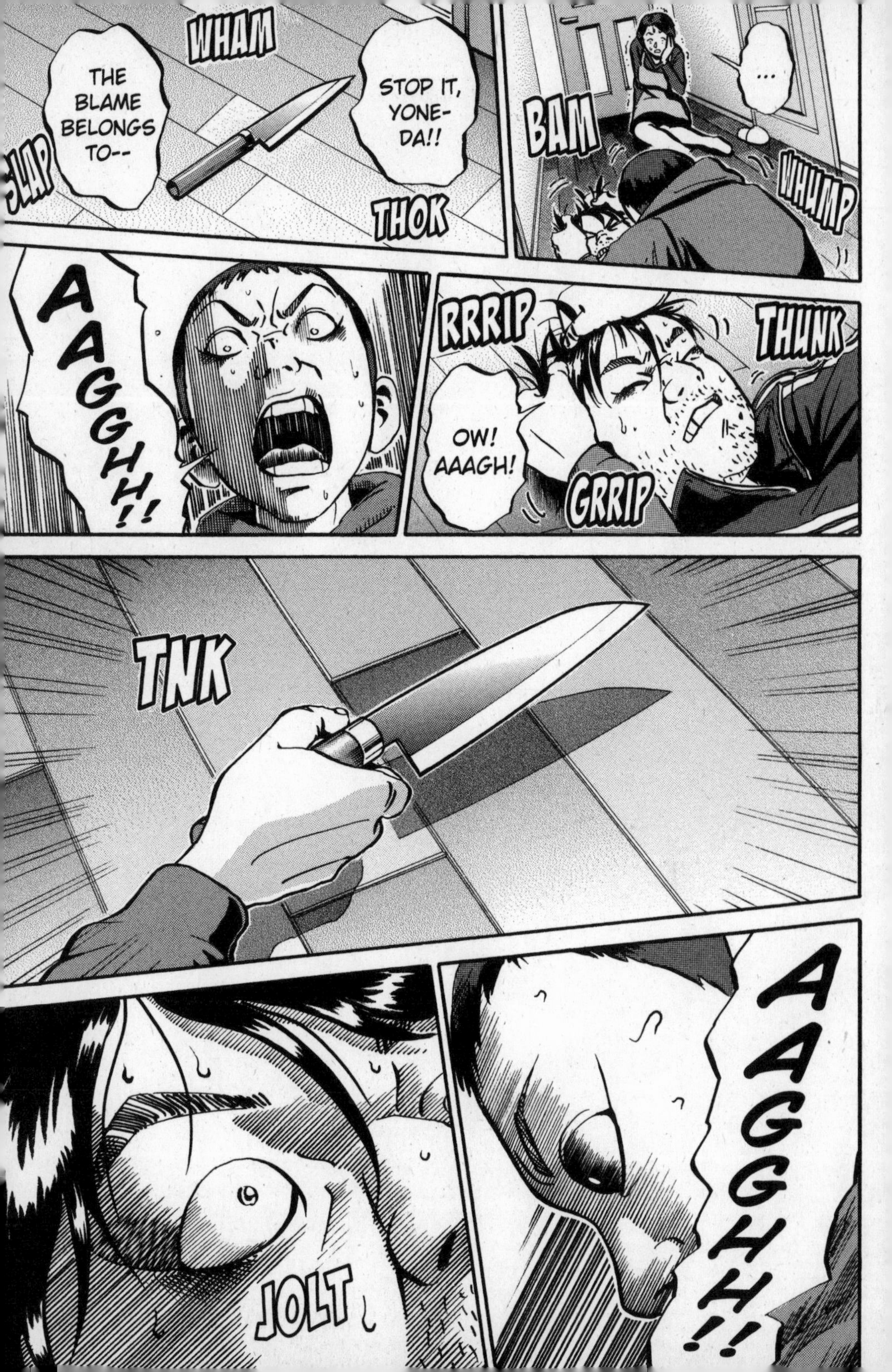

...
BAM
WHUMP
WHAM
STOP IT, YONE-DA!!
THE BLAME BELONGS TO--
SLAP
THOK
THUNK
RRRIP
OW! AAAGH!
GRRIP
AAGGHH!!
TNK
AAGGHH!!
JOLT

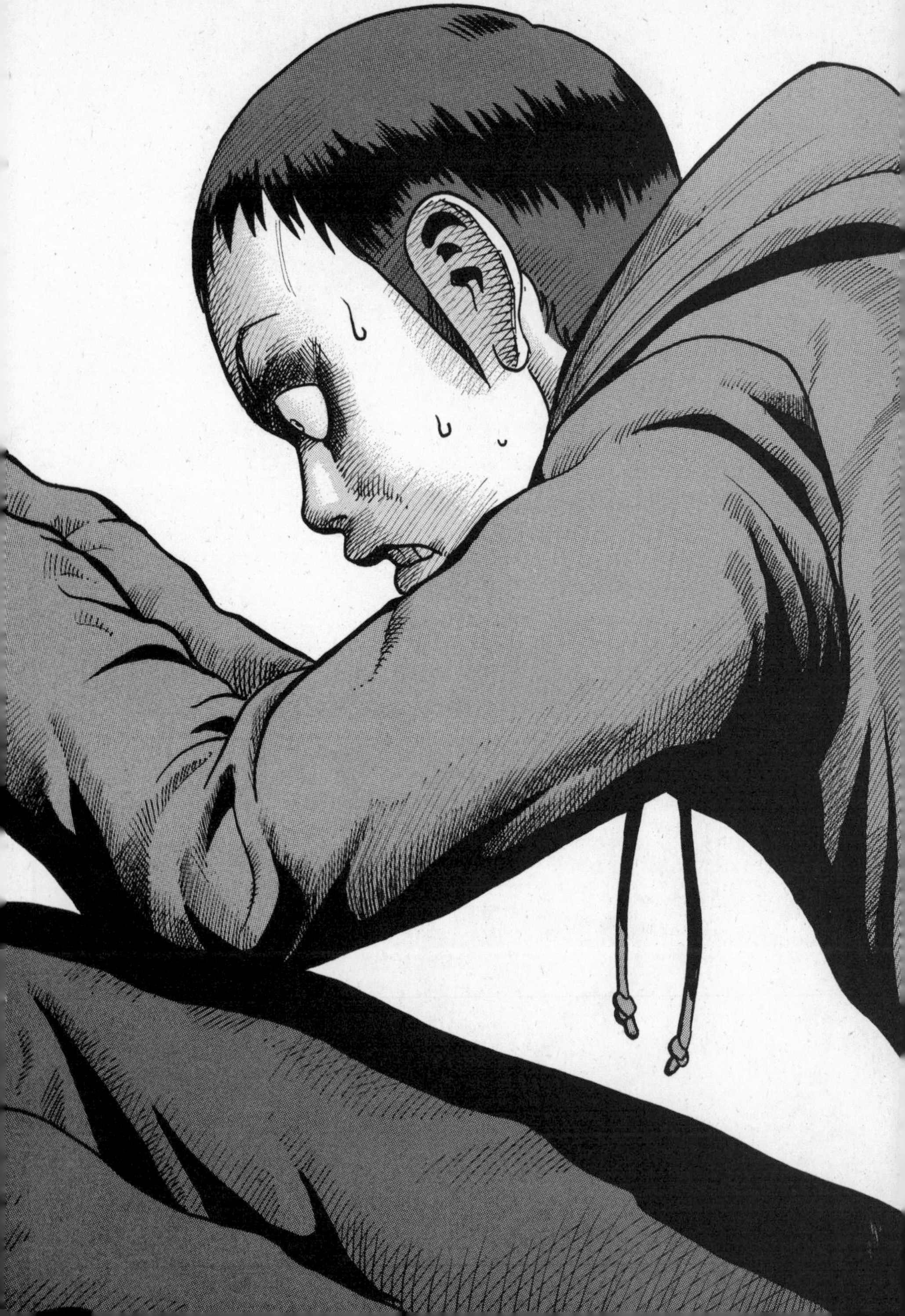

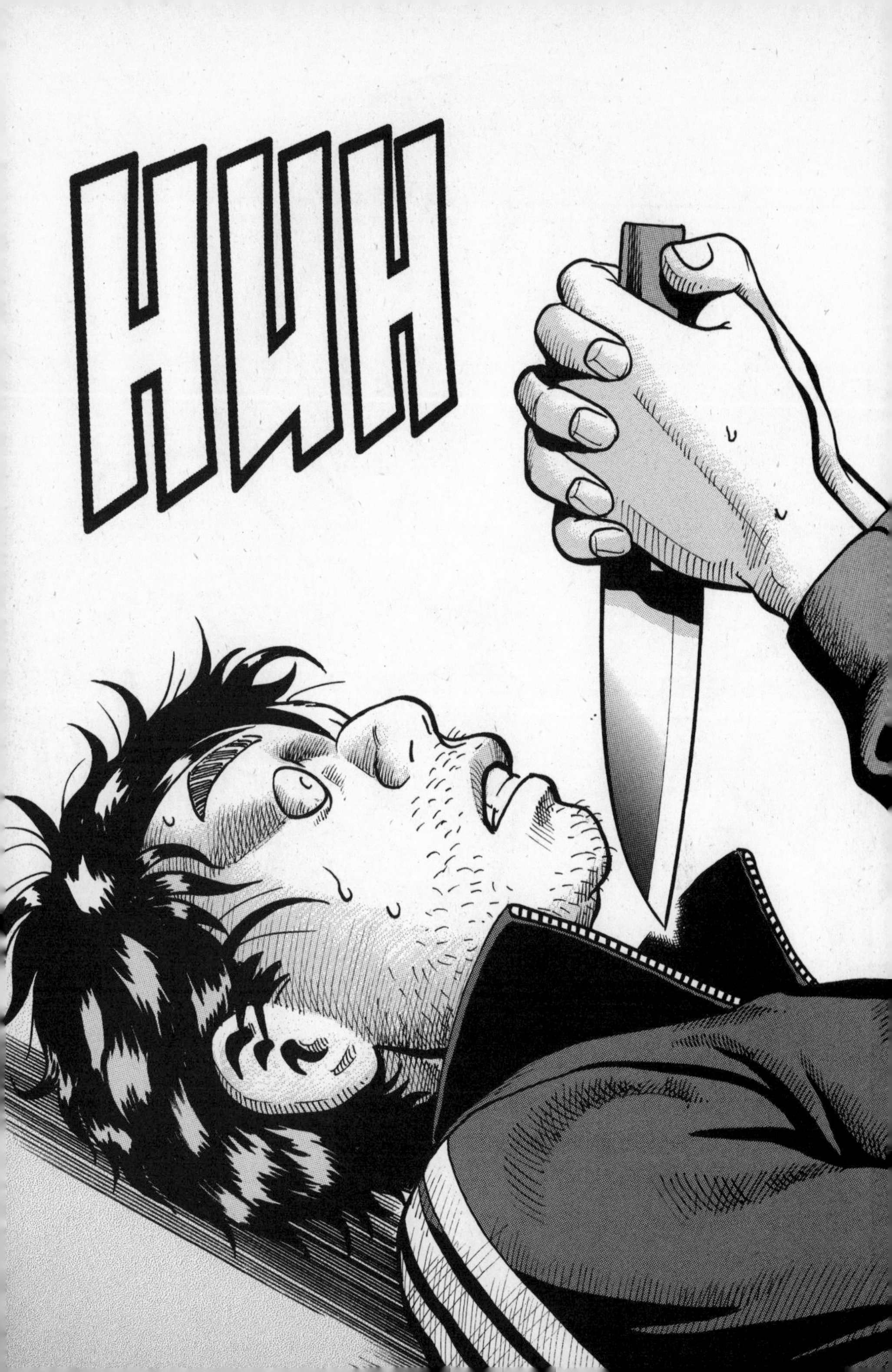
HUH

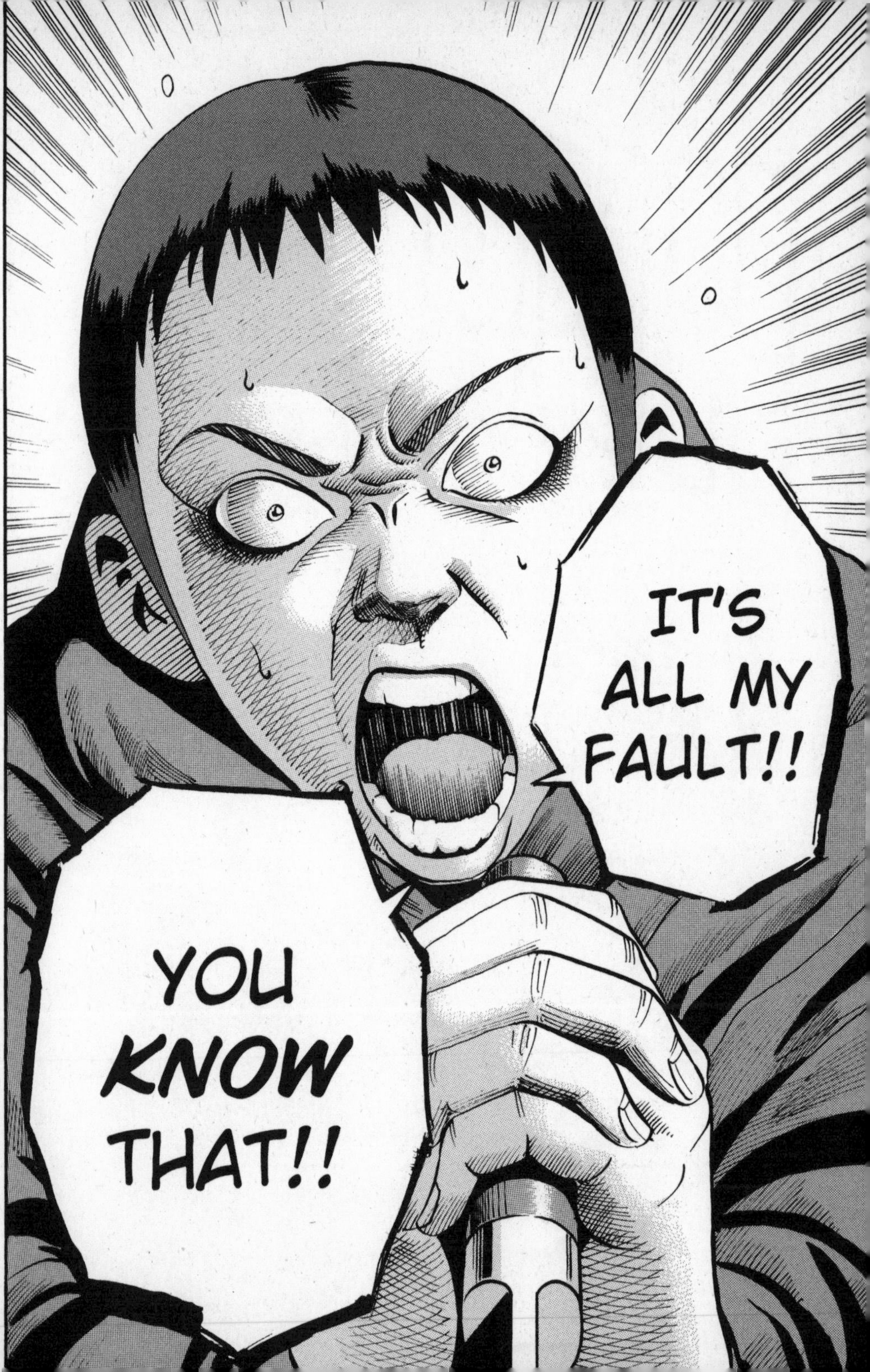
IT'S ALL MY FAULT!!
YOU KNOW THAT!!

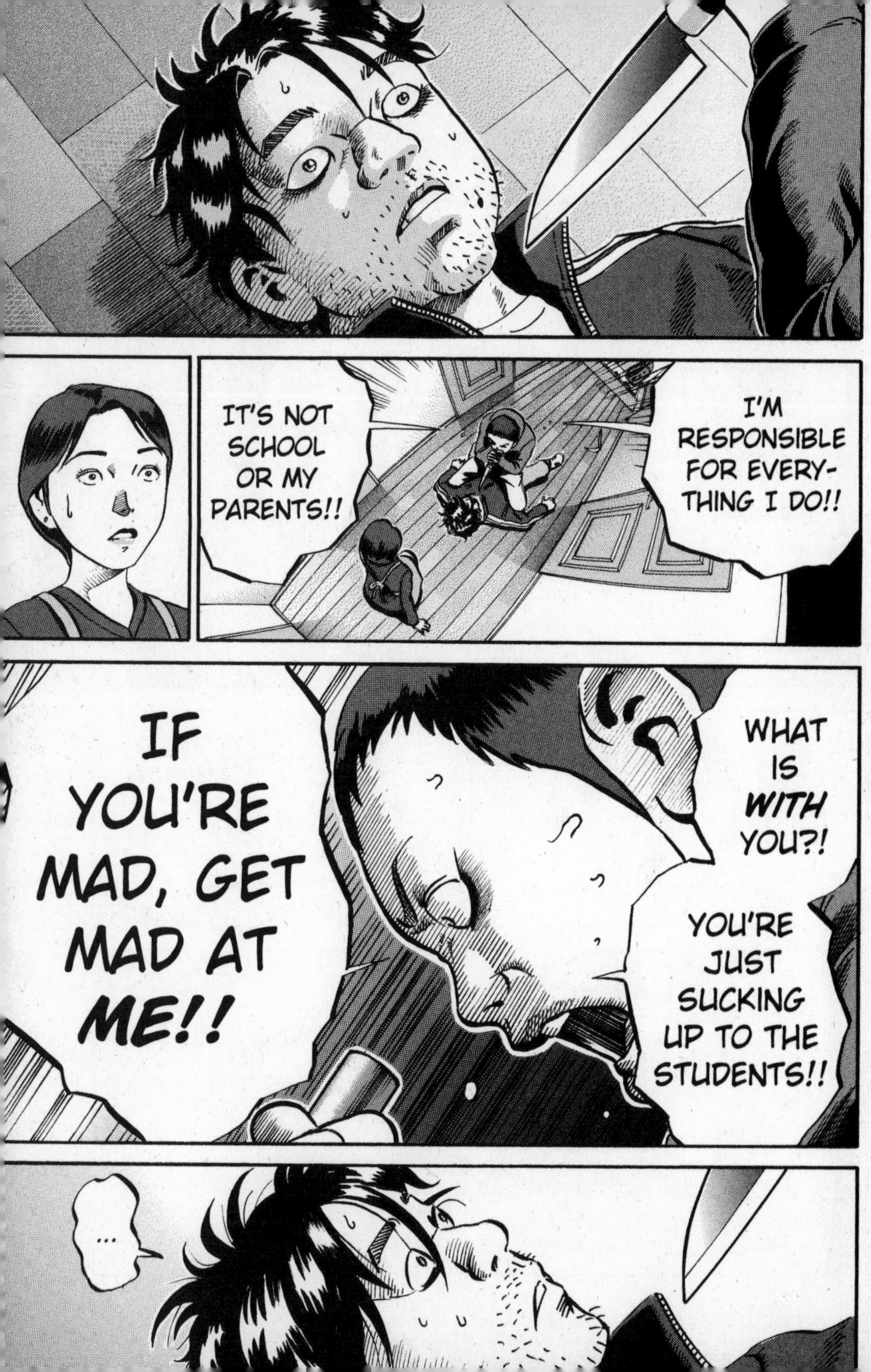
I'M RESPONSIBLE FOR EVERY-THING I DO!!
IT'S NOT SCHOOL OR MY PARENTS!!
WHAT IS *WITH* YOU?!
YOU'RE JUST SUCKING UP TO THE STUDENTS!!
IF YOU'RE MAD, GET MAD AT *ME!!*
...

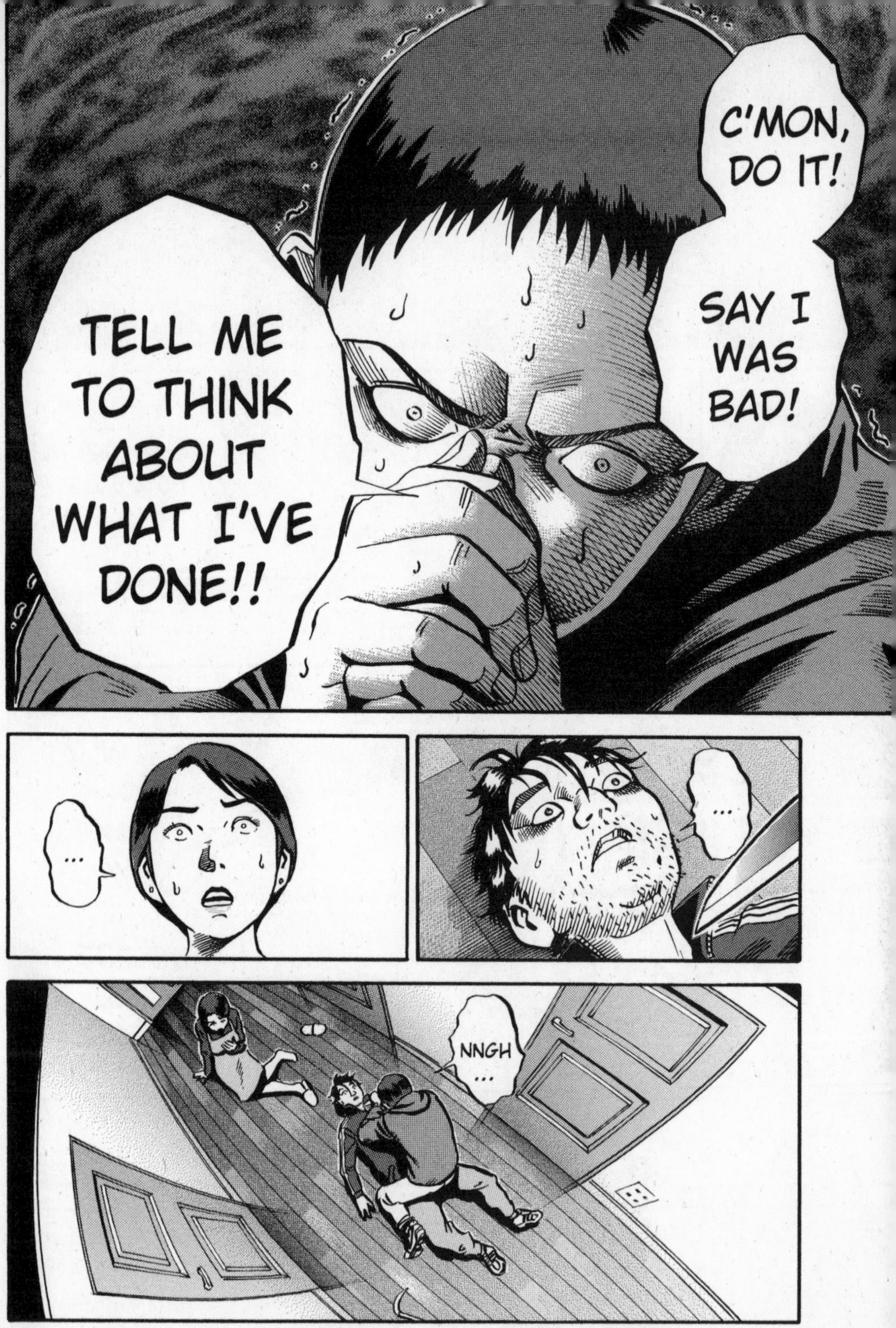

C'MON, DO IT!
SAY I WAS BAD!
TELL ME TO THINK ABOUT WHAT I'VE DONE!!
...
...
NNGH ...

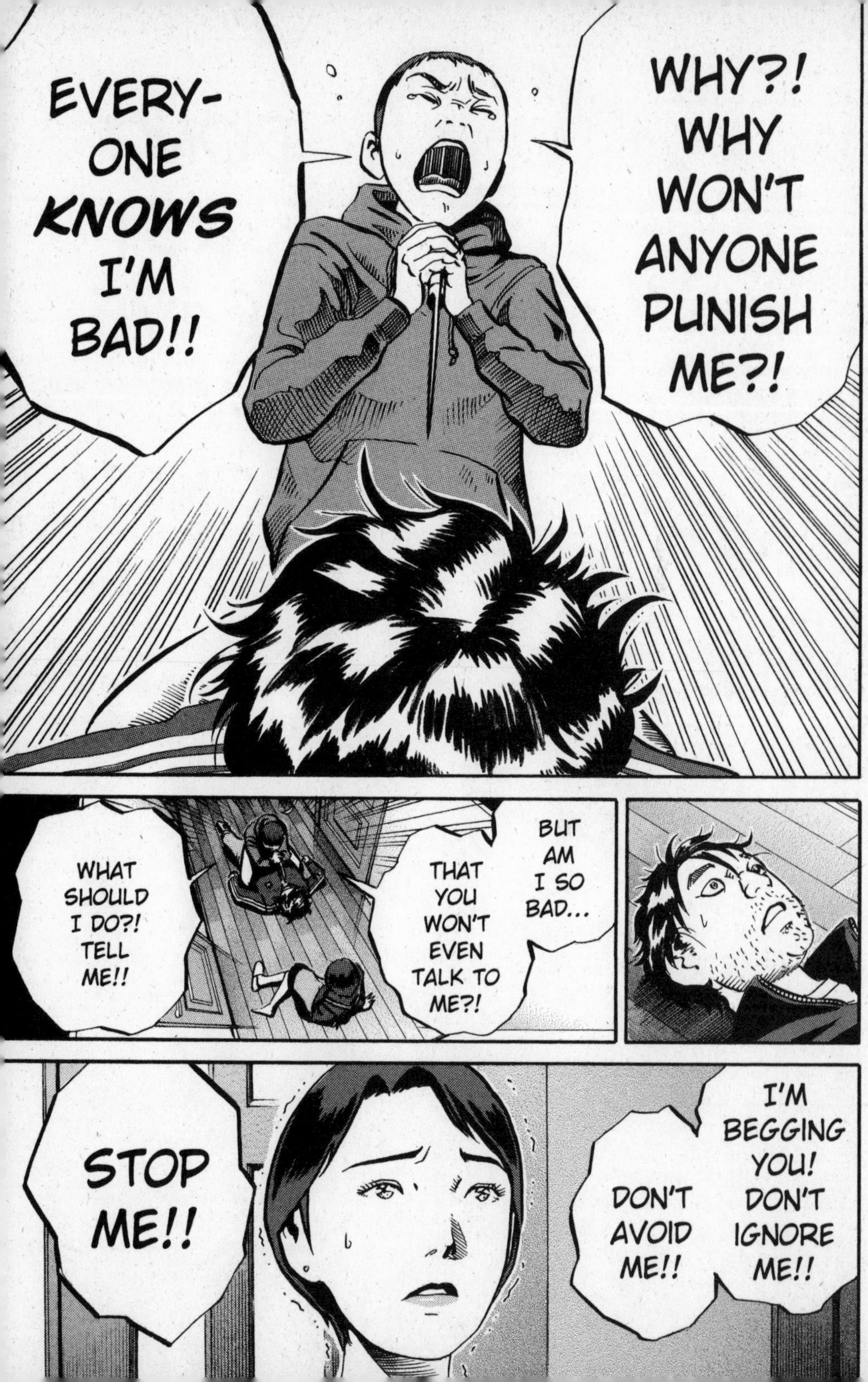
WHY?! WHY WON'T ANYONE PUNISH ME?!
EVERY-ONE *KNOWS* I'M BAD!!
BUT AM I SO BAD...
THAT YOU WON'T EVEN TALK TO ME?!
WHAT SHOULD I DO?! TELL ME!!
I'M BEGGING YOU! DON'T IGNORE ME!!
DON'T AVOID ME!!
STOP ME!!

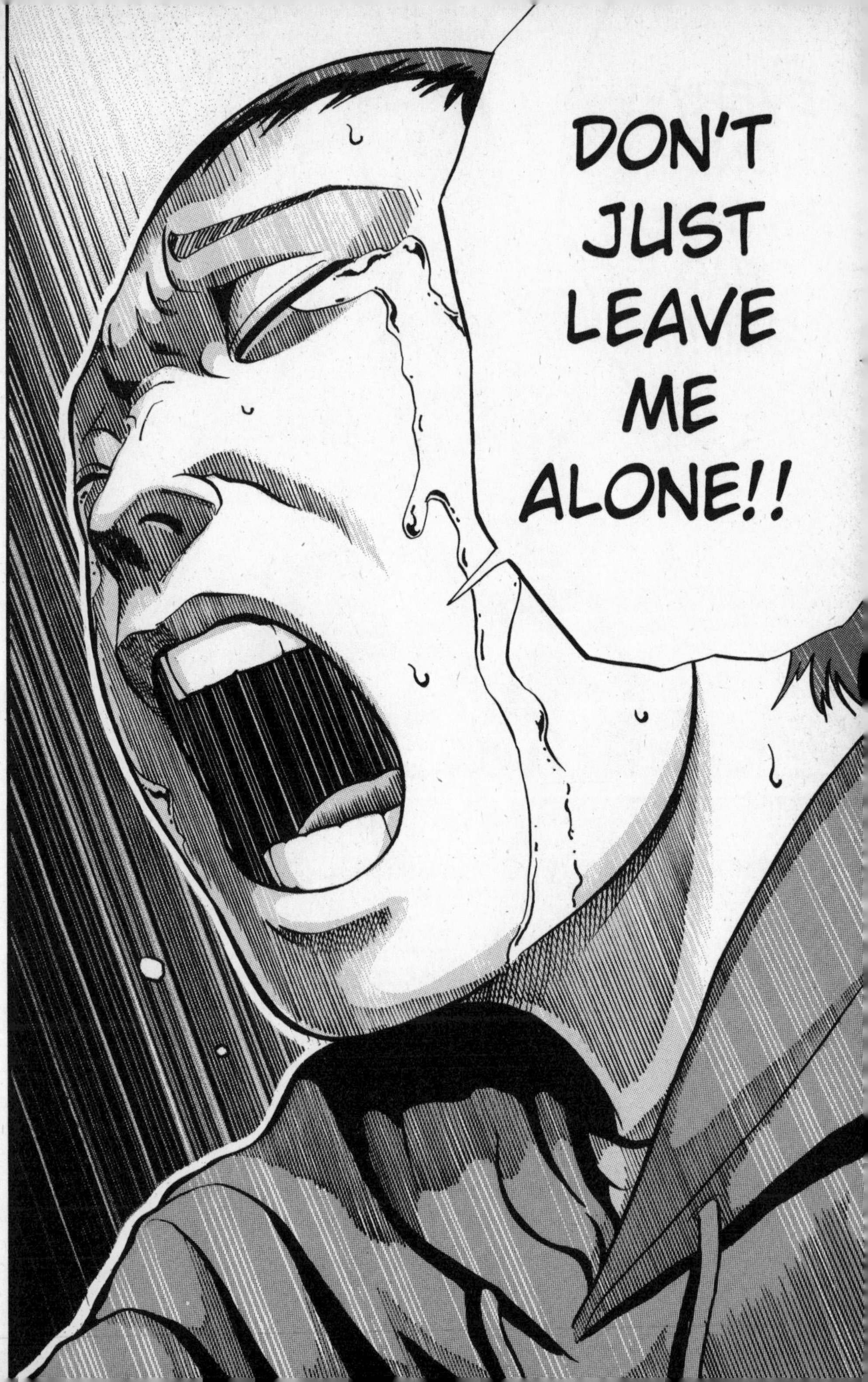
DON'T JUST LEAVE ME ALONE!!

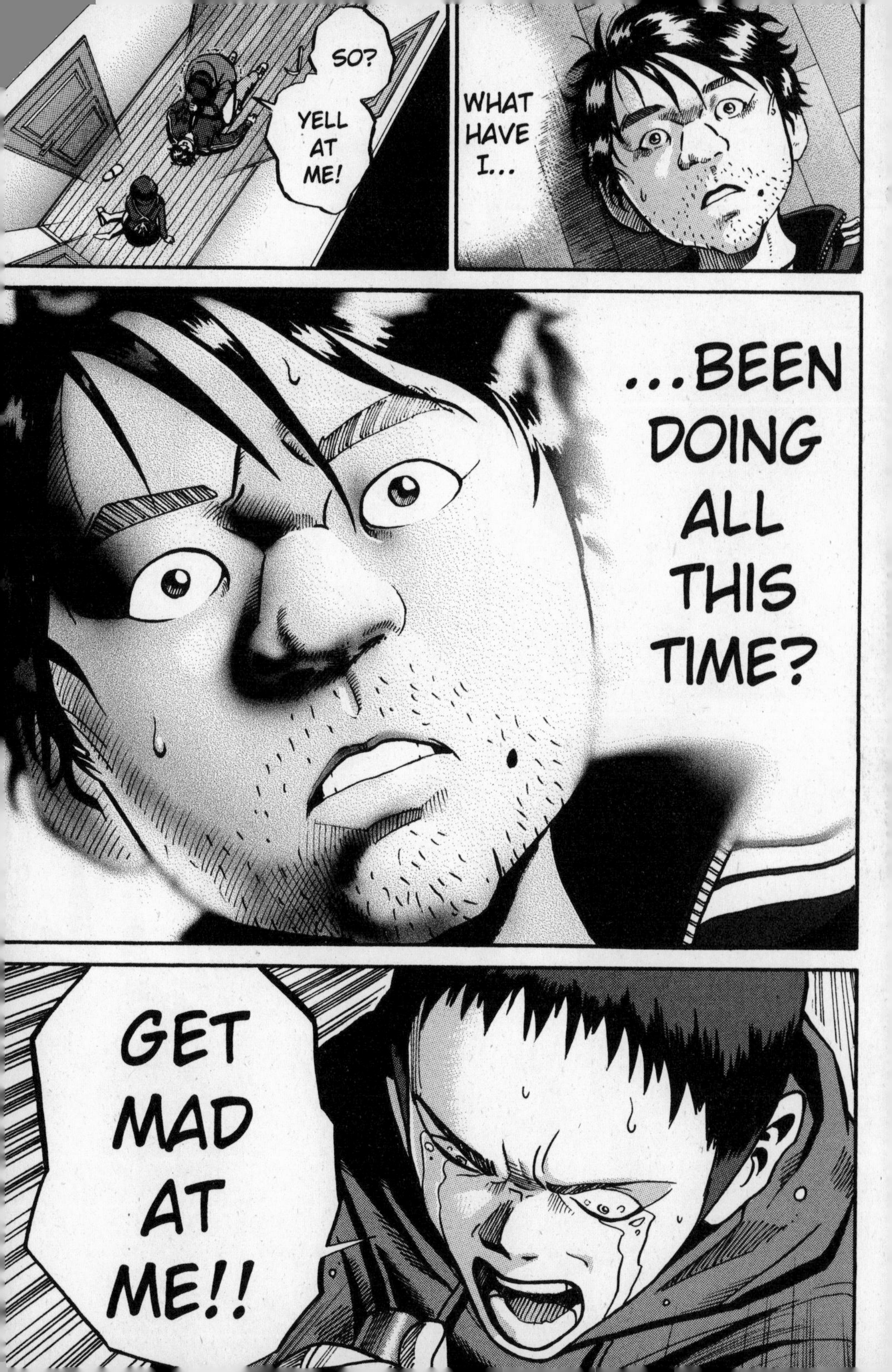
WHAT HAVE I...
SO?
YELL AT ME!
...BEEN DOING ALL THIS TIME?
GET MAD AT ME!!

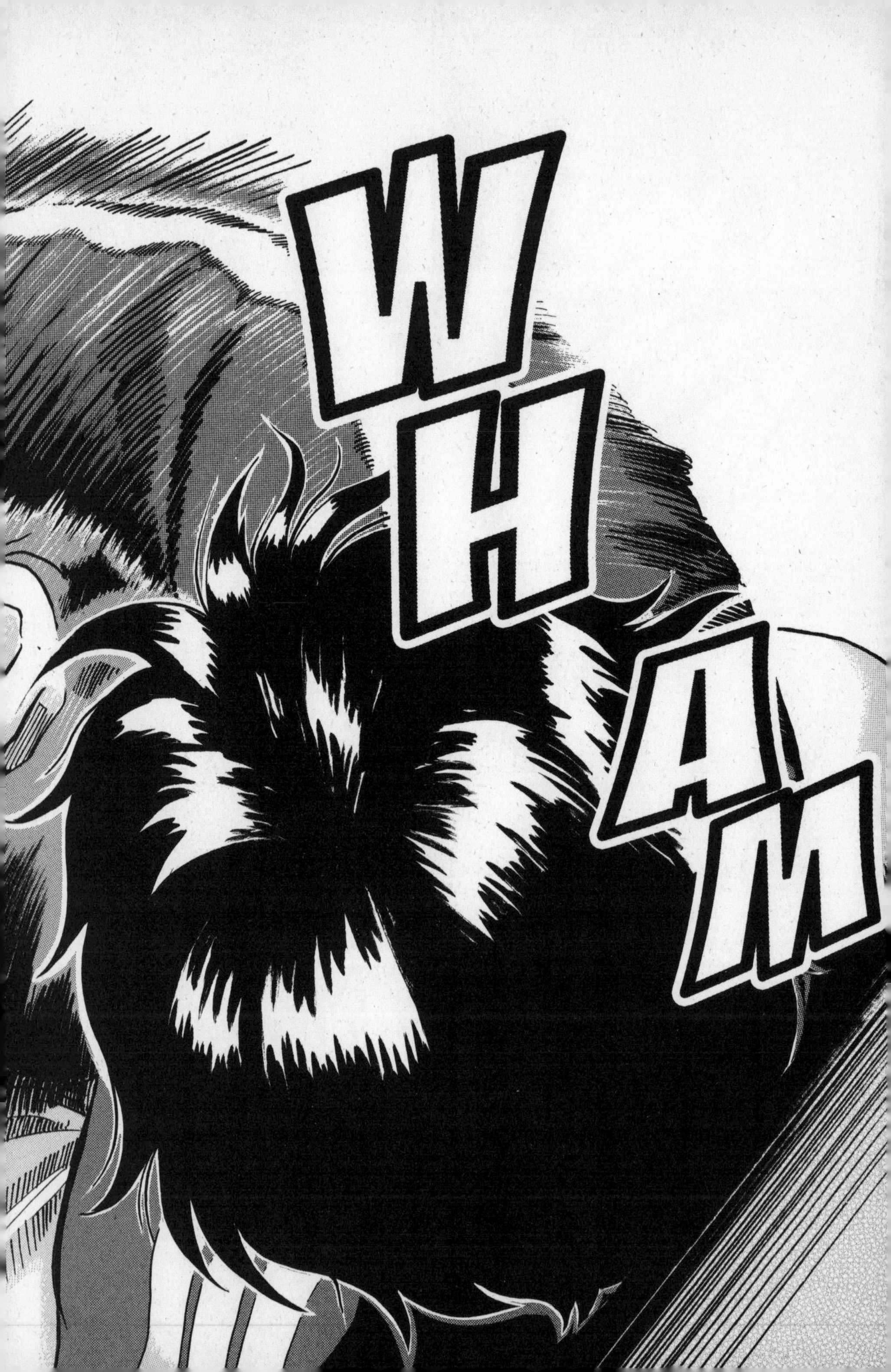
WHAM

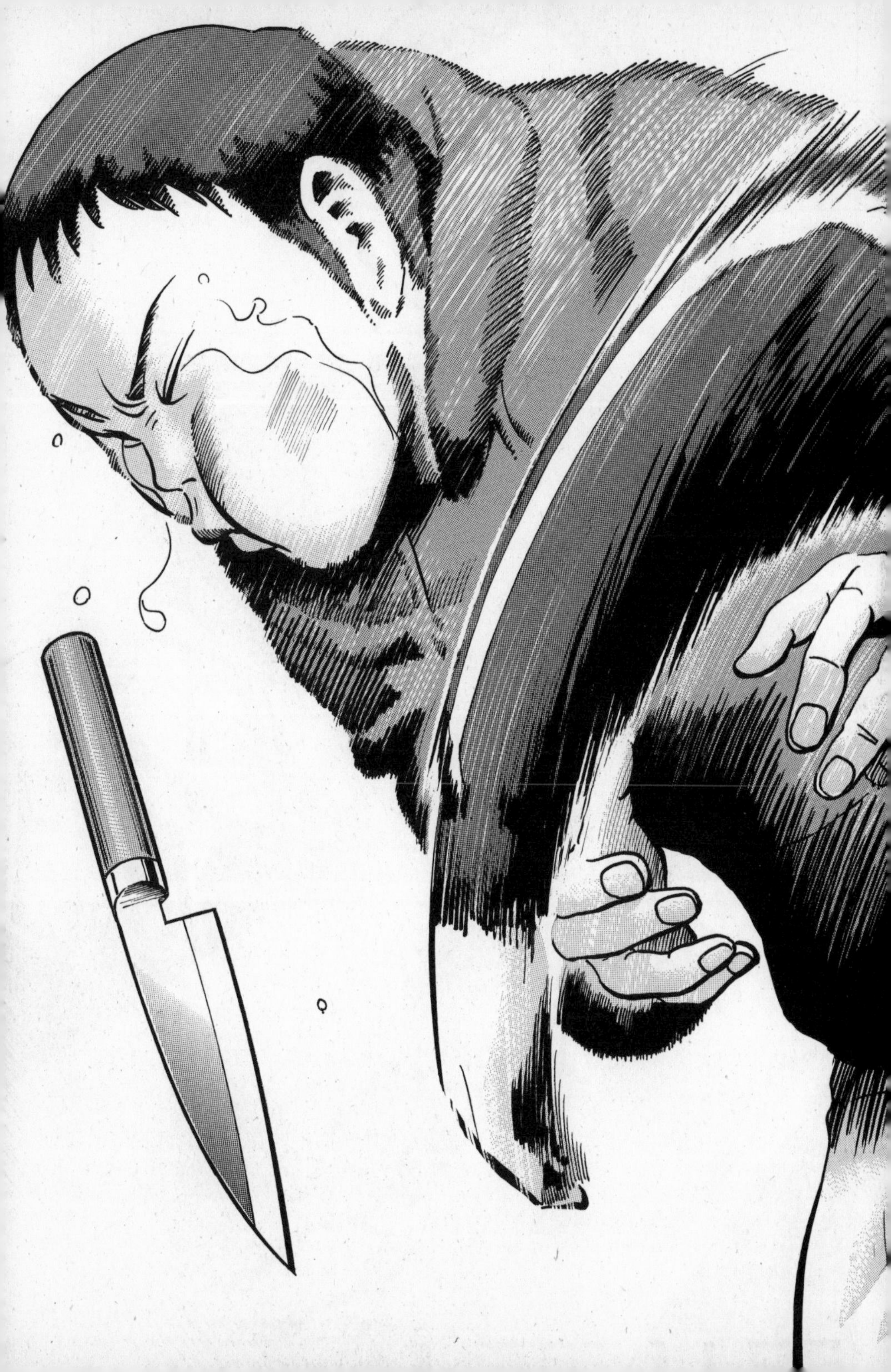

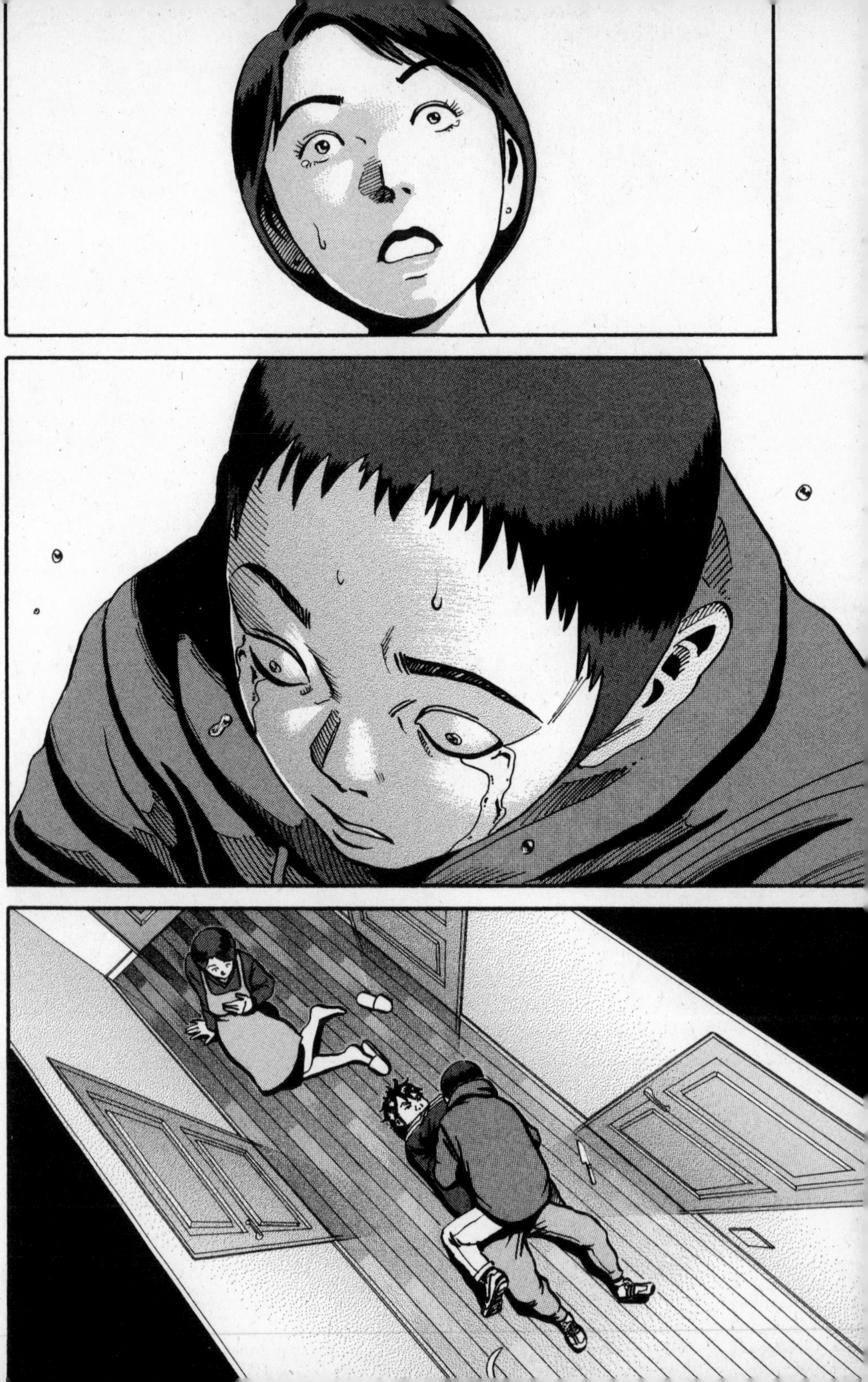

...

Y-YES.

YONE- DA...

...YOU THINK YOU'RE BAD?

ARE YOU TRULY SORRY...

...FROM THE BOTTOM OF YOUR HEART?

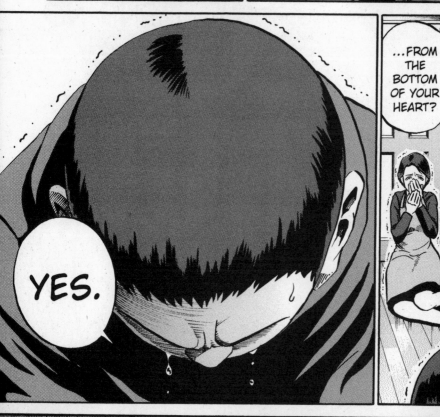

YES.

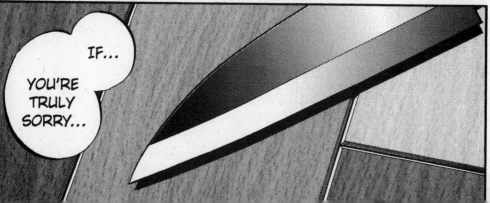

IF...

YOU'RE TRULY SORRY...

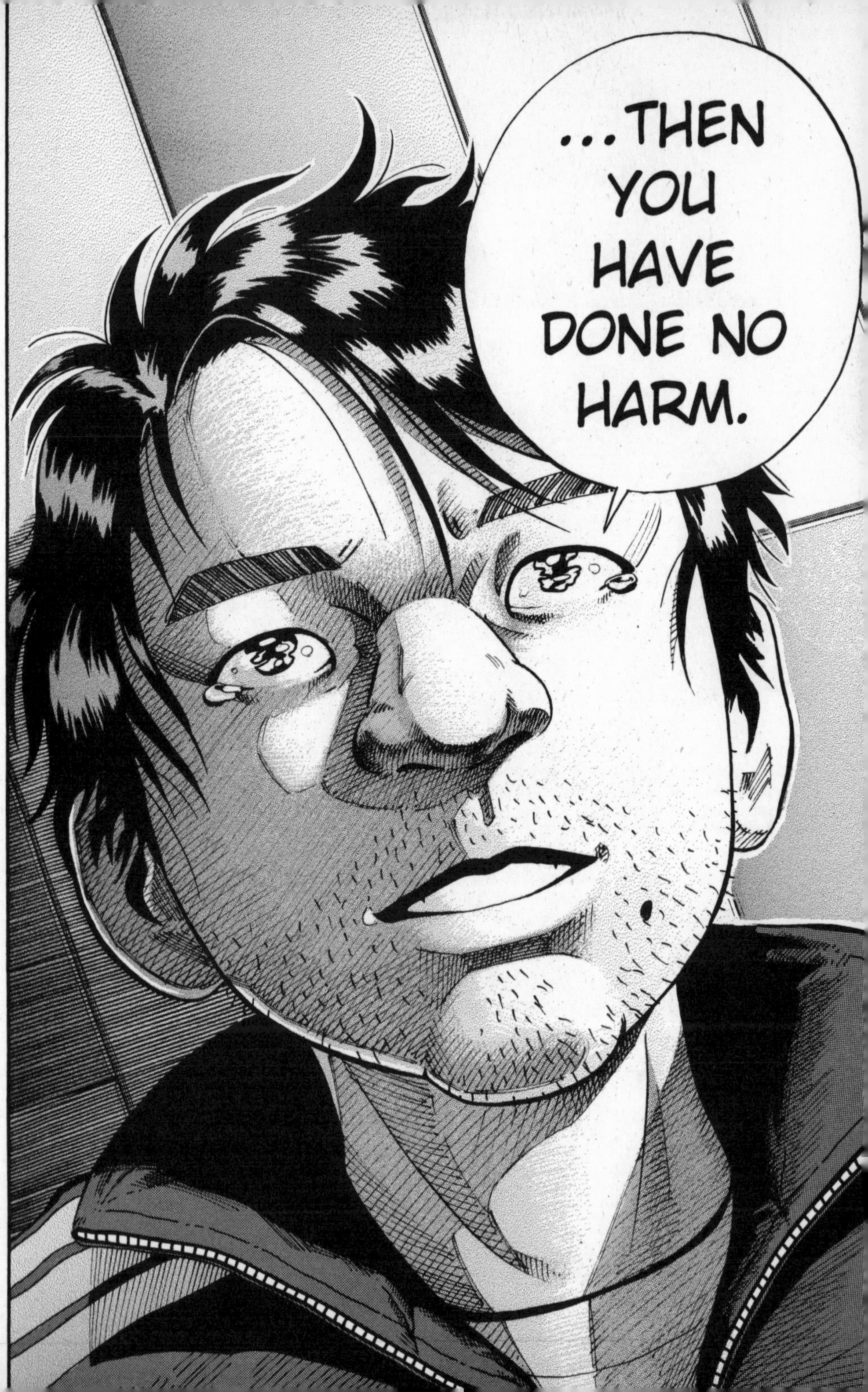
...THEN YOU HAVE DONE NO HARM.

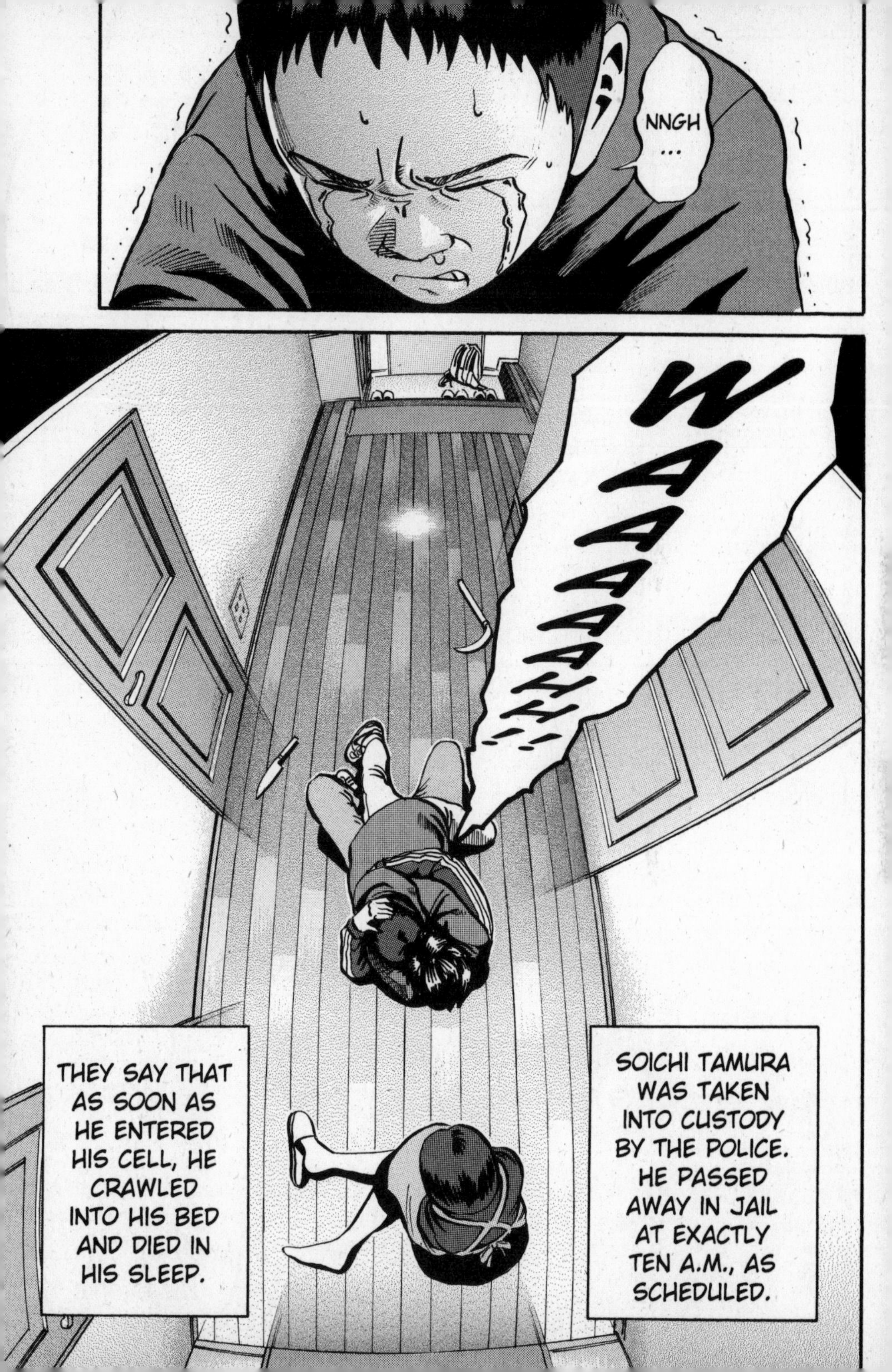
NNGH ...
WAAAAAAH!!!
SOICHI TAMURA WAS TAKEN INTO CUSTODY BY THE POLICE. HE PASSED AWAY IN JAIL AT EXACTLY TEN A.M., AS SCHEDULED.
THEY SAY THAT AS SOON AS HE ENTERED HIS CELL, HE CRAWLED INTO HIS BED AND DIED IN HIS SLEEP.

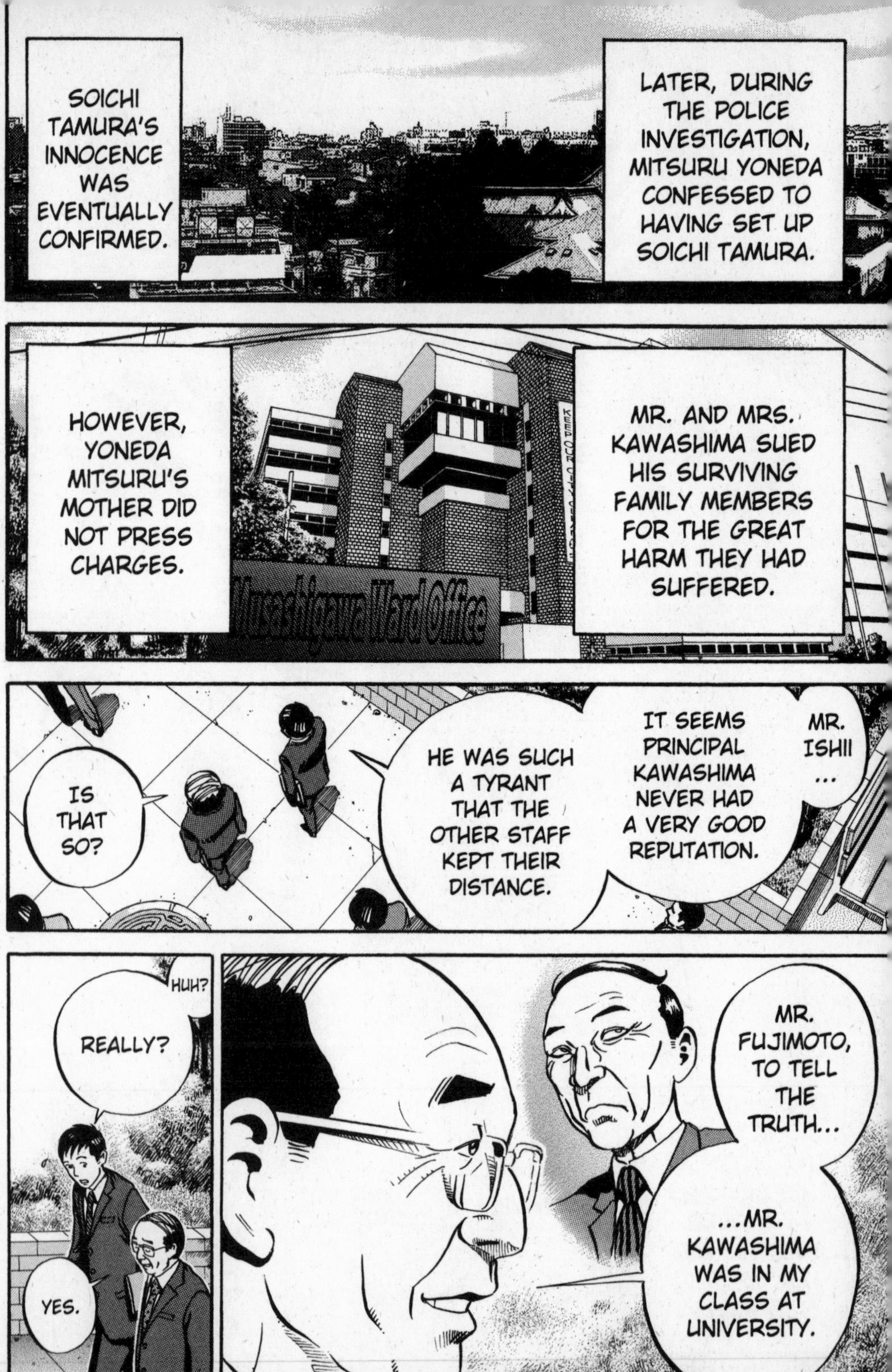
LATER, DURING THE POLICE INVESTIGATION, MITSURU YONEDA CONFESSED TO HAVING SET UP SOICHI TAMURA.
SOICHI TAMURA'S INNOCENCE WAS EVENTUALLY CONFIRMED.
MR. AND MRS. KAWASHIMA SUED HIS SURVIVING FAMILY MEMBERS FOR THE GREAT HARM THEY HAD SUFFERED.
HOWEVER, YONEDA MITSURU'S MOTHER DID NOT PRESS CHARGES.
Musashigawa Ward Office
MR. ISHII ...
IT SEEMS PRINCIPAL KAWASHIMA NEVER HAD A VERY GOOD REPUTATION.
HE WAS SUCH A TYRANT THAT THE OTHER STAFF KEPT THEIR DISTANCE.
IS THAT SO?
MR. FUJIMOTO, TO TELL THE TRUTH...
...MR. KAWASHIMA WAS IN MY CLASS AT UNIVERSITY.
HUH?
REALLY?
YES.

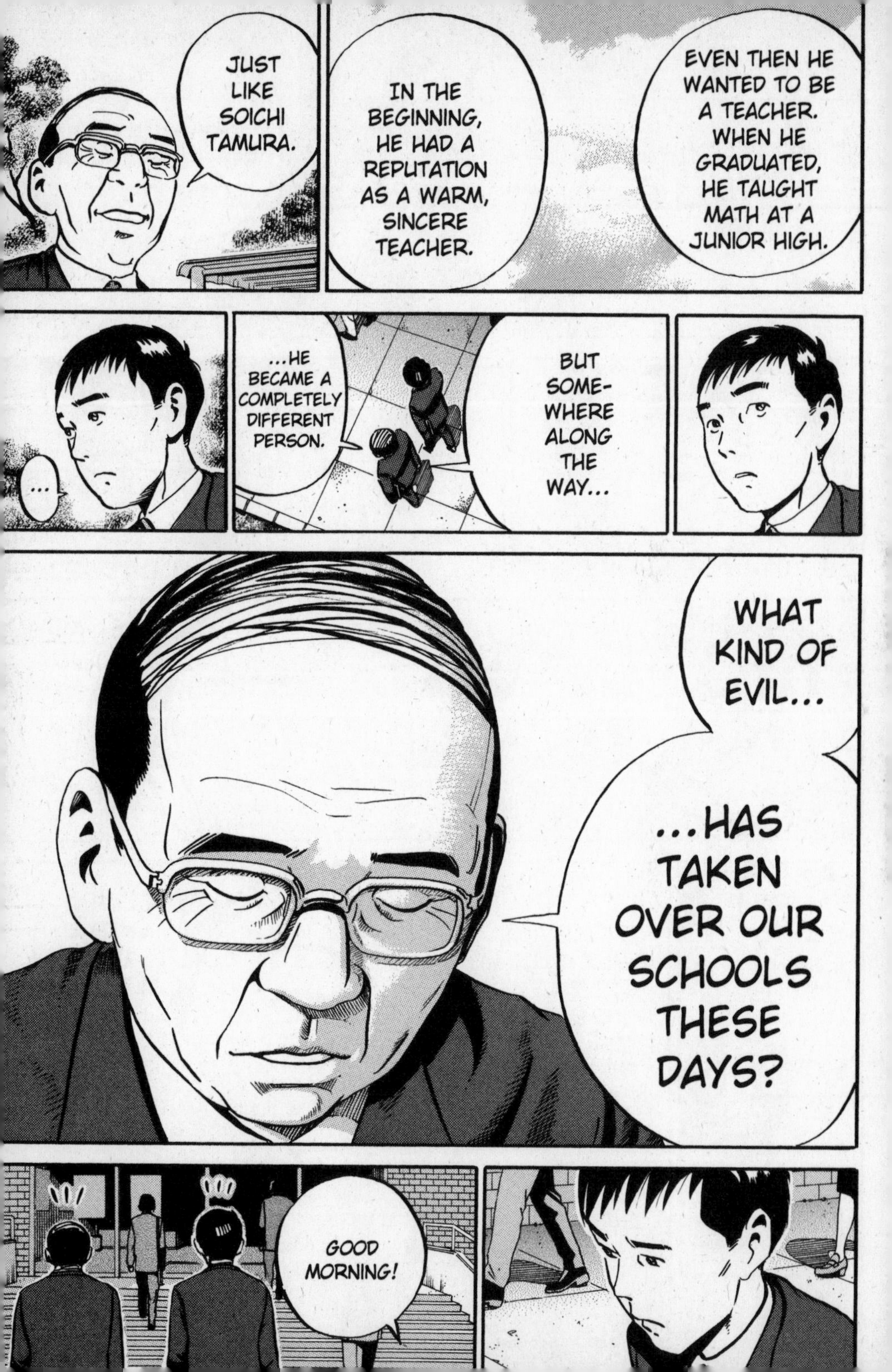
EVEN THEN HE WANTED TO BE A TEACHER. WHEN HE GRADUATED, HE TAUGHT MATH AT A JUNIOR HIGH.
IN THE BEGINNING, HE HAD A REPUTATION AS A WARM, SINCERE TEACHER.
JUST LIKE SOICHI TAMURA.
BUT SOME-WHERE ALONG THE WAY...
...HE BECAME A COMPLETELY DIFFERENT PERSON.
...
WHAT KIND OF EVIL...
...HAS TAKEN OVER OUR SCHOOLS THESE DAYS?
GOOD MORNING!

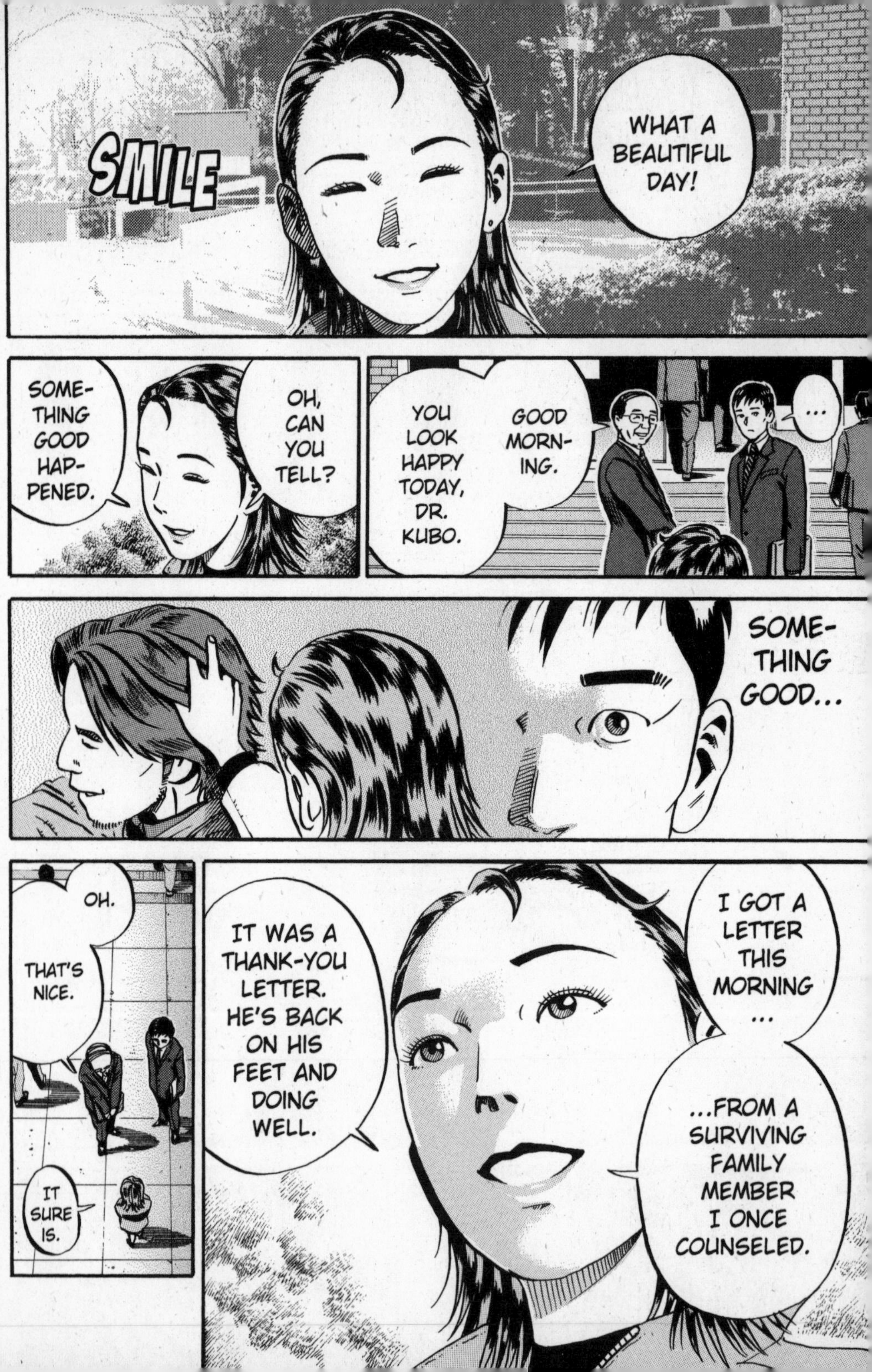
WHAT A BEAUTIFUL DAY!
SMILE
...
GOOD MORNING.
YOU LOOK HAPPY TODAY, DR. KUBO.
OH, CAN YOU TELL?
SOMETHING GOOD HAPPENED.
SOMETHING GOOD...
I GOT A LETTER THIS MORNING...
...FROM A SURVIVING FAMILY MEMBER I ONCE COUNSELED.
IT WAS A THANK-YOU LETTER. HE'S BACK ON HIS FEET AND DOING WELL.
OH.
THAT'S NICE.
IT SURE IS.

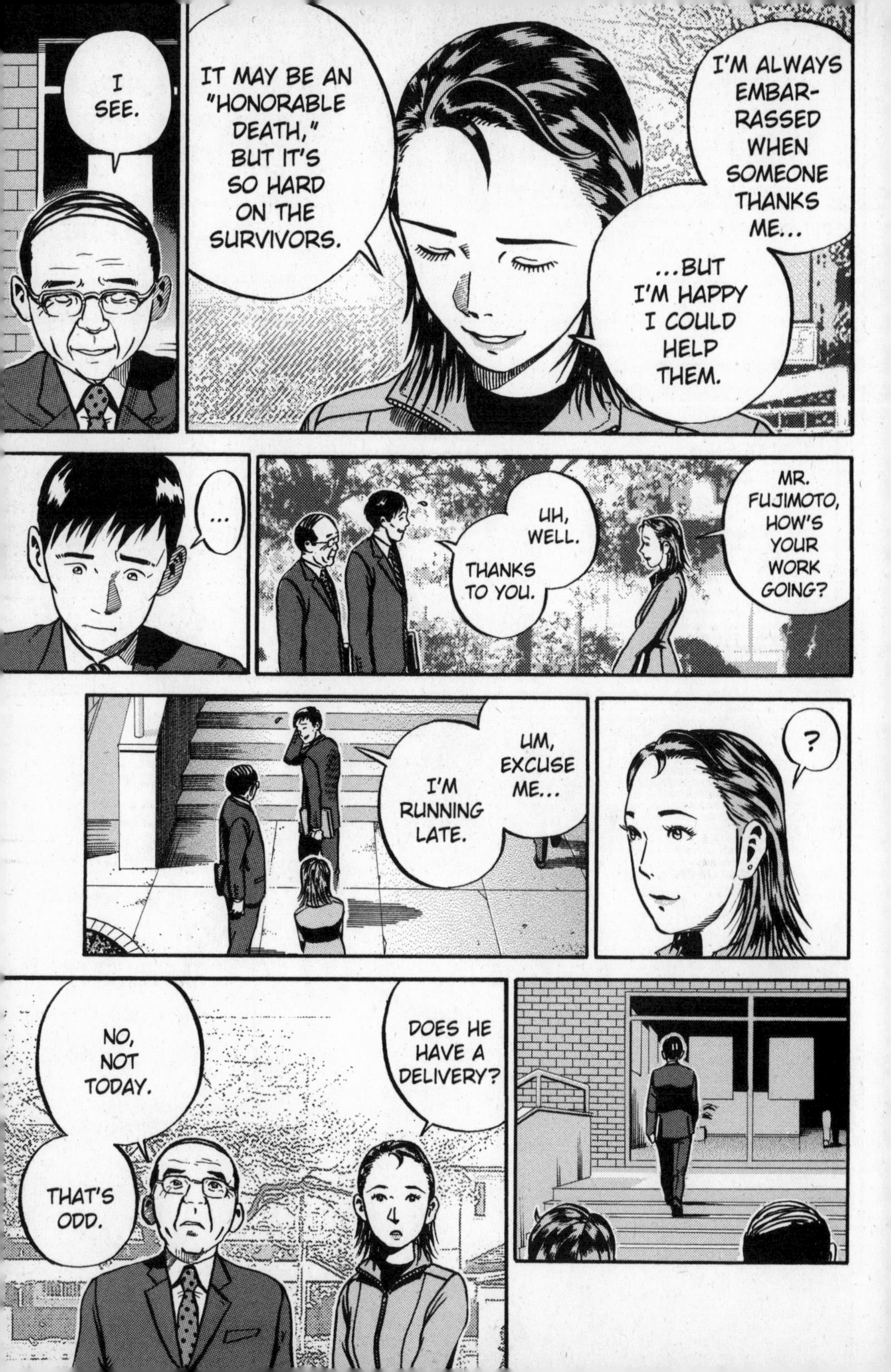
IT MAY BE AN "HONORABLE DEATH," BUT IT'S SO HARD ON THE SURVIVORS.
I'M ALWAYS EMBARRASSED WHEN SOMEONE THANKS ME...
...BUT I'M HAPPY I COULD HELP THEM.
I SEE.
MR. FUJIMOTO, HOW'S YOUR WORK GOING?
UH, WELL.
THANKS TO YOU.
...
?
UM, EXCUSE ME...
I'M RUNNING LATE.
DOES HE HAVE A DELIVERY?
NO, NOT TODAY.
THAT'S ODD.

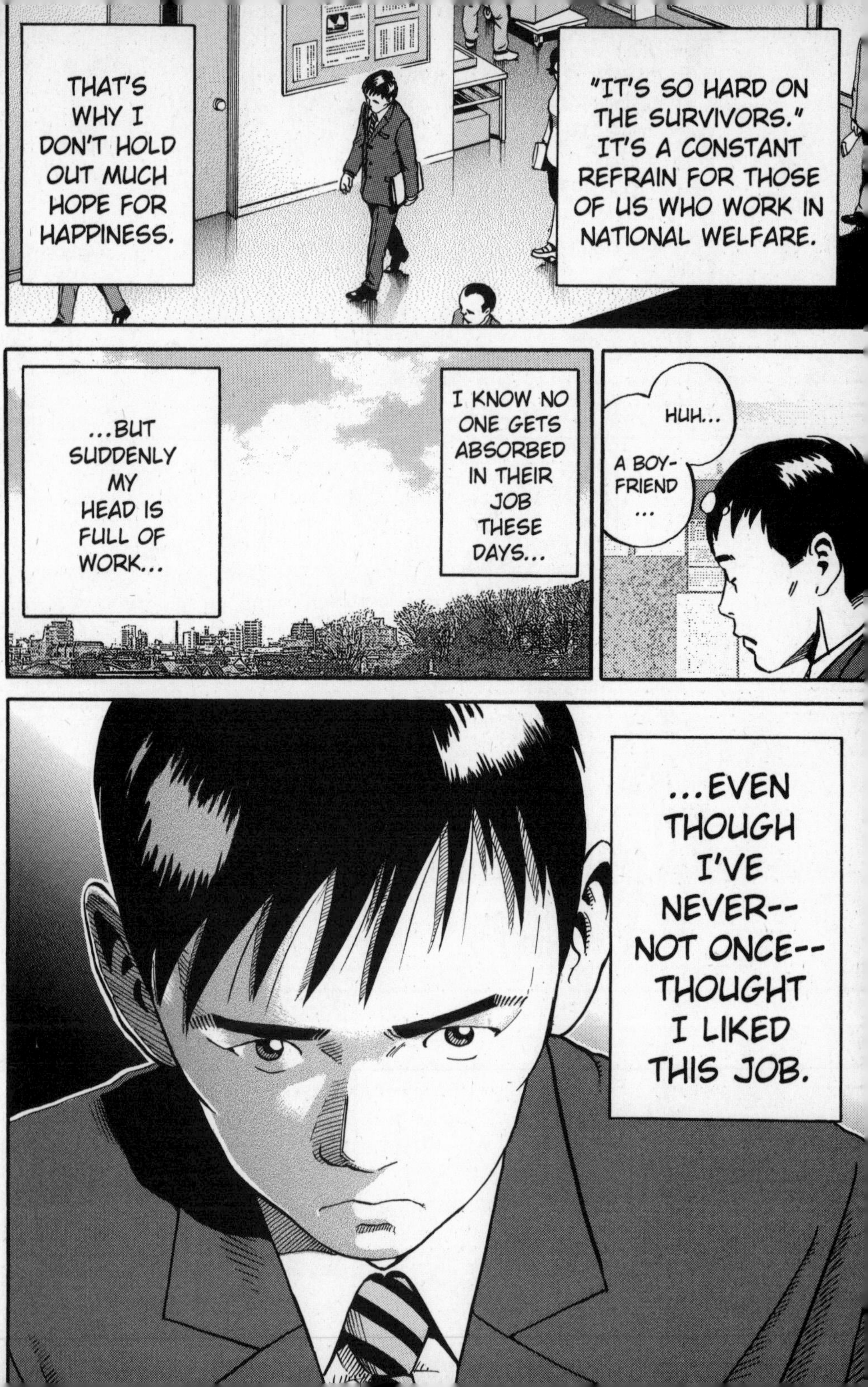
"IT'S SO HARD ON THE SURVIVORS." IT'S A CONSTANT REFRAIN FOR THOSE OF US WHO WORK IN NATIONAL WELFARE.
THAT'S WHY I DON'T HOLD OUT MUCH HOPE FOR HAPPINESS.
HUH...
A BOY-FRIEND...
I KNOW NO ONE GETS ABSORBED IN THEIR JOB THESE DAYS...
...BUT SUDDENLY MY HEAD IS FULL OF WORK...
...EVEN THOUGH I'VE NEVER--NOT ONCE--THOUGHT I LIKED THIS JOB.

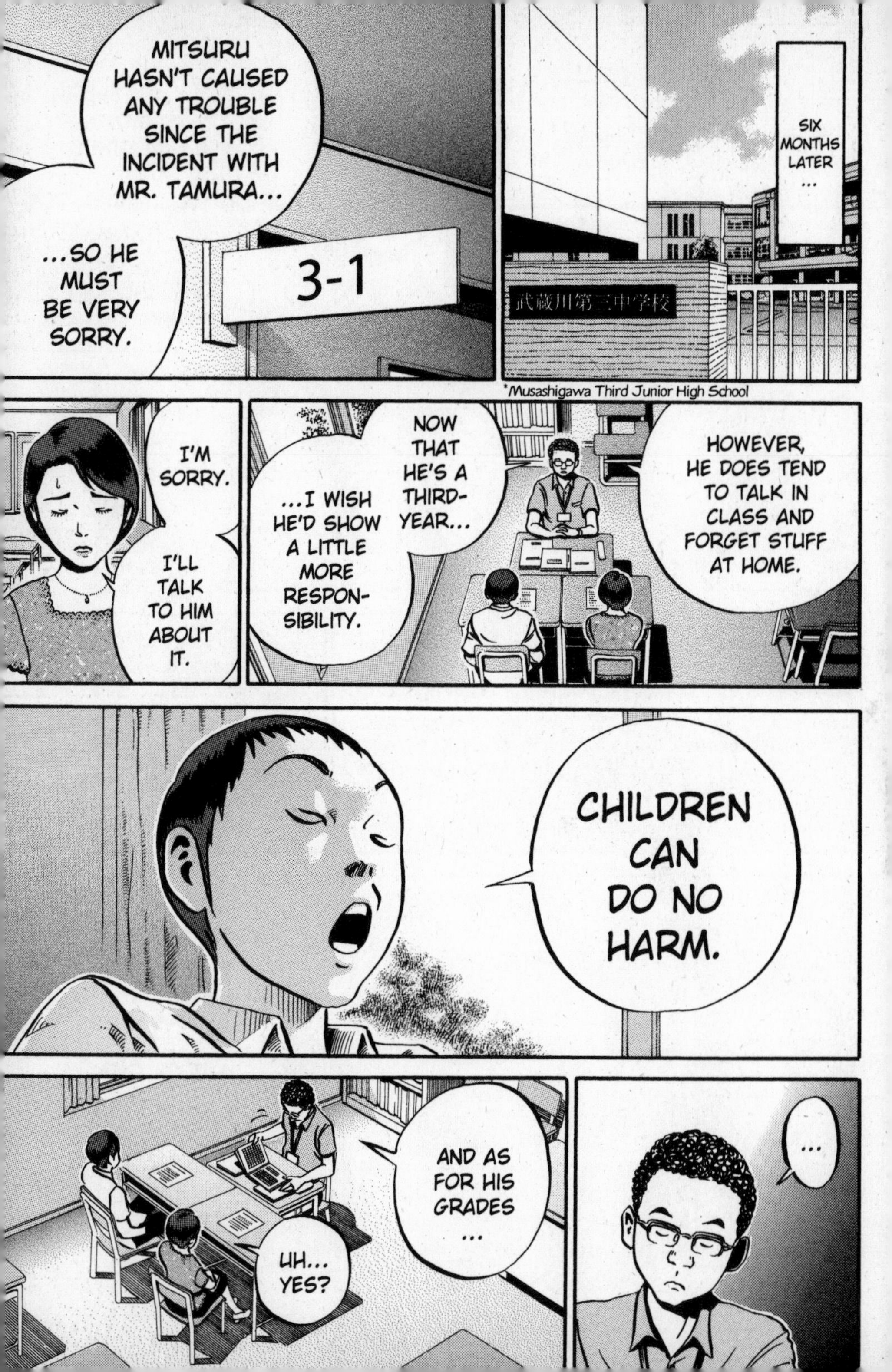
SIX MONTHS LATER ...
武蔵川第三中学校
*Musashigawa Third Junior High School
3-1
MITSURU HASN'T CAUSED ANY TROUBLE SINCE THE INCIDENT WITH MR. TAMURA...
...SO HE MUST BE VERY SORRY.
HOWEVER, HE DOES TEND TO TALK IN CLASS AND FORGET STUFF AT HOME.
NOW THAT HE'S A THIRD-YEAR...
...I WISH HE'D SHOW A LITTLE MORE RESPON-SIBILITY.
I'M SORRY.
I'LL TALK TO HIM ABOUT IT.
CHILDREN CAN DO NO HARM.
...
AND AS FOR HIS GRADES ...
UH... YES?

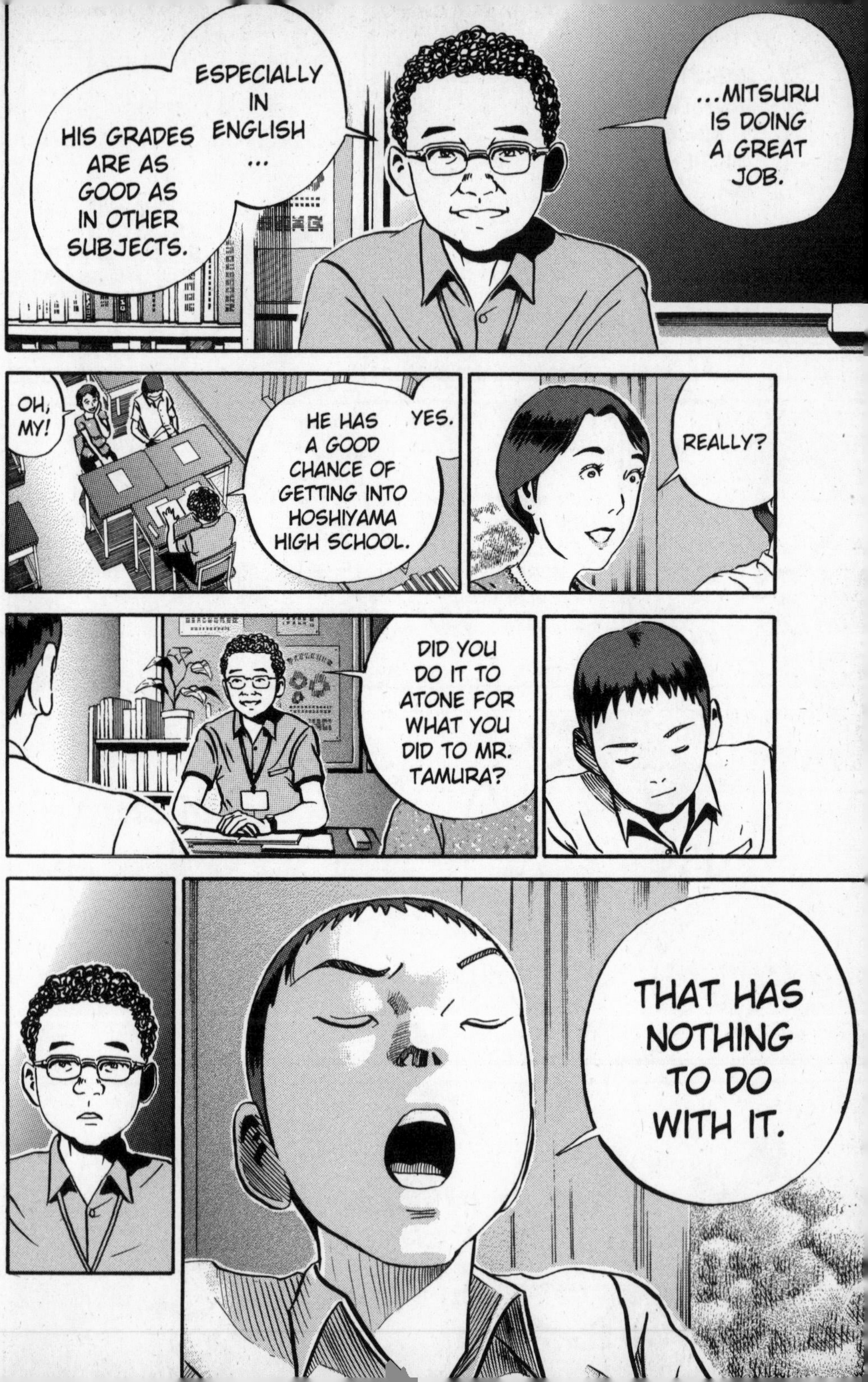
...MITSURU IS DOING A GREAT JOB.
ESPECIALLY IN ENGLISH ...
HIS GRADES ARE AS GOOD AS IN OTHER SUBJECTS.
REALLY?
YES.
HE HAS A GOOD CHANCE OF GETTING INTO HOSHIYAMA HIGH SCHOOL.
OH, MY!
DID YOU DO IT TO ATONE FOR WHAT YOU DID TO MR. TAMURA?
THAT HAS NOTHING TO DO WITH IT.

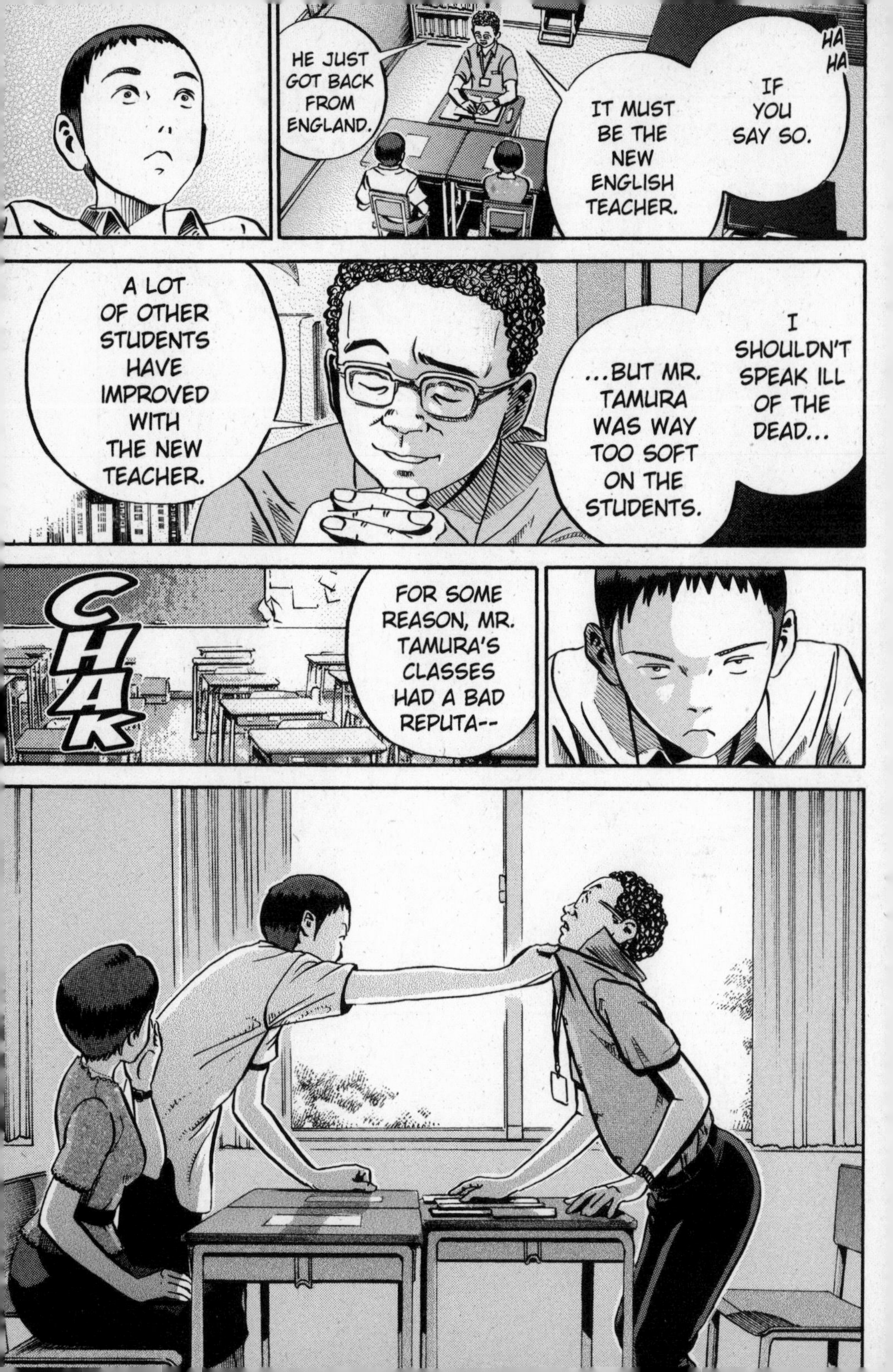
HA HA
IF YOU SAY SO.
IT MUST BE THE NEW ENGLISH TEACHER.
HE JUST GOT BACK FROM ENGLAND.
I SHOULDN'T SPEAK ILL OF THE DEAD...
...BUT MR. TAMURA WAS WAY TOO SOFT ON THE STUDENTS.
A LOT OF OTHER STUDENTS HAVE IMPROVED WITH THE NEW TEACHER.
FOR SOME REASON, MR. TAMURA'S CLASSES HAD A BAD REPUTA--
CHAK

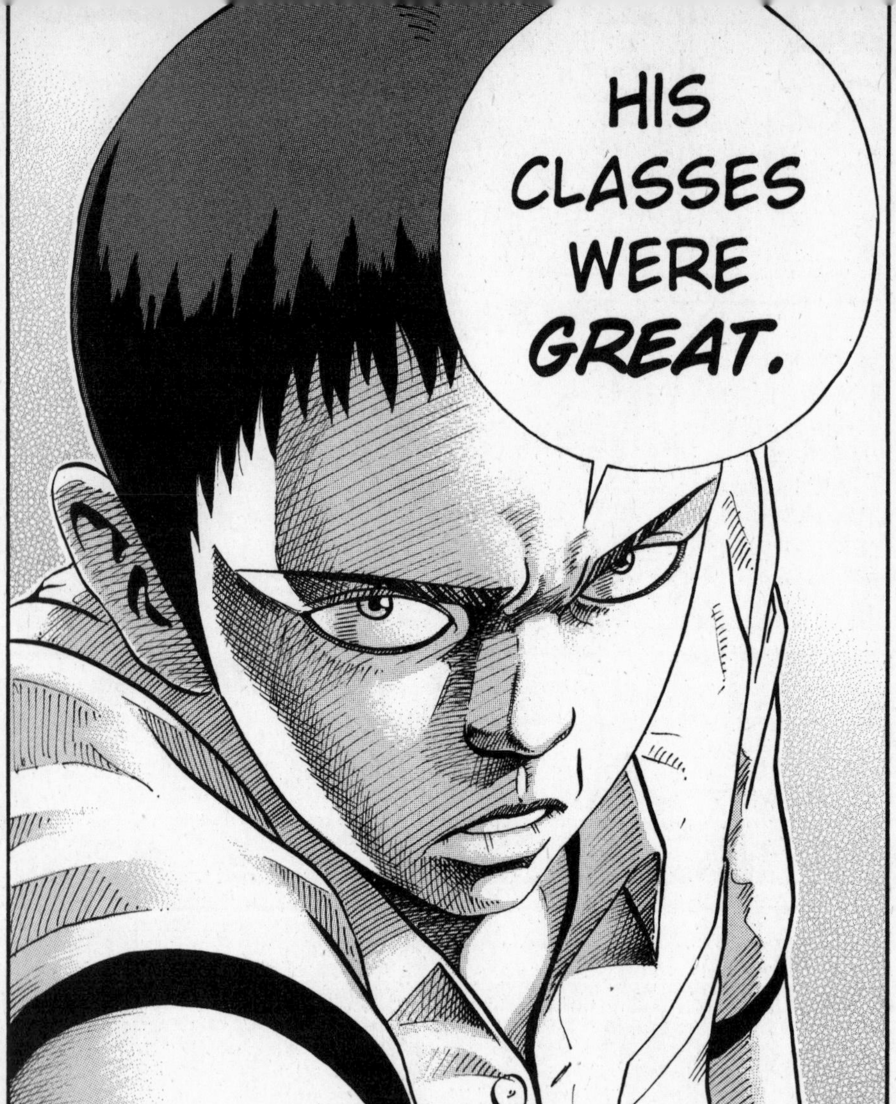
HIS CLASSES WERE *GREAT.*

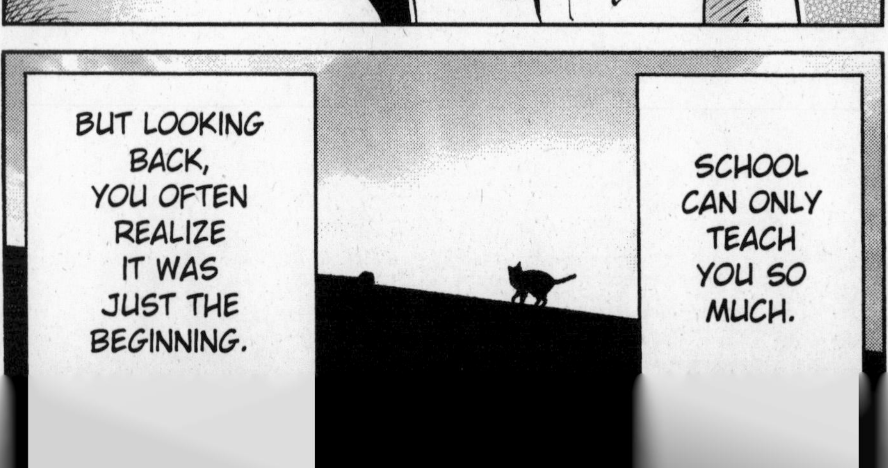
SCHOOL CAN ONLY TEACH YOU SO MUCH.
BUT LOOKING BACK, YOU OFTEN REALIZE IT WAS JUST THE BEGINNING.

Episode 8 A Place of Peace Act1

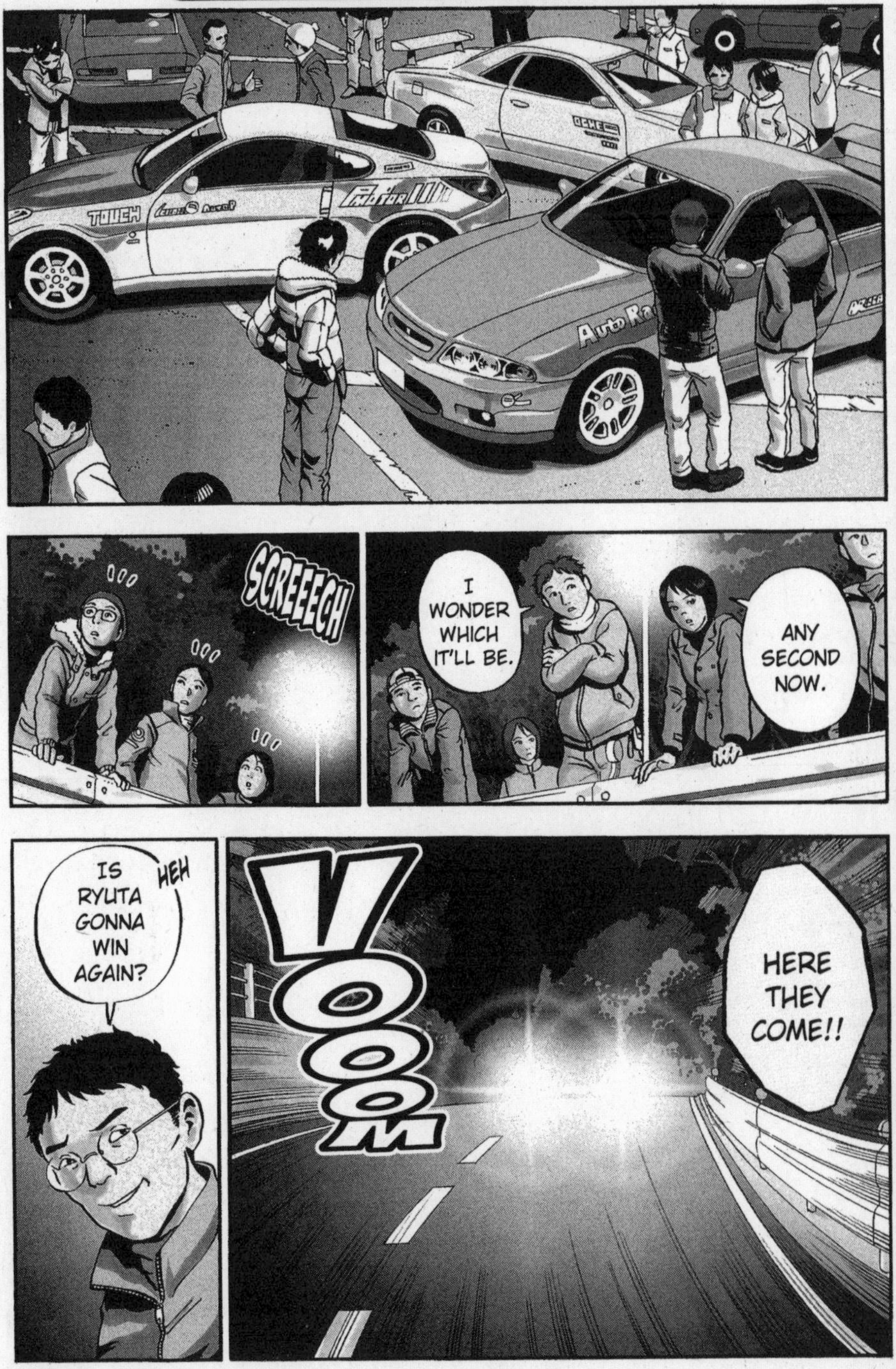
ANY SECOND NOW.
I WONDER WHICH IT'LL BE.
SCREEEECH
HERE THEY COME!!
VOOOOM
IS RYUTA GONNA WIN AGAIN?
HEH

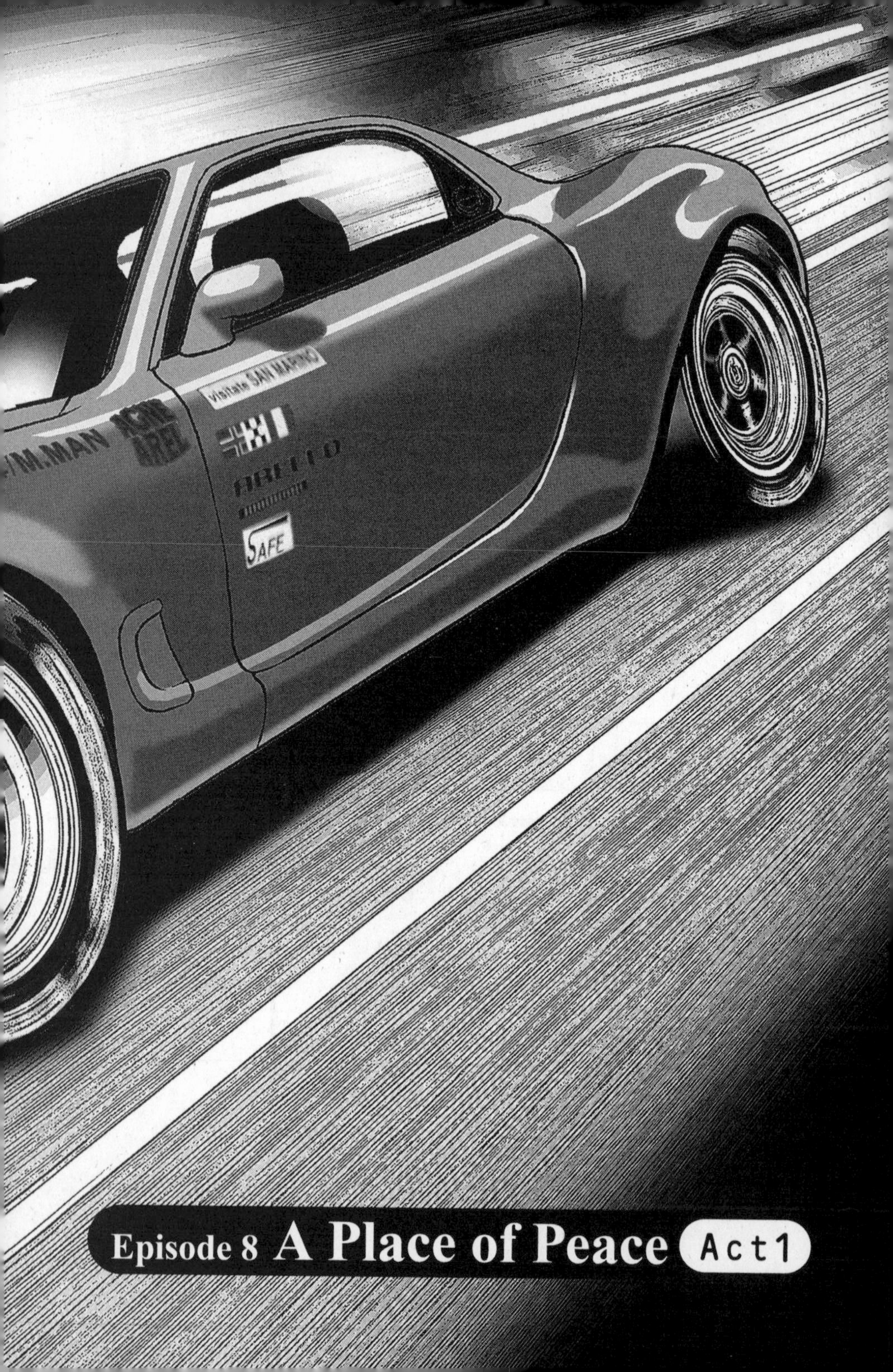
visitate SAN MARINO
SAFE

Episode 8 A Place of Peace Act1

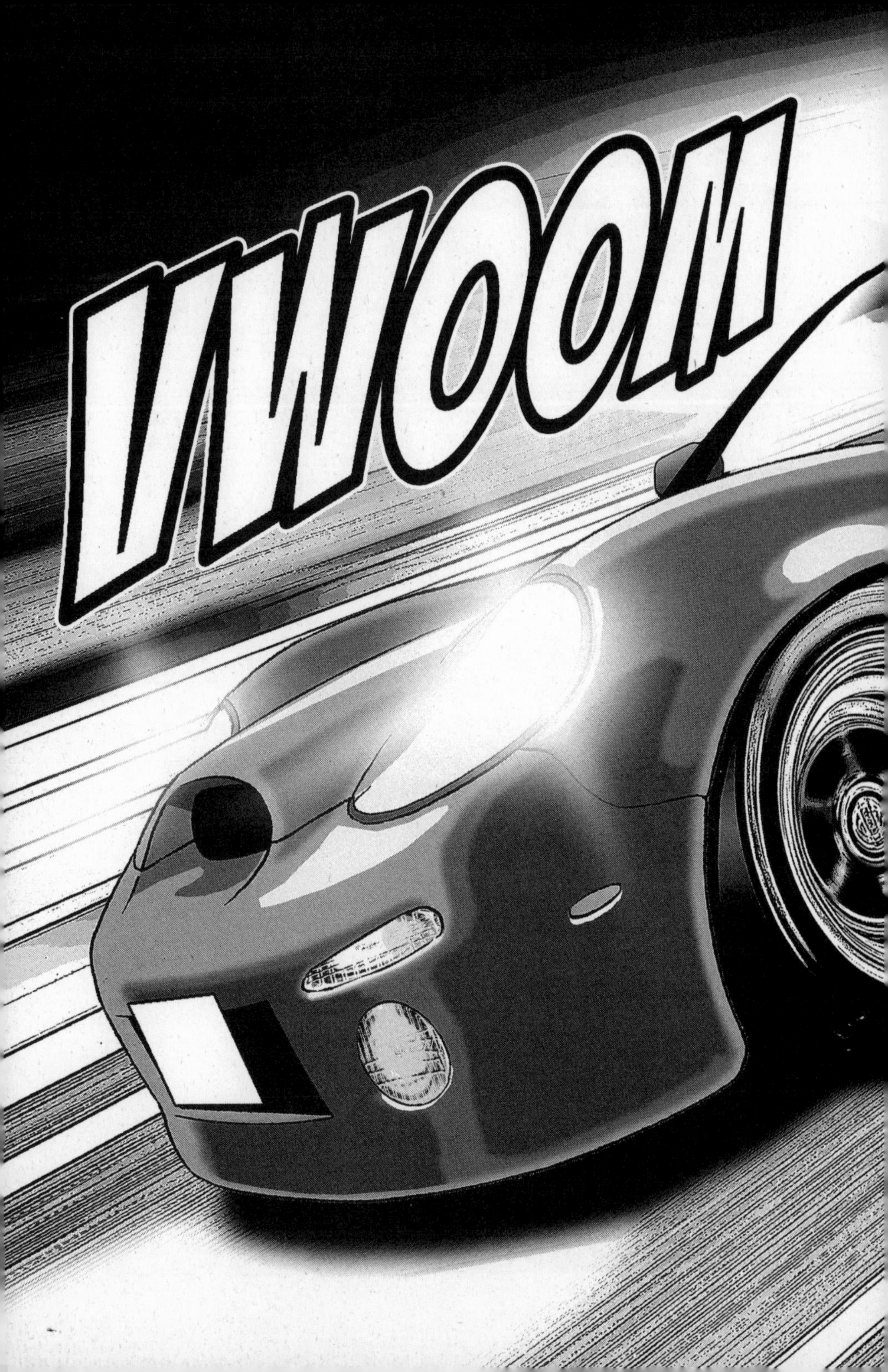
VROOM

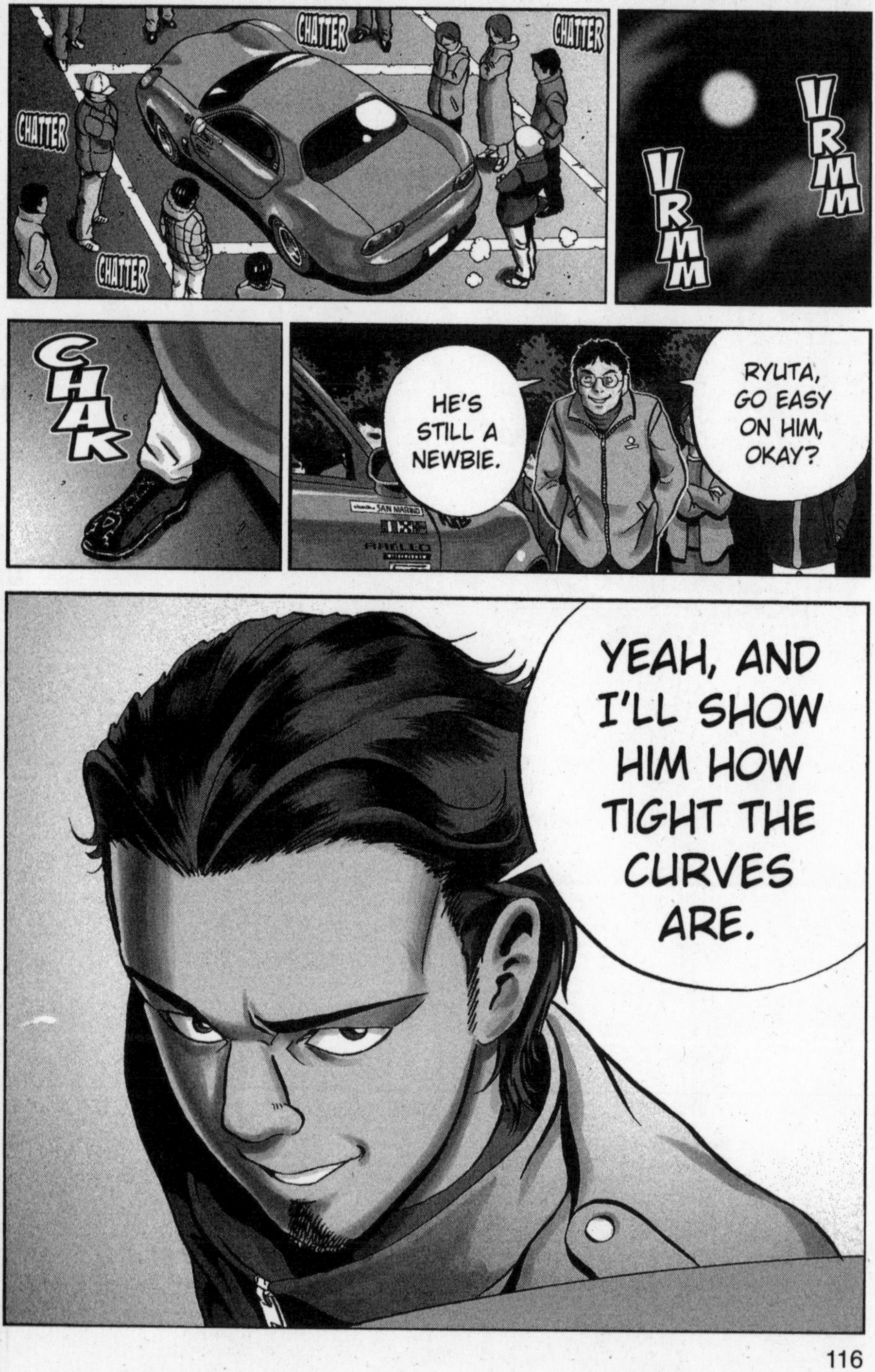
VRMM
VRMM
CHATTER
CHATTER
CHATTER
CHATTER
RYUTA, GO EASY ON HIM, OKAY?
HE'S STILL A NEWBIE.
CHAK
YEAH, AND I'LL SHOW HIM HOW TIGHT THE CURVES ARE.

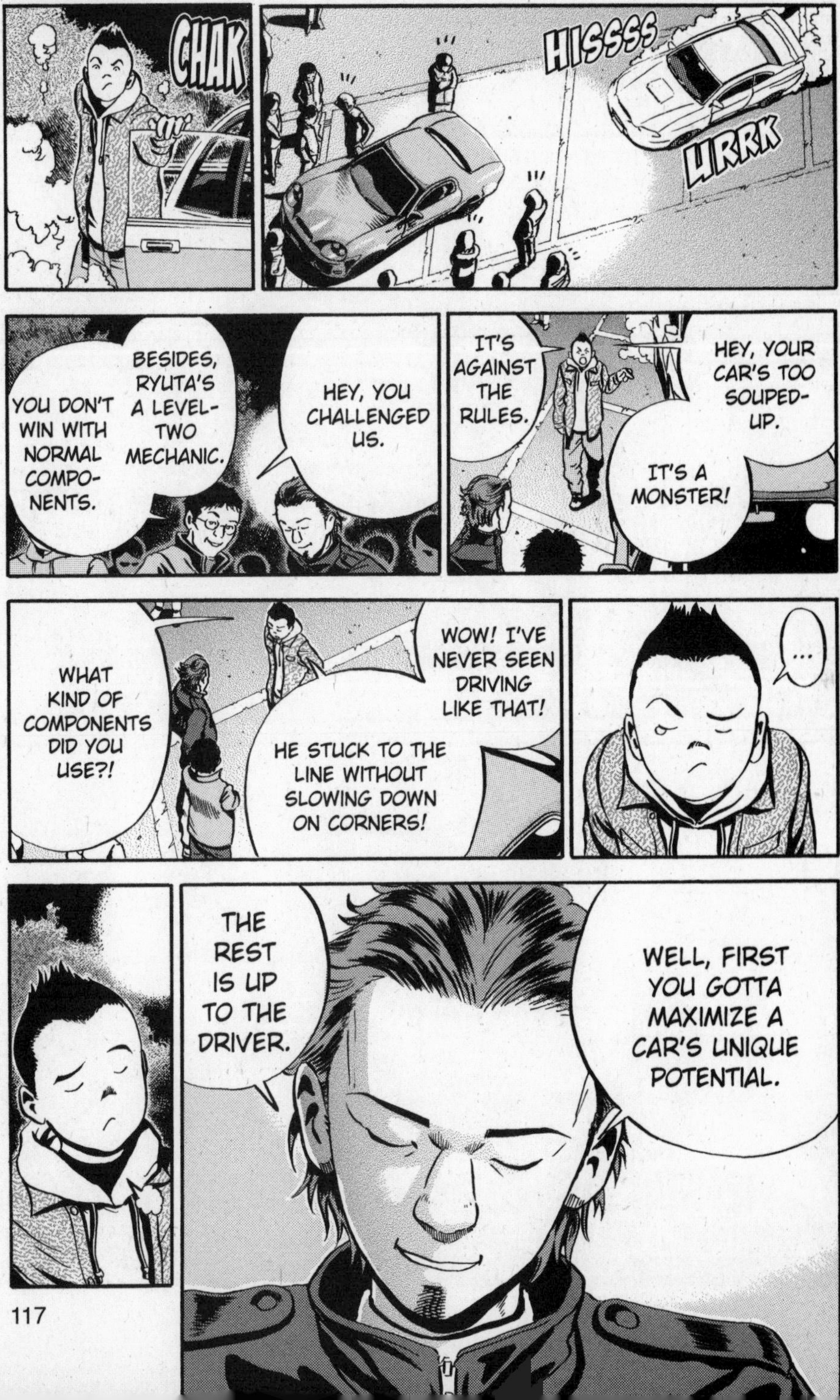
HISSSS
URRK
CHAK
HEY, YOUR CAR'S TOO SOUPED-UP.
IT'S A MONSTER!
IT'S AGAINST THE RULES.
HEY, YOU CHALLENGED US.
BESIDES, RYUTA'S A LEVEL-TWO MECHANIC.
YOU DON'T WIN WITH NORMAL COMPONENTS.
...
WOW! I'VE NEVER SEEN DRIVING LIKE THAT!
HE STUCK TO THE LINE WITHOUT SLOWING DOWN ON CORNERS!
WHAT KIND OF COMPONENTS DID YOU USE?!
WELL, FIRST YOU GOTTA MAXIMIZE A CAR'S UNIQUE POTENTIAL.
THE REST IS UP TO THE DRIVER.

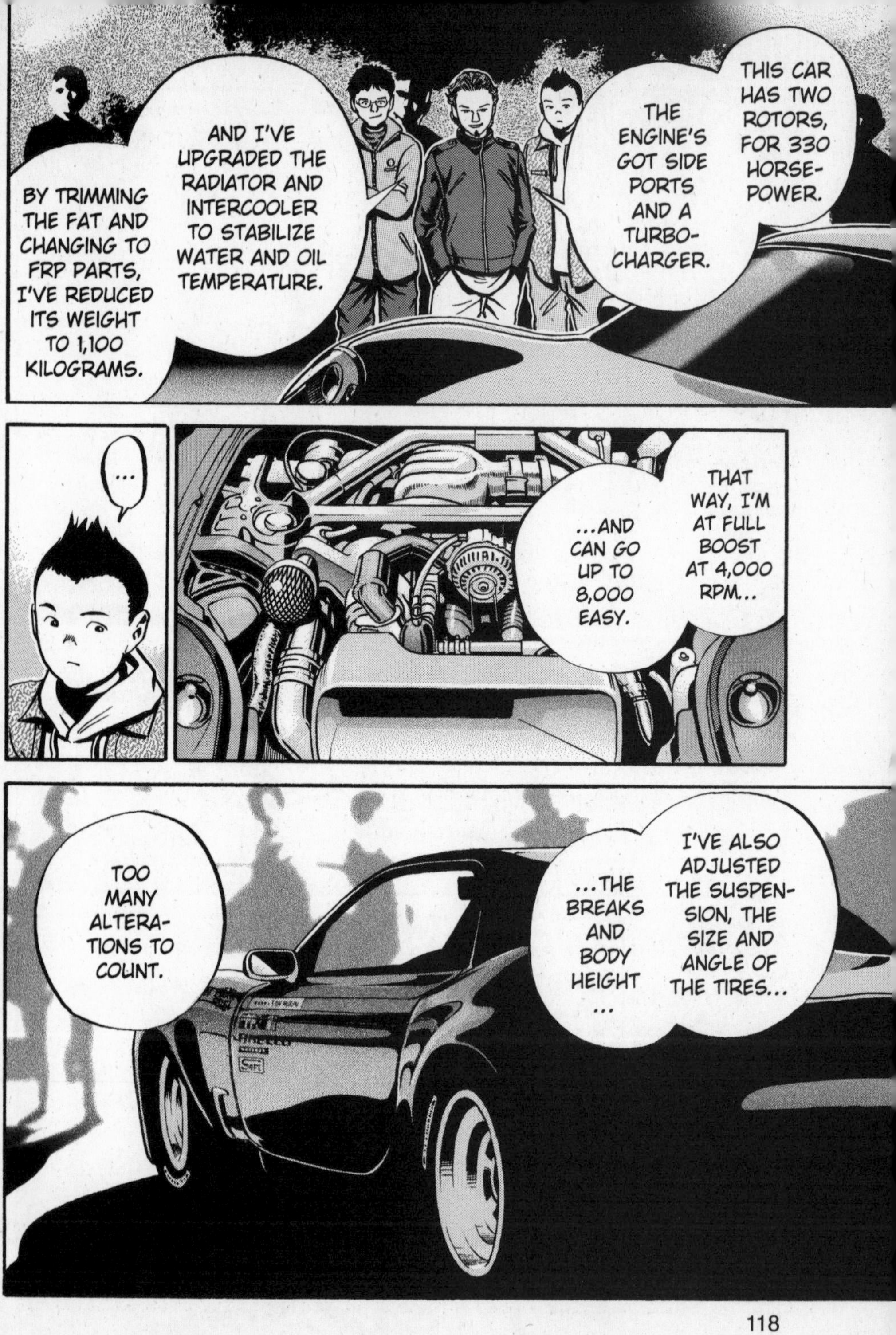
THIS CAR HAS TWO ROTORS, FOR 330 HORSEPOWER.
THE ENGINE'S GOT SIDE PORTS AND A TURBOCHARGER.
AND I'VE UPGRADED THE RADIATOR AND INTERCOOLER TO STABILIZE WATER AND OIL TEMPERATURE.
BY TRIMMING THE FAT AND CHANGING TO FRP PARTS, I'VE REDUCED ITS WEIGHT TO 1,100 KILOGRAMS.
THAT WAY, I'M AT FULL BOOST AT 4,000 RPM...
...AND CAN GO UP TO 8,000 EASY.
...
I'VE ALSO ADJUSTED THE SUSPENSION, THE SIZE AND ANGLE OF THE TIRES...
...THE BREAKS AND BODY HEIGHT...
TOO MANY ALTERATIONS TO COUNT.

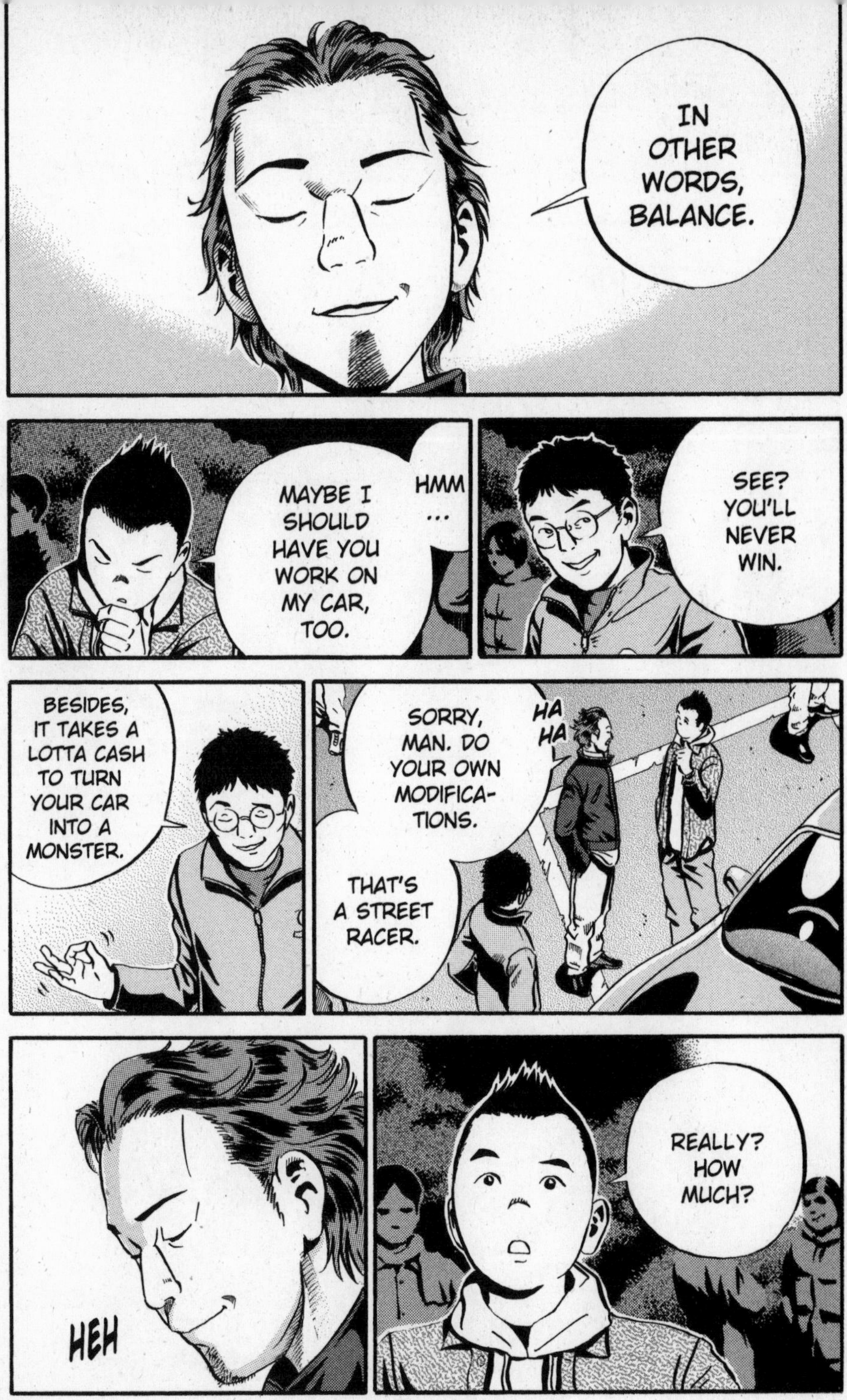
IN OTHER WORDS, BALANCE.
SEE? YOU'LL NEVER WIN.
HMM ...
MAYBE I SHOULD HAVE YOU WORK ON MY CAR, TOO.
HA HA
SORRY, MAN. DO YOUR OWN MODIFICA-TIONS.
THAT'S A STREET RACER.
BESIDES, IT TAKES A LOTTA CASH TO TURN YOUR CAR INTO A MONSTER.
REALLY? HOW MUCH?
HEH

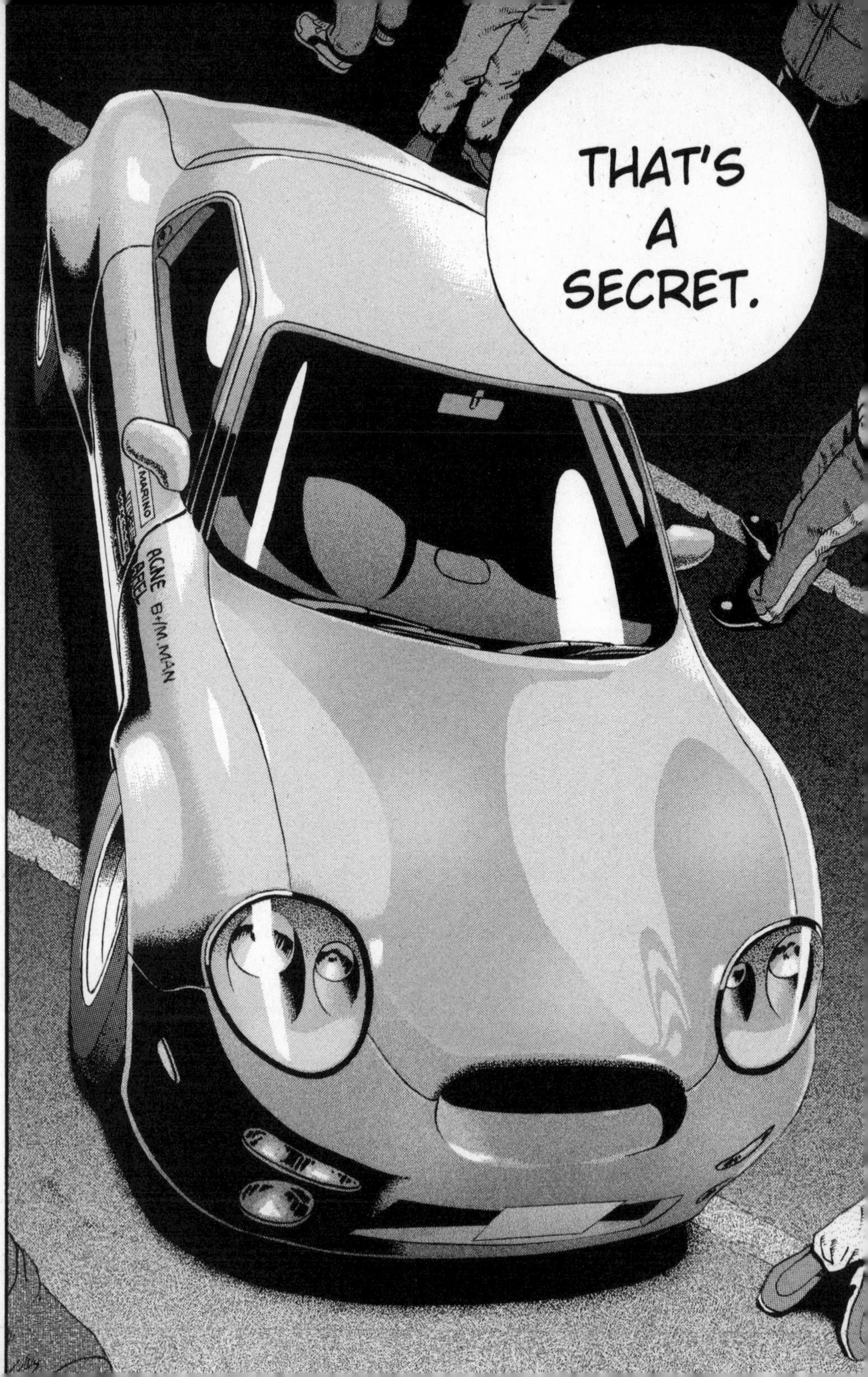
THAT'S A SECRET.

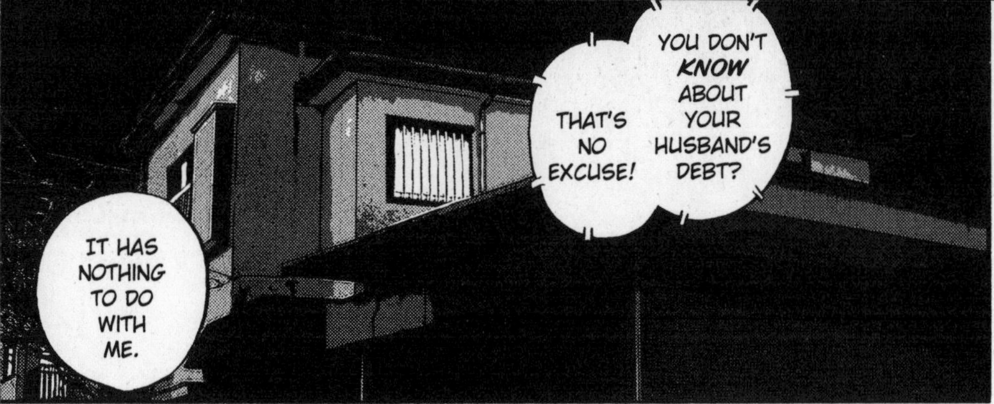
YOU DON'T *KNOW* ABOUT YOUR HUSBAND'S DEBT?
THAT'S NO EXCUSE!
IT HAS NOTHING TO DO WITH ME.

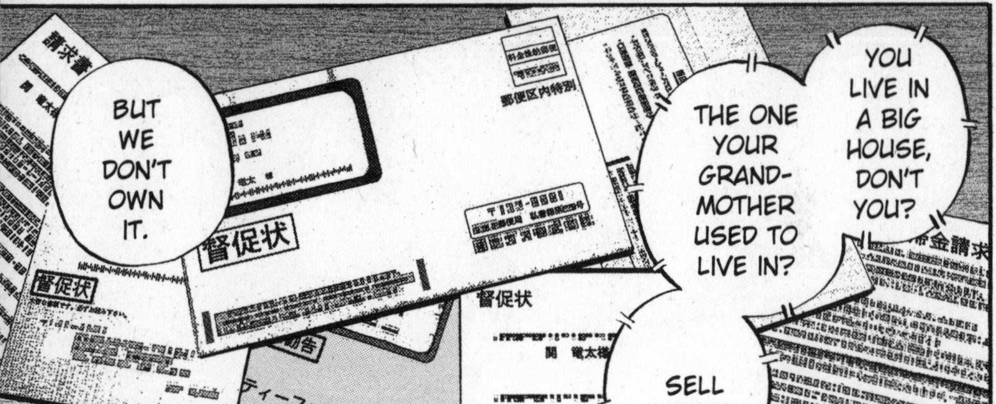
YOU LIVE IN A BIG HOUSE, DON'T YOU?
THE ONE YOUR GRANDMOTHER USED TO LIVE IN?
SELL THAT!
BUT WE DON'T OWN IT.
督促状
請求書
ディーファイナンス

*Papers: Bills and overdue statements

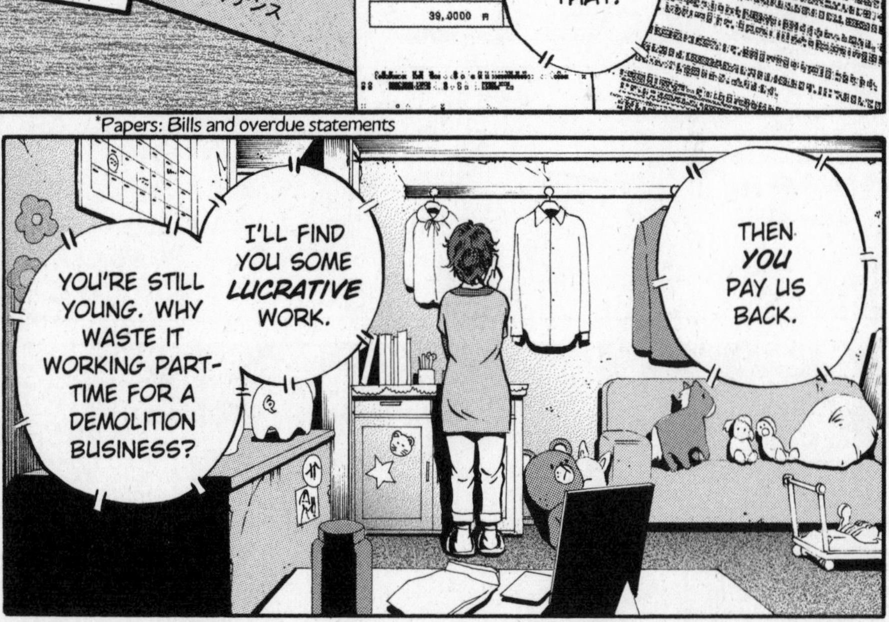
THEN *YOU* PAY US BACK.
I'LL FIND YOU SOME *LUCRATIVE* WORK.
YOU'RE STILL YOUNG. WHY WASTE IT WORKING PART-TIME FOR A DEMOLITION BUSINESS?

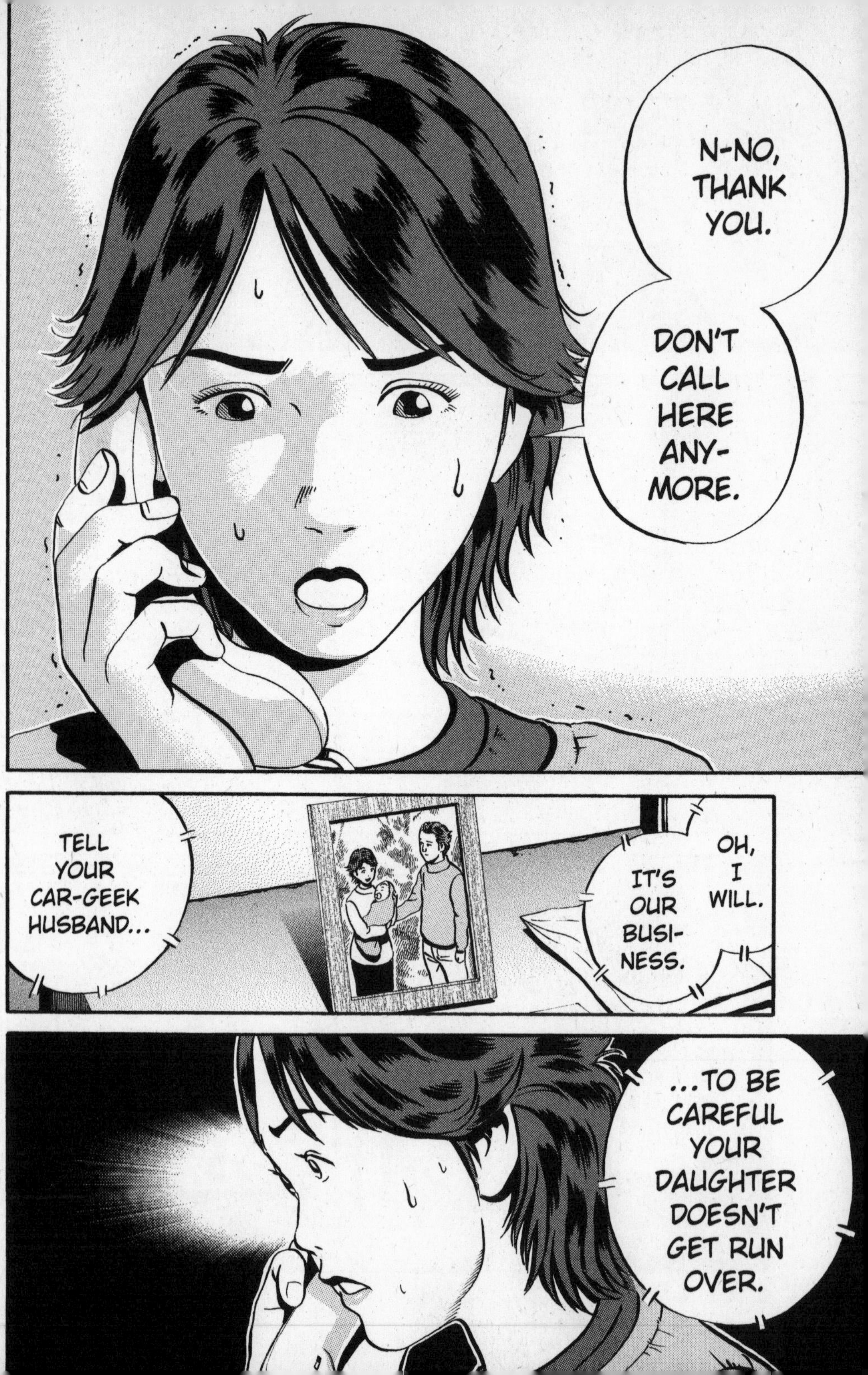
N-NO, THANK YOU.
DON'T CALL HERE ANYMORE.
OH, I WILL.
IT'S OUR BUSINESS.
TELL YOUR CAR-GEEK HUSBAND...
...TO BE CAREFUL YOUR DAUGHTER DOESN'T GET RUN OVER.

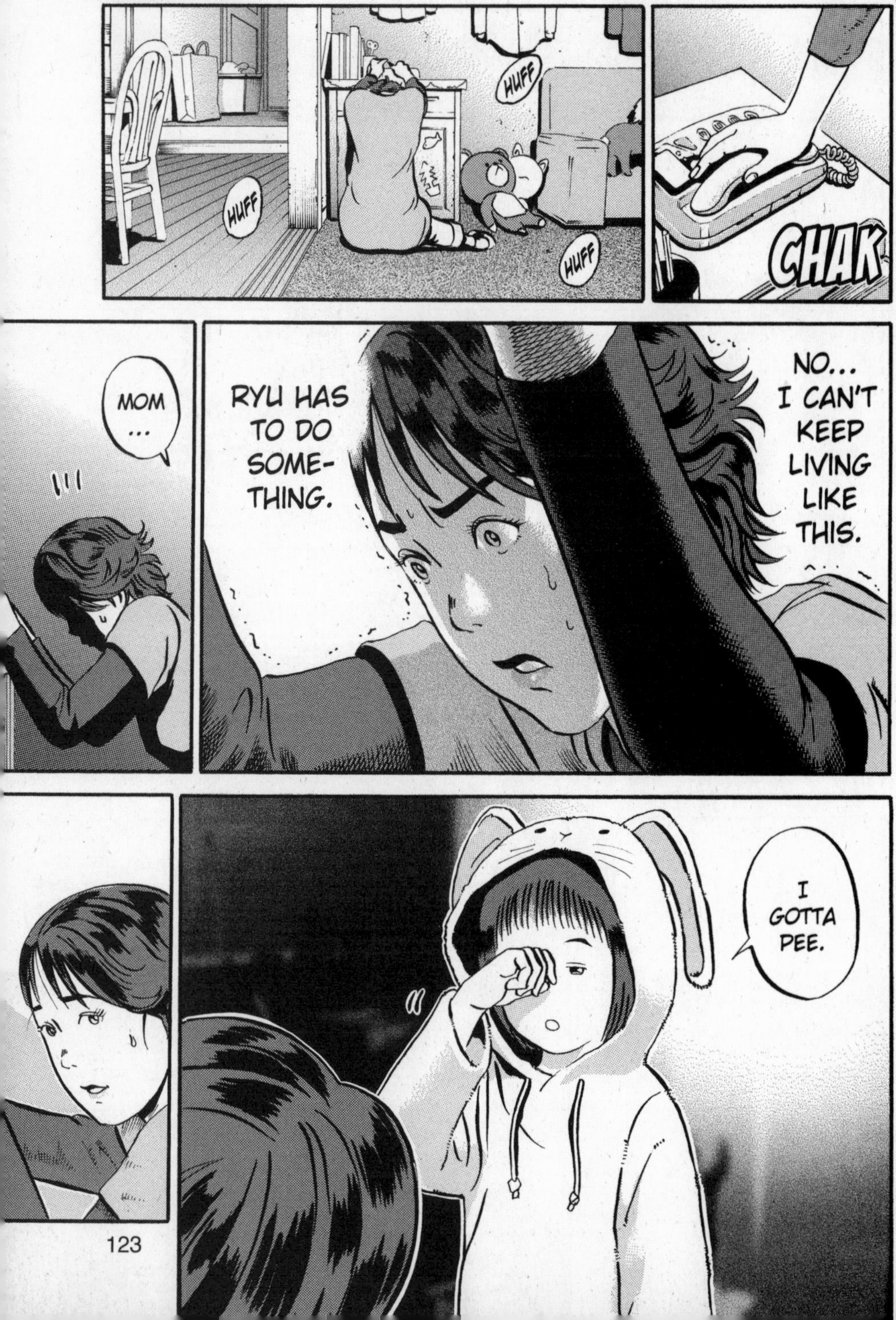
CHAK
HUFF
HUFF
HUFF
NO... I CAN'T KEEP LIVING LIKE THIS.
RYU HAS TO DO SOME-THING.
MOM ...
I GOTTA PEE.

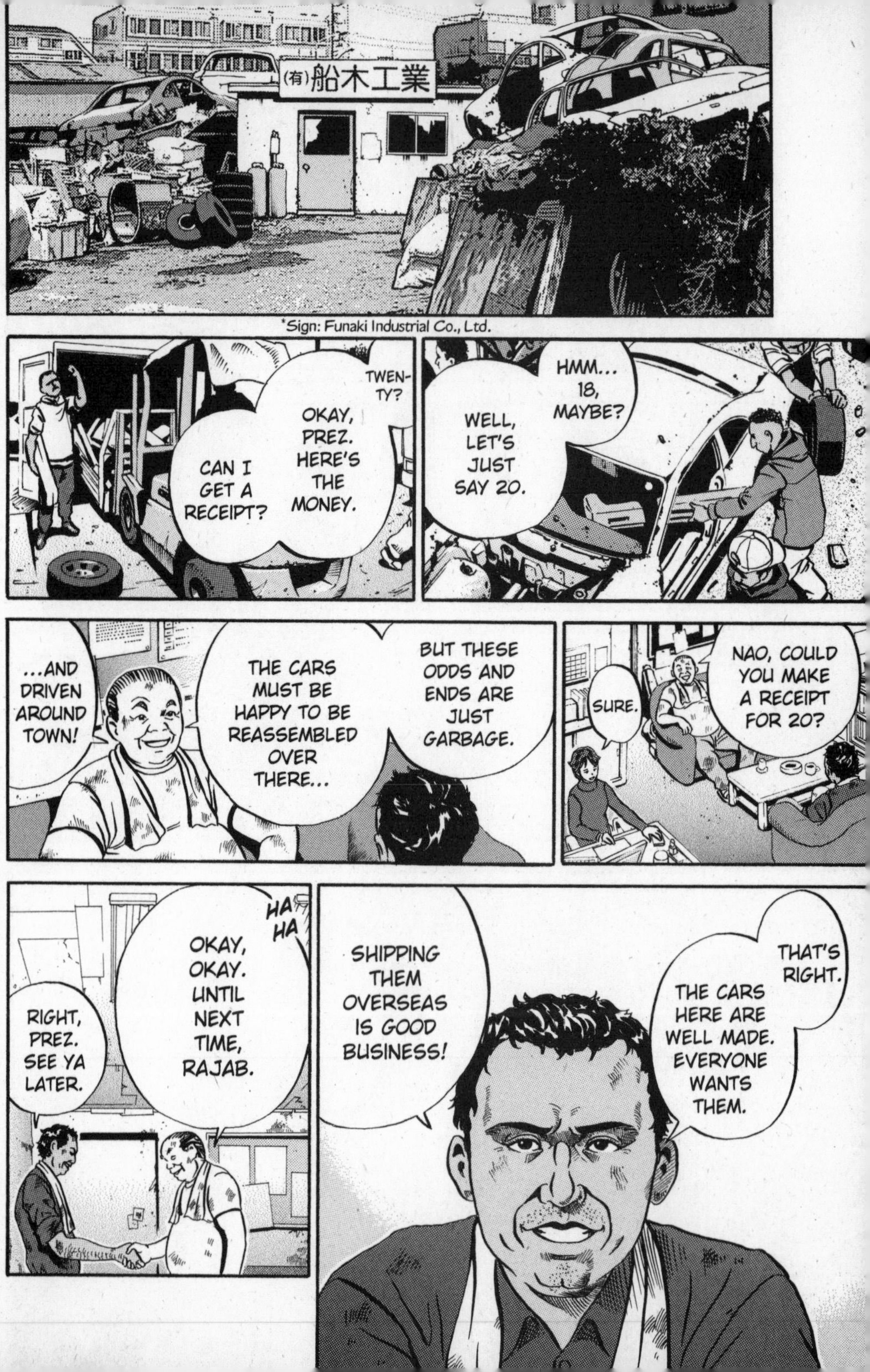
(有)船木工業
*Sign: Funaki Industrial Co., Ltd.
HMM... 18, MAYBE?
WELL, LET'S JUST SAY 20.
TWENTY?
OKAY, PREZ. HERE'S THE MONEY.
CAN I GET A RECEIPT?
NAO, COULD YOU MAKE A RECEIPT FOR 20?
SURE.
BUT THESE ODDS AND ENDS ARE JUST GARBAGE.
THE CARS MUST BE HAPPY TO BE REASSEMBLED OVER THERE...
...AND DRIVEN AROUND TOWN!
THAT'S RIGHT.
THE CARS HERE ARE WELL MADE. EVERYONE WANTS THEM.
SHIPPING THEM OVERSEAS IS GOOD BUSINESS!
HA HA
OKAY, OKAY. UNTIL NEXT TIME, RAJAB.
RIGHT, PREZ. SEE YA LATER.

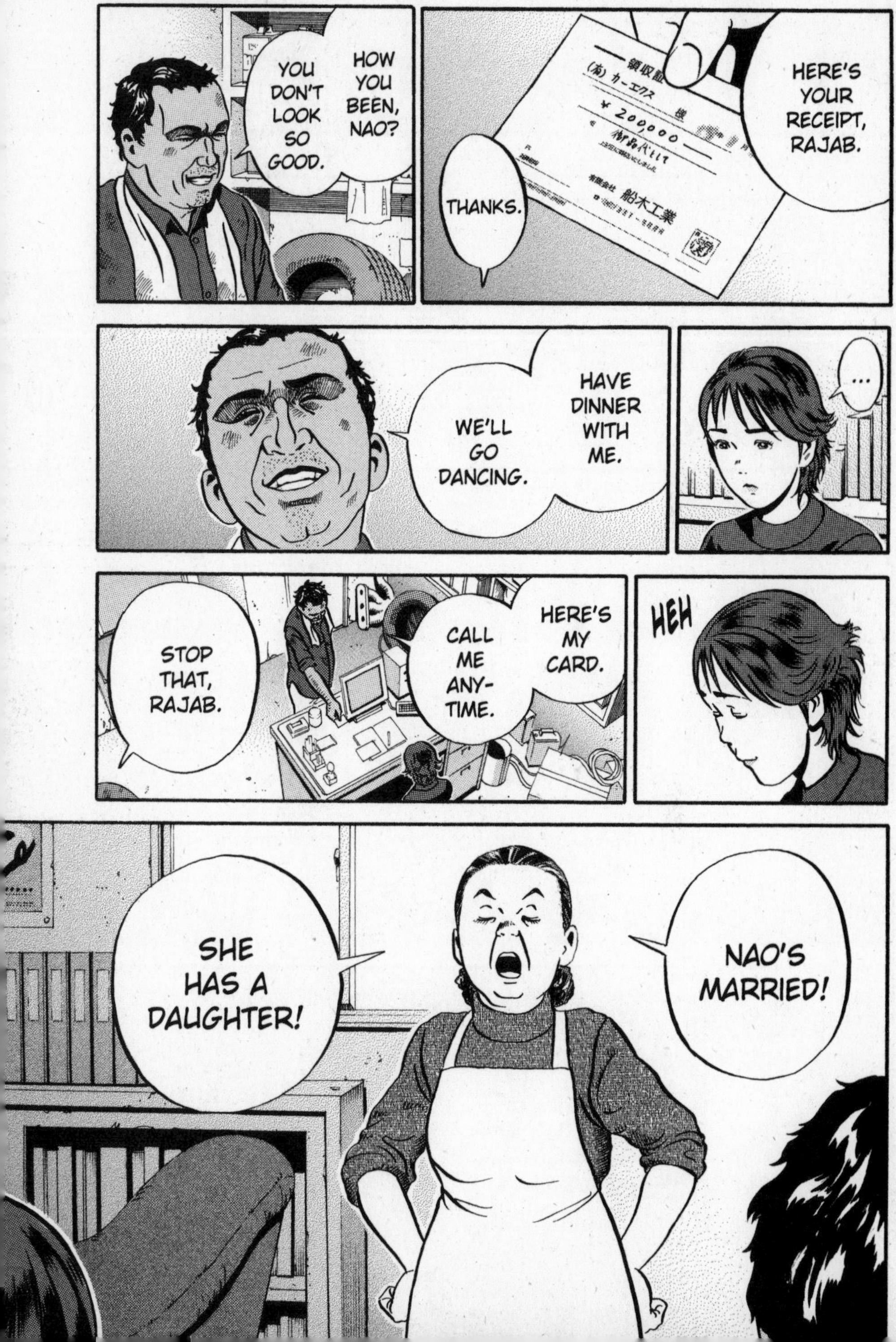
HERE'S YOUR RECEIPT, RAJAB.
THANKS.
HOW YOU BEEN, NAO?
YOU DON'T LOOK SO GOOD.
...
HAVE DINNER WITH ME.
WE'LL GO DANCING.
HEH
HERE'S MY CARD.
CALL ME ANY-TIME.
STOP THAT, RAJAB.
NAO'S MARRIED!
SHE HAS A DAUGHTER!

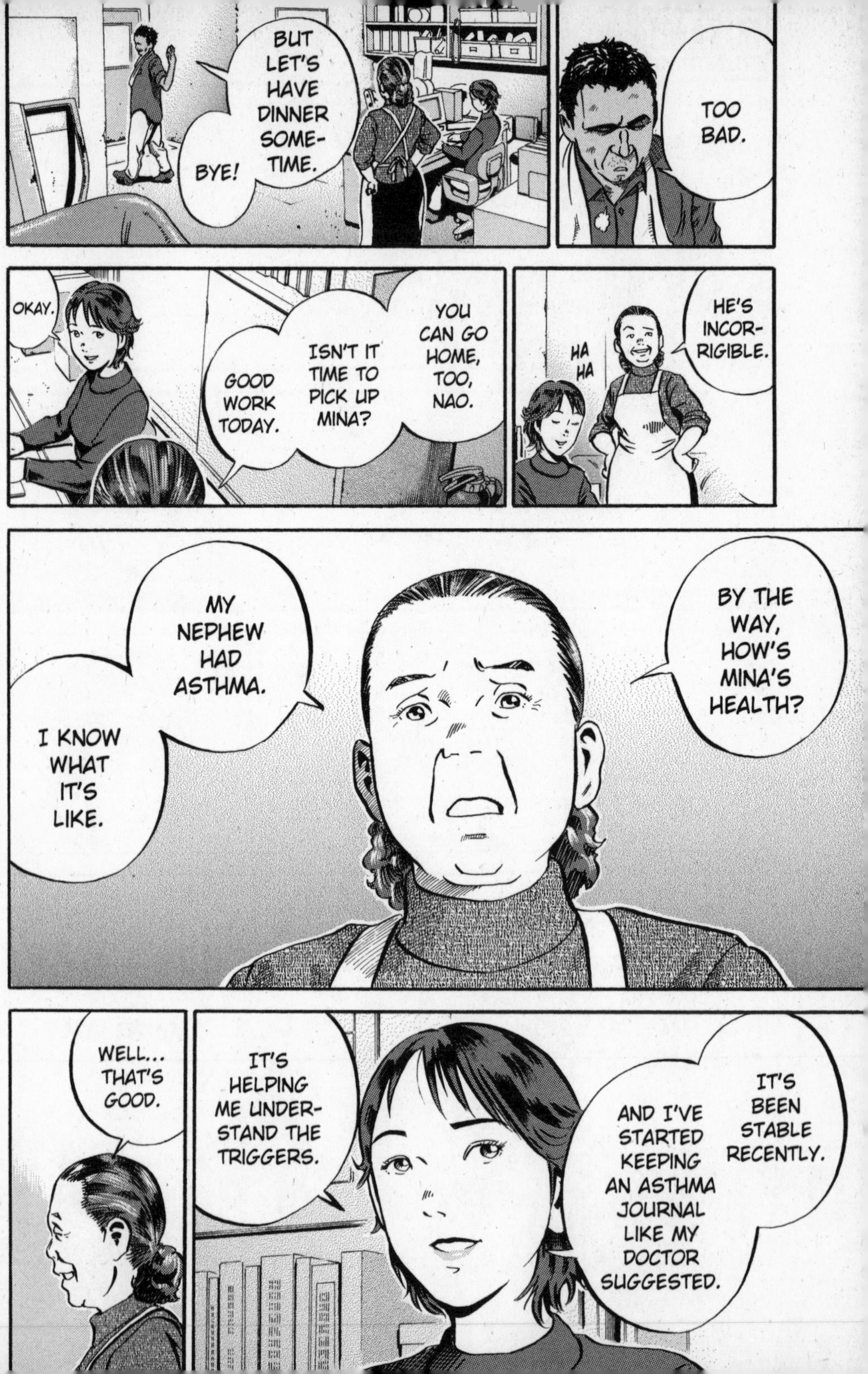
TOO BAD.
BUT LET'S HAVE DINNER SOME-TIME.
BYE!
HE'S INCOR-RIGIBLE.
HA HA
YOU CAN GO HOME, TOO, NAO.
ISN'T IT TIME TO PICK UP MINA?
GOOD WORK TODAY.
OKAY.
BY THE WAY, HOW'S MINA'S HEALTH?
MY NEPHEW HAD ASTHMA.
I KNOW WHAT IT'S LIKE.
IT'S BEEN STABLE RECENTLY.
AND I'VE STARTED KEEPING AN ASTHMA JOURNAL LIKE MY DOCTOR SUGGESTED.
IT'S HELPING ME UNDER-STAND THE TRIGGERS.
WELL... THAT'S GOOD.

YEAH.

STILL, YUTA REALLY NEEDS TO SHAPE UP.

HE DOESN'T SEEM TO ACT LIKE A PARENT AT ALL.

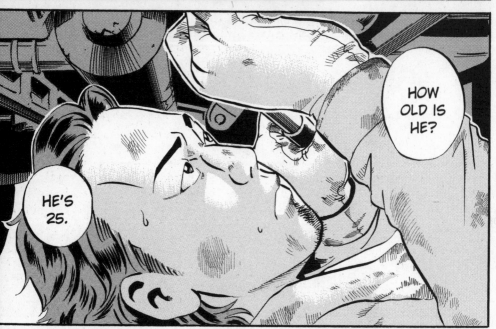

HOW OLD IS HE?

HE'S 25.

...

OH... WELL, THAT EXPLAINS IT...

...BUT HE NEEDS TO GROW UP.

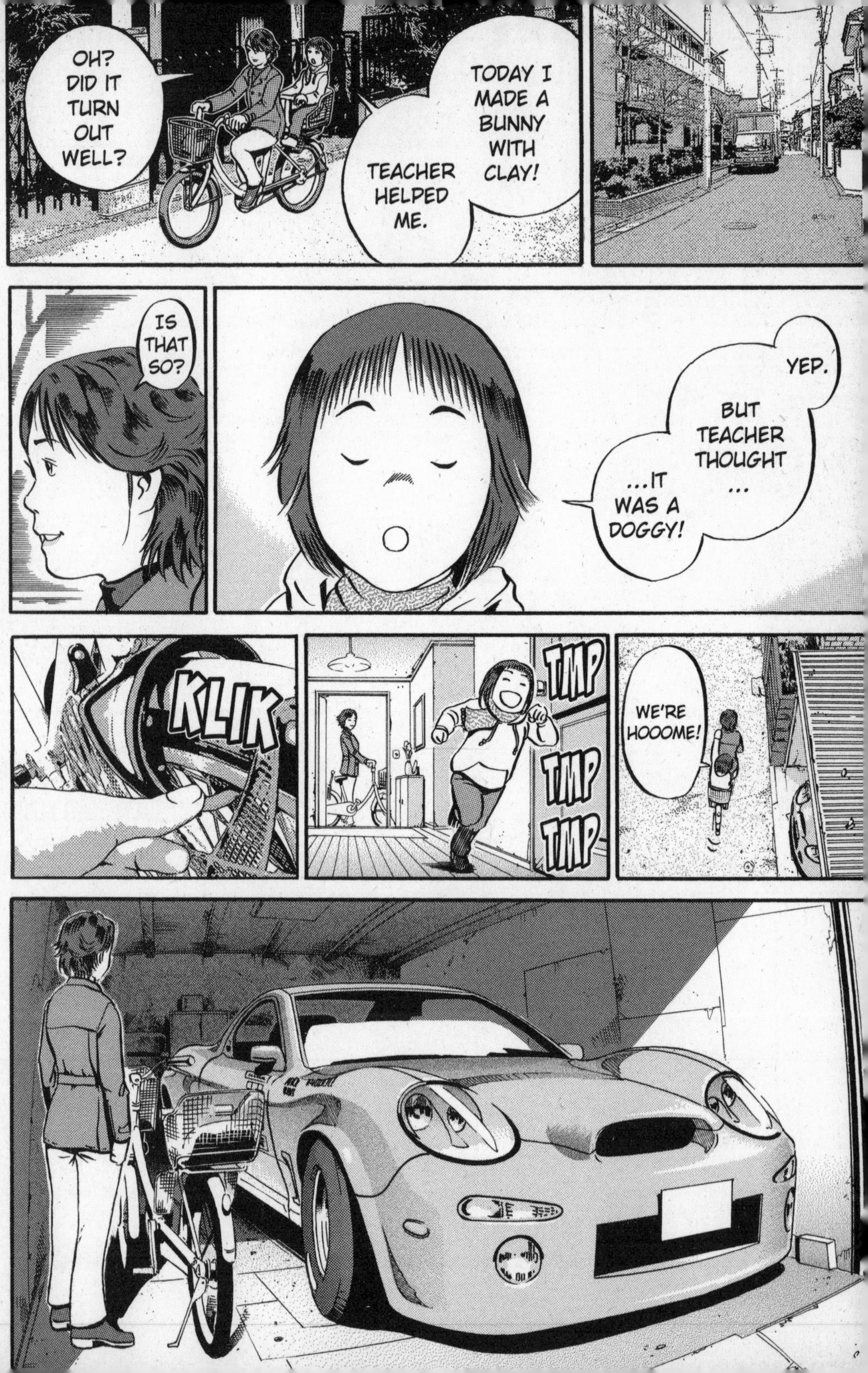
TODAY I MADE A BUNNY WITH CLAY!
TEACHER HELPED ME.
OH? DID IT TURN OUT WELL?
YEP.
BUT TEACHER THOUGHT ...
...IT WAS A DOGGY!
IS THAT SO?
WE'RE HOOOME!
TMP TMP TMP
KLIK

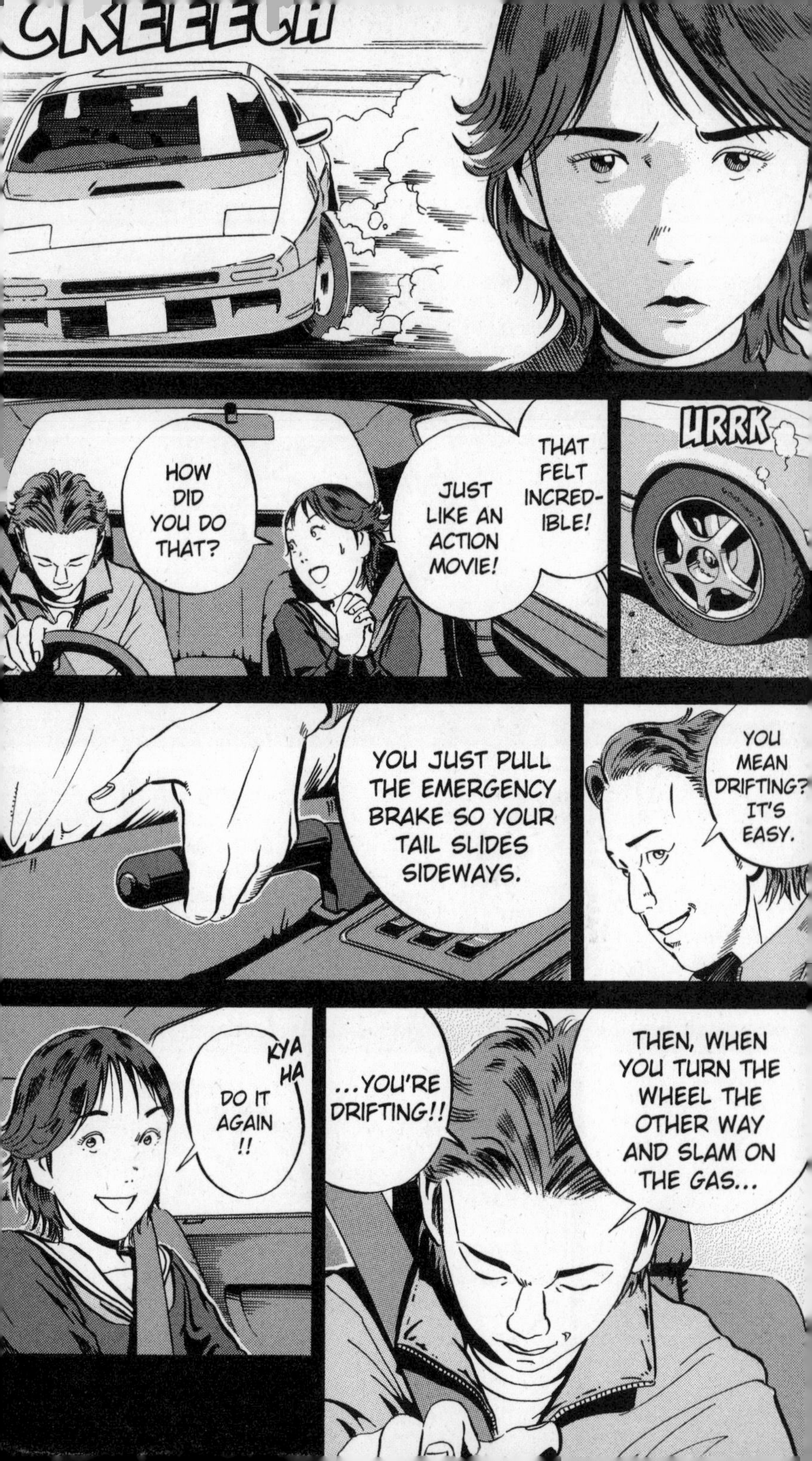
CREEECH
URRK
THAT FELT INCREDIBLE!
JUST LIKE AN ACTION MOVIE!
HOW DID YOU DO THAT?
YOU MEAN DRIFTING? IT'S EASY.
YOU JUST PULL THE EMERGENCY BRAKE SO YOUR TAIL SLIDES SIDEWAYS.
THEN, WHEN YOU TURN THE WHEEL THE OTHER WAY AND SLAM ON THE GAS...
...YOU'RE DRIFTING!!
KYA HA
DO IT AGAIN !!

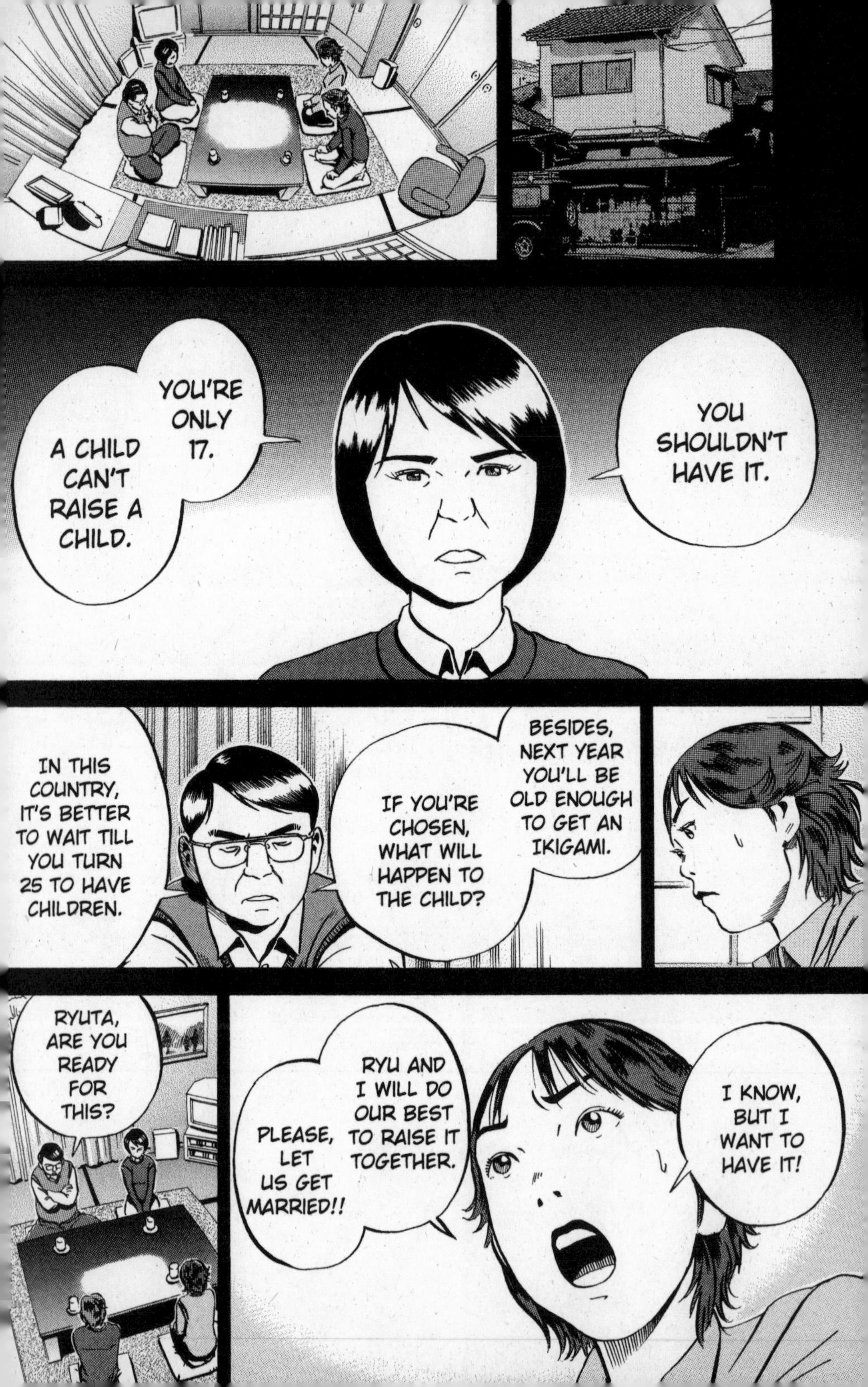
YOU SHOULDN'T HAVE IT.
YOU'RE ONLY 17. A CHILD CAN'T RAISE A CHILD.
BESIDES, NEXT YEAR YOU'LL BE OLD ENOUGH TO GET AN IKIGAMI.
IF YOU'RE CHOSEN, WHAT WILL HAPPEN TO THE CHILD?
IN THIS COUNTRY, IT'S BETTER TO WAIT TILL YOU TURN 25 TO HAVE CHILDREN.
I KNOW, BUT I WANT TO HAVE IT!
RYU AND I WILL DO OUR BEST TO RAISE IT TOGETHER. PLEASE, LET US GET MARRIED!!
RYUTA, ARE YOU READY FOR THIS?

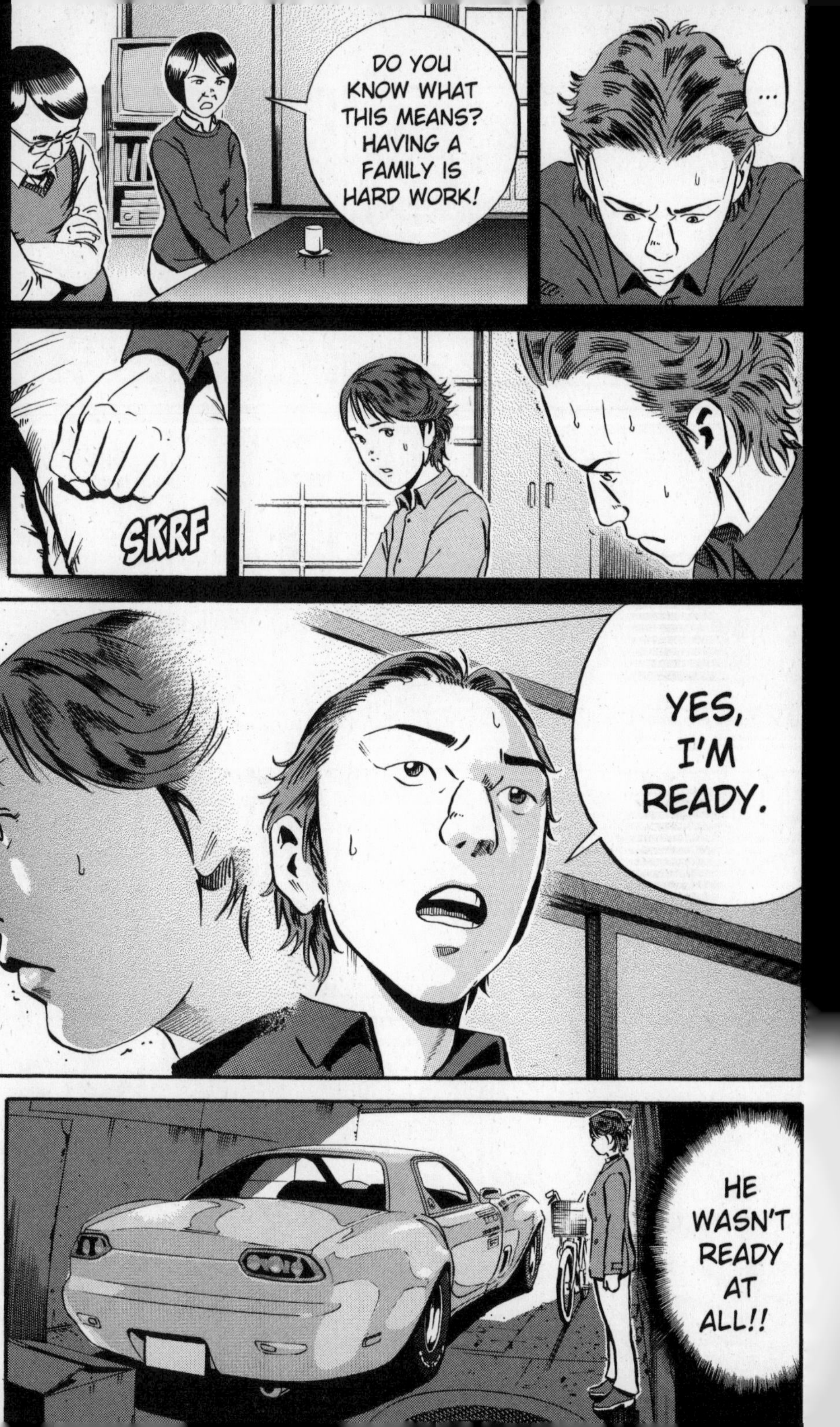
...
DO YOU KNOW WHAT THIS MEANS? HAVING A FAMILY IS HARD WORK!
SKRF
YES, I'M READY.
HE WASN'T READY AT ALL!!

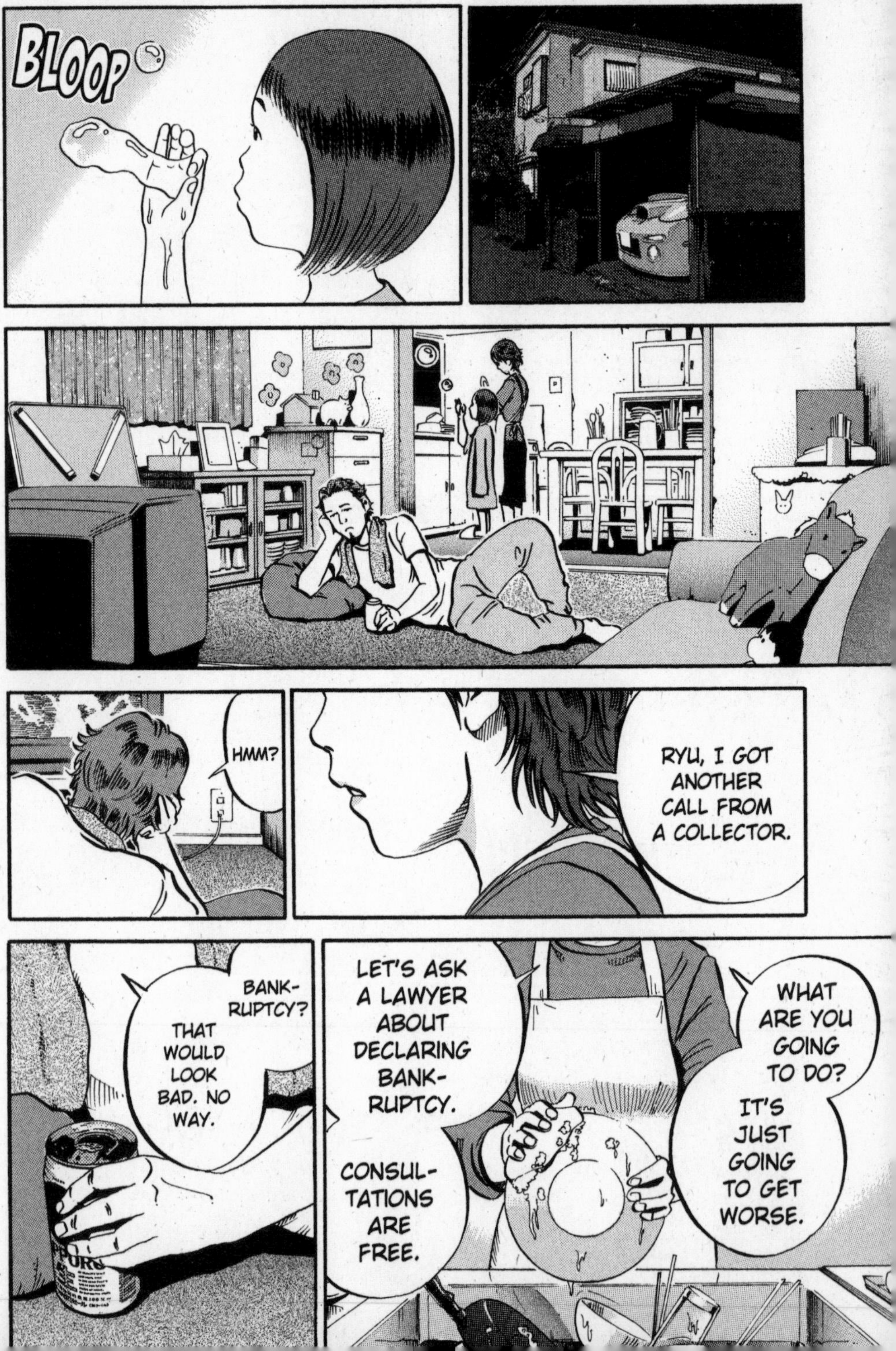
BLOOP
RYU, I GOT ANOTHER CALL FROM A COLLECTOR.
HMM?
WHAT ARE YOU GOING TO DO?
IT'S JUST GOING TO GET WORSE.
LET'S ASK A LAWYER ABOUT DECLARING BANKRUPTCY.
CONSULTATIONS ARE FREE.
BANKRUPTCY?
THAT WOULD LOOK BAD. NO WAY.

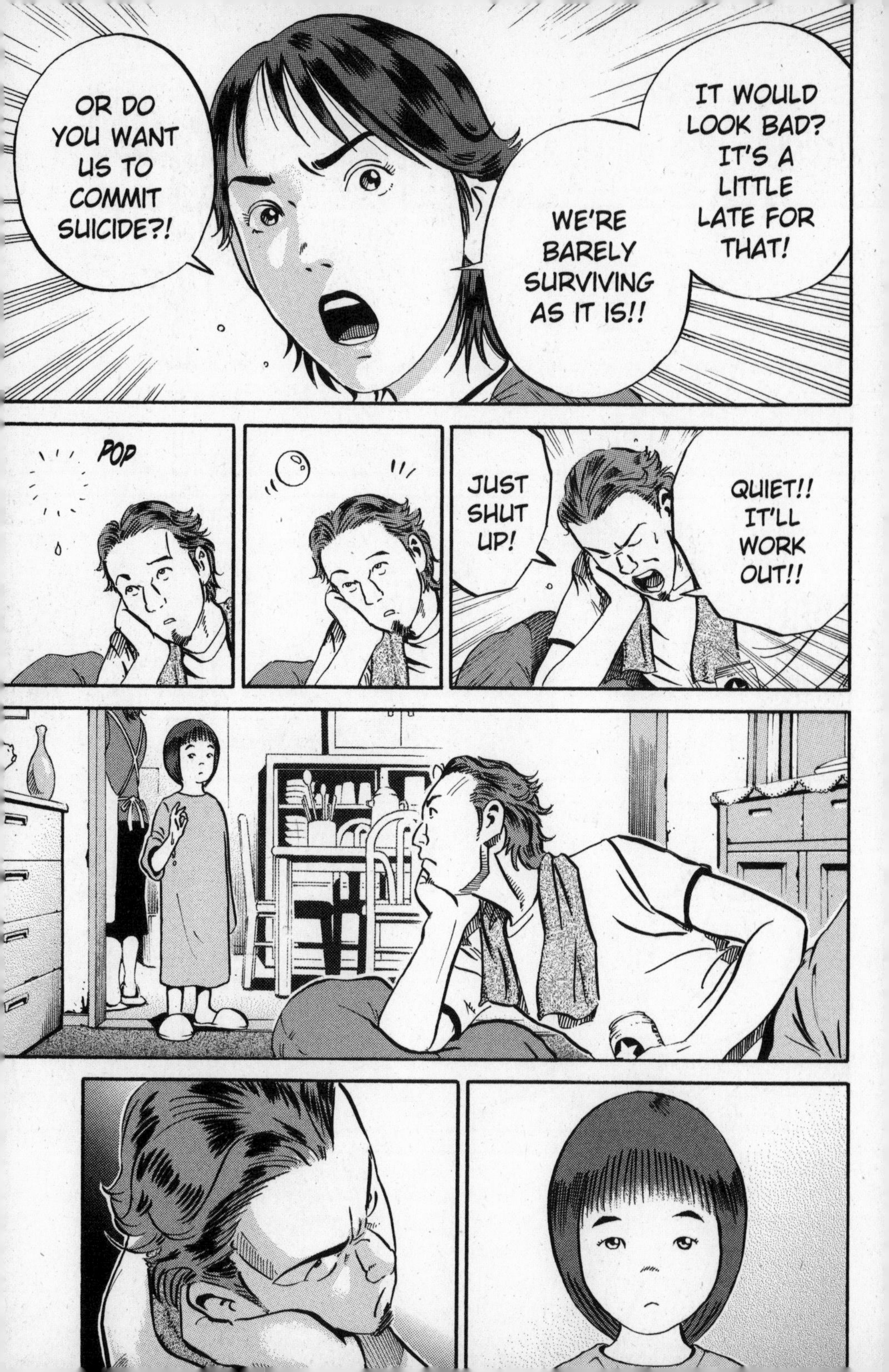
IT WOULD LOOK BAD? IT'S A LITTLE LATE FOR THAT!
WE'RE BARELY SURVIVING AS IT IS!!
OR DO YOU WANT US TO COMMIT SUICIDE?!
QUIET!! IT'LL WORK OUT!!
JUST SHUT UP!
POP

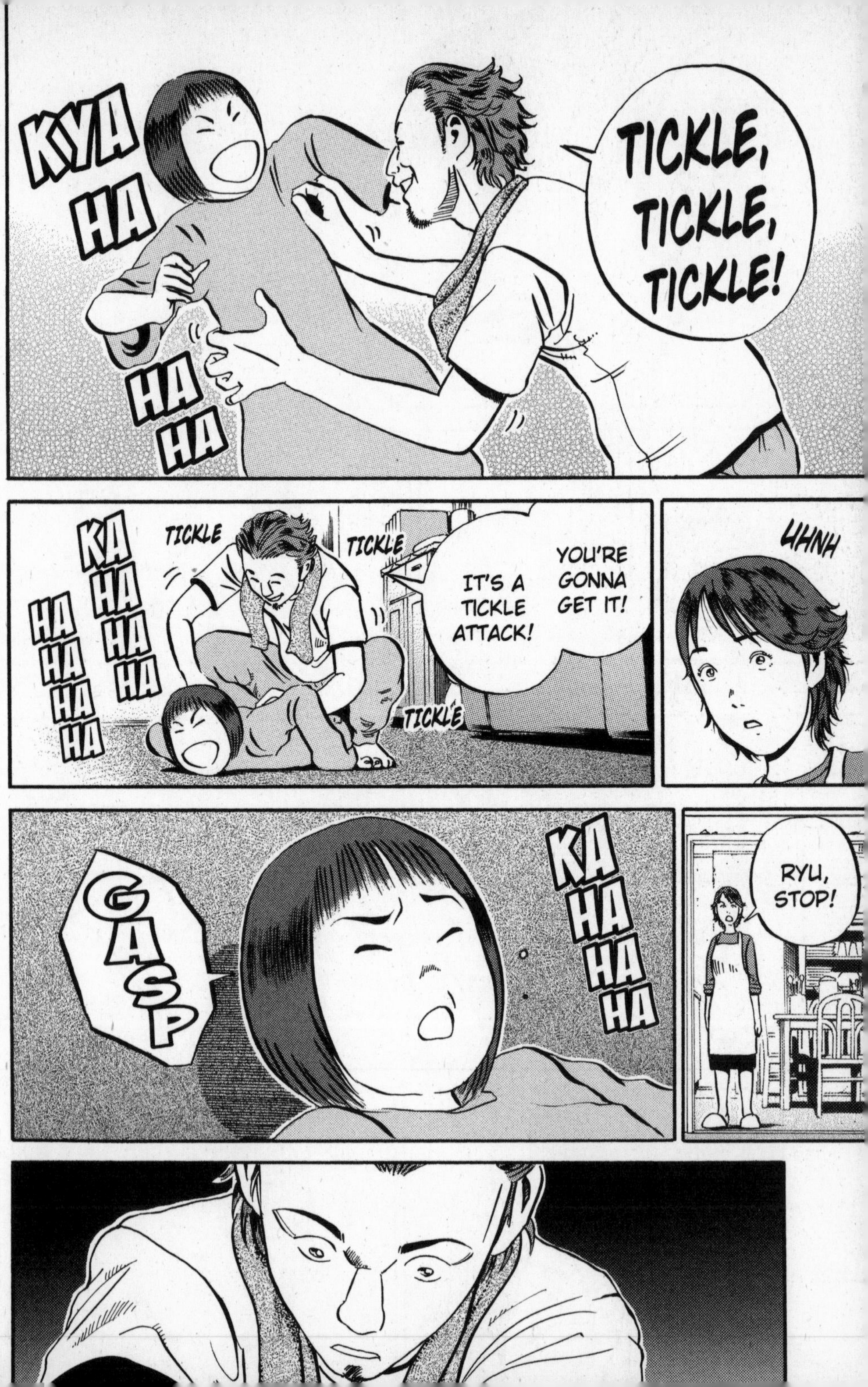
TICKLE, TICKLE, TICKLE!
KYA HA
HA HA
UHNH
YOU'RE GONNA GET IT!
IT'S A TICKLE ATTACK!
TICKLE
KA HA HA HA HA
TICKLE
HA HA HA HA HA
TICKLE
RYU, STOP!
KA HA HA HA HA
GASP

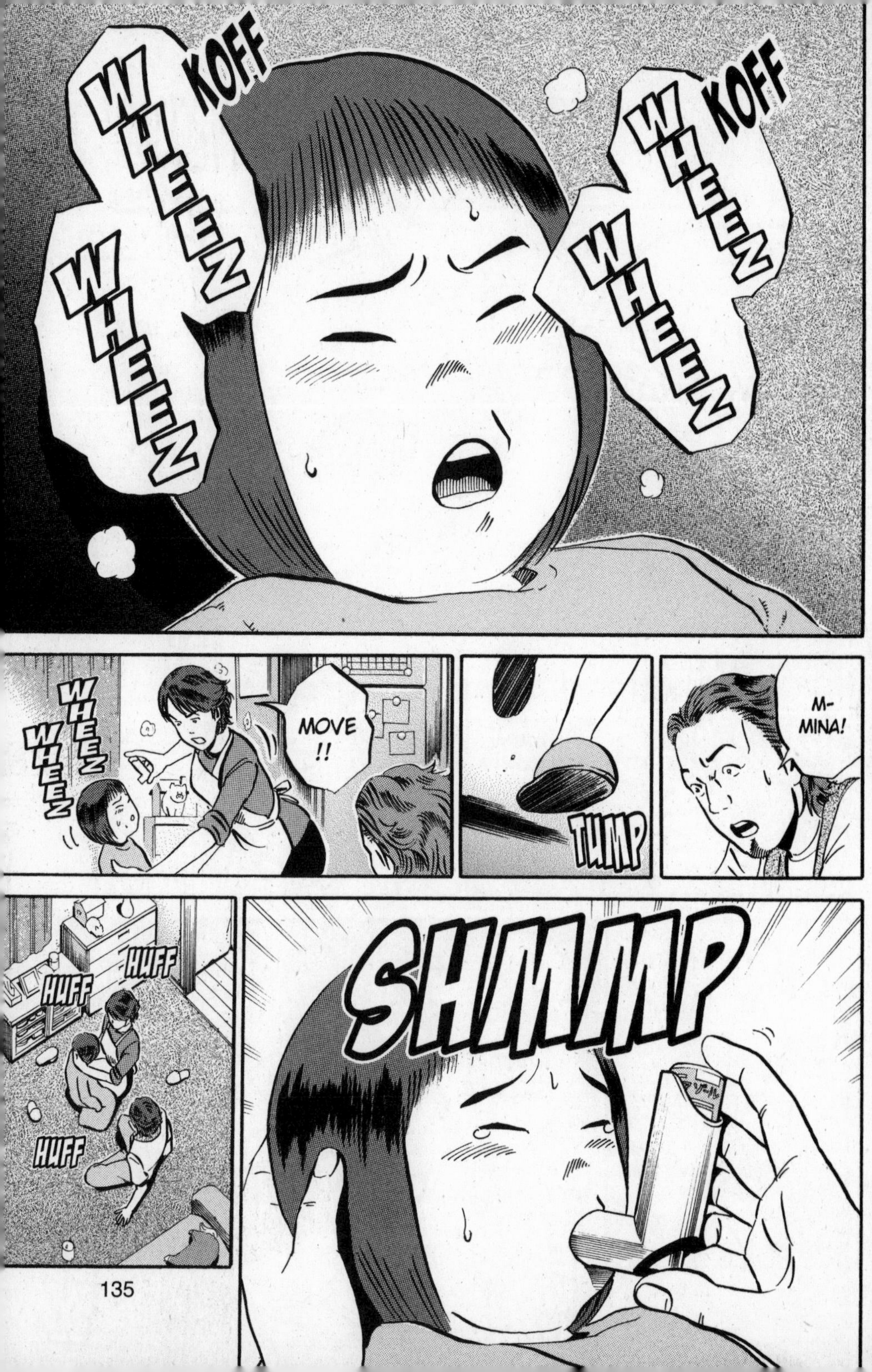
KOFF
WHEEZ WHEEZ
KOFF
WHEEZ WHEEZ
M-MINA!
TUMP
MOVE !!
WHEEZ WHEEZ
SHMMP
HUFF
HUFF
HUFF

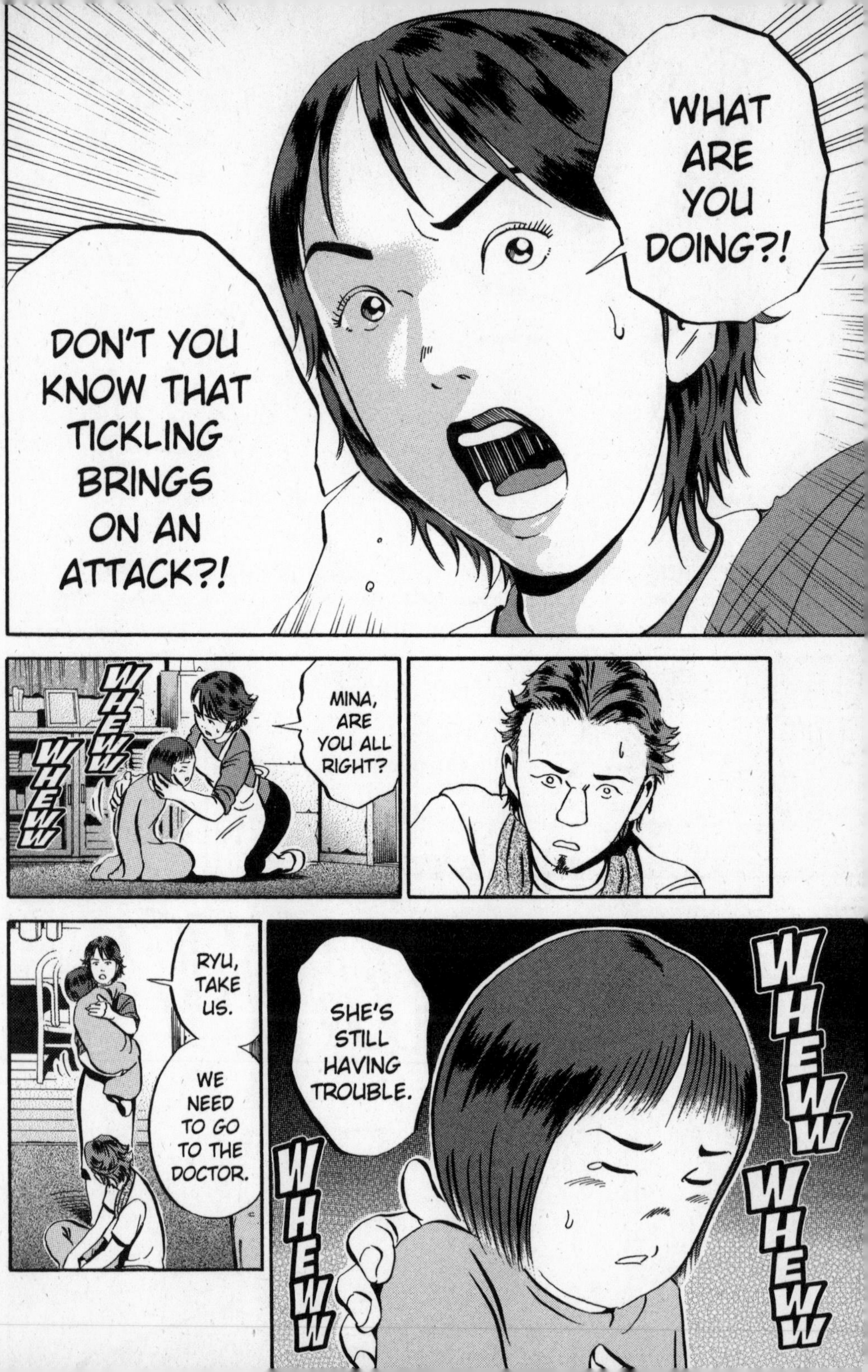
WHAT ARE YOU DOING?!
DON'T YOU KNOW THAT TICKLING BRINGS ON AN ATTACK?!
MINA, ARE YOU ALL RIGHT?
WHEWW
WHEWW
WHEWW
WHEWW
SHE'S STILL HAVING TROUBLE.
WHEWW
RYU, TAKE US.
WE NEED TO GO TO THE DOCTOR.

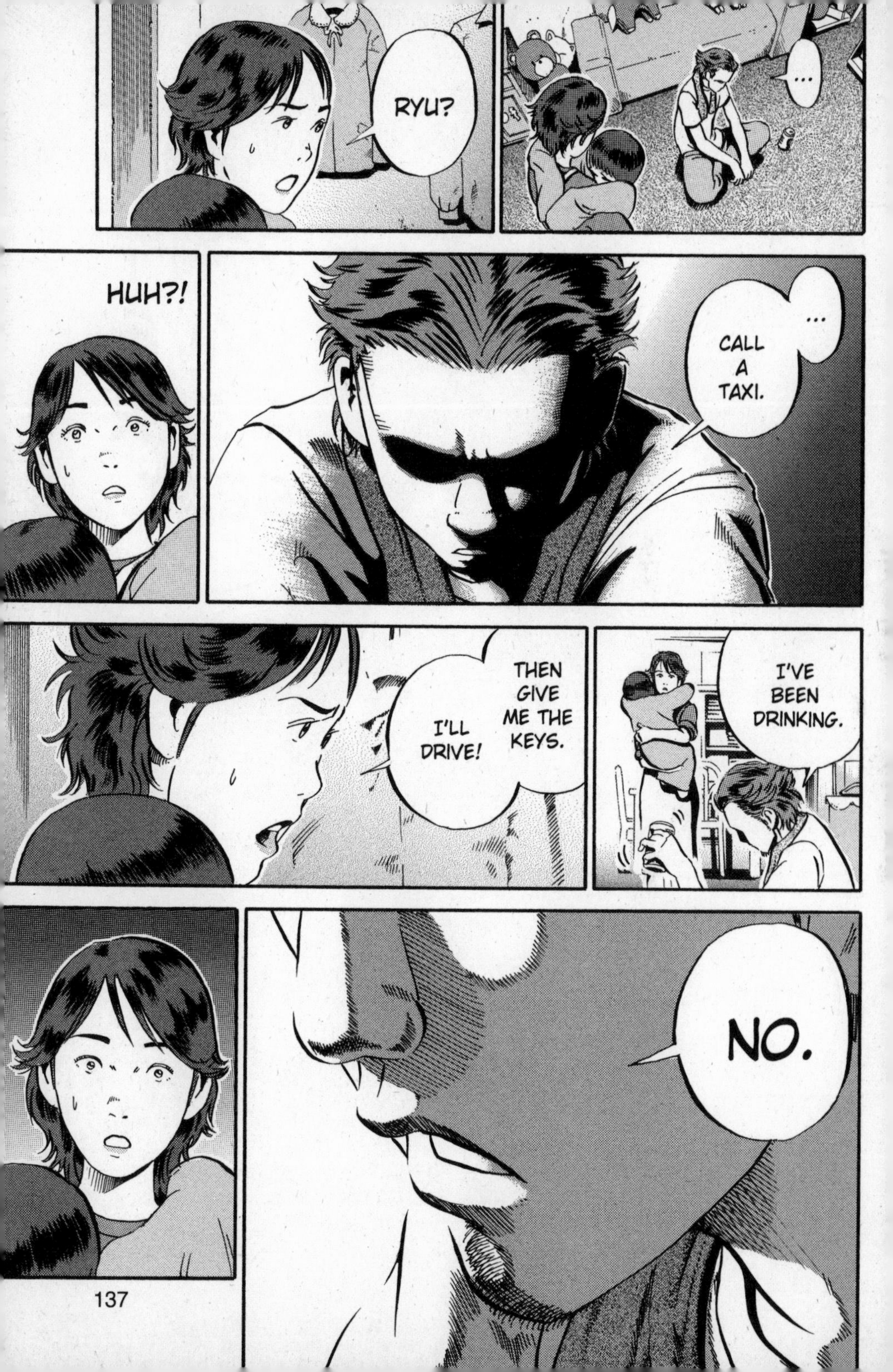
...
RYU?
...
CALL A TAXI.
HUH?!
I'VE BEEN DRINKING.
THEN GIVE ME THE KEYS.
I'LL DRIVE!
NO.

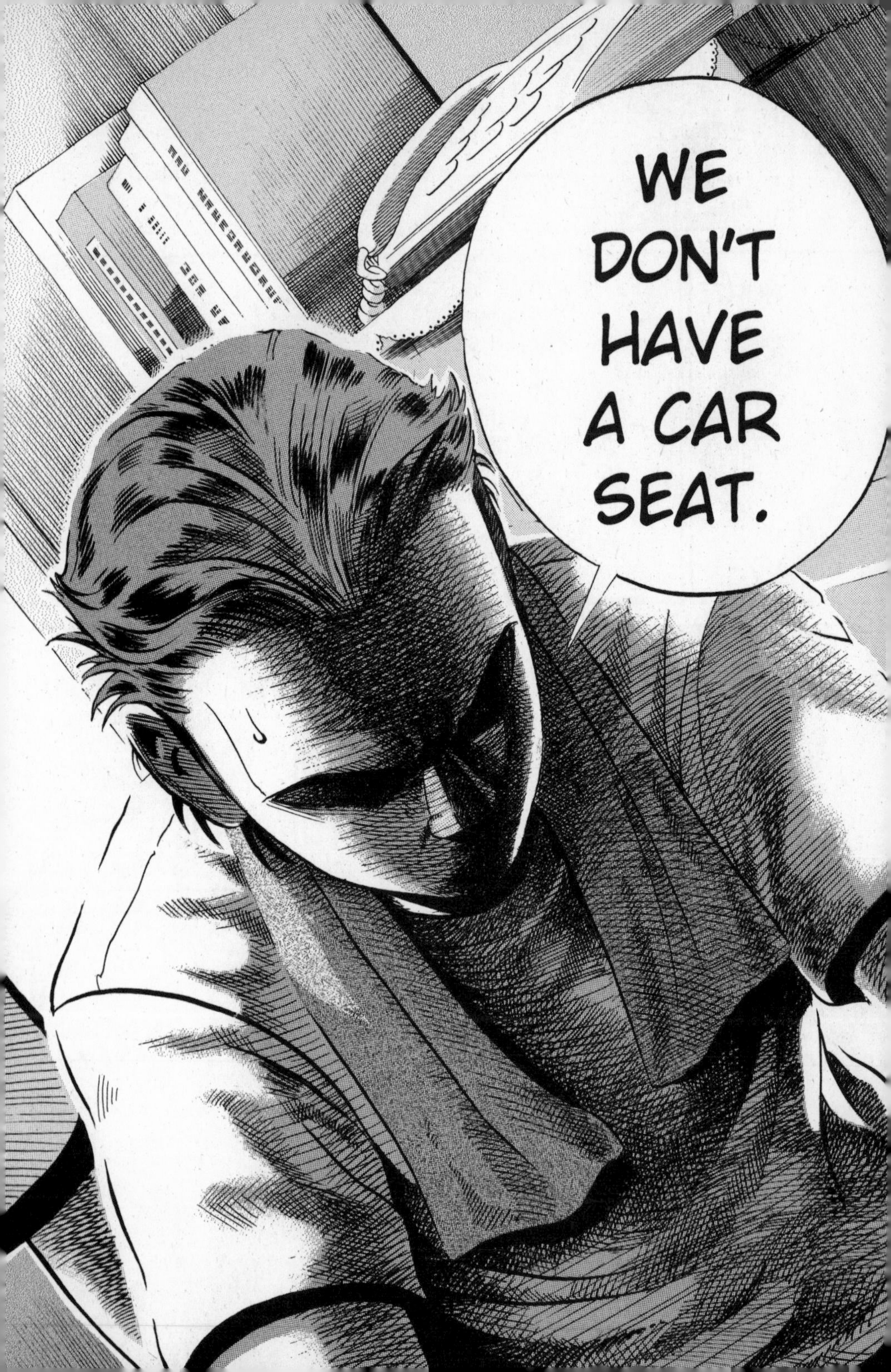
WE DON'T HAVE A CAR SEAT.

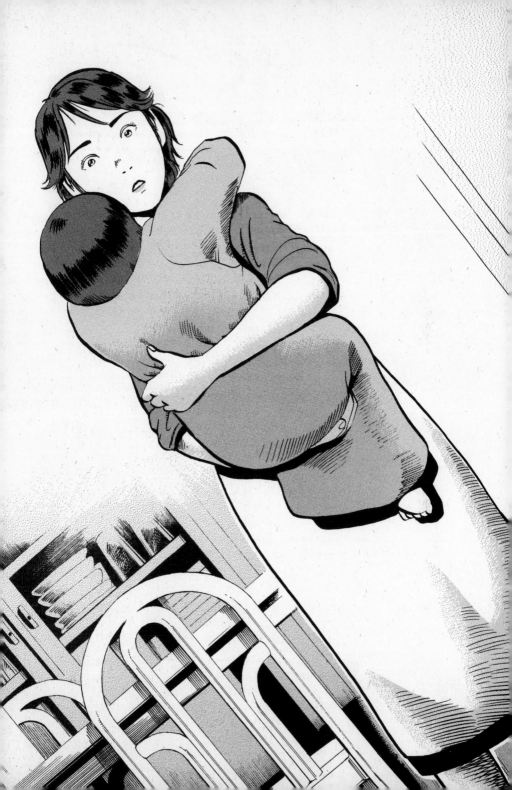

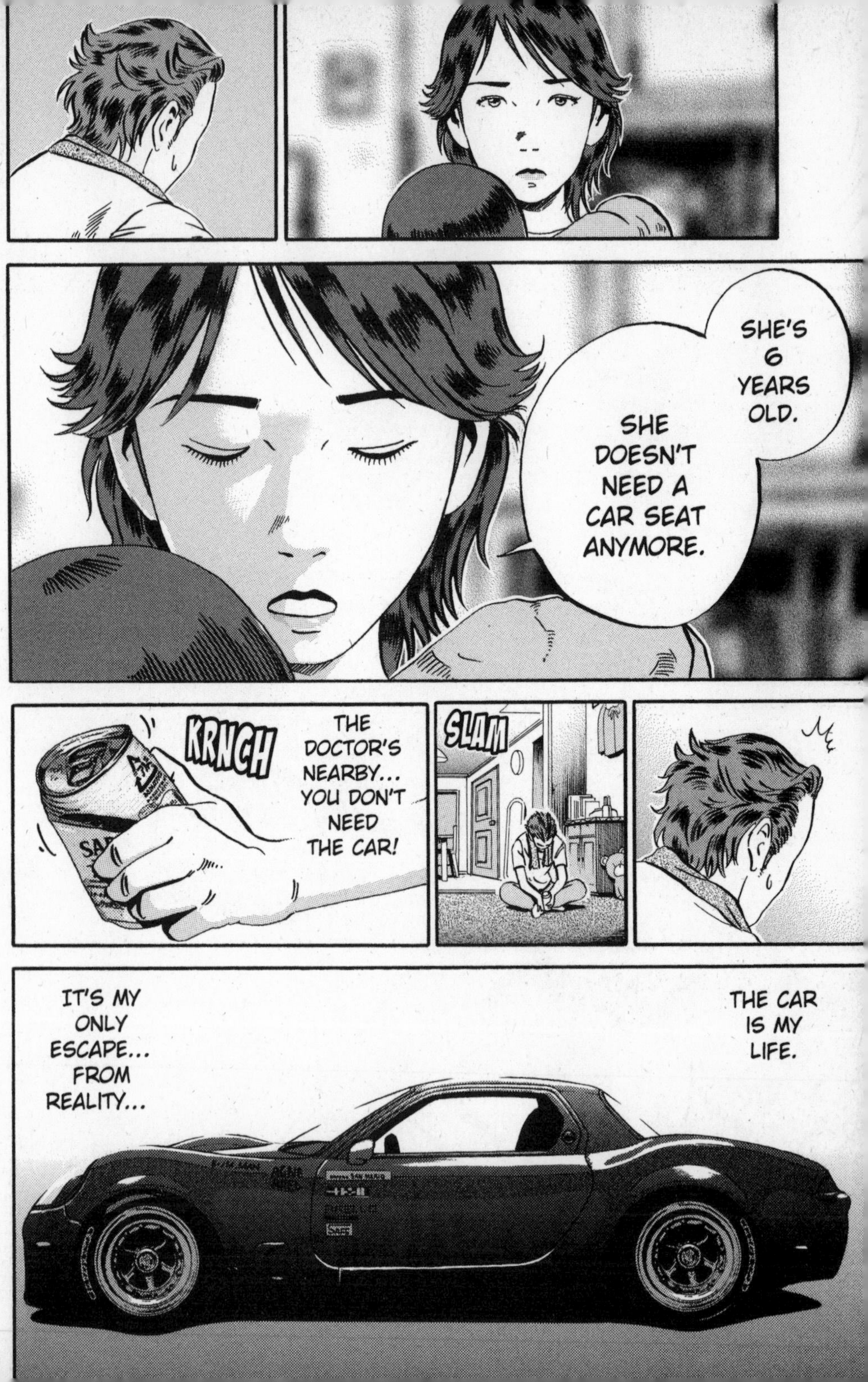
SHE'S 6 YEARS OLD.
SHE DOESN'T NEED A CAR SEAT ANYMORE.
SLAM
THE DOCTOR'S NEARBY... YOU DON'T NEED THE CAR!
KRNCH
THE CAR IS MY LIFE.
IT'S MY ONLY ESCAPE... FROM REALITY...

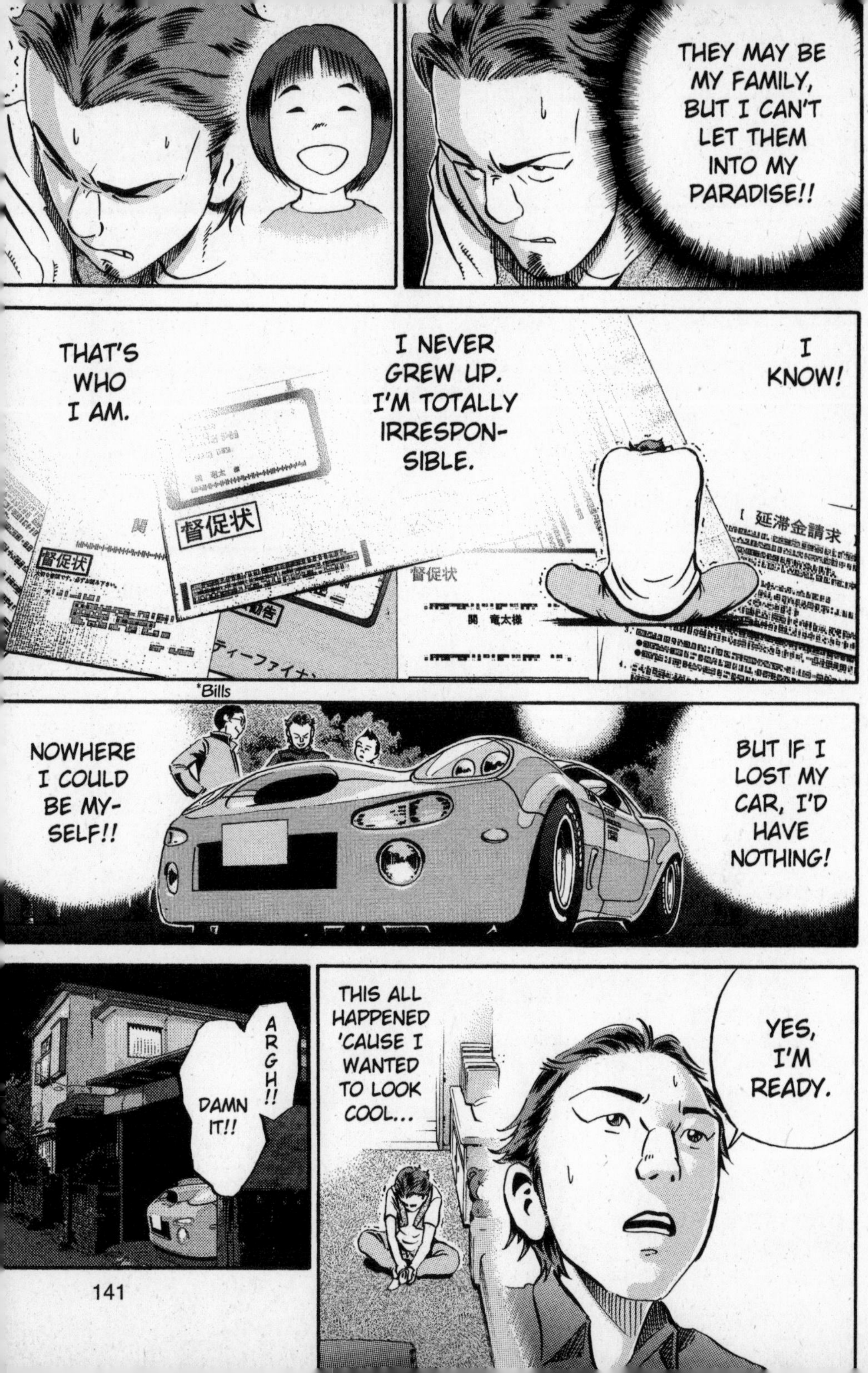

THEY MAY BE MY FAMILY, BUT I CAN'T LET THEM INTO MY PARADISE!!
I KNOW!
I NEVER GREW UP. I'M TOTALLY IRRESPONSIBLE.
THAT'S WHO I AM.
延滞金請求
督促状
関 竜太様
督促状
督促状
*Bills
BUT IF I LOST MY CAR, I'D HAVE NOTHING!
NOWHERE I COULD BE MYSELF!!
YES, I'M READY.
THIS ALL HAPPENED 'CAUSE I WANTED TO LOOK COOL...
ARGH!!
DAMN IT!!

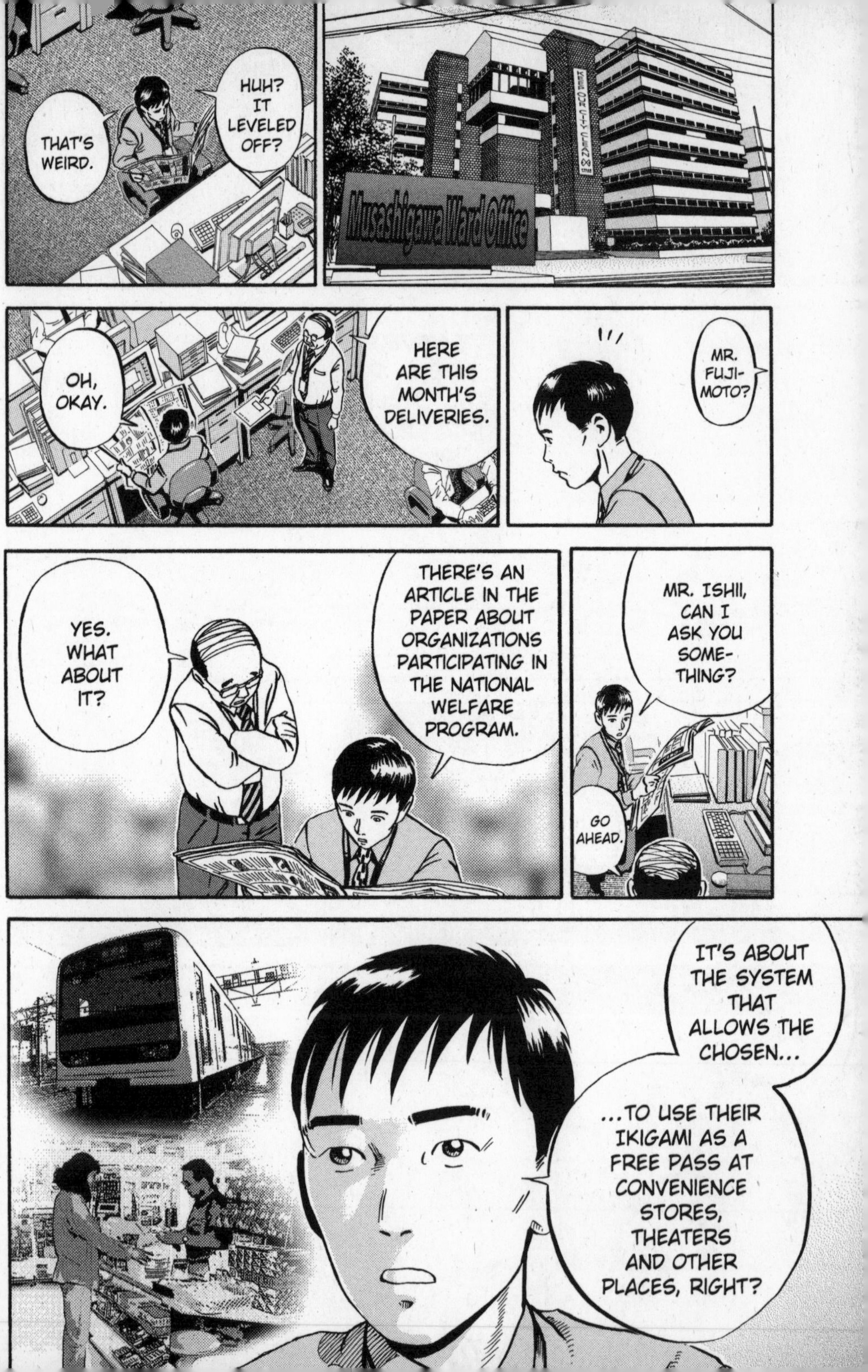
KEEP OUR CITY CLEAN
Musashigawa Ward Office
HUH? IT LEVELED OFF?
THAT'S WEIRD.
MR. FUJIMOTO?
HERE ARE THIS MONTH'S DELIVERIES.
OH, OKAY.
MR. ISHII, CAN I ASK YOU SOMETHING?
GO AHEAD.
THERE'S AN ARTICLE IN THE PAPER ABOUT ORGANIZATIONS PARTICIPATING IN THE NATIONAL WELFARE PROGRAM.
YES. WHAT ABOUT IT?
IT'S ABOUT THE SYSTEM THAT ALLOWS THE CHOSEN...
...TO USE THEIR IKIGAMI AS A FREE PASS AT CONVENIENCE STORES, THEATERS AND OTHER PLACES, RIGHT?

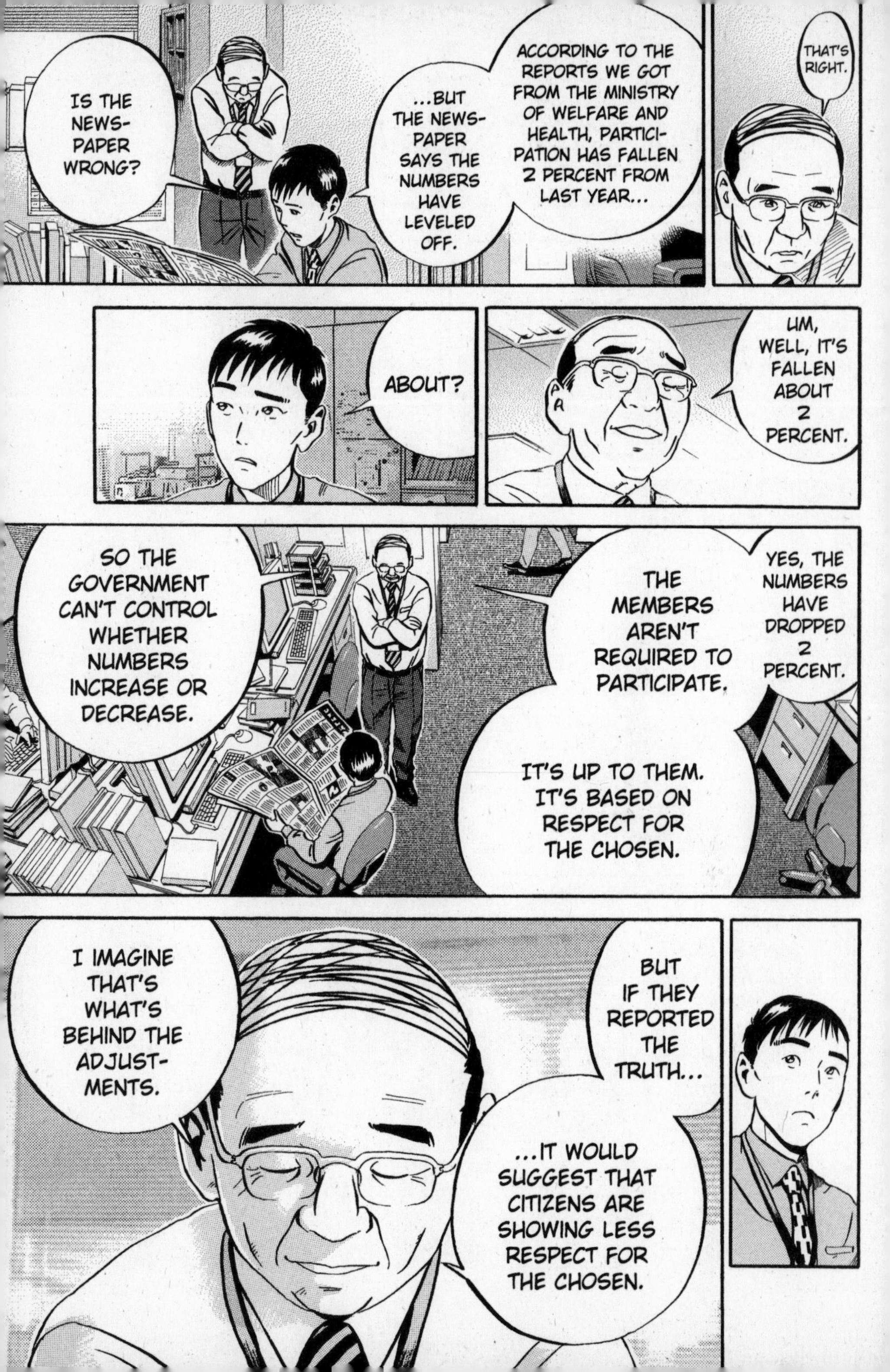
ACCORDING TO THE REPORTS WE GOT FROM THE MINISTRY OF WELFARE AND HEALTH, PARTICI-PATION HAS FALLEN 2 PERCENT FROM LAST YEAR...
...BUT THE NEWS-PAPER SAYS THE NUMBERS HAVE LEVELED OFF.
IS THE NEWS-PAPER WRONG?
THAT'S RIGHT.
ABOUT?
UM, WELL, IT'S FALLEN ABOUT 2 PERCENT.
YES, THE NUMBERS HAVE DROPPED 2 PERCENT.
THE MEMBERS AREN'T REQUIRED TO PARTICIPATE.
IT'S UP TO THEM. IT'S BASED ON RESPECT FOR THE CHOSEN.
SO THE GOVERNMENT CAN'T CONTROL WHETHER NUMBERS INCREASE OR DECREASE.
I IMAGINE THAT'S WHAT'S BEHIND THE ADJUST-MENTS.
BUT IF THEY REPORTED THE TRUTH...
...IT WOULD SUGGEST THAT CITIZENS ARE SHOWING LESS RESPECT FOR THE CHOSEN.

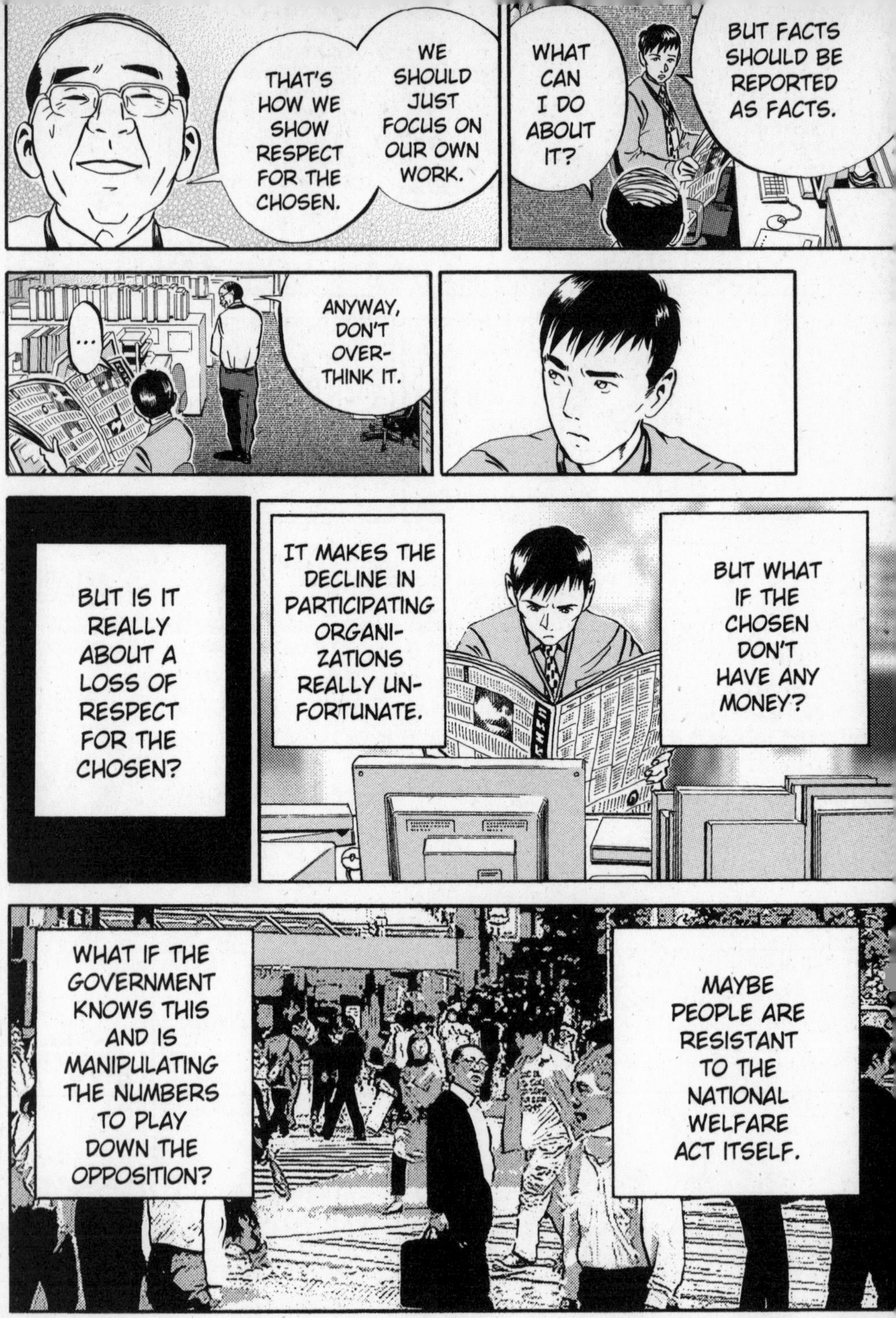
BUT FACTS SHOULD BE REPORTED AS FACTS.
WHAT CAN I DO ABOUT IT?
WE SHOULD JUST FOCUS ON OUR OWN WORK.
THAT'S HOW WE SHOW RESPECT FOR THE CHOSEN.
ANYWAY, DON'T OVER-THINK IT.
...
BUT WHAT IF THE CHOSEN DON'T HAVE ANY MONEY?
IT MAKES THE DECLINE IN PARTICIPATING ORGANI-ZATIONS REALLY UN-FORTUNATE.
BUT IS IT REALLY ABOUT A LOSS OF RESPECT FOR THE CHOSEN?
MAYBE PEOPLE ARE RESISTANT TO THE NATIONAL WELFARE ACT ITSELF.
WHAT IF THE GOVERNMENT KNOWS THIS AND IS MANIPULATING THE NUMBERS TO PLAY DOWN THE OPPOSITION?

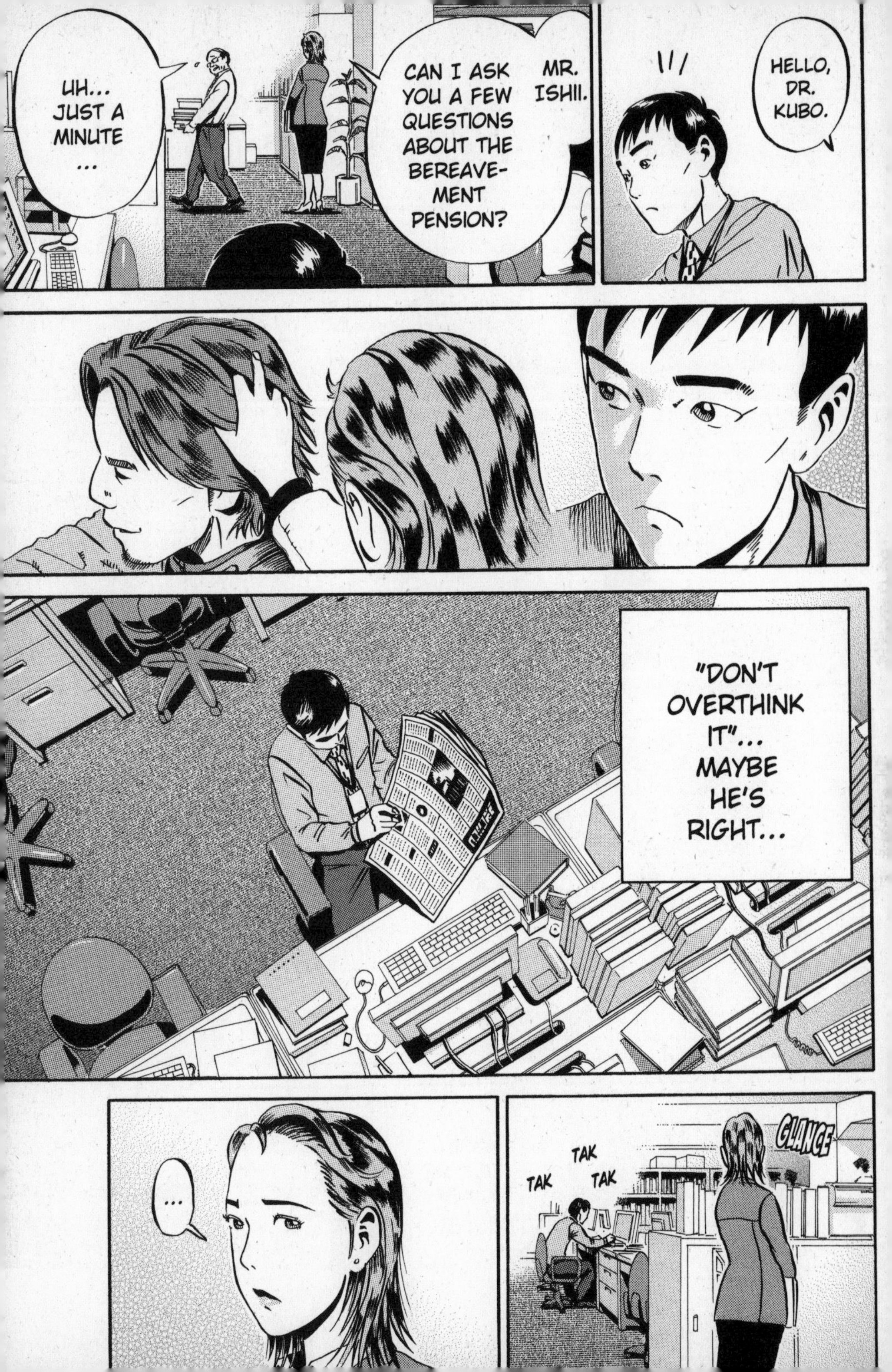
HELLO, DR. KUBO.
MR. ISHII.
CAN I ASK YOU A FEW QUESTIONS ABOUT THE BEREAVE-MENT PENSION?
UH... JUST A MINUTE ...
"DON'T OVERTHINK IT"... MAYBE HE'S RIGHT...
GLANCE
TAK
TAK
TAK
...

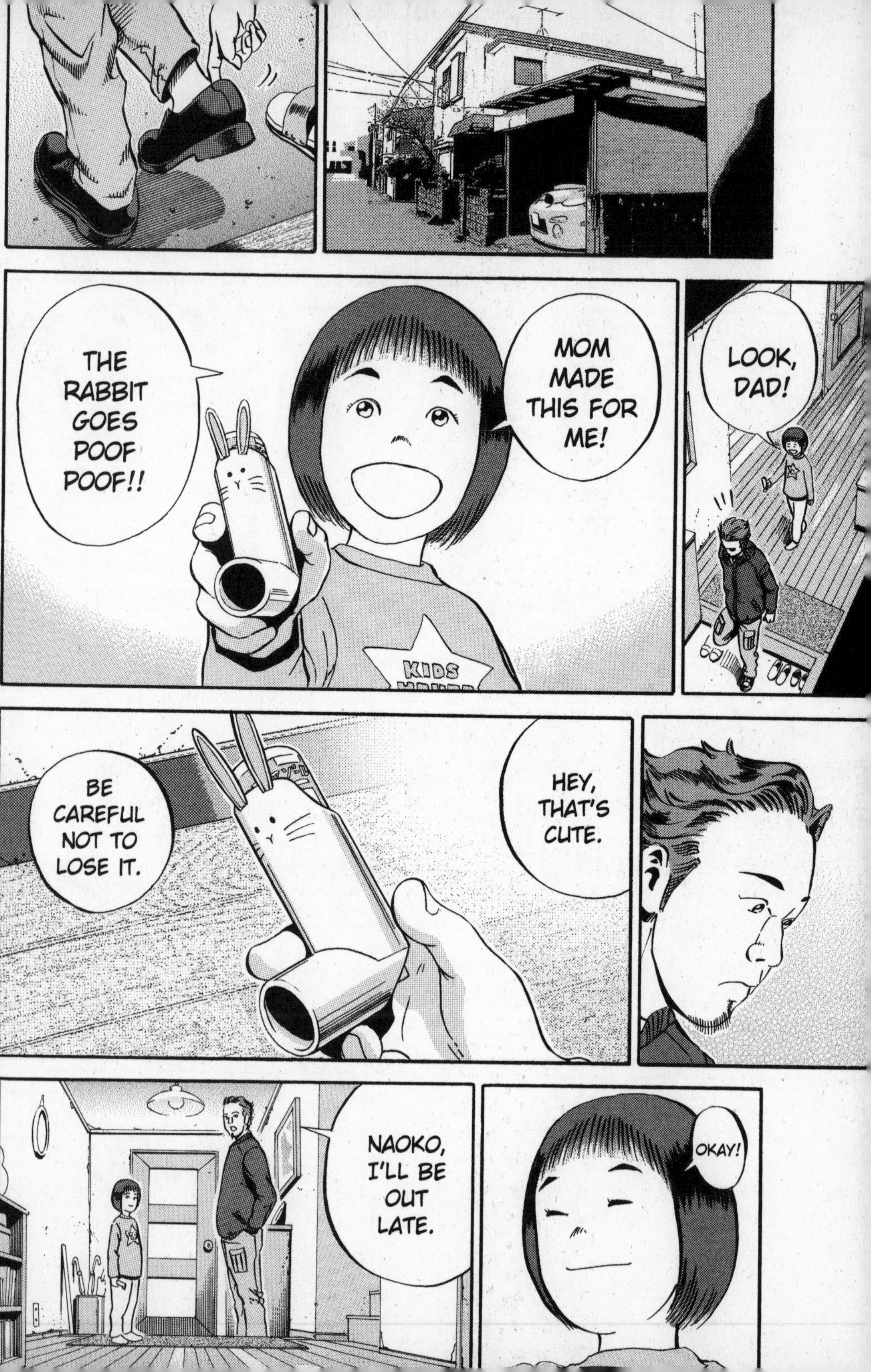

LOOK, DAD!
MOM MADE THIS FOR ME!
THE RABBIT GOES POOF POOF!!
KIDS
HEY, THAT'S CUTE.
BE CAREFUL NOT TO LOSE IT.
OKAY!
NAOKO, I'LL BE OUT LATE.

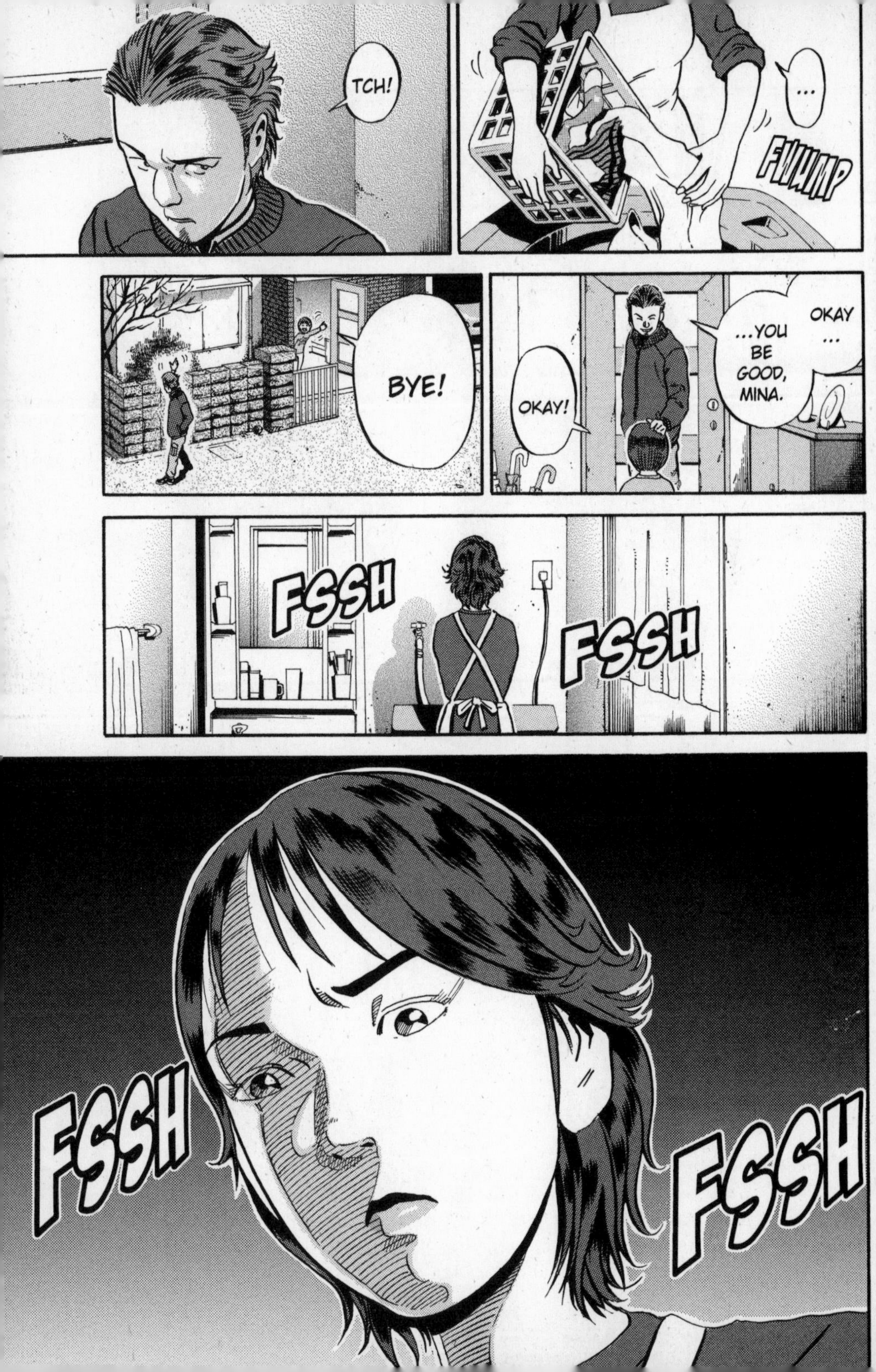
...
FWUMP
TCH!
OKAY ...
...YOU BE GOOD, MINA.
OKAY!
BYE!
FSSH
FSSH
FSSH
FSSH

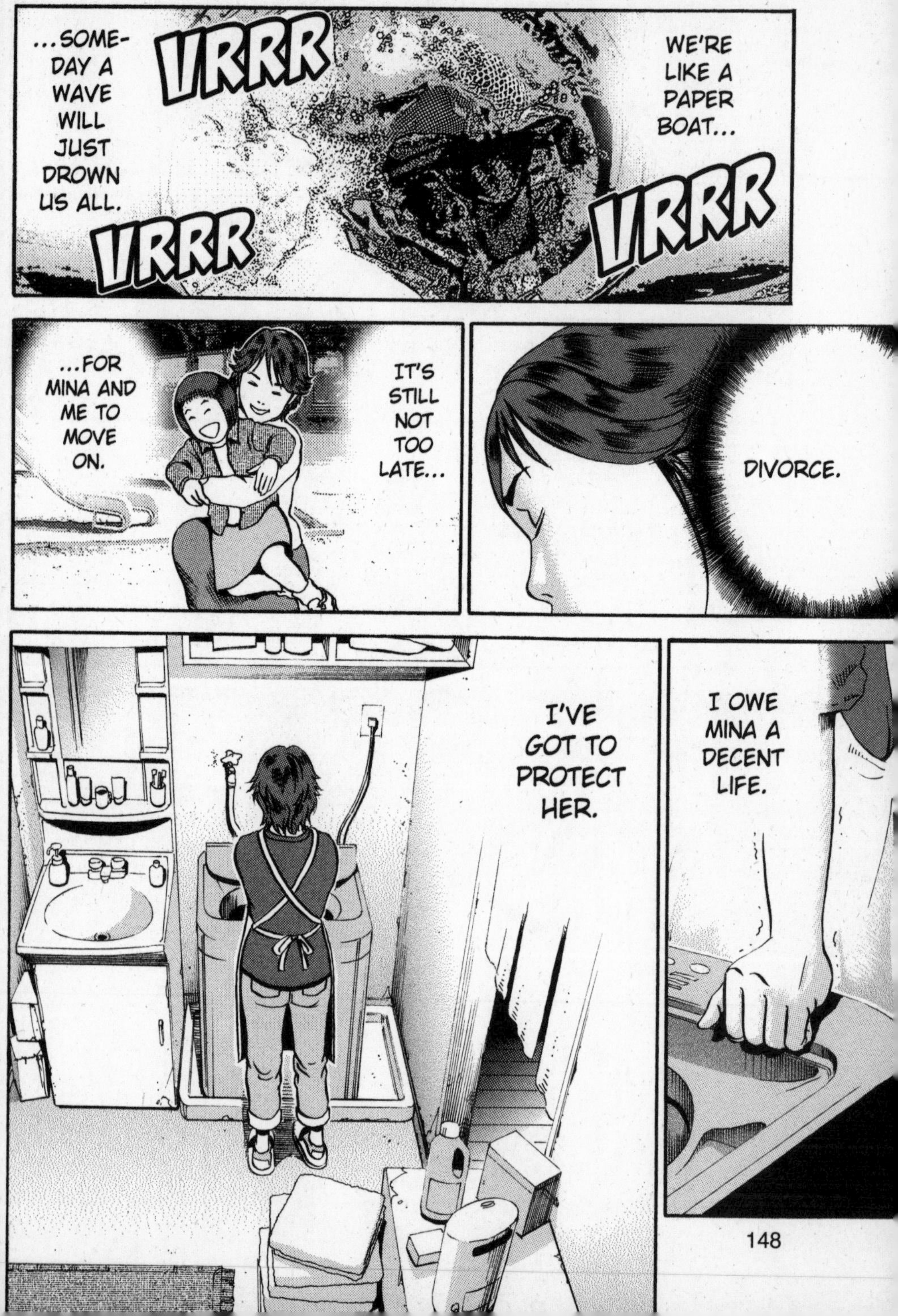
WE'RE LIKE A PAPER BOAT...
VRRR
VRRR
...SOME-DAY A WAVE WILL JUST DROWN US ALL.
VRRR
DIVORCE.
IT'S STILL NOT TOO LATE...
...FOR MINA AND ME TO MOVE ON.
I OWE MINA A DECENT LIFE.
I'VE GOT TO PROTECT HER.

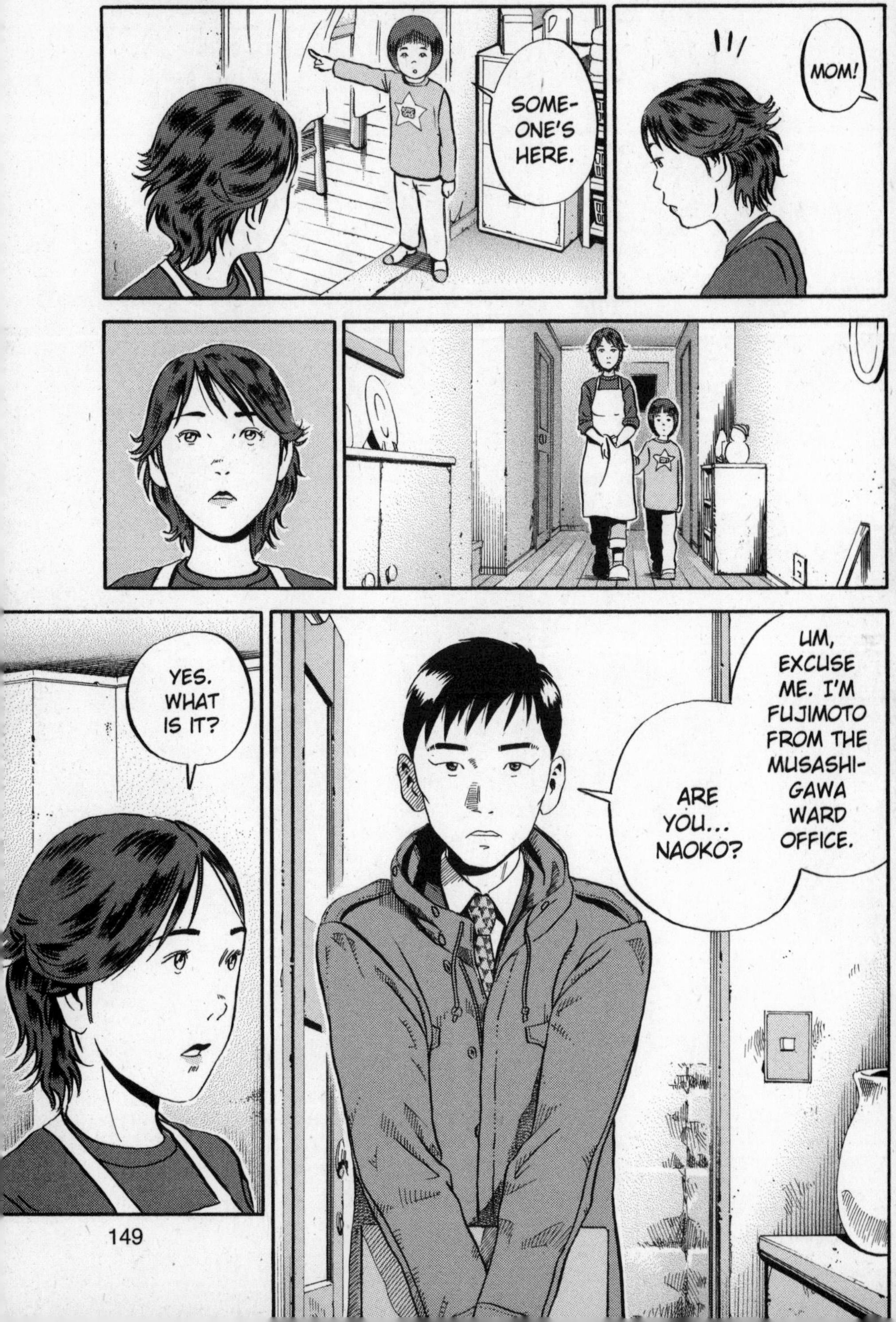
MOM!
SOME-ONE'S HERE.
UM, EXCUSE ME. I'M FUJIMOTO FROM THE MUSASHI-GAWA WARD OFFICE.
ARE YOU... NAOKO?
YES. WHAT IS IT?

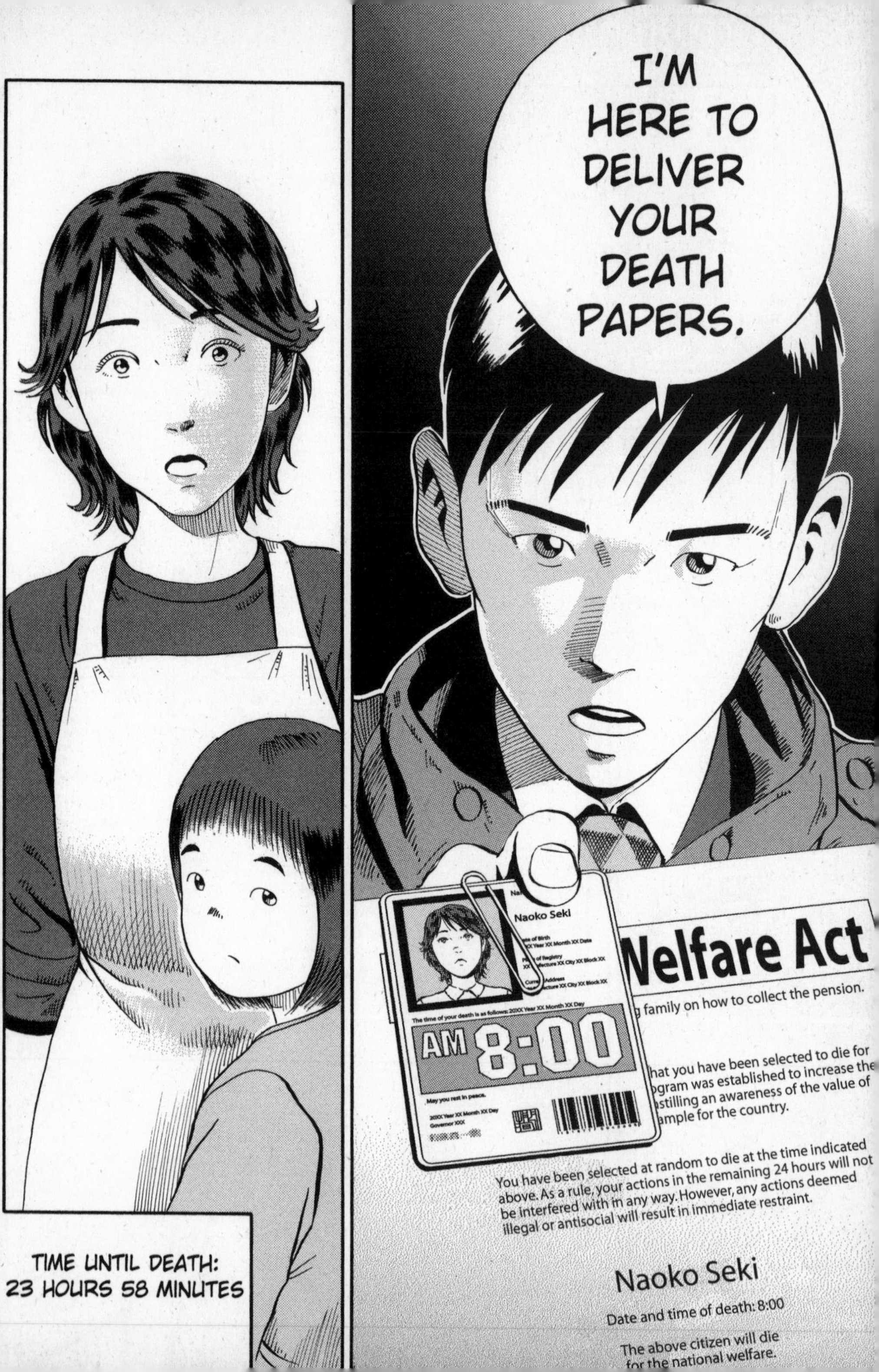

I'M HERE TO DELIVER YOUR DEATH PAPERS.
Naoko Seki
AM 8:00
Welfare Act
You have been selected at random to die at the time indicated above. As a rule, your actions in the remaining 24 hours will not be interfered with in any way. However, any actions deemed illegal or antisocial will result in immediate restraint.
Naoko Seki
Date and time of death: 8:00
The above citizen will die
TIME UNTIL DEATH: 23 HOURS 58 MINUTES

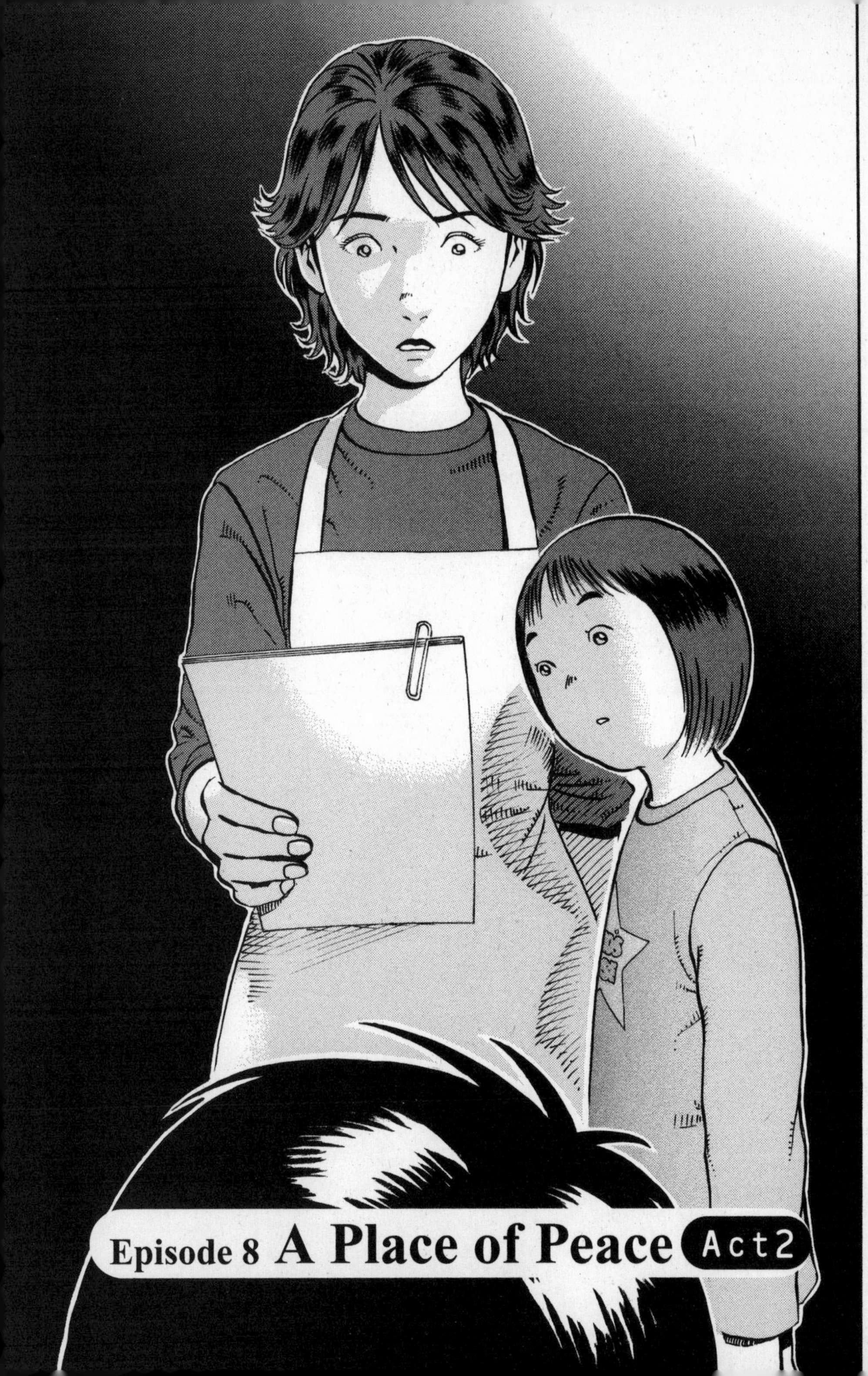

Episode 8 A Place of Peace Act2

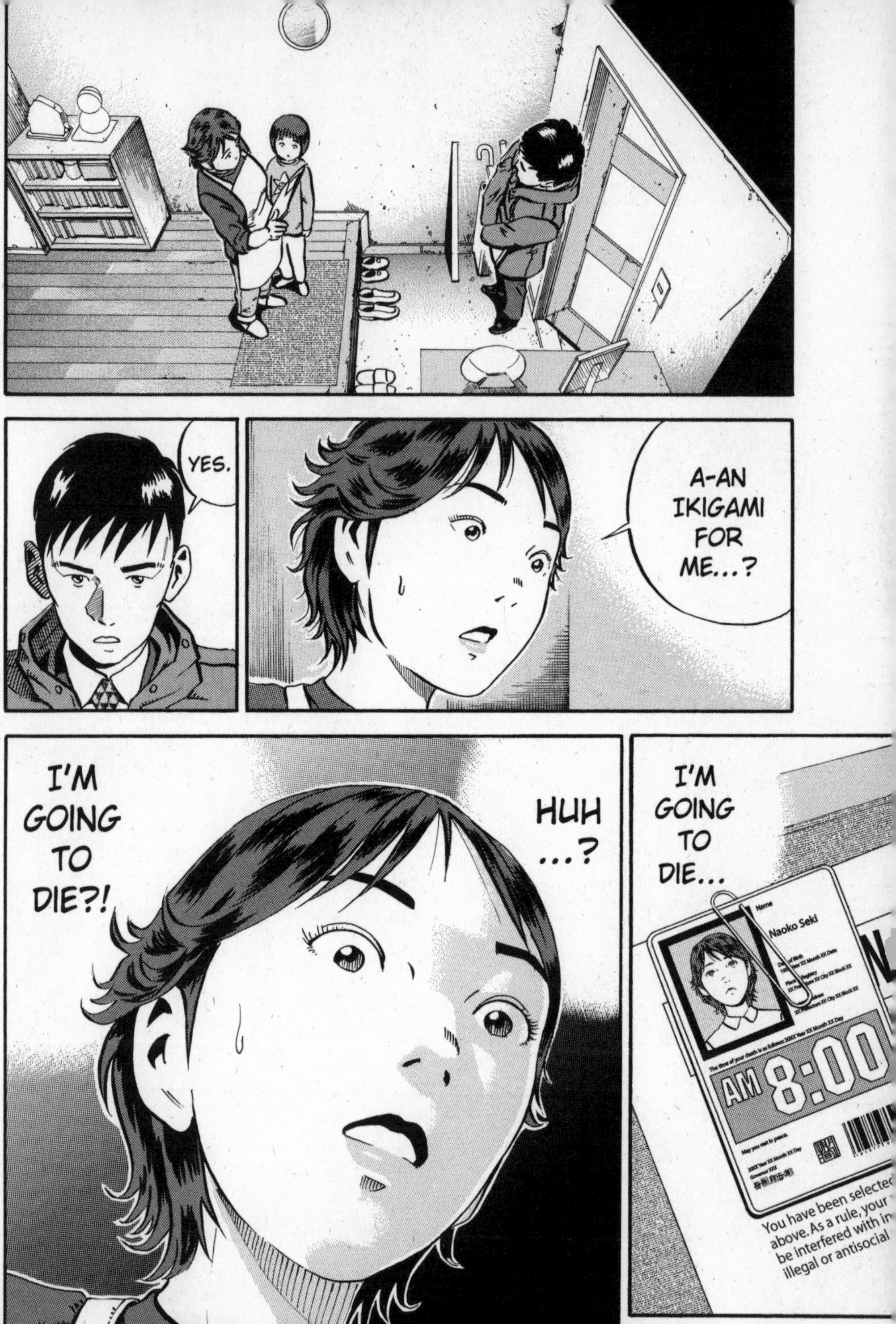

A-AN IKIGAMI FOR ME...?
YES.
I'M GOING TO DIE...
Name
Naoko Seki
AM 8:00
May you rest in peace.
You have been selected
above. As a rule, your
be interfered with in
illegal or antisocial
HUH ...?
I'M GOING TO DIE?!

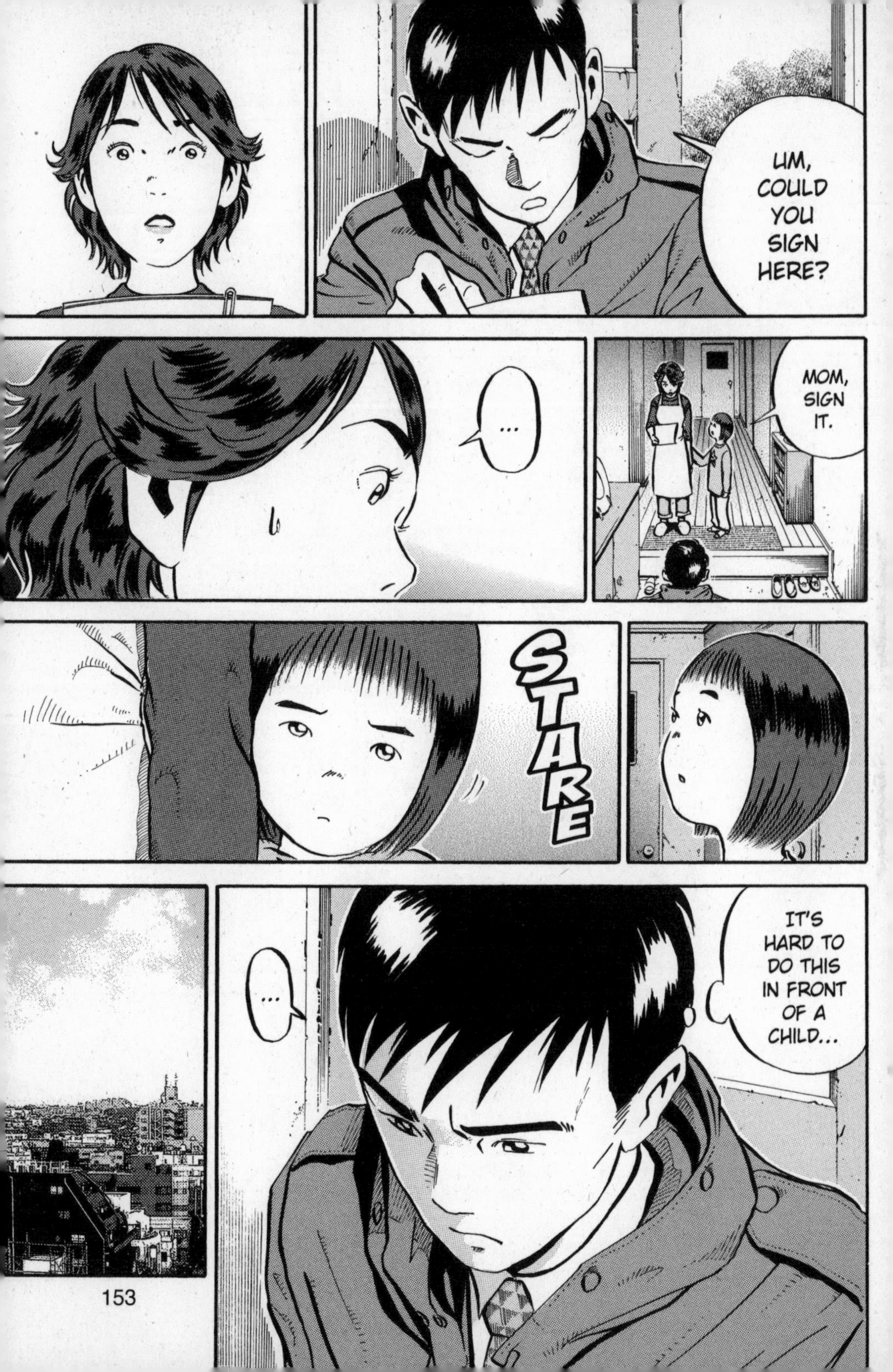
UM, COULD YOU SIGN HERE?
MOM, SIGN IT.
...
STARE
IT'S HARD TO DO THIS IN FRONT OF A CHILD...
...

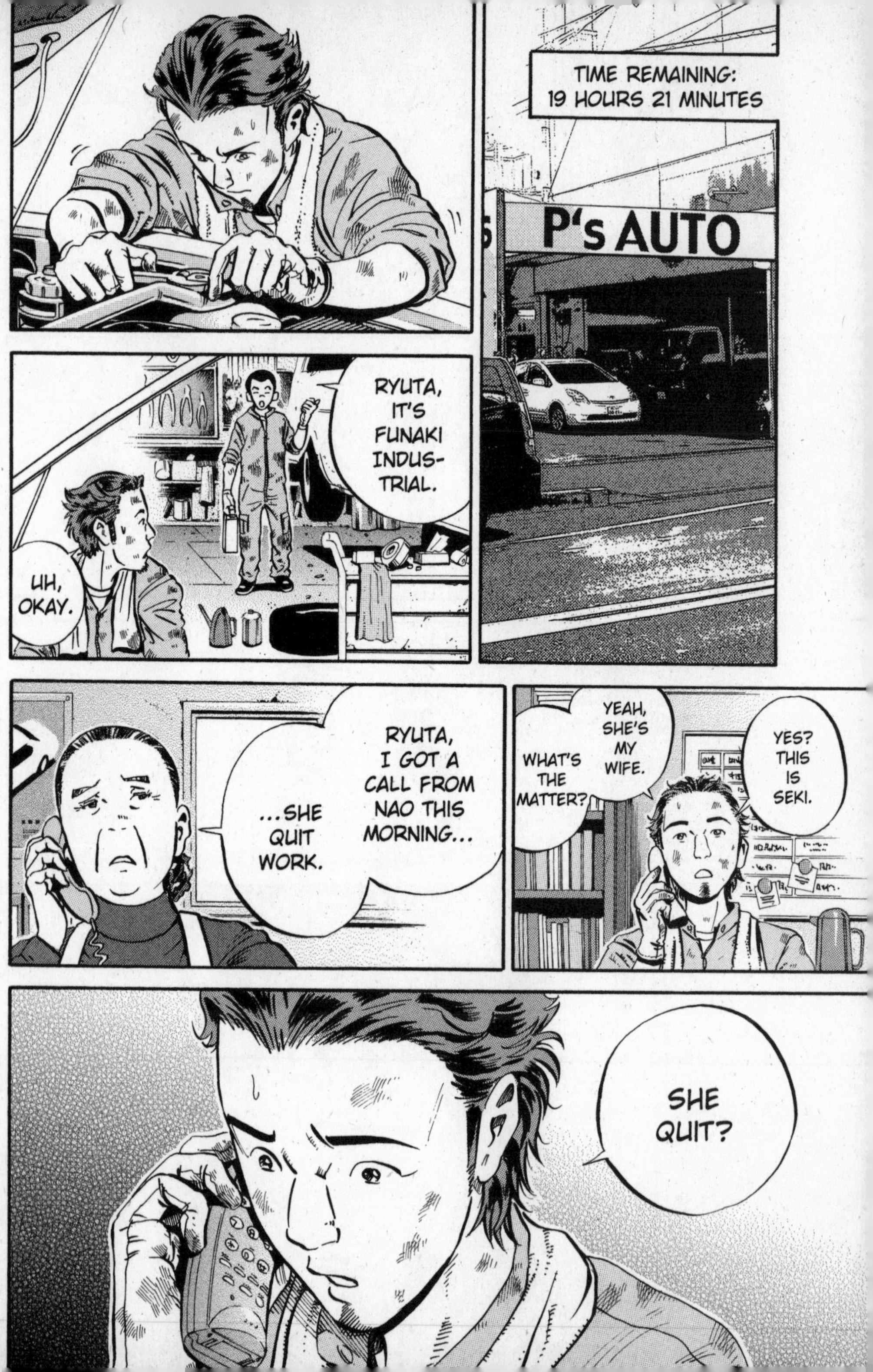
TIME REMAINING:
19 HOURS 21 MINUTES
P's AUTO
RYUTA, IT'S FUNAKI INDUSTRIAL.
UH, OKAY.
YES? THIS IS SEKI.
YEAH, SHE'S MY WIFE.
WHAT'S THE MATTER?
RYUTA, I GOT A CALL FROM NAO THIS MORNING...
...SHE QUIT WORK.
SHE QUIT?

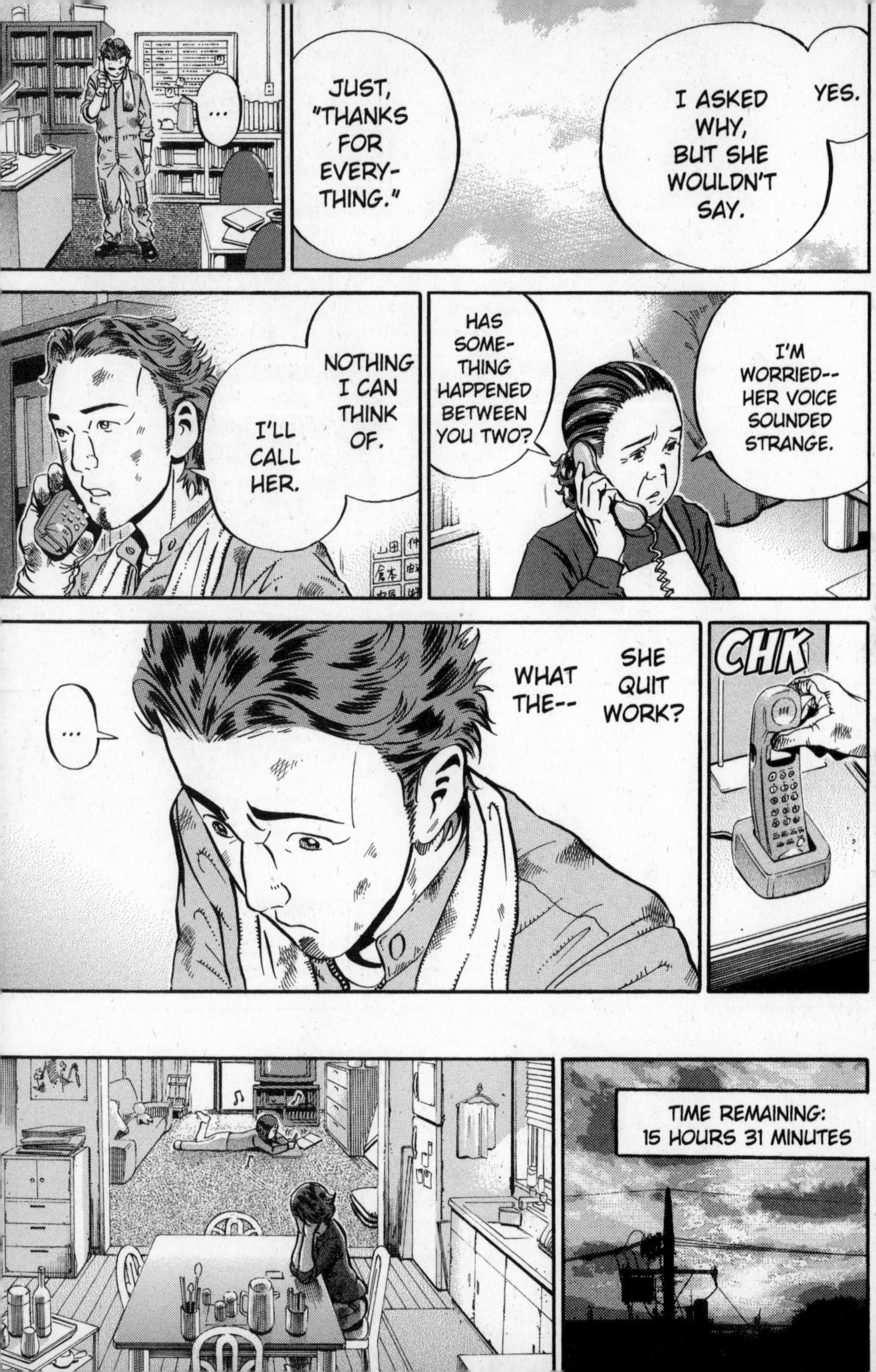
YES.
I ASKED WHY, BUT SHE WOULDN'T SAY.
JUST, "THANKS FOR EVERY-THING."
...
I'M WORRIED--HER VOICE SOUNDED STRANGE.
HAS SOME-THING HAPPENED BETWEEN YOU TWO?
NOTHING I CAN THINK OF.
I'LL CALL HER.
CHK
SHE QUIT WORK?
WHAT THE--
...
TIME REMAINING:
15 HOURS 31 MINUTES

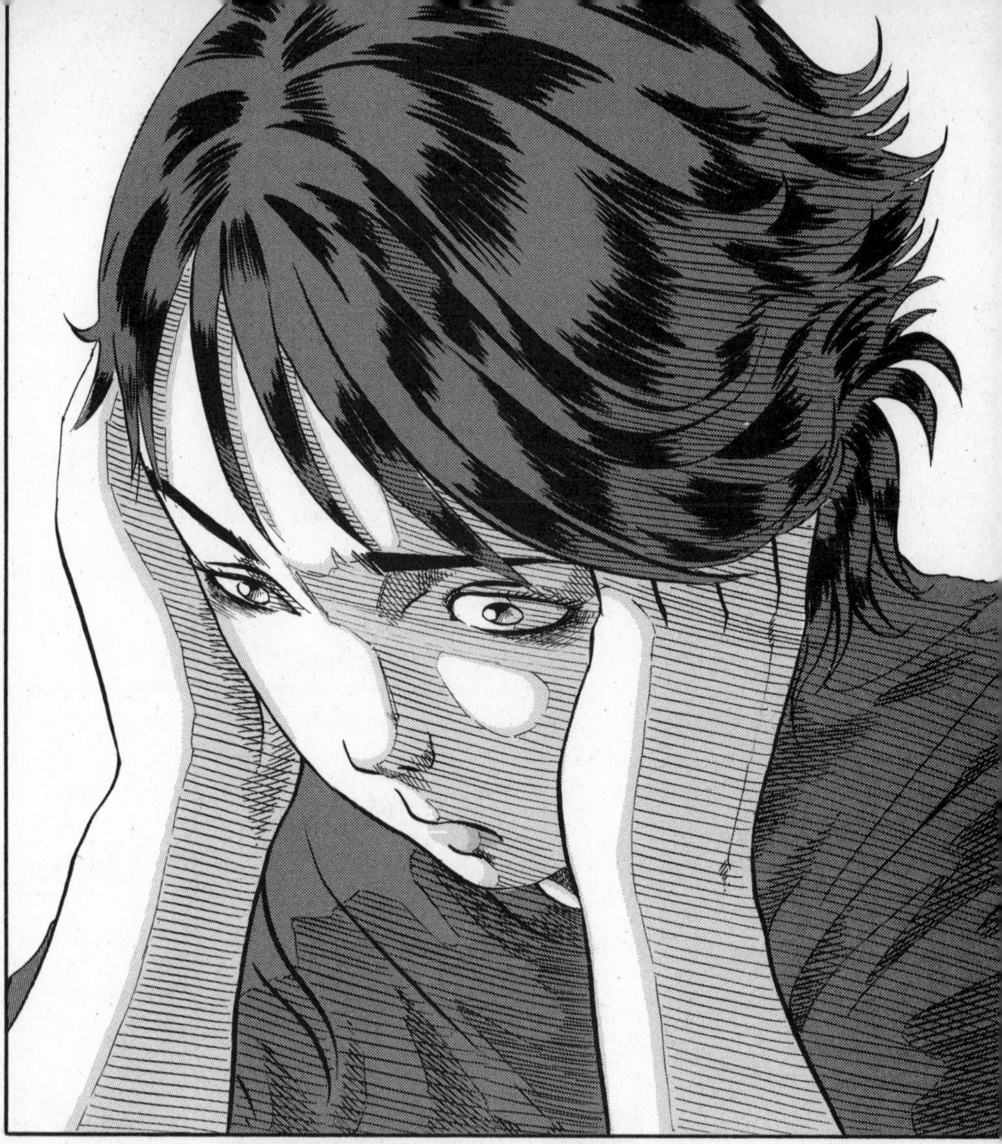

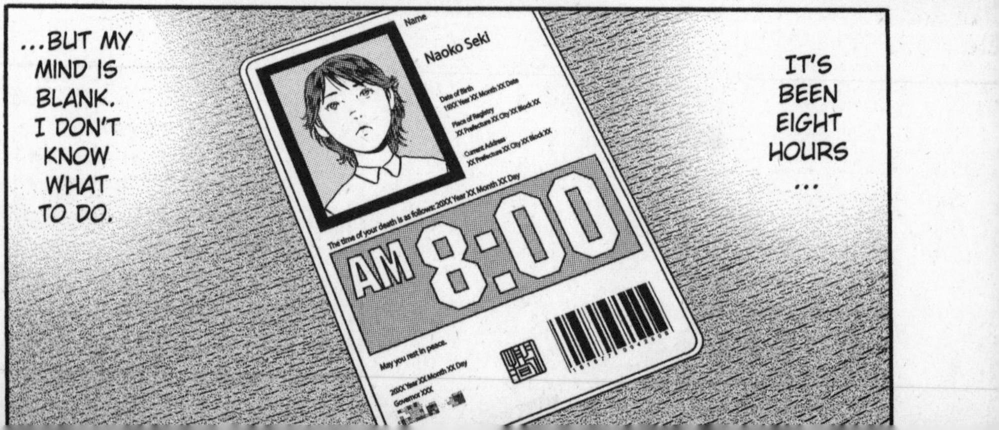
IT'S BEEN EIGHT HOURS ...
...BUT MY MIND IS BLANK. I DON'T KNOW WHAT TO DO.
Name
Naoko Seki
The time of your death is as follows: 20XX Year XX Month XX Day
AM 8:00
May you rest in peace.

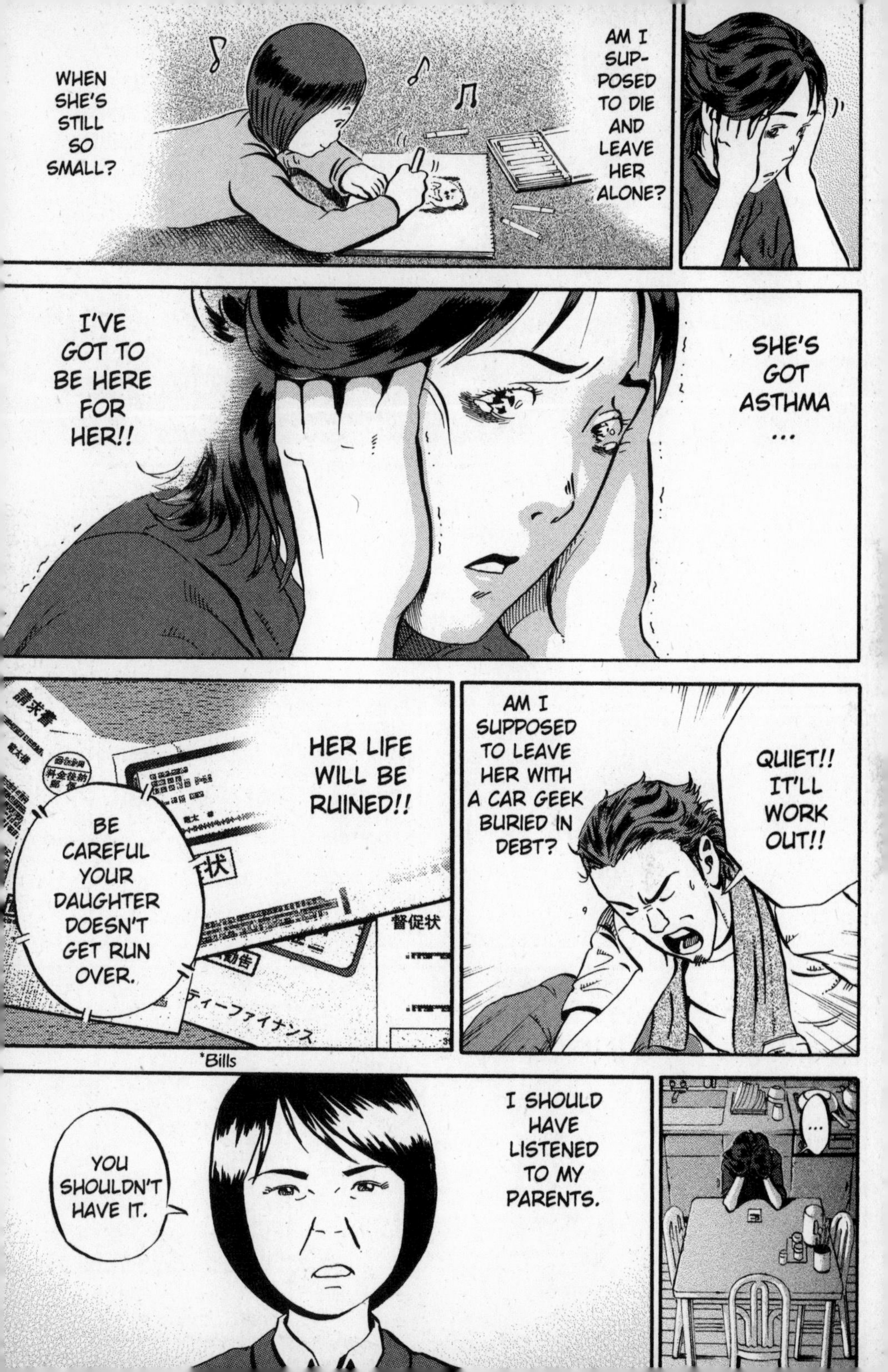
AM I SUP-POSED TO DIE AND LEAVE HER ALONE?
WHEN SHE'S STILL SO SMALL?
SHE'S GOT ASTHMA ...
I'VE GOT TO BE HERE FOR HER!!
AM I SUPPOSED TO LEAVE HER WITH A CAR GEEK BURIED IN DEBT?
QUIET!! IT'LL WORK OUT!!
HER LIFE WILL BE RUINED!!
BE CAREFUL YOUR DAUGHTER DOESN'T GET RUN OVER.
請求書
督促状
ティーファイナンス
*Bills
...
I SHOULD HAVE LISTENED TO MY PARENTS.
YOU SHOULDN'T HAVE IT.

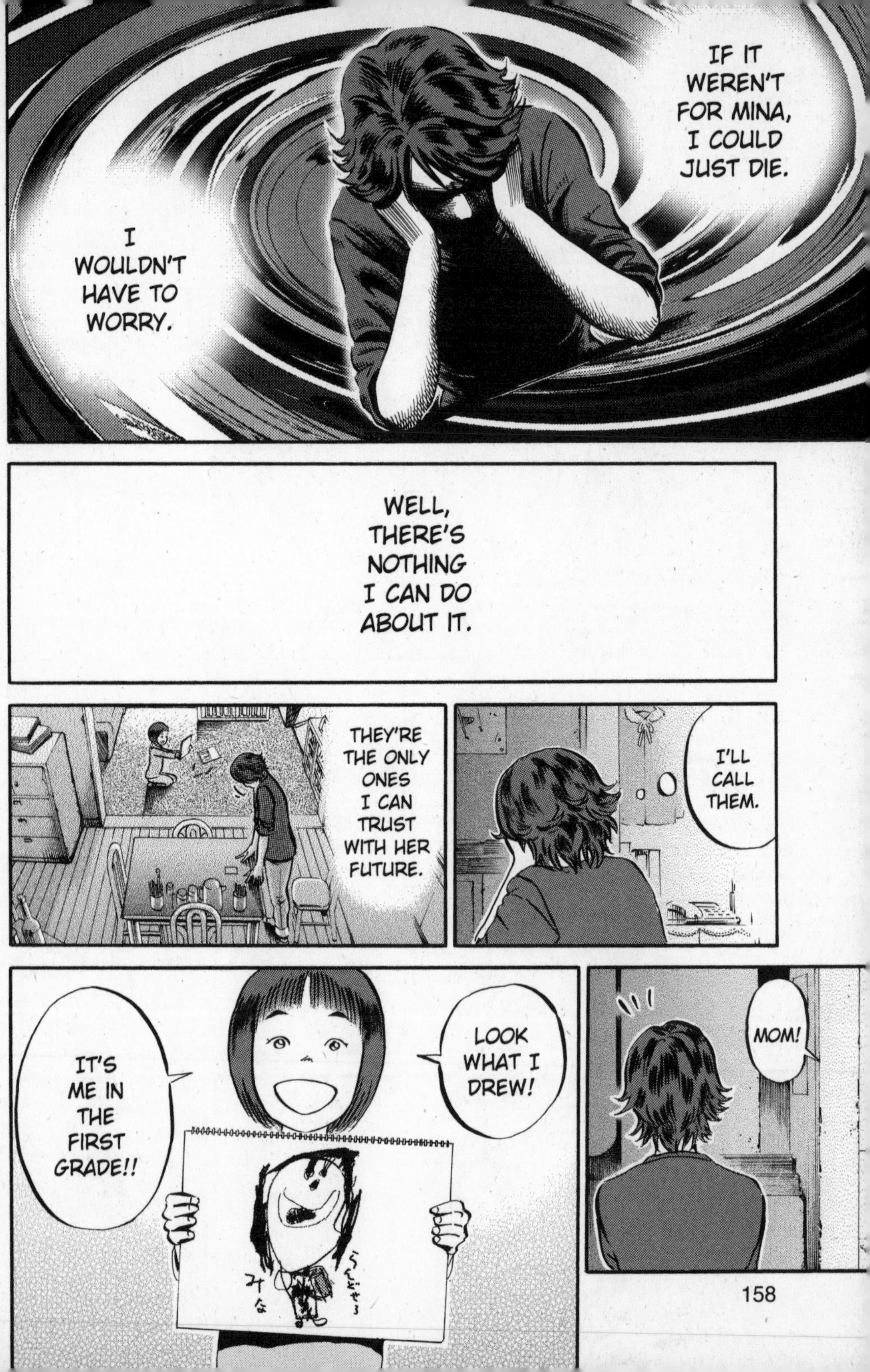
IF IT WEREN'T FOR MINA, I COULD JUST DIE.
I WOULDN'T HAVE TO WORRY.
WELL, THERE'S NOTHING I CAN DO ABOUT IT.
I'LL CALL THEM.
THEY'RE THE ONLY ONES I CAN TRUST WITH HER FUTURE.
MOM!
LOOK WHAT I DREW!
IT'S ME IN THE FIRST GRADE!!
らんどせる
みな

*Mina   *Backpack

FIRST
GRADE
...

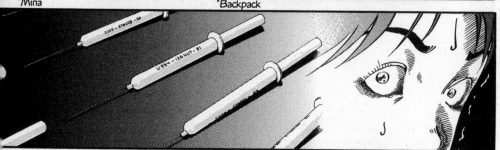

NATIONAL
WELFARE
IMMUNI-
ZATION.

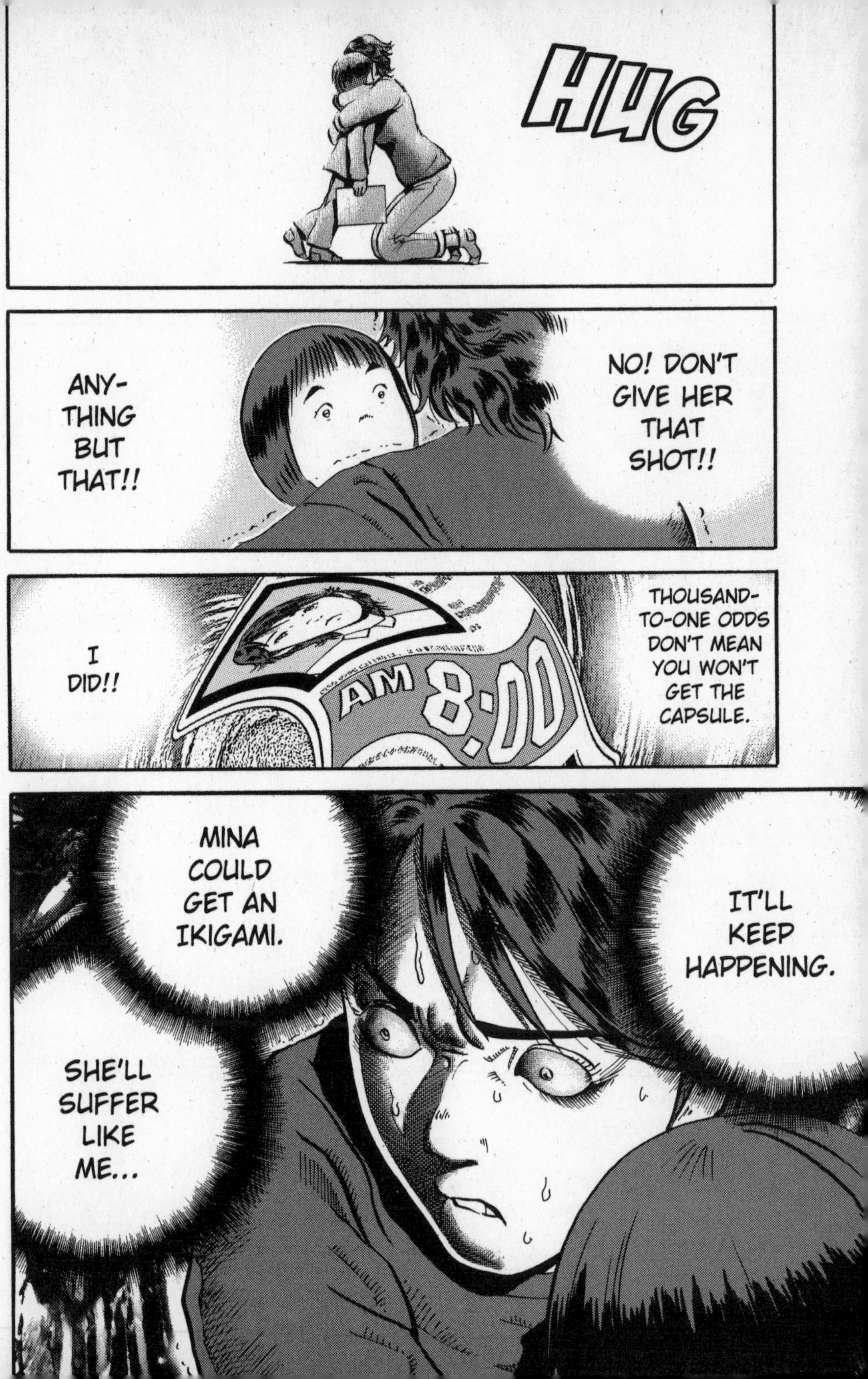
HUG
NO! DON'T GIVE HER THAT SHOT!!
ANY-THING BUT THAT!!
THOUSAND-TO-ONE ODDS DON'T MEAN YOU WON'T GET THE CAPSULE.
AM 8:00
I DID!!
IT'LL KEEP HAPPENING.
MINA COULD GET AN IKIGAMI.
SHE'LL SUFFER LIKE ME...

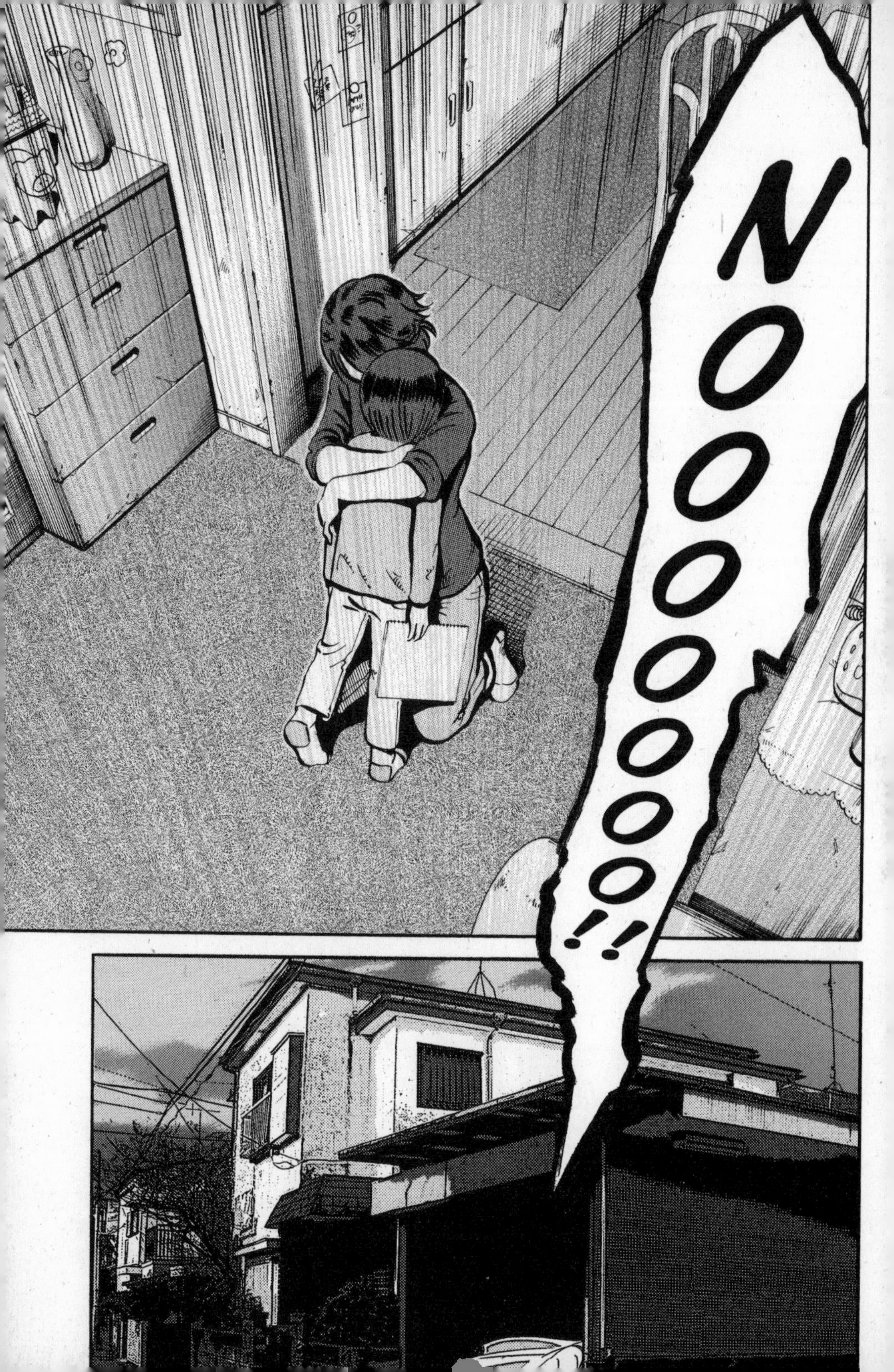
NOOOOOOOOO!!

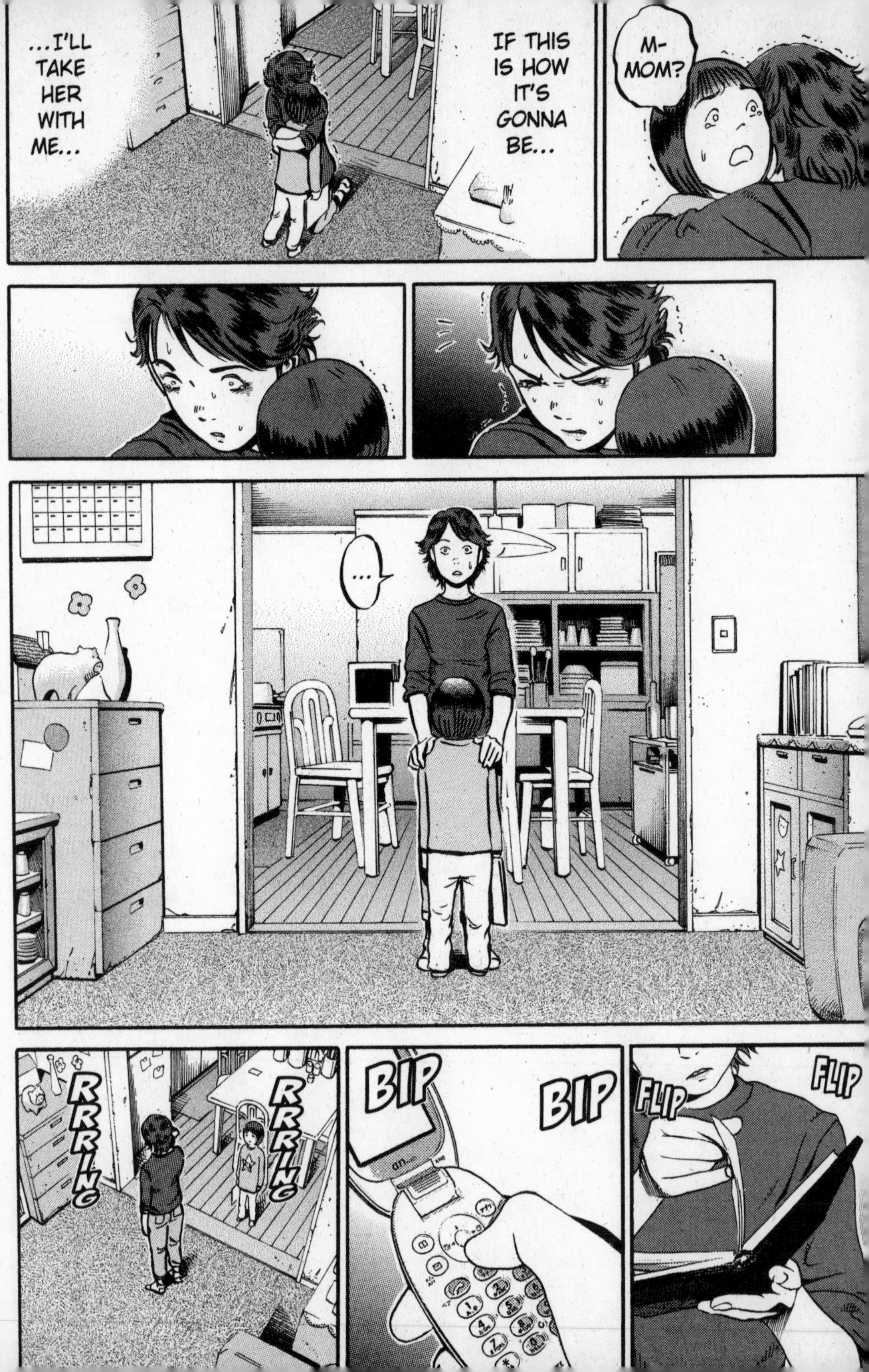

M-MOM?
IF THIS IS HOW IT'S GONNA BE...
...I'LL TAKE HER WITH ME...
...
FLIP
FLIP
BIP
BIP
RRRING
RRRING

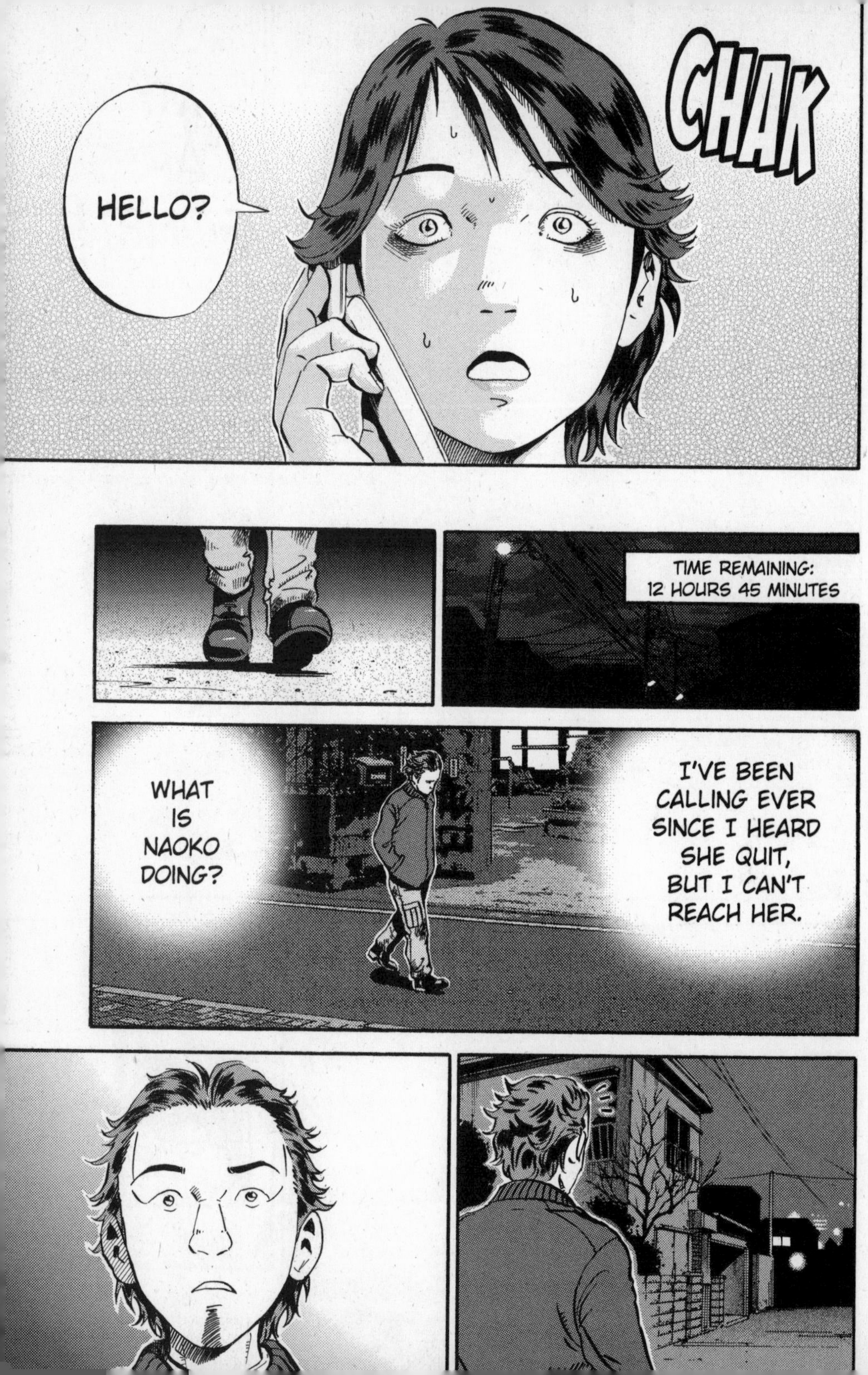
CHAK
HELLO?
TIME REMAINING:
12 HOURS 45 MINUTES
I'VE BEEN CALLING EVER SINCE I HEARD SHE QUIT, BUT I CAN'T REACH HER.
WHAT IS NAOKO DOING?

MY CAR'S GONE!!

THEIR SHOES ARE GONE...

FLIK

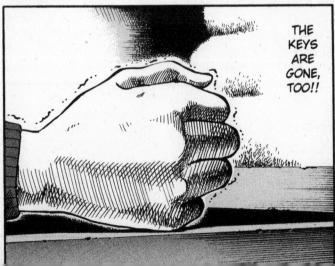

THE KEYS ARE GONE, TOO!!

RUSTLE RUSTLE

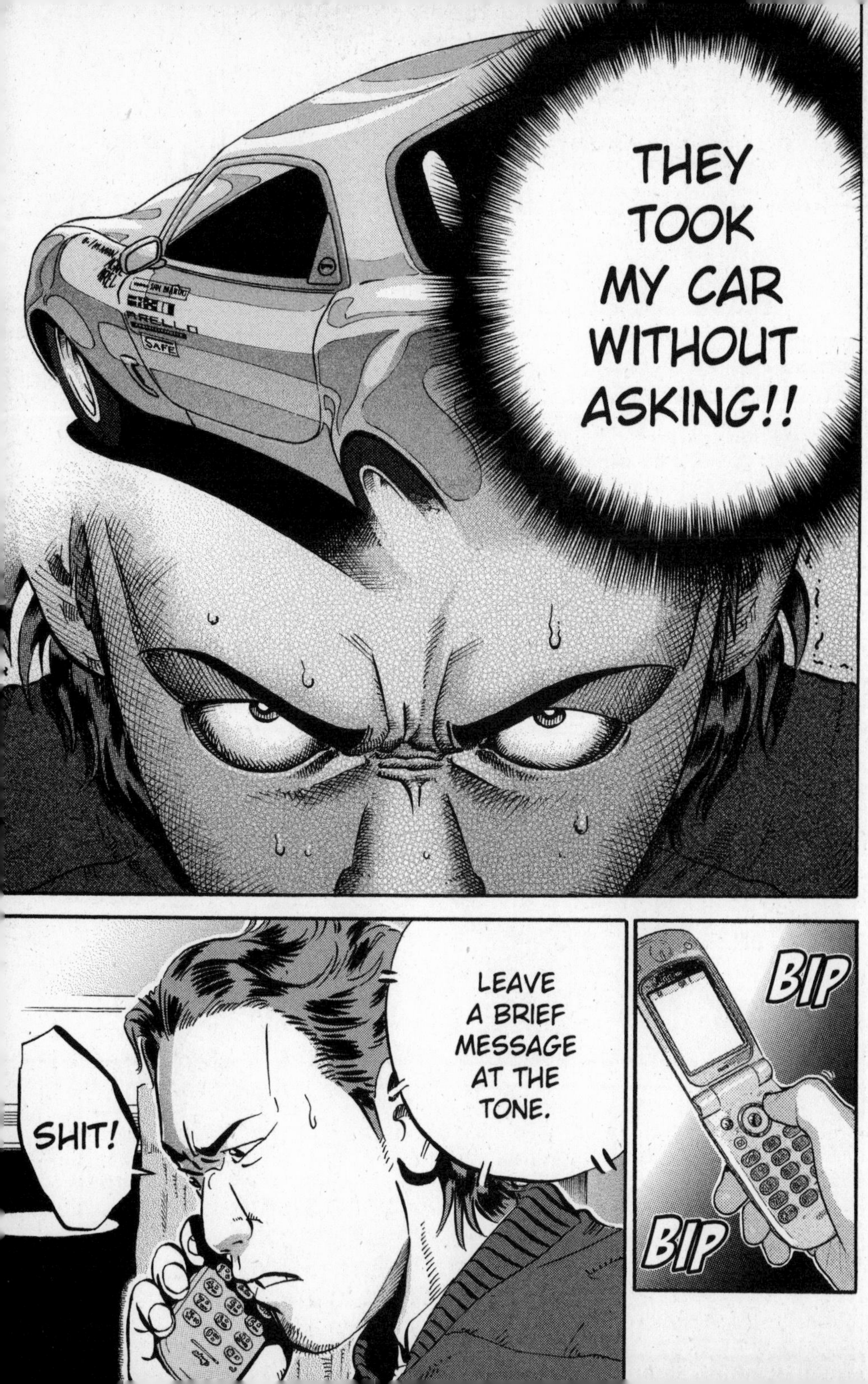
THEY TOOK MY CAR WITHOUT ASKING!!
BIP
BIP
LEAVE A BRIEF MESSAGE AT THE TONE.
SHIT!

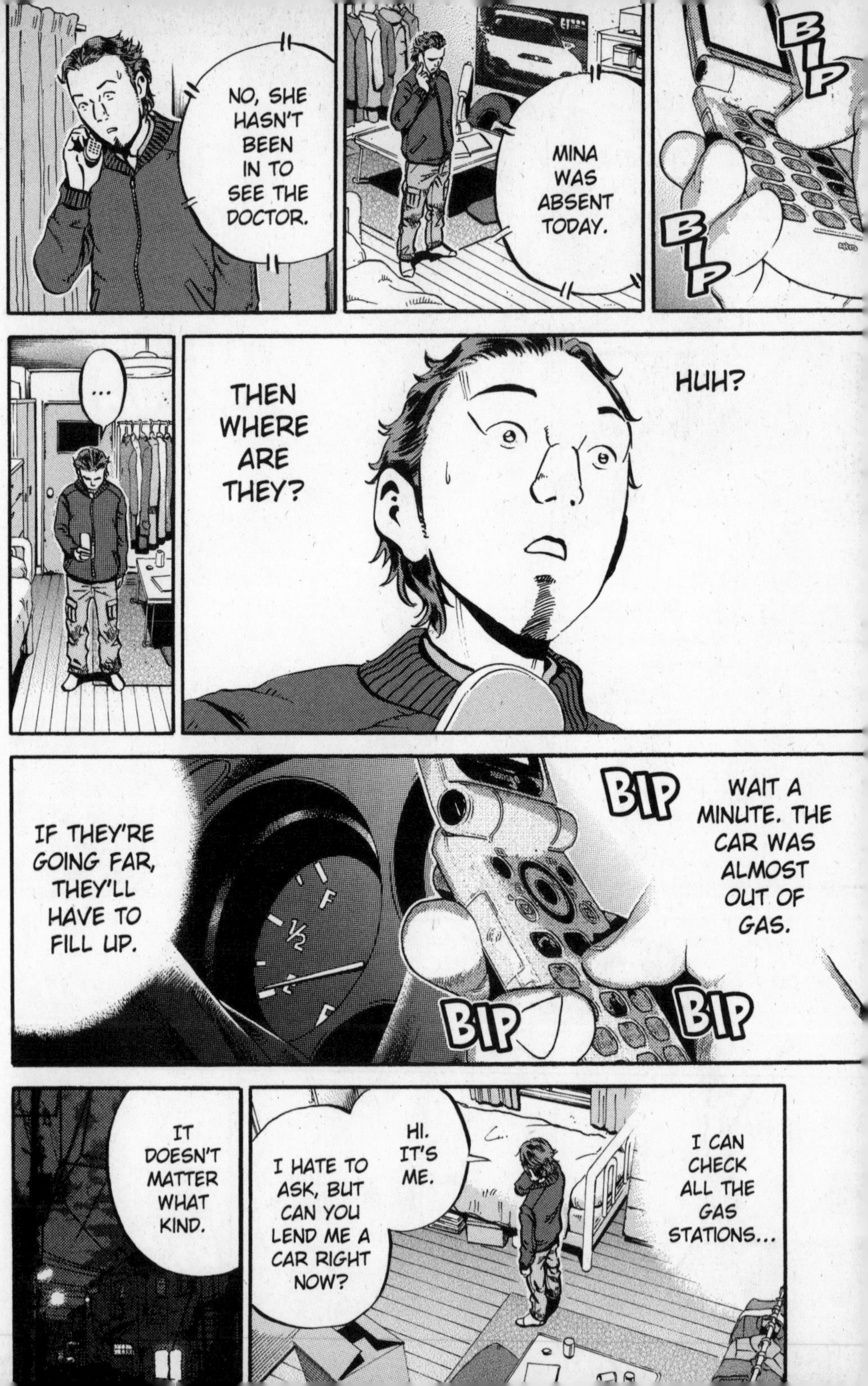
BIP
BIP
MINA WAS ABSENT TODAY.
NO, SHE HASN'T BEEN IN TO SEE THE DOCTOR.
HUH?
THEN WHERE ARE THEY?
...
BIP
WAIT A MINUTE. THE CAR WAS ALMOST OUT OF GAS.
IF THEY'RE GOING FAR, THEY'LL HAVE TO FILL UP.
BIP
BIP
I CAN CHECK ALL THE GAS STATIONS...
HI. IT'S ME.
I HATE TO ASK, BUT CAN YOU LEND ME A CAR RIGHT NOW?
IT DOESN'T MATTER WHAT KIND.

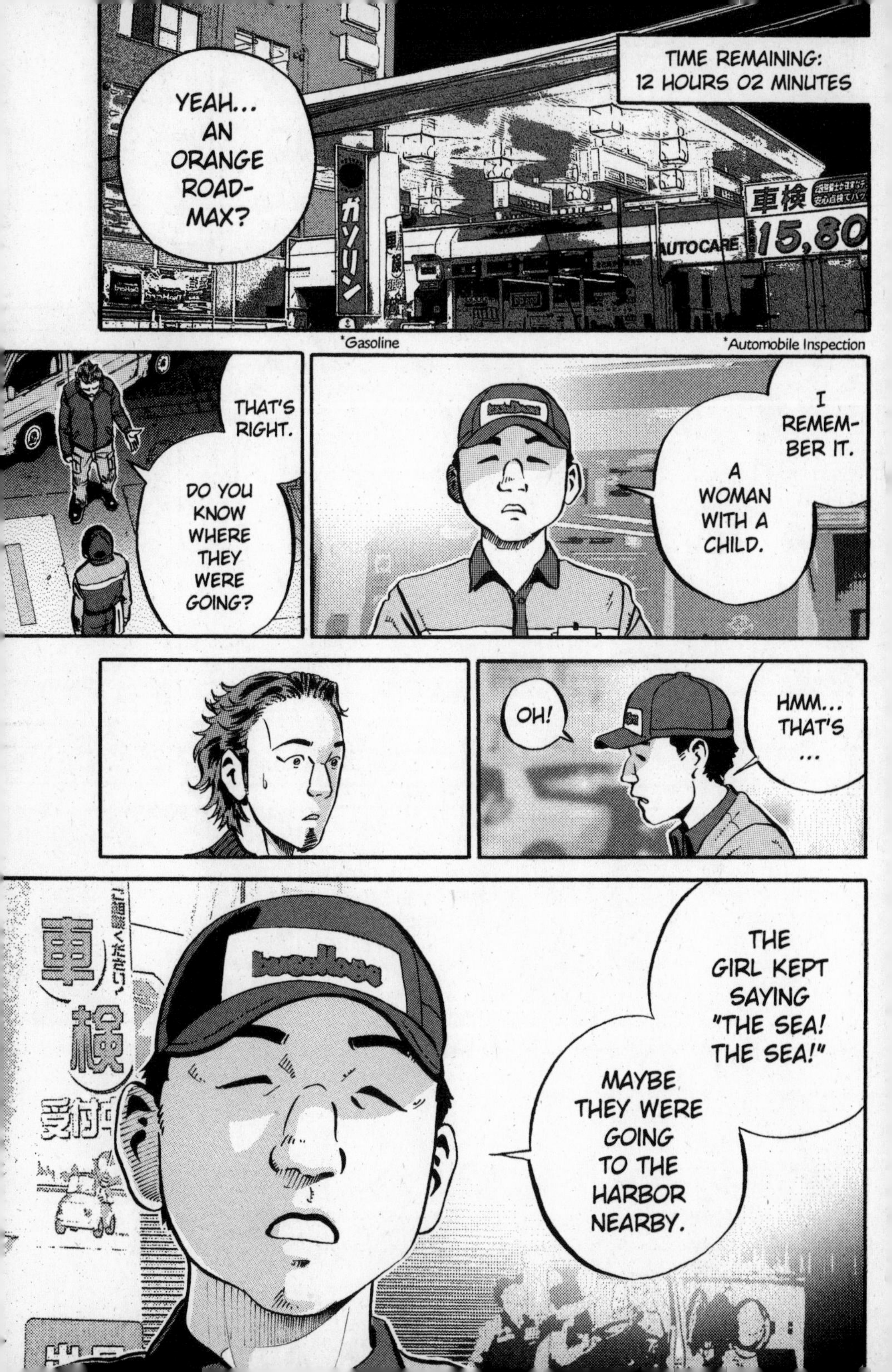
TIME REMAINING: 12 HOURS 02 MINUTES
YEAH... AN ORANGE ROAD-MAX?
ガソリン
車検
15,80
AUTO CARE
I REMEMBER IT.
A WOMAN WITH A CHILD.
THAT'S RIGHT.
DO YOU KNOW WHERE THEY WERE GOING?
HMM... THAT'S ...
OH!
THE GIRL KEPT SAYING "THE SEA! THE SEA!"
MAYBE THEY WERE GOING TO THE HARBOR NEARBY.
車検
受付中
*Gasoline
*Automobile Inspection

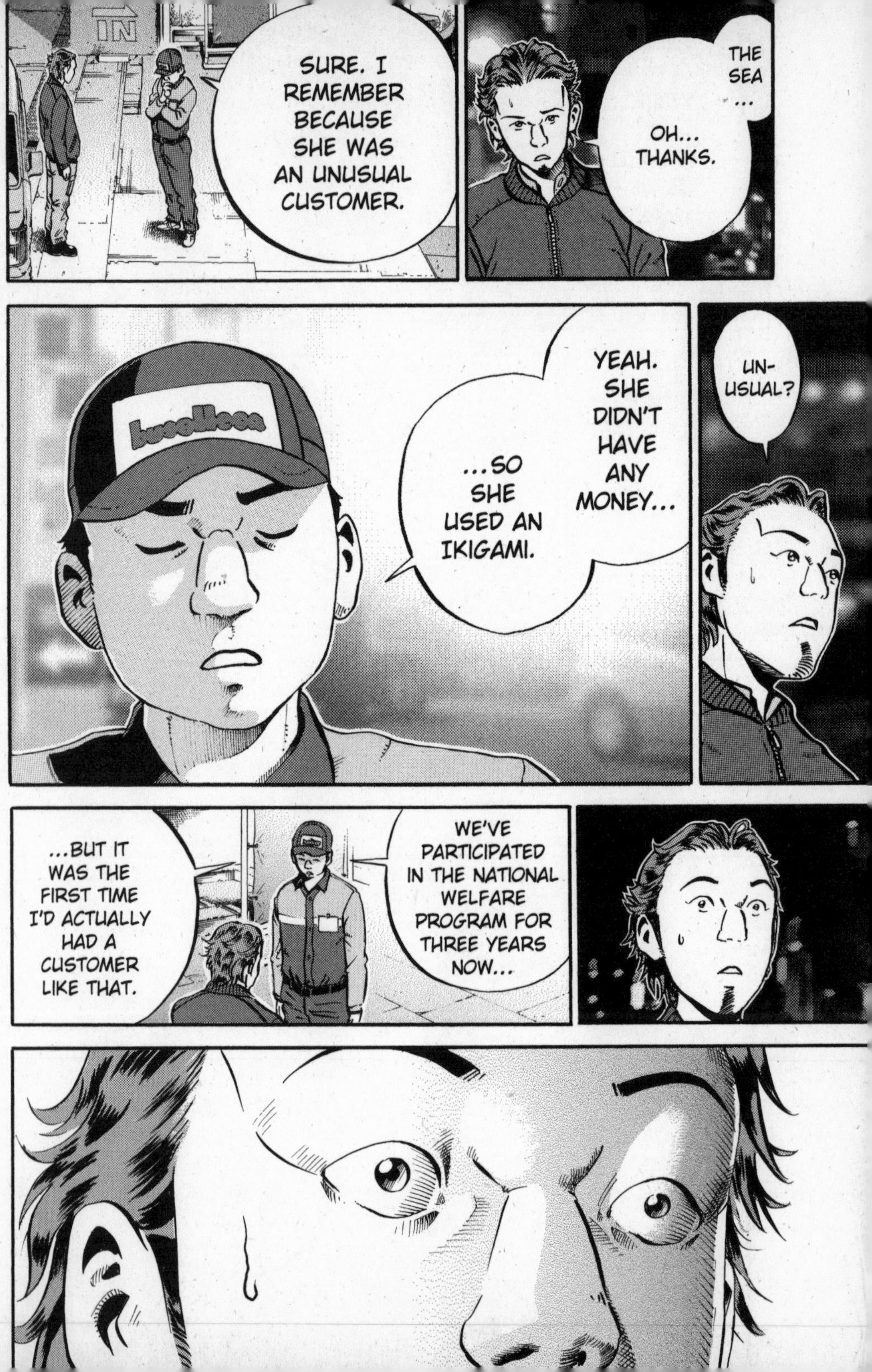
THE SEA...
OH... THANKS.
SURE. I REMEMBER BECAUSE SHE WAS AN UNUSUAL CUSTOMER.
UN-USUAL?
YEAH. SHE DIDN'T HAVE ANY MONEY...
...SO SHE USED AN IKIGAMI.
WE'VE PARTICIPATED IN THE NATIONAL WELFARE PROGRAM FOR THREE YEARS NOW...
...BUT IT WAS THE FIRST TIME I'D ACTUALLY HAD A CUSTOMER LIKE THAT.

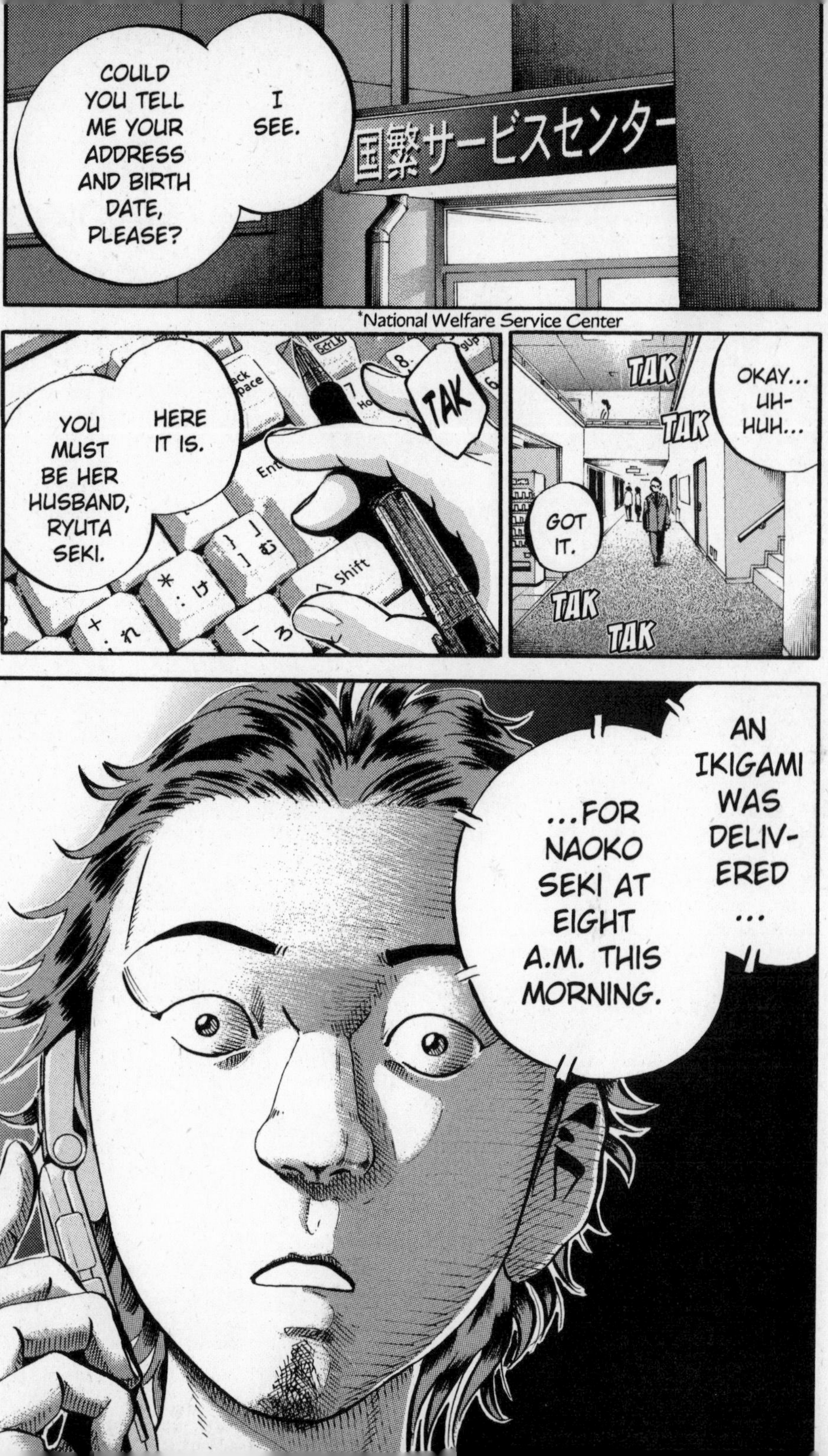
国繁サービスセンター
I SEE.
COULD YOU TELL ME YOUR ADDRESS AND BIRTH DATE, PLEASE?
OKAY... UH-HUH...
TAK
TAK
GOT IT.
TAK
TAK
HERE IT IS.
YOU MUST BE HER HUSBAND, RYUTA SEKI.
TAK
AN IKIGAMI WAS DELIVERED...
...FOR NAOKO SEKI AT EIGHT A.M. THIS MORNING.

*National Welfare Service Center

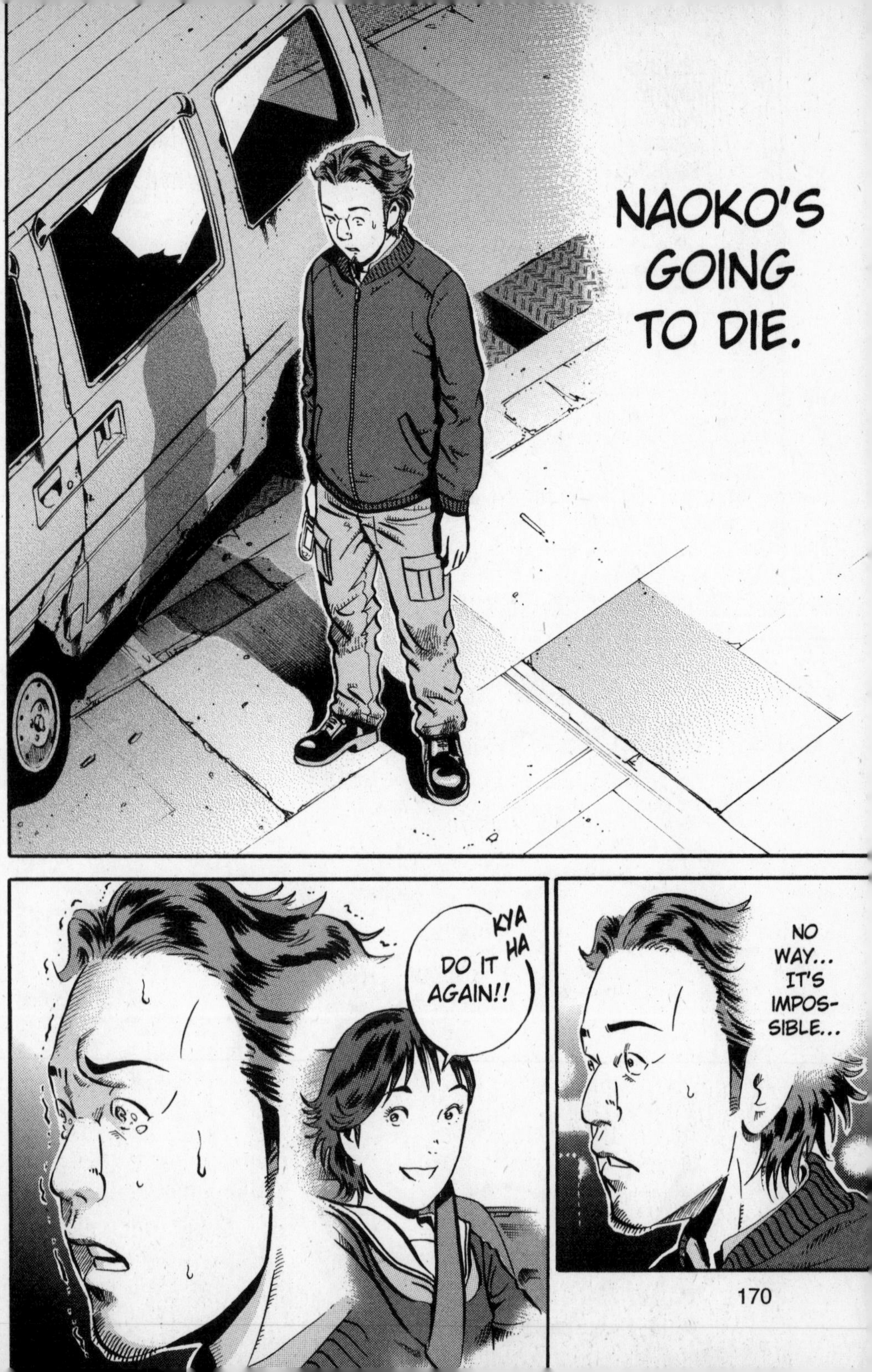
NAOKO'S GOING TO DIE.
NO WAY... IT'S IMPOS-SIBLE...
KYA HA
DO IT AGAIN!!

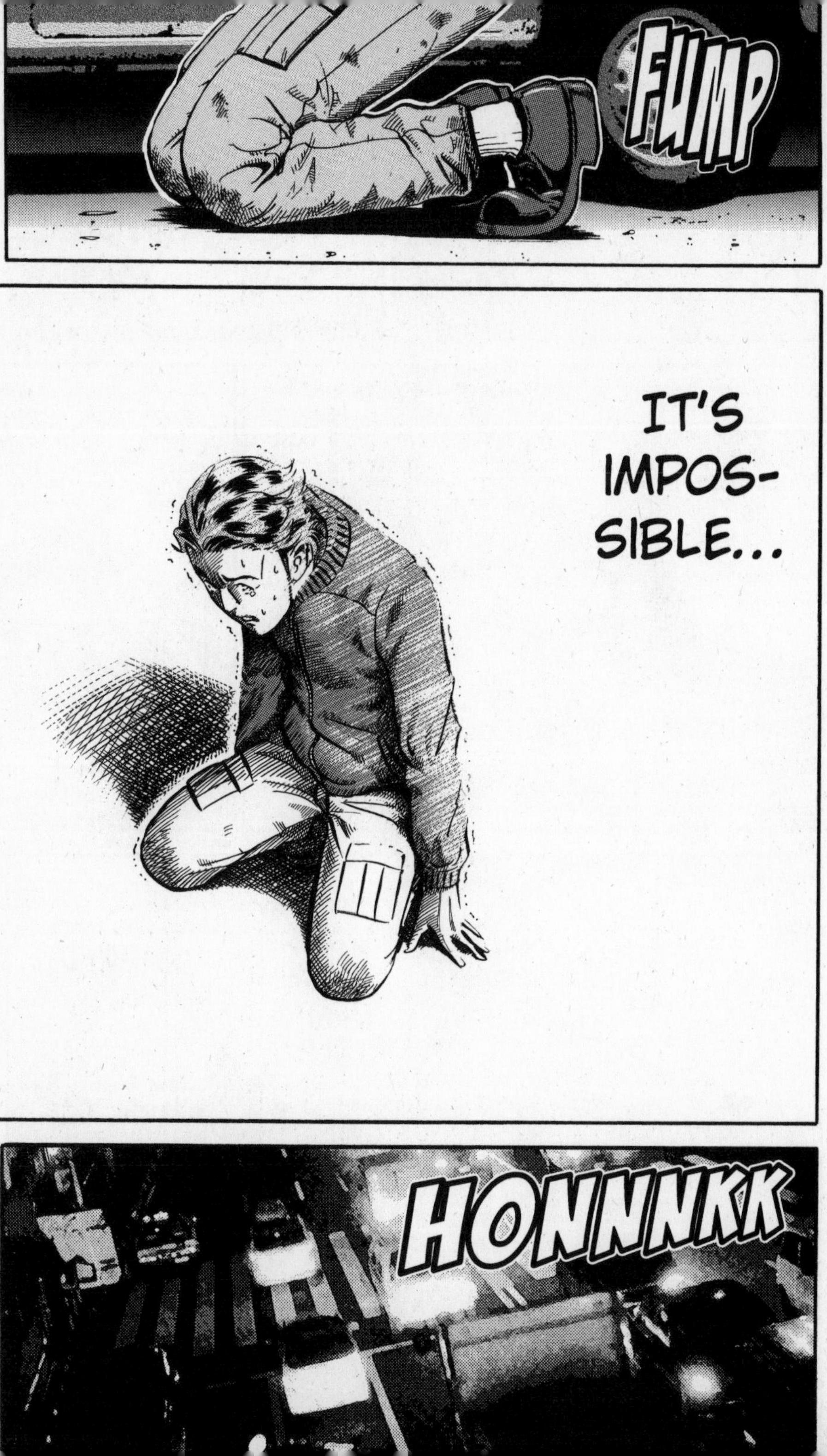
FUMP
IT'S IMPOSSIBLE...
HONNNKK

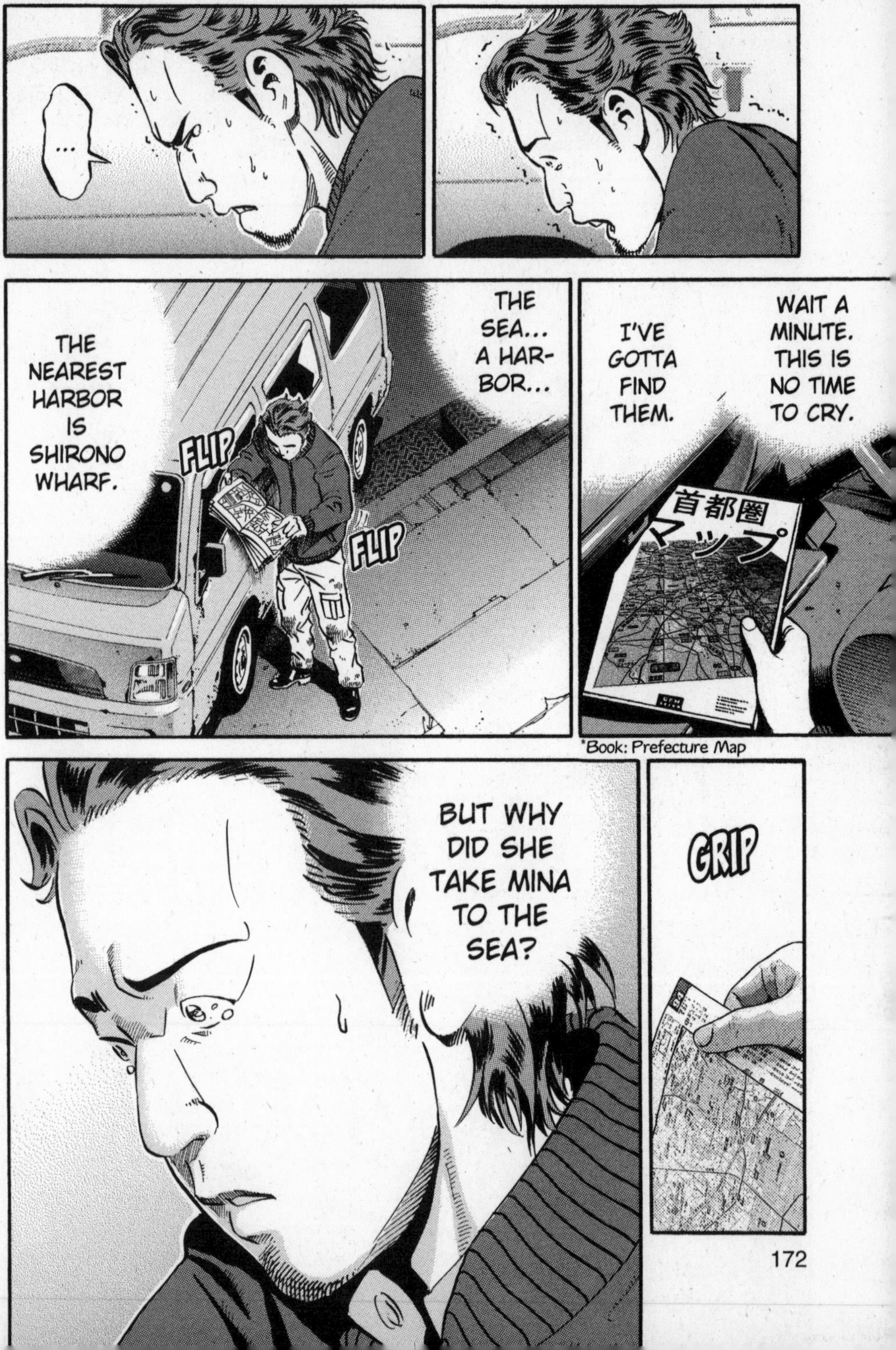
...
WAIT A MINUTE. THIS IS NO TIME TO CRY.
I'VE GOTTA FIND THEM.
首都圏マップ
THE SEA... A HARBOR...
THE NEAREST HARBOR IS SHIRONO WHARF.
FLIP
FLIP
GRIP
BUT WHY DID SHE TAKE MINA TO THE SEA?

*Book: Prefecture Map

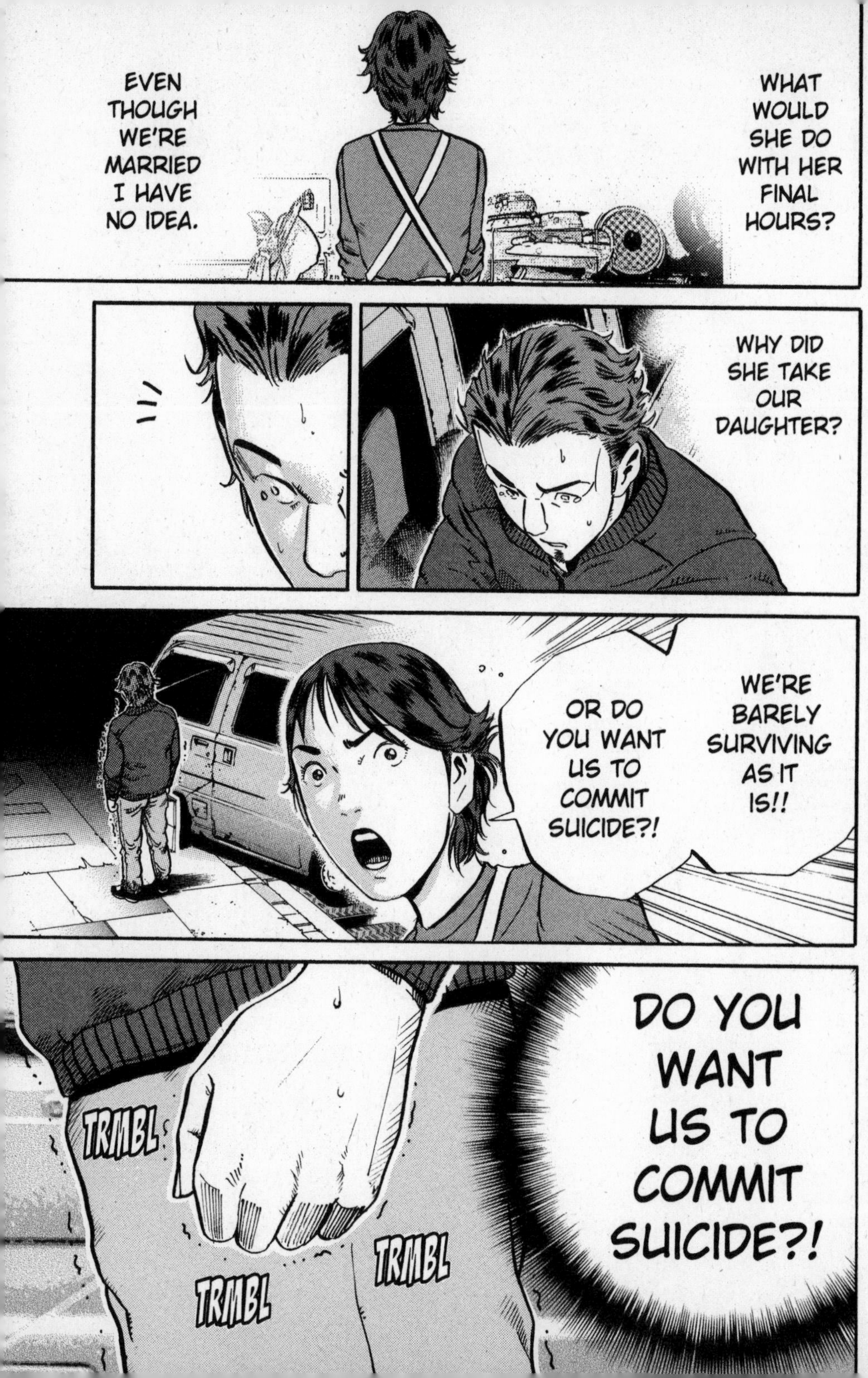
WHAT WOULD SHE DO WITH HER FINAL HOURS?
EVEN THOUGH WE'RE MARRIED I HAVE NO IDEA.
WHY DID SHE TAKE OUR DAUGHTER?
WE'RE BARELY SURVIVING AS IT IS!!
OR DO YOU WANT US TO COMMIT SUICIDE?!
DO YOU WANT US TO COMMIT SUICIDE?!
TRMBL
TRMBL
TRMBL

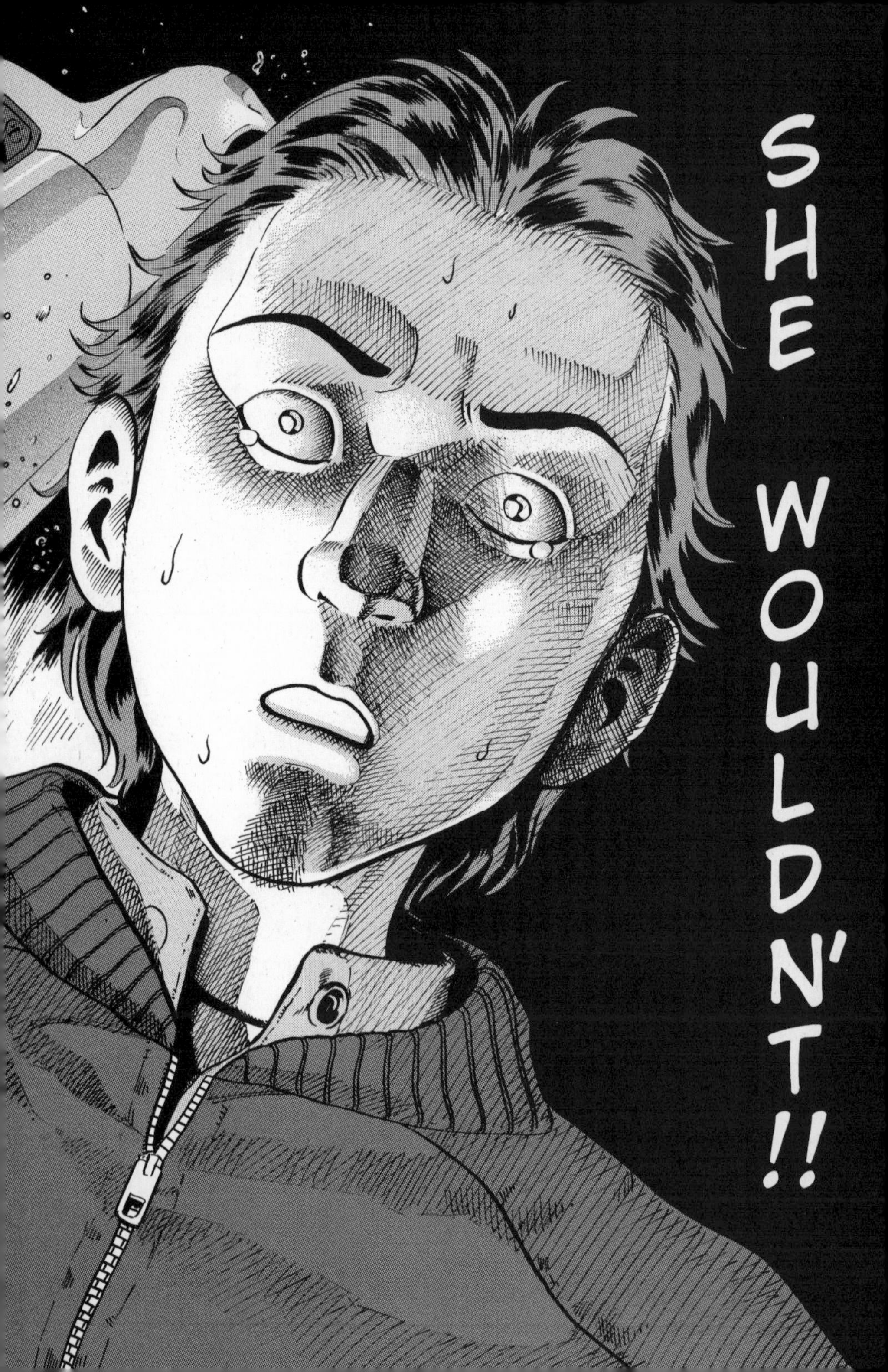
SHE WOULDN'T!!

**TIME REMAINING:
11 HOURS 45 MINUTES**

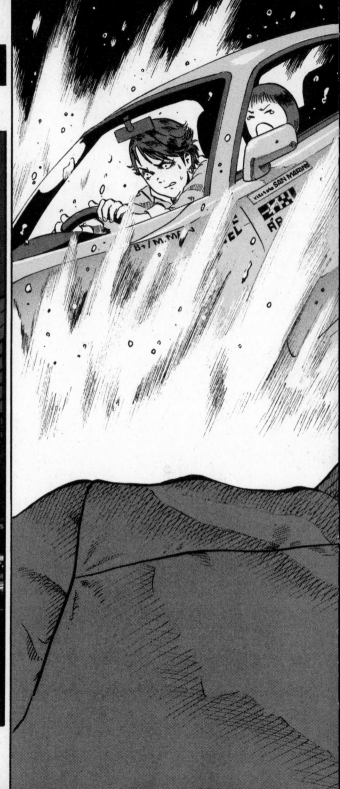

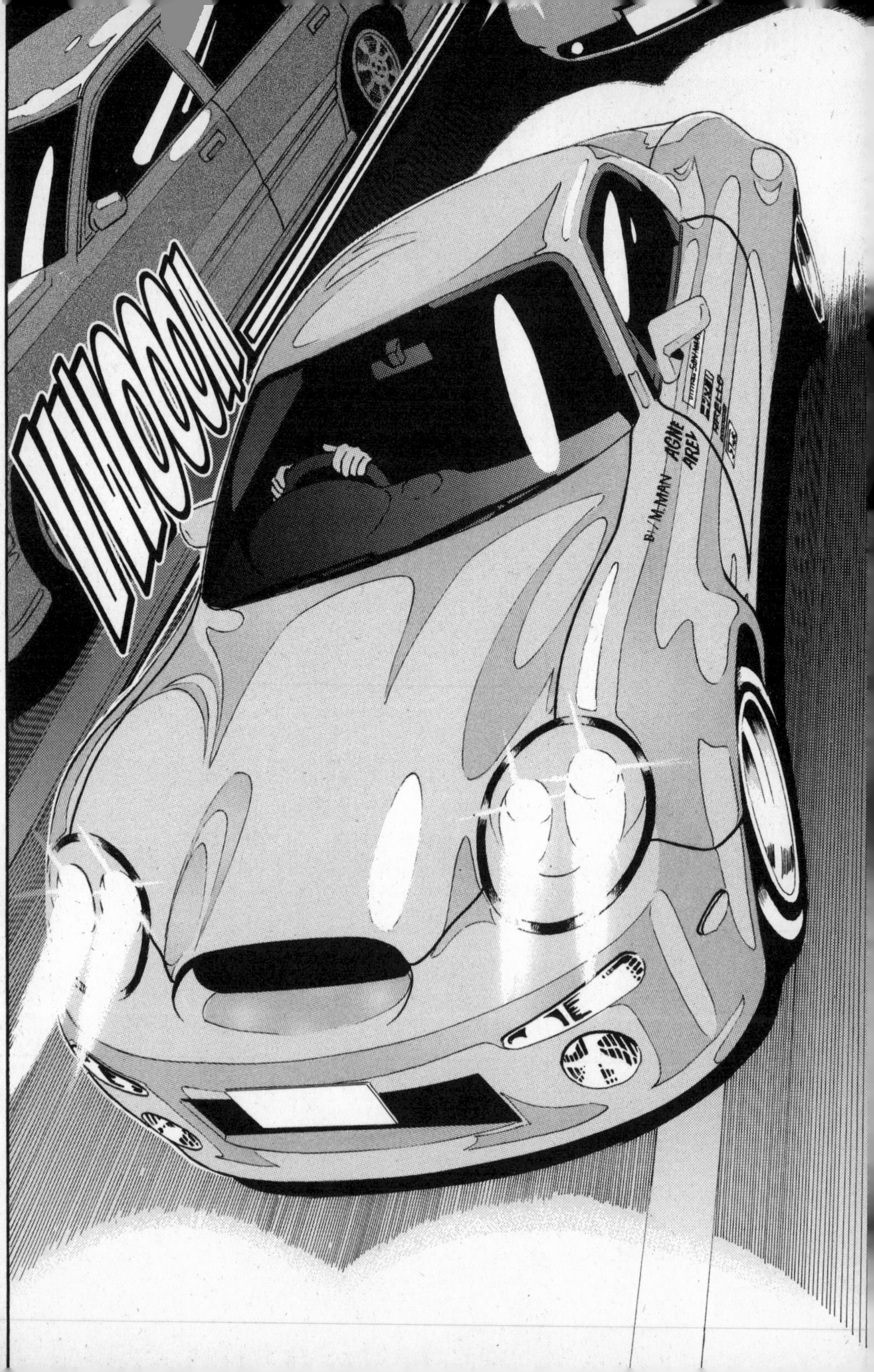
VROOOM!
B-/M.MAN
AGNE
AREV

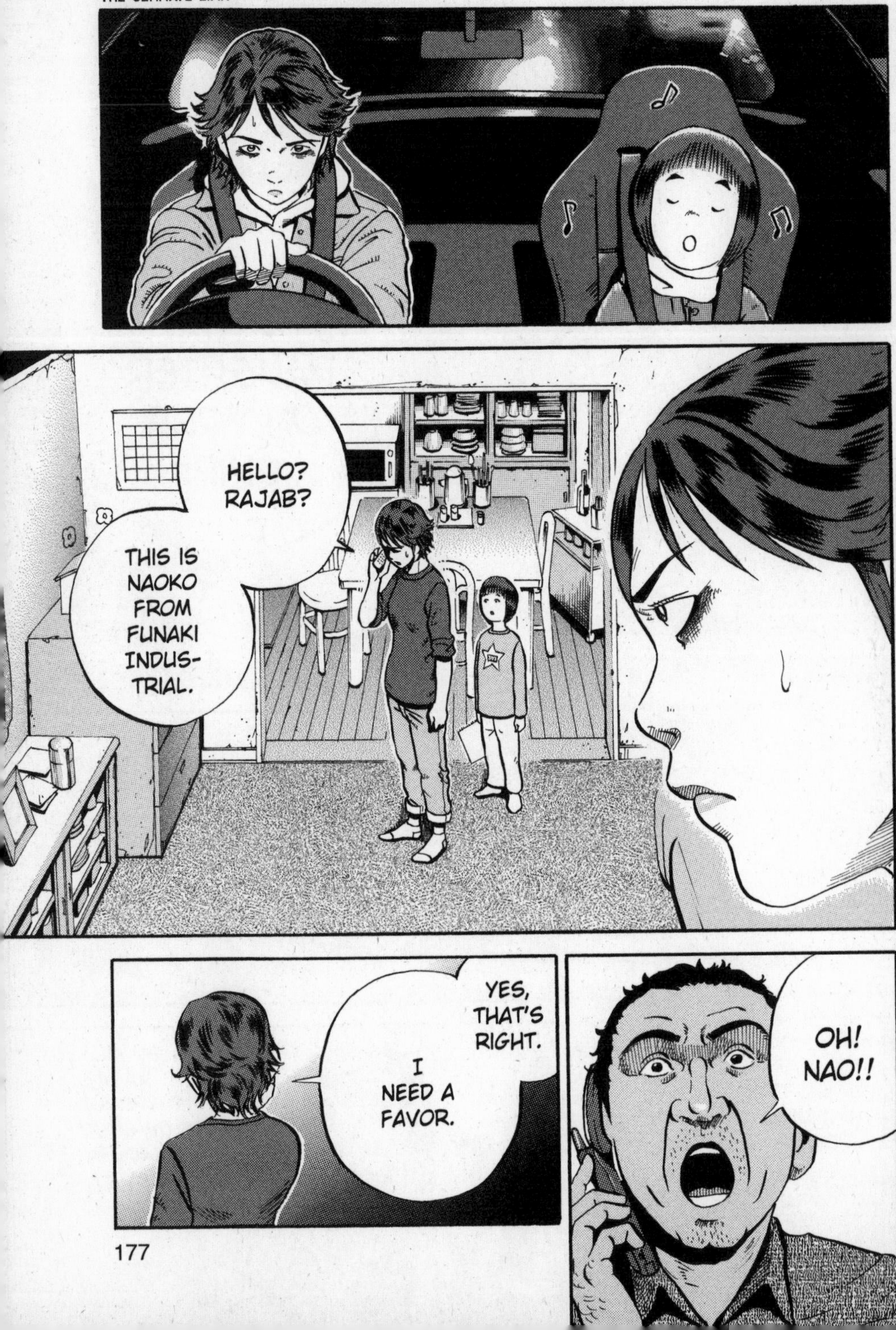
HELLO? RAJAB?
THIS IS NAOKO FROM FUNAKI INDUS-TRIAL.
OH! NAO!!
YES, THAT'S RIGHT.
I NEED A FAVOR.

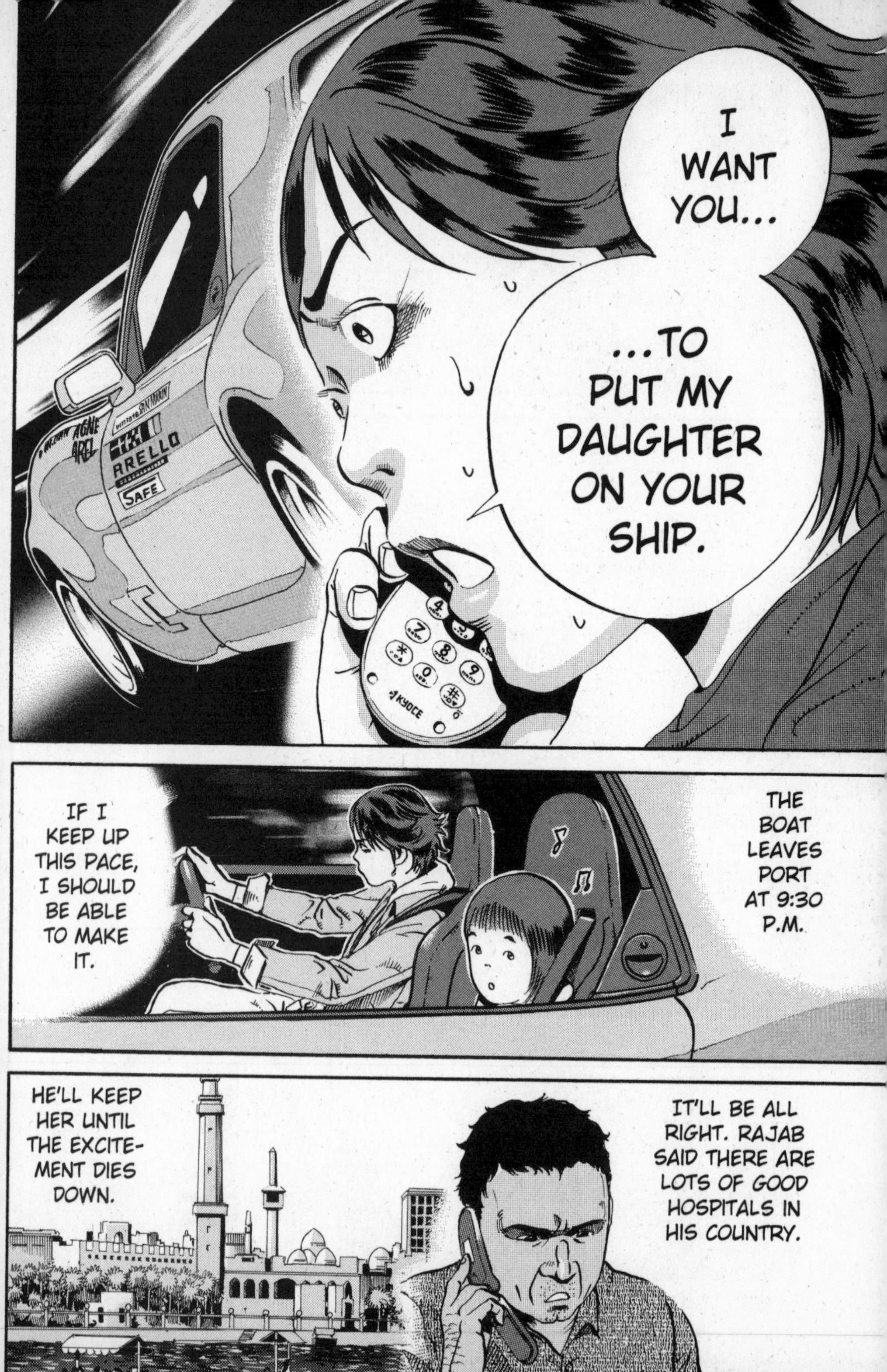
I WANT YOU...
...TO PUT MY DAUGHTER ON YOUR SHIP.
THE BOAT LEAVES PORT AT 9:30 P.M.
IF I KEEP UP THIS PACE, I SHOULD BE ABLE TO MAKE IT.
IT'LL BE ALL RIGHT. RAJAB SAID THERE ARE LOTS OF GOOD HOSPITALS IN HIS COUNTRY.
HE'LL KEEP HER UNTIL THE EXCITE-MENT DIES DOWN.

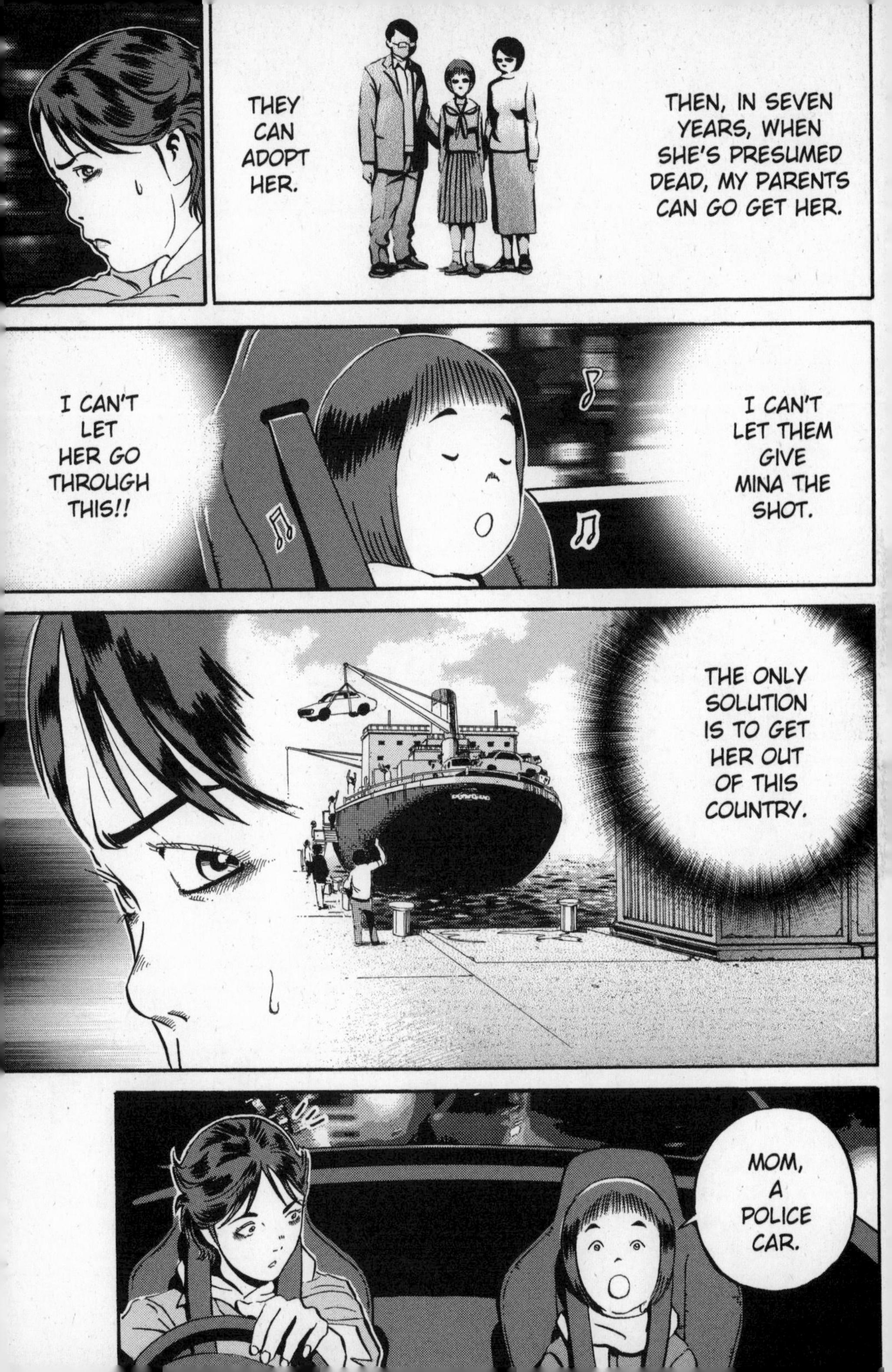

THEN, IN SEVEN YEARS, WHEN SHE'S PRESUMED DEAD, MY PARENTS CAN GO GET HER.
THEY CAN ADOPT HER.
I CAN'T LET THEM GIVE MINA THE SHOT.
I CAN'T LET HER GO THROUGH THIS!!
THE ONLY SOLUTION IS TO GET HER OUT OF THIS COUNTRY.
MOM, A POLICE CAR.

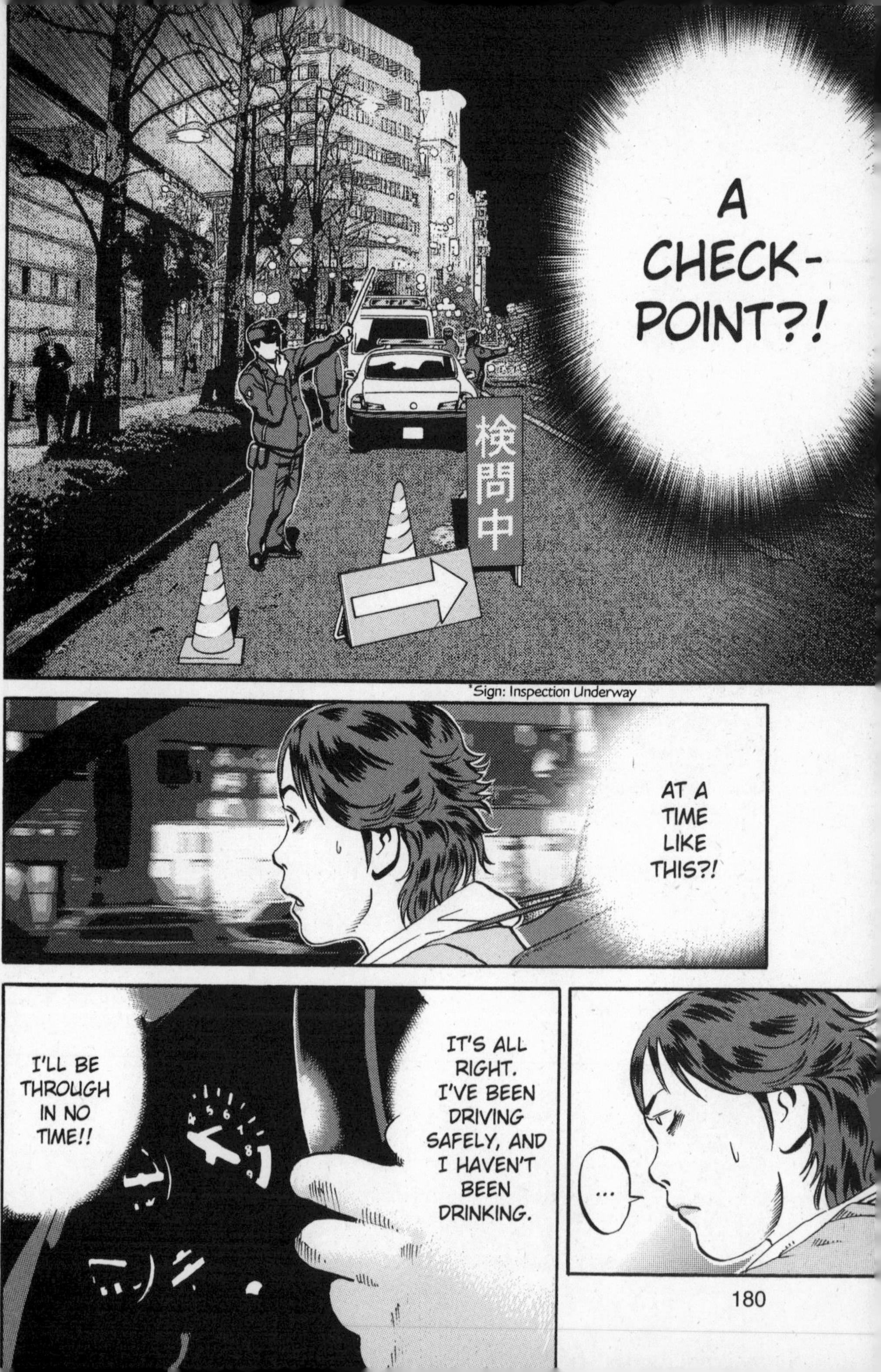
A CHECK-POINT?!
検問中
*Sign: Inspection Underway
AT A TIME LIKE THIS?!
...
IT'S ALL RIGHT. I'VE BEEN DRIVING SAFELY, AND I HAVEN'T BEEN DRINKING.
I'LL BE THROUGH IN NO TIME!!

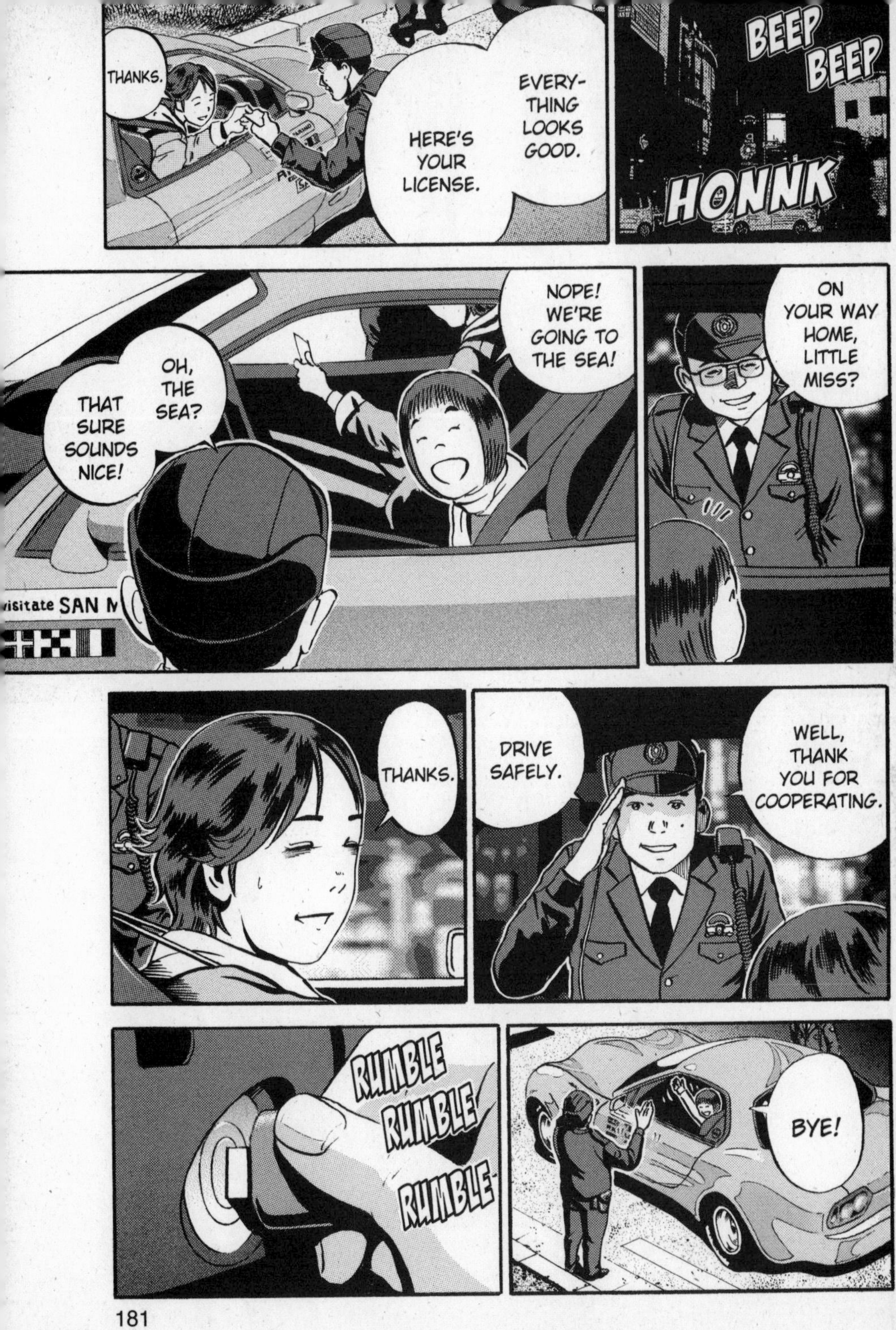
BEEP
BEEP
HONNK
EVERY-THING LOOKS GOOD.
HERE'S YOUR LICENSE.
THANKS.
ON YOUR WAY HOME, LITTLE MISS?
NOPE! WE'RE GOING TO THE SEA!
OH, THE SEA?
THAT SURE SOUNDS NICE!
WELL, THANK YOU FOR COOPERATING.
DRIVE SAFELY.
THANKS.
BYE!
RUMBLE
RUMBLE
RUMBLE

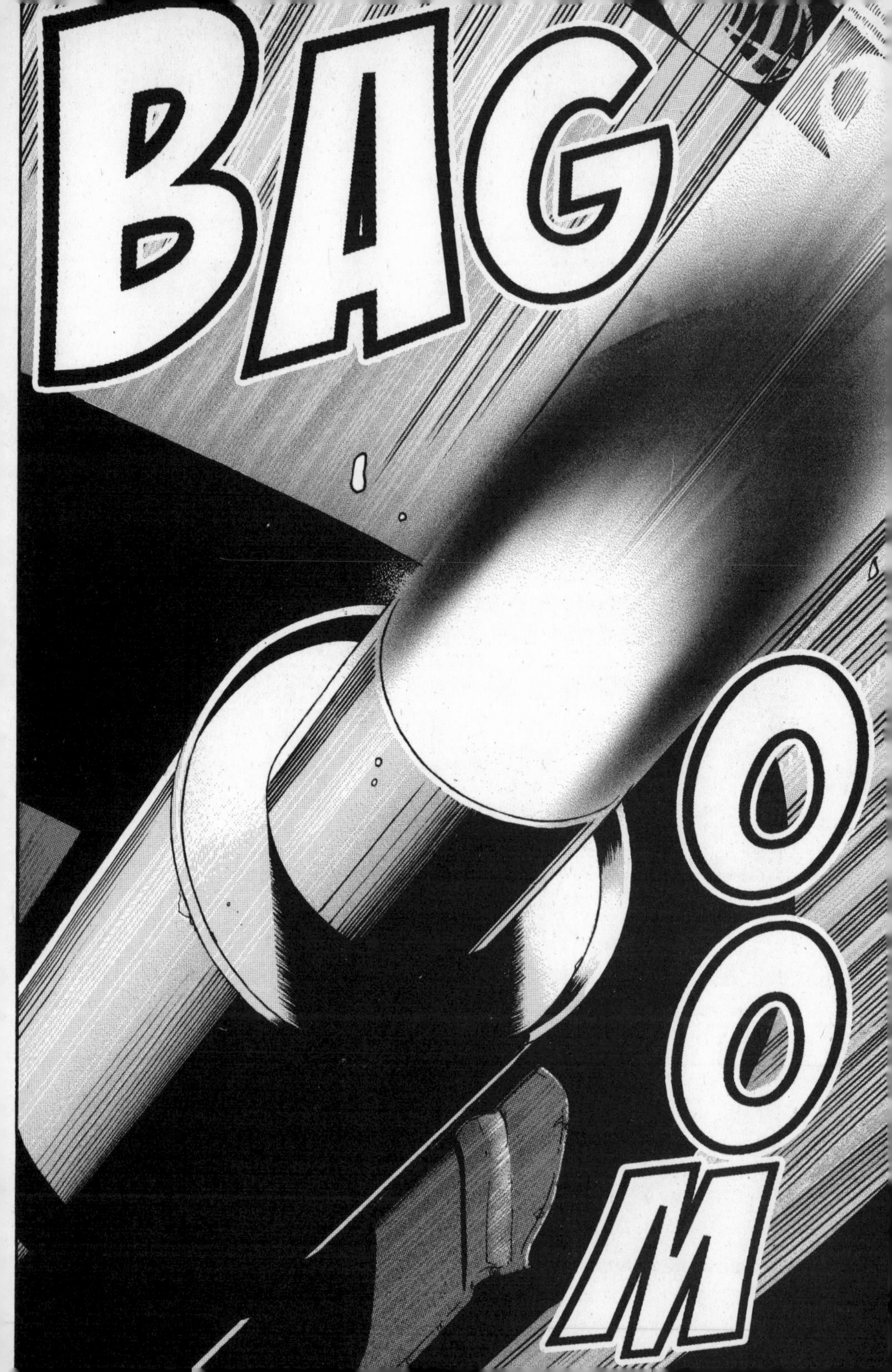
BAGOOM

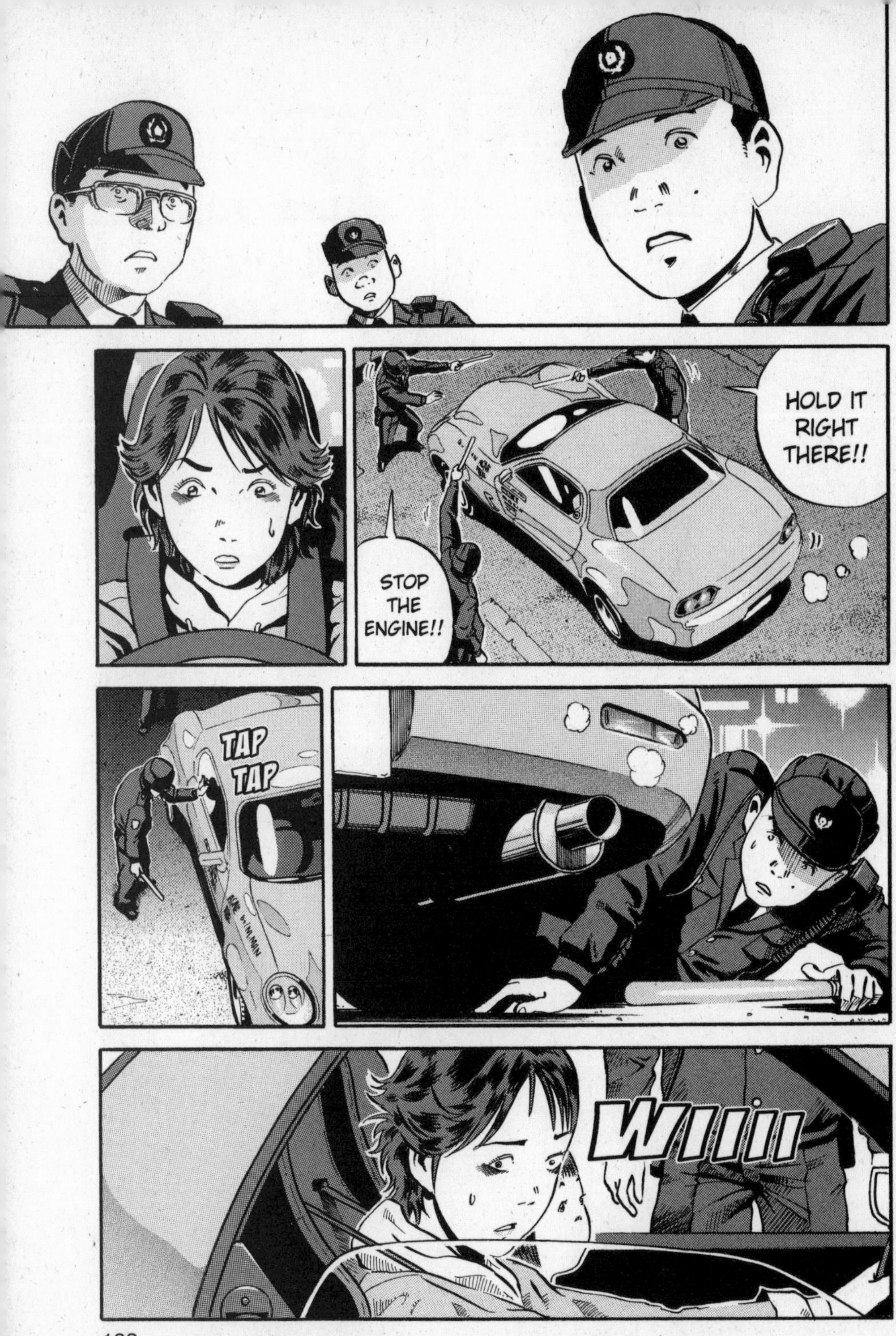
HOLD IT RIGHT THERE!!
STOP THE ENGINE!!
TAP TAP
WIIII

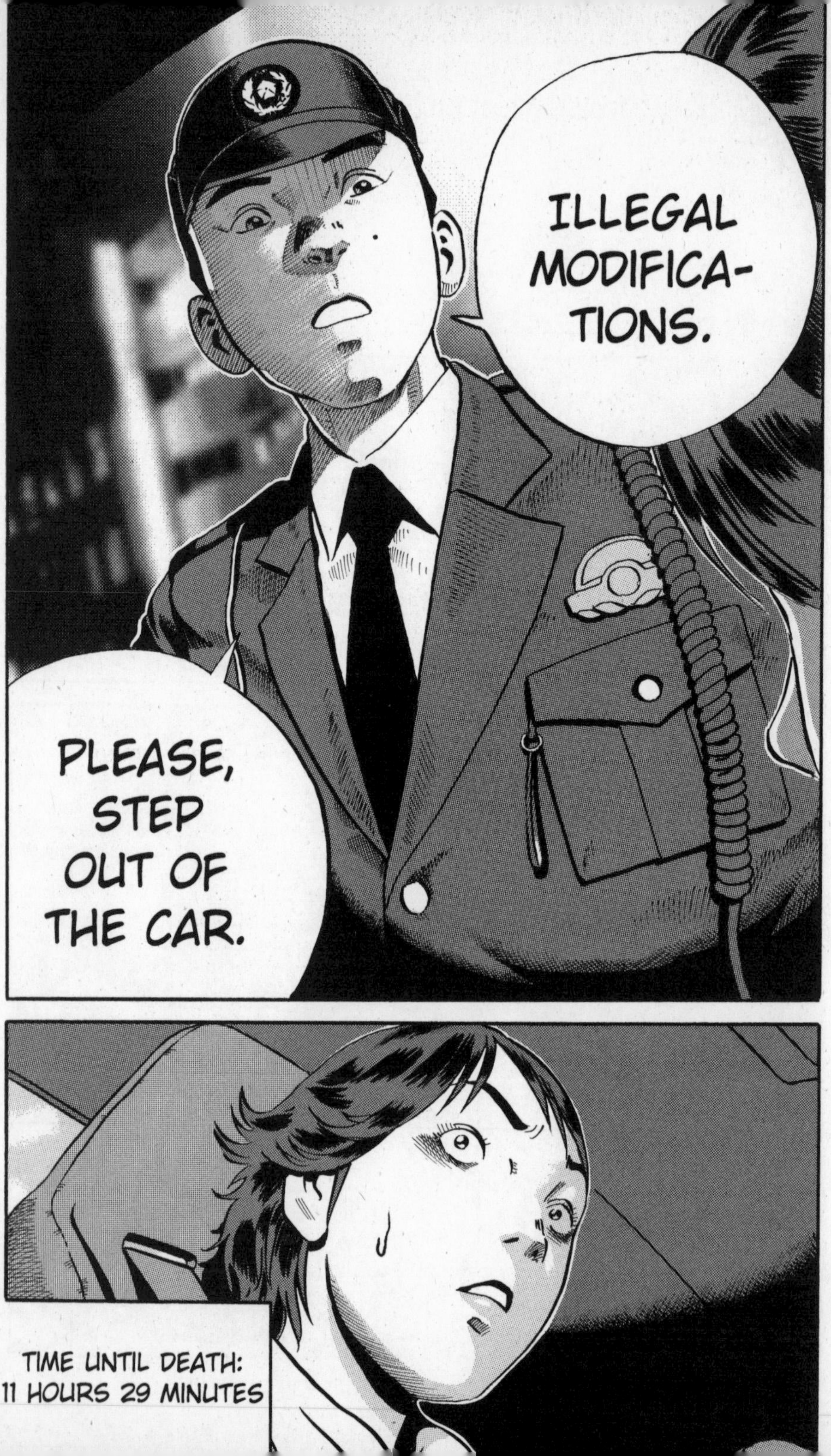
ILLEGAL MODIFICA-TIONS.
PLEASE, STEP OUT OF THE CAR.
TIME UNTIL DEATH: 11 HOURS 29 MINUTES

Episode 8 A Place of Peace Act3

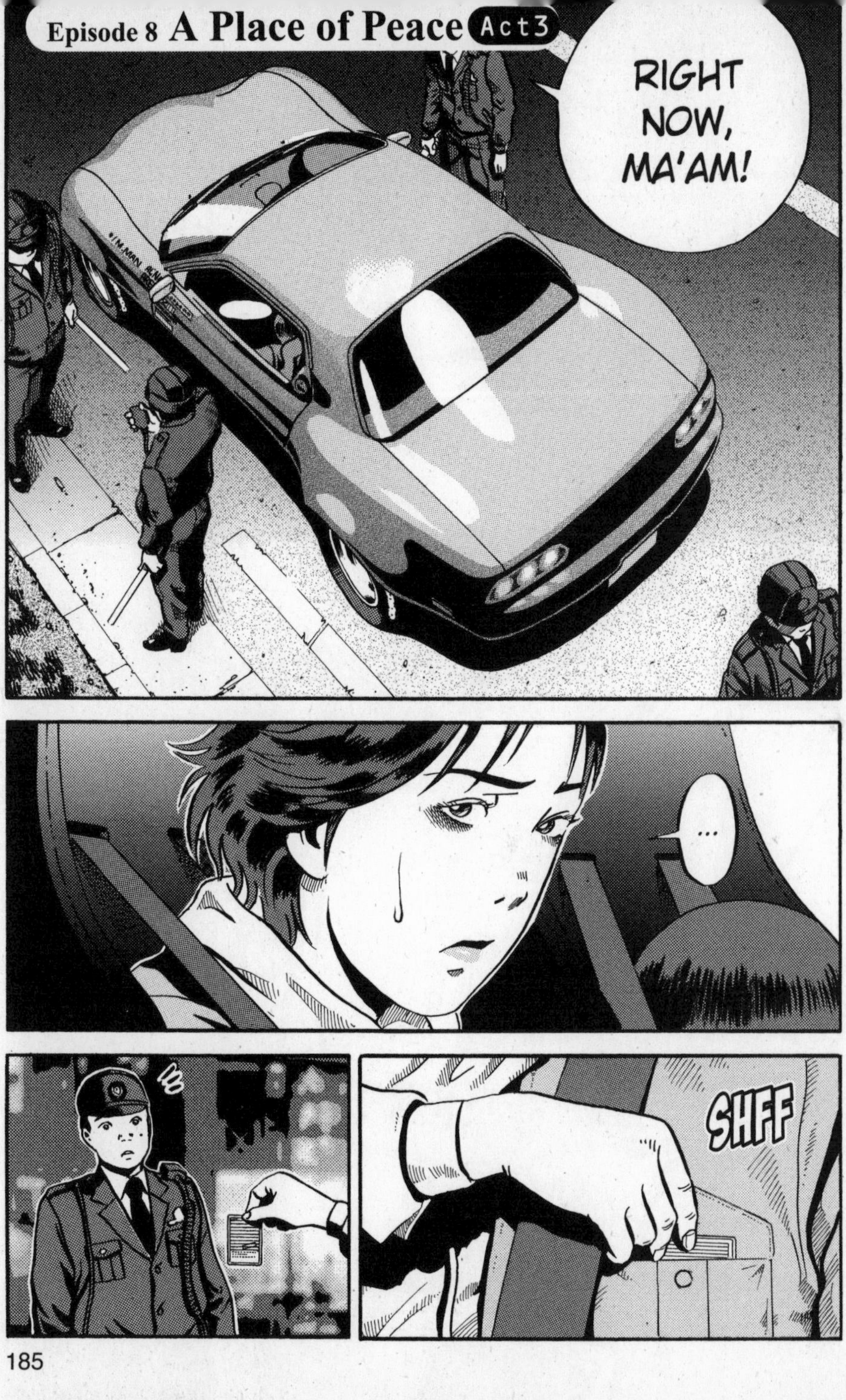
RIGHT NOW, MA'AM!
...
SHFF

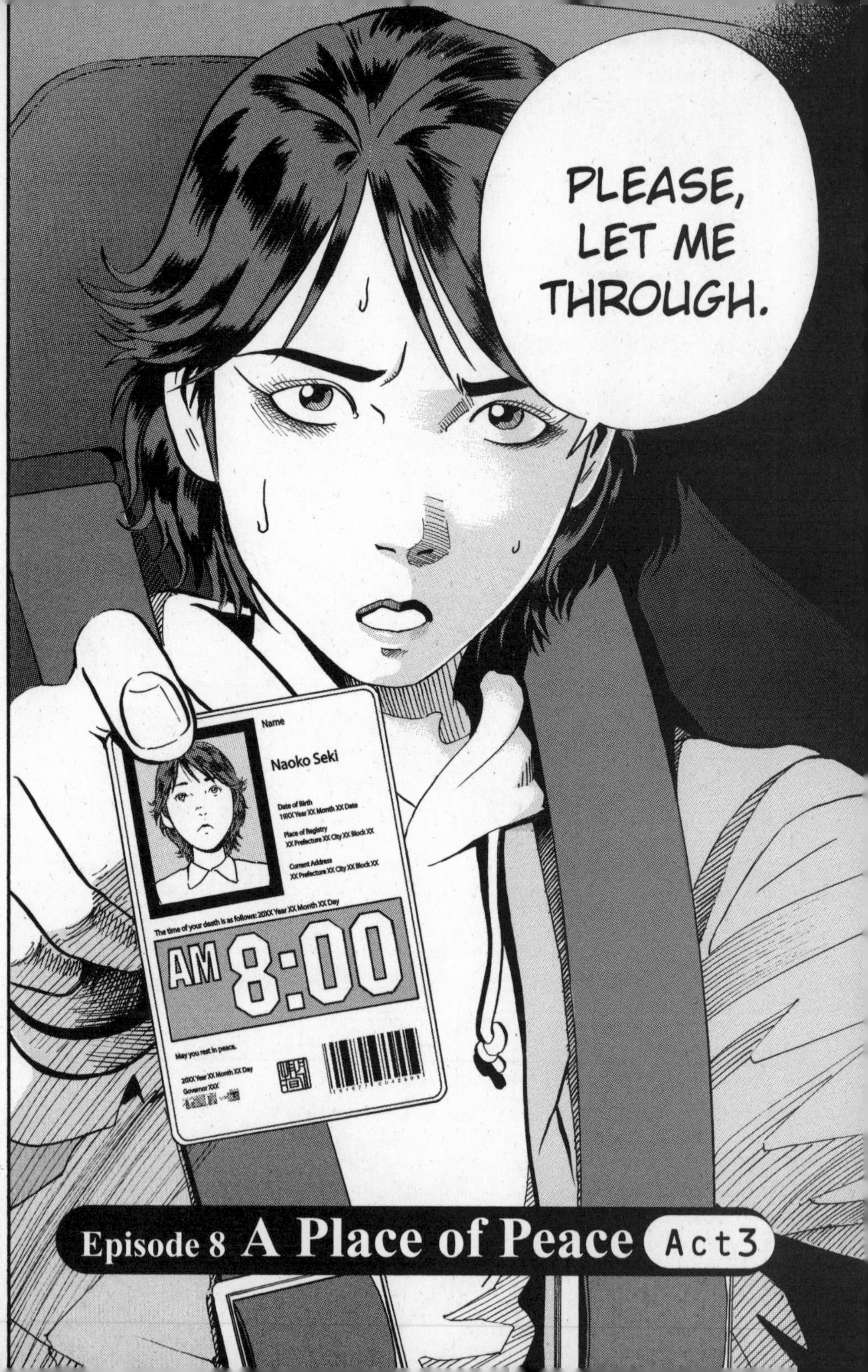
PLEASE, LET ME THROUGH.
Name
Naoko Seki
Date of Birth
19XX Year XX Month XX Date
Place of Registry
XX Prefecture XX City XX Block XX
Current Address
XX Prefecture XX City XX Block XX
The time of your death is as follows: 20XX Year XX Month XX Day
AM 8:00
May you rest in peace.
20XX Year XX Month XX Day
Governor XXX
Episode 8 A Place of Peace Act3

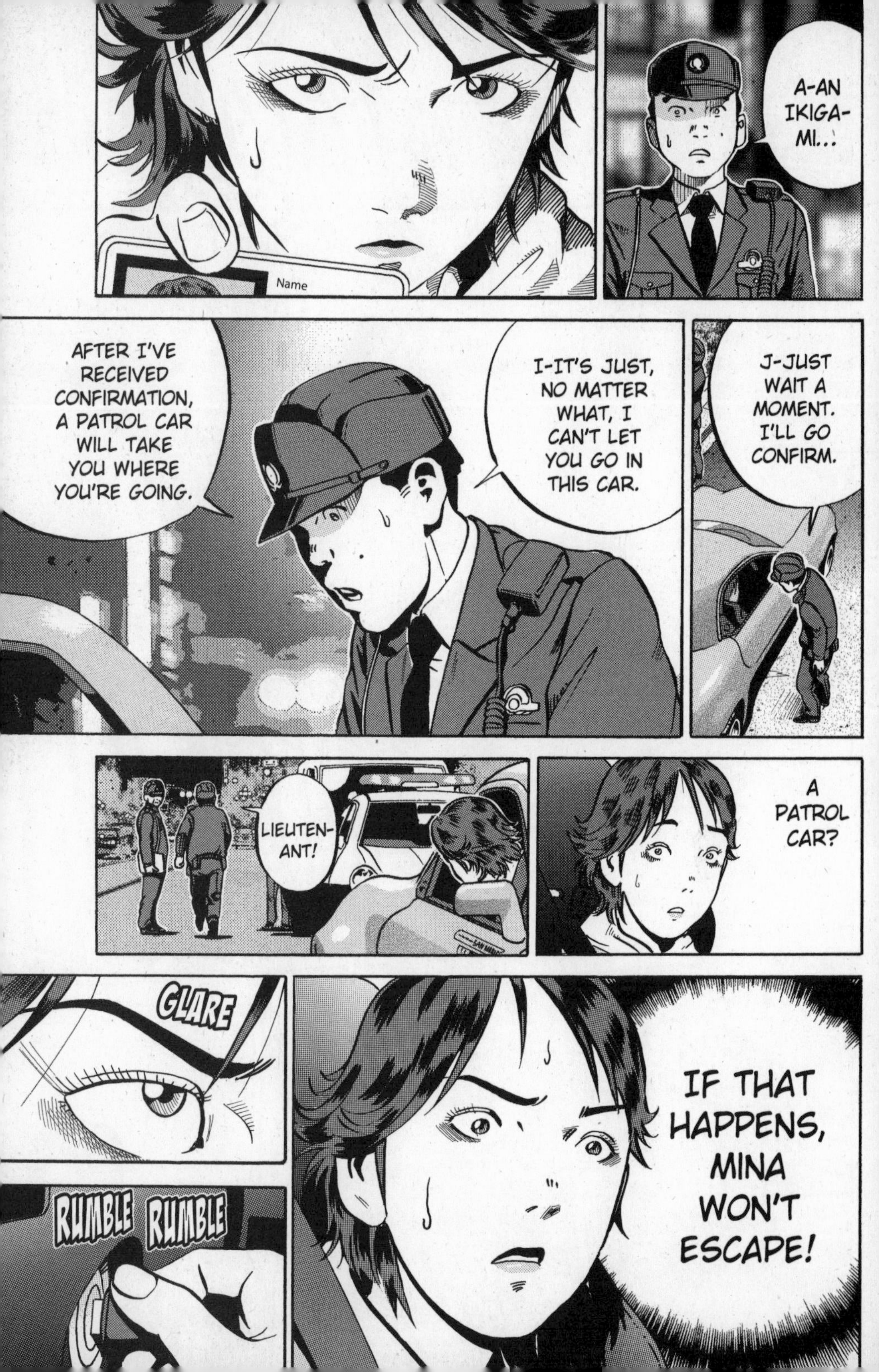
A-AN IKIGA-MI...
Name
J-JUST WAIT A MOMENT. I'LL GO CONFIRM.
I-IT'S JUST, NO MATTER WHAT, I CAN'T LET YOU GO IN THIS CAR.
AFTER I'VE RECEIVED CONFIRMATION, A PATROL CAR WILL TAKE YOU WHERE YOU'RE GOING.
A PATROL CAR?
LIEUTEN-ANT!
IF THAT HAPPENS, MINA WON'T ESCAPE!
GLARE
RUMBLE RUMBLE

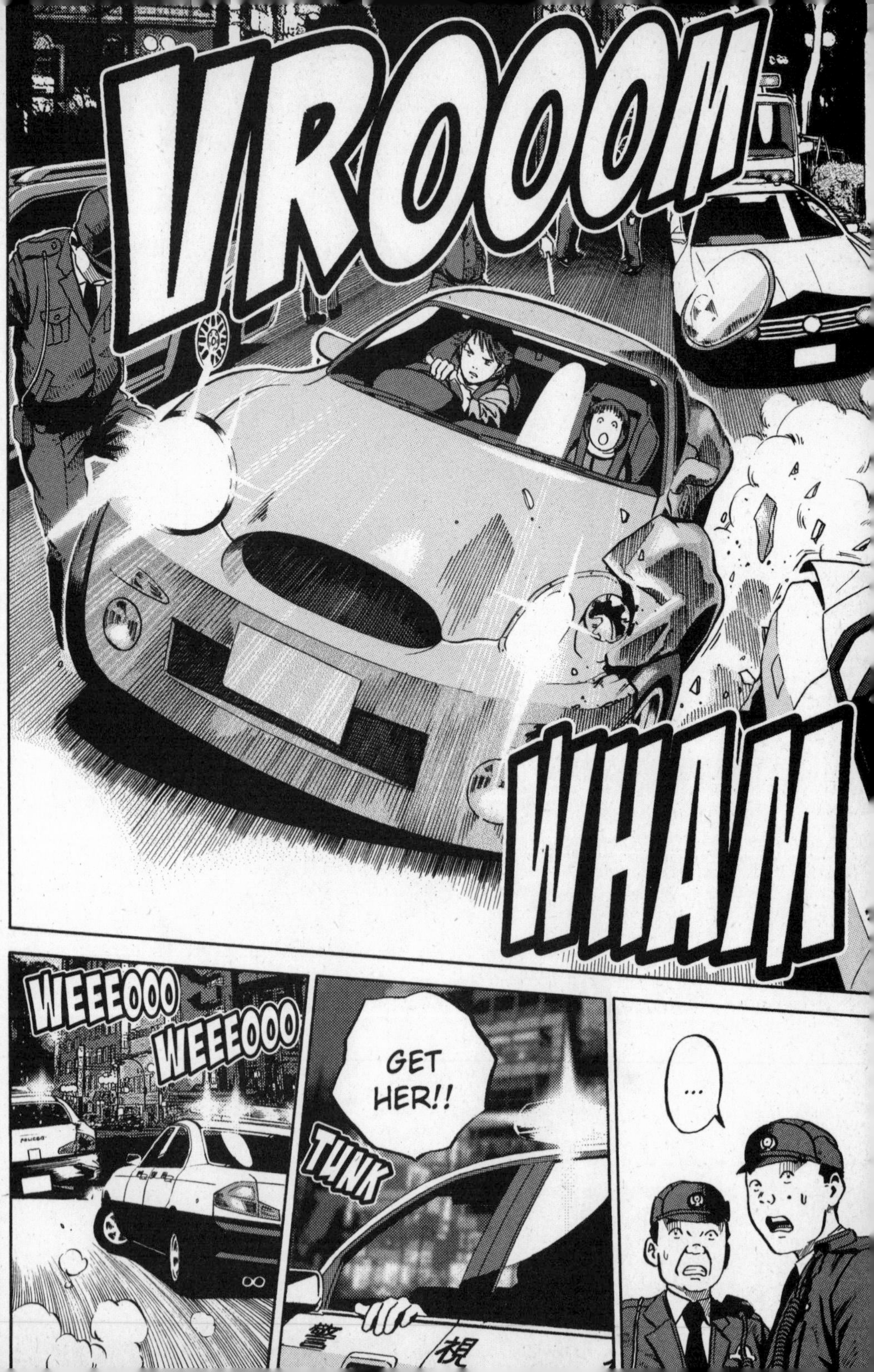
VROOOM
WHAM
...
GET HER!!
TUNK
警
視
WEEEOOO
WEEEOOO

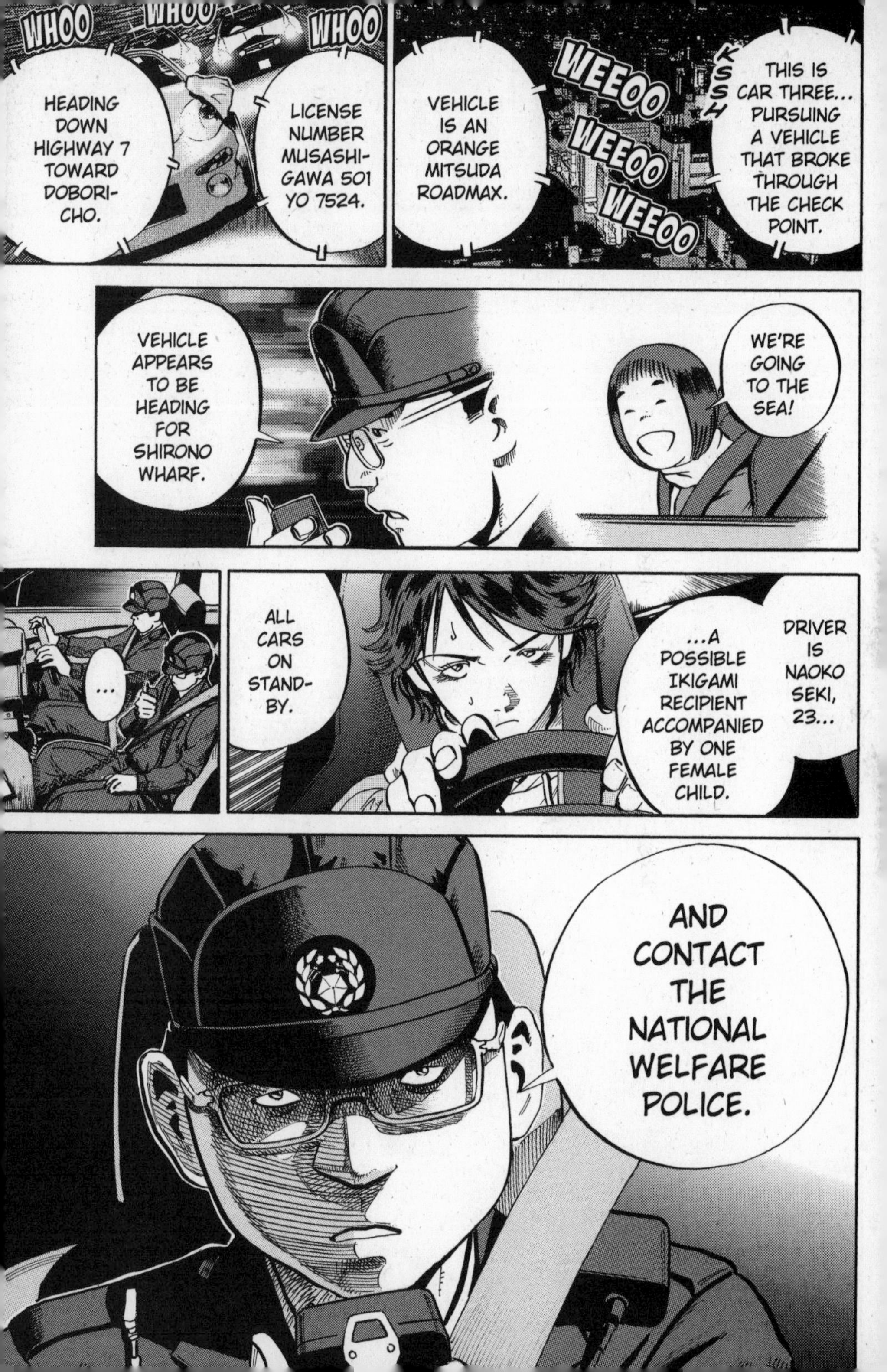
WEEOO
WEEOO
WEEOO
KSH
THIS IS CAR THREE... PURSUING A VEHICLE THAT BROKE THROUGH THE CHECK POINT.
VEHICLE IS AN ORANGE MITSUDA ROADMAX.
WHOO
WHOO
WHOO
LICENSE NUMBER MUSASHI-GAWA 501 YO 7524.
HEADING DOWN HIGHWAY 7 TOWARD DOBORI-CHO.
WE'RE GOING TO THE SEA!
VEHICLE APPEARS TO BE HEADING FOR SHIRONO WHARF.
DRIVER IS NAOKO SEKI, 23...
...A POSSIBLE IKIGAMI RECIPIENT ACCOMPANIED BY ONE FEMALE CHILD.
ALL CARS ON STAND-BY.
...
AND CONTACT THE NATIONAL WELFARE POLICE.

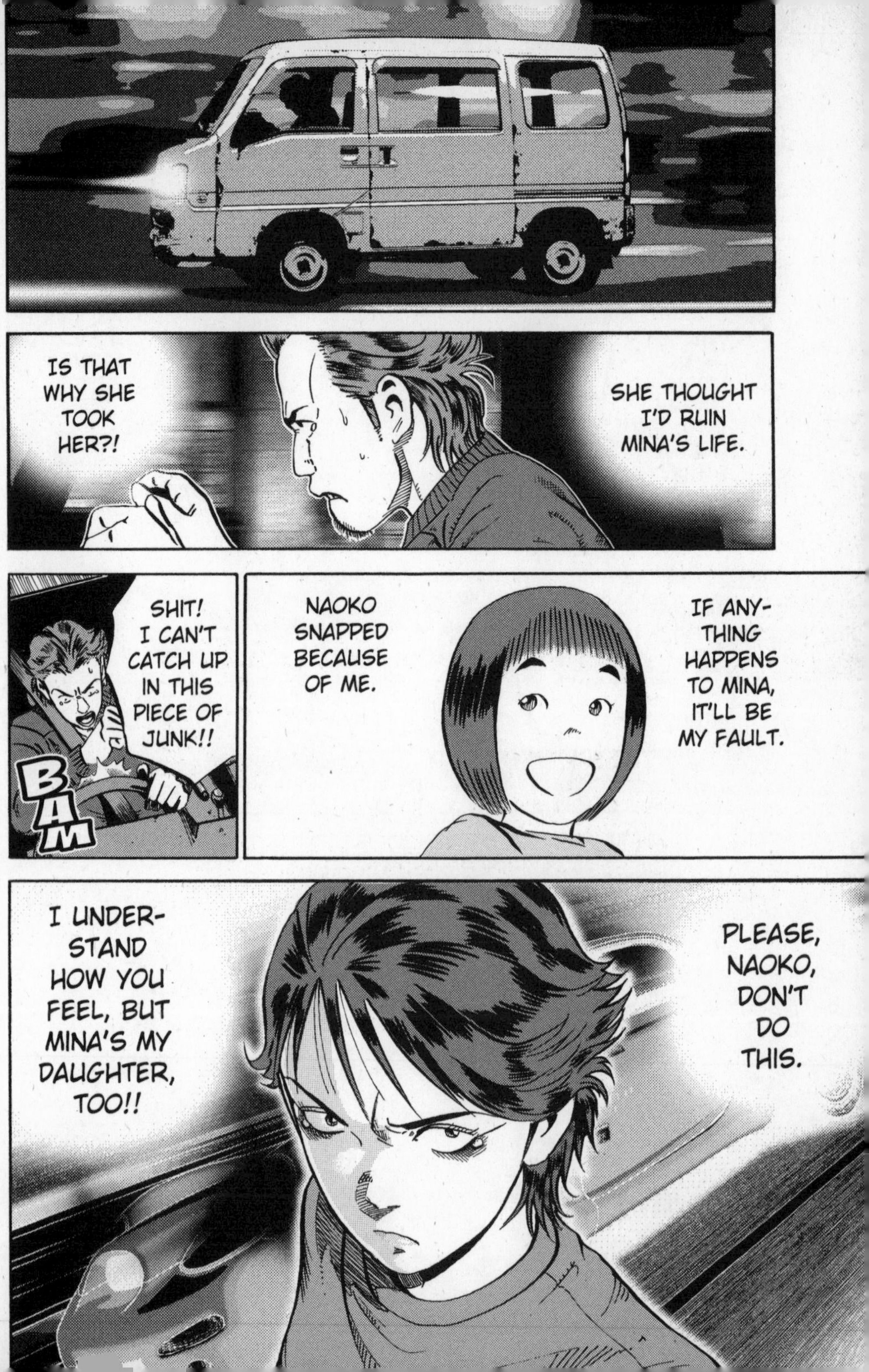
SHE THOUGHT I'D RUIN MINA'S LIFE.
IS THAT WHY SHE TOOK HER?!
IF ANY-THING HAPPENS TO MINA, IT'LL BE MY FAULT.
NAOKO SNAPPED BECAUSE OF ME.
SHIT! I CAN'T CATCH UP IN THIS PIECE OF JUNK!!
BAM
PLEASE, NAOKO, DON'T DO THIS.
I UNDER-STAND HOW YOU FEEL, BUT MINA'S MY DAUGHTER, TOO!!

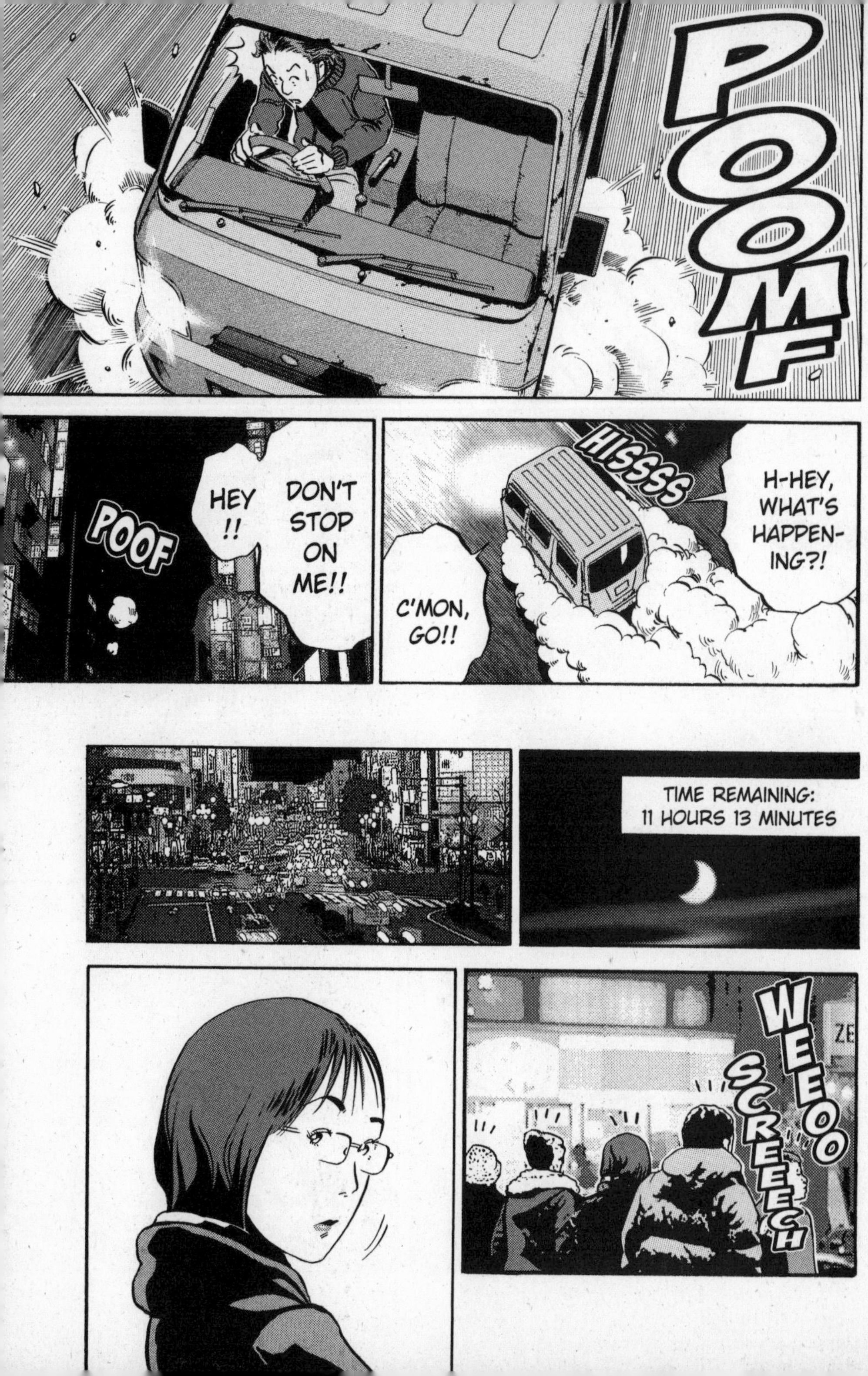
POOMF
HISSSS
H-HEY, WHAT'S HAPPEN-ING?!
C'MON, GO!!
HEY !! DON'T STOP ON ME!!
POOF
TIME REMAINING: 11 HOURS 13 MINUTES
WEEEOO
SCREEECH

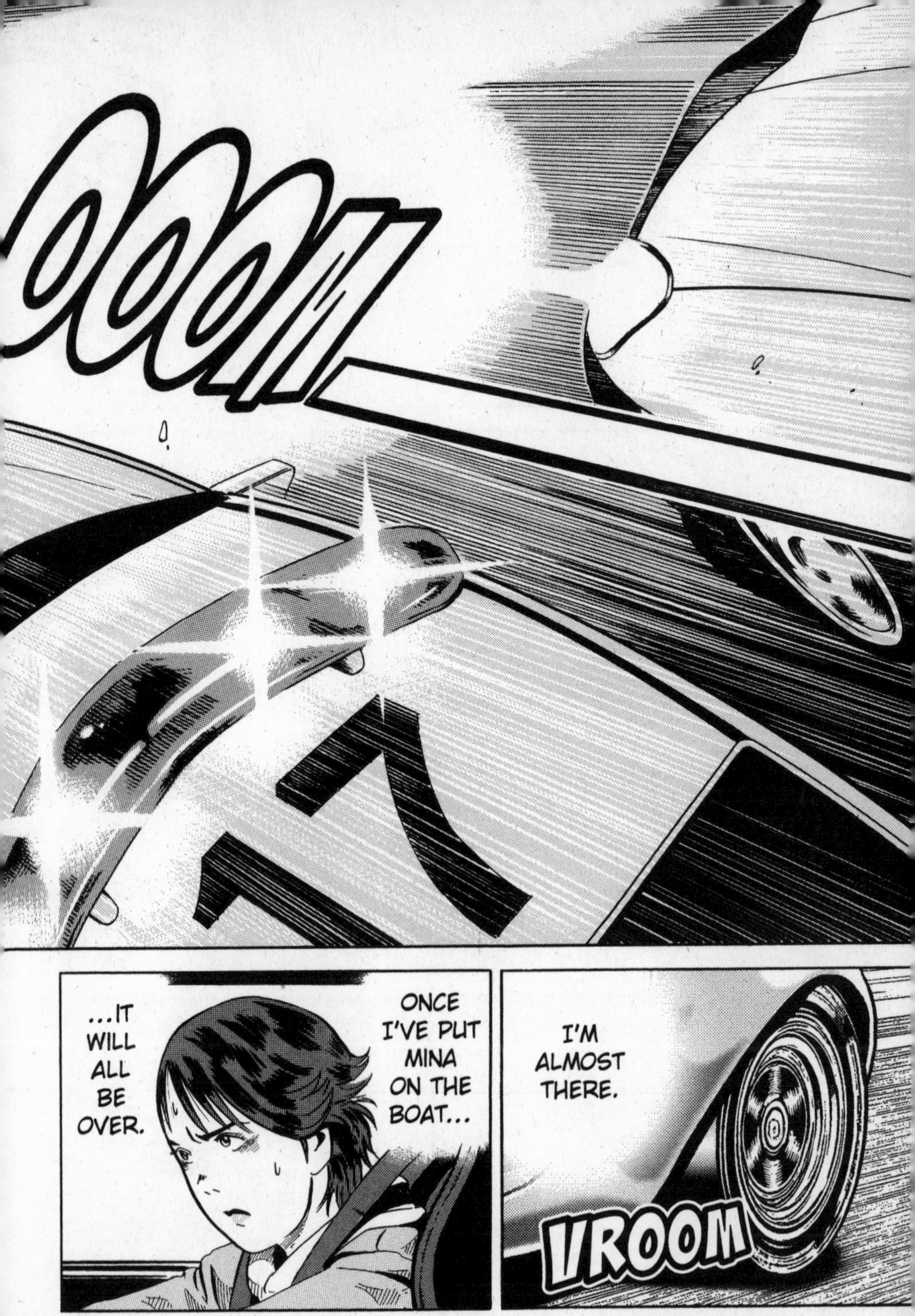
I'M ALMOST THERE.
VROOM
ONCE I'VE PUT MINA ON THE BOAT...
...IT WILL ALL BE OVER.

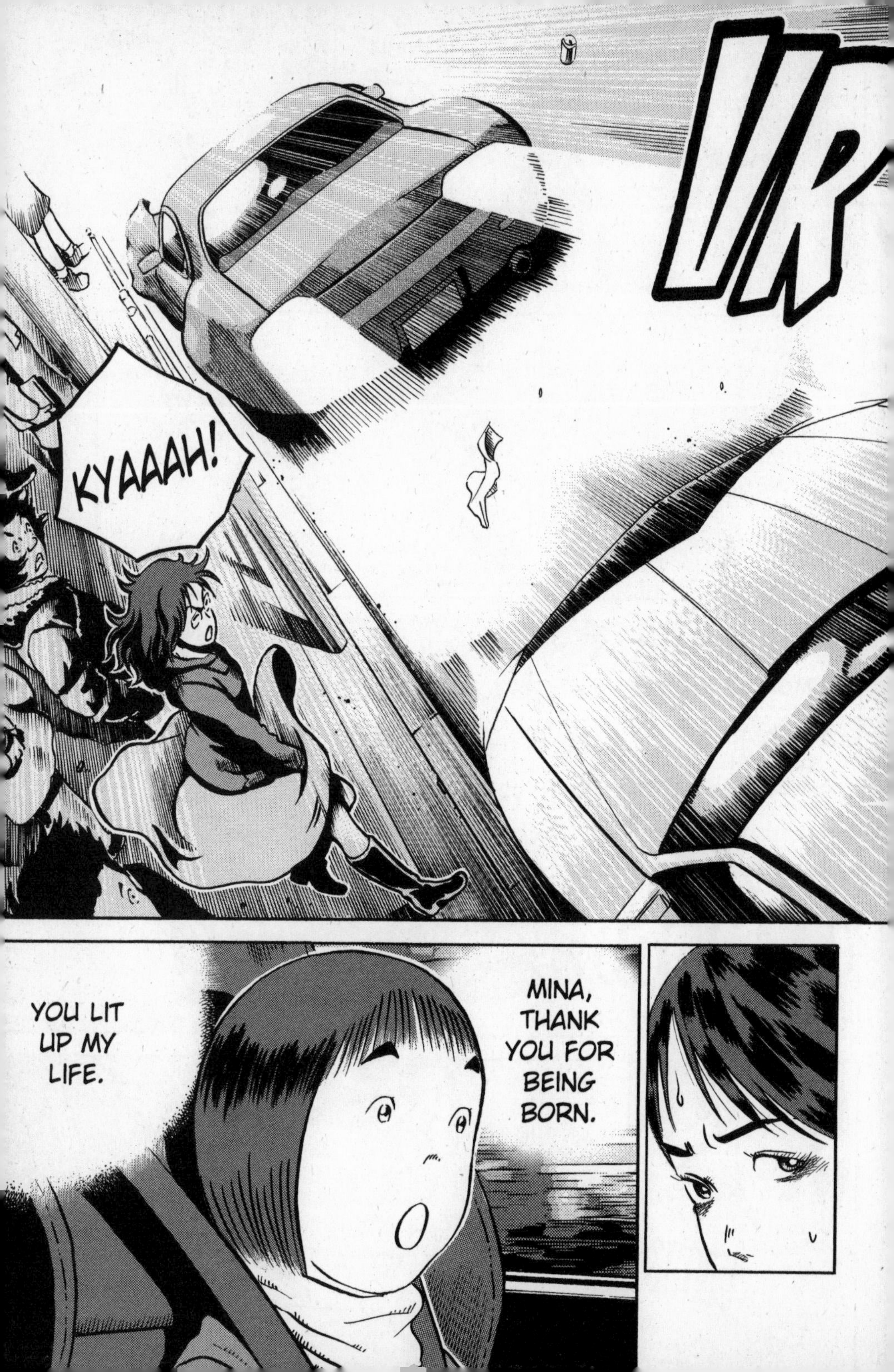
KYAAAH!
MINA, THANK YOU FOR BEING BORN.
YOU LIT UP MY LIFE.

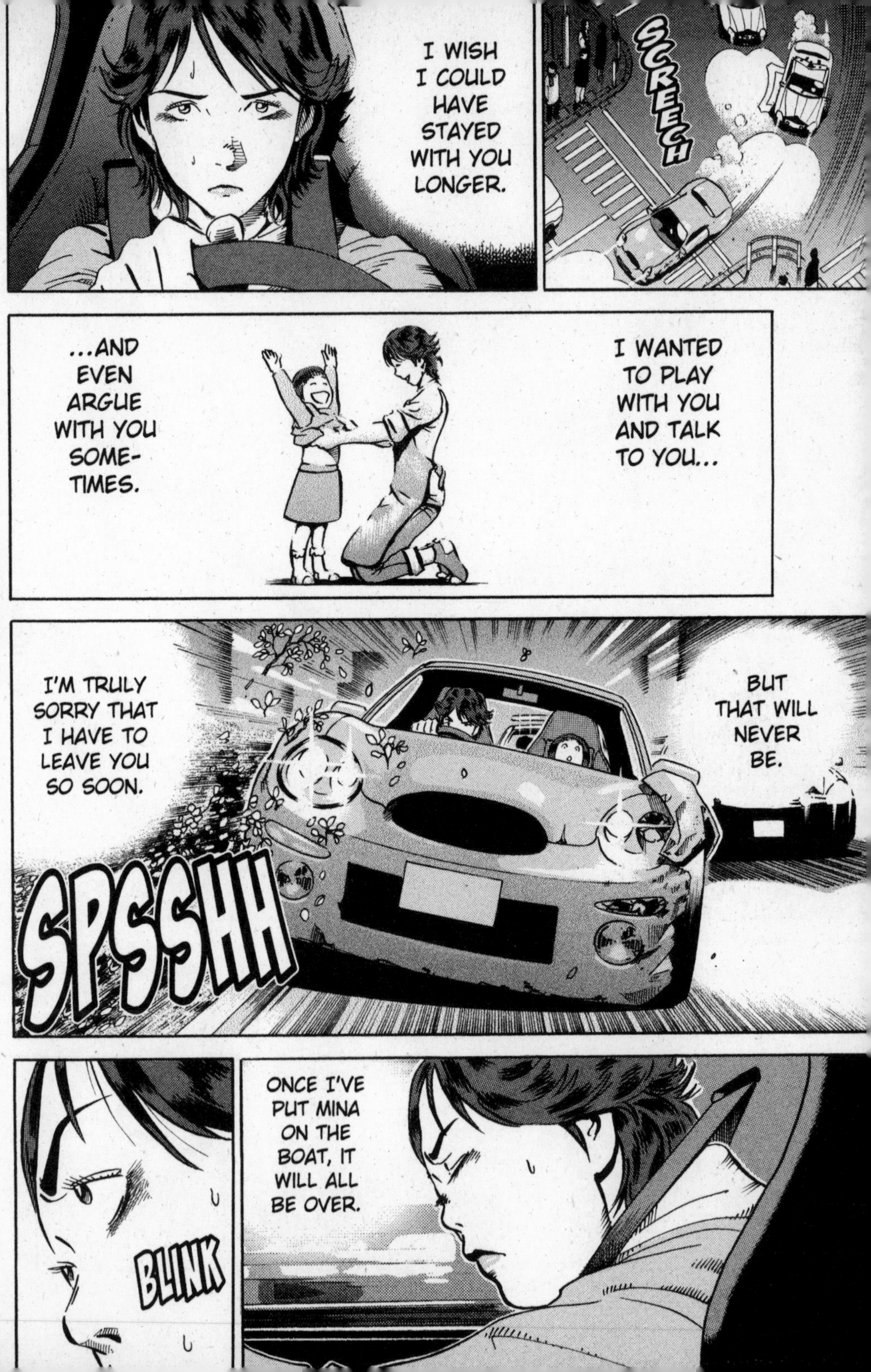
SCREECH
I WISH I COULD HAVE STAYED WITH YOU LONGER.
I WANTED TO PLAY WITH YOU AND TALK TO YOU...
...AND EVEN ARGUE WITH YOU SOME-TIMES.
BUT THAT WILL NEVER BE.
I'M TRULY SORRY THAT I HAVE TO LEAVE YOU SO SOON.
SPSSHH
ONCE I'VE PUT MINA ON THE BOAT, IT WILL ALL BE OVER.
BLINK

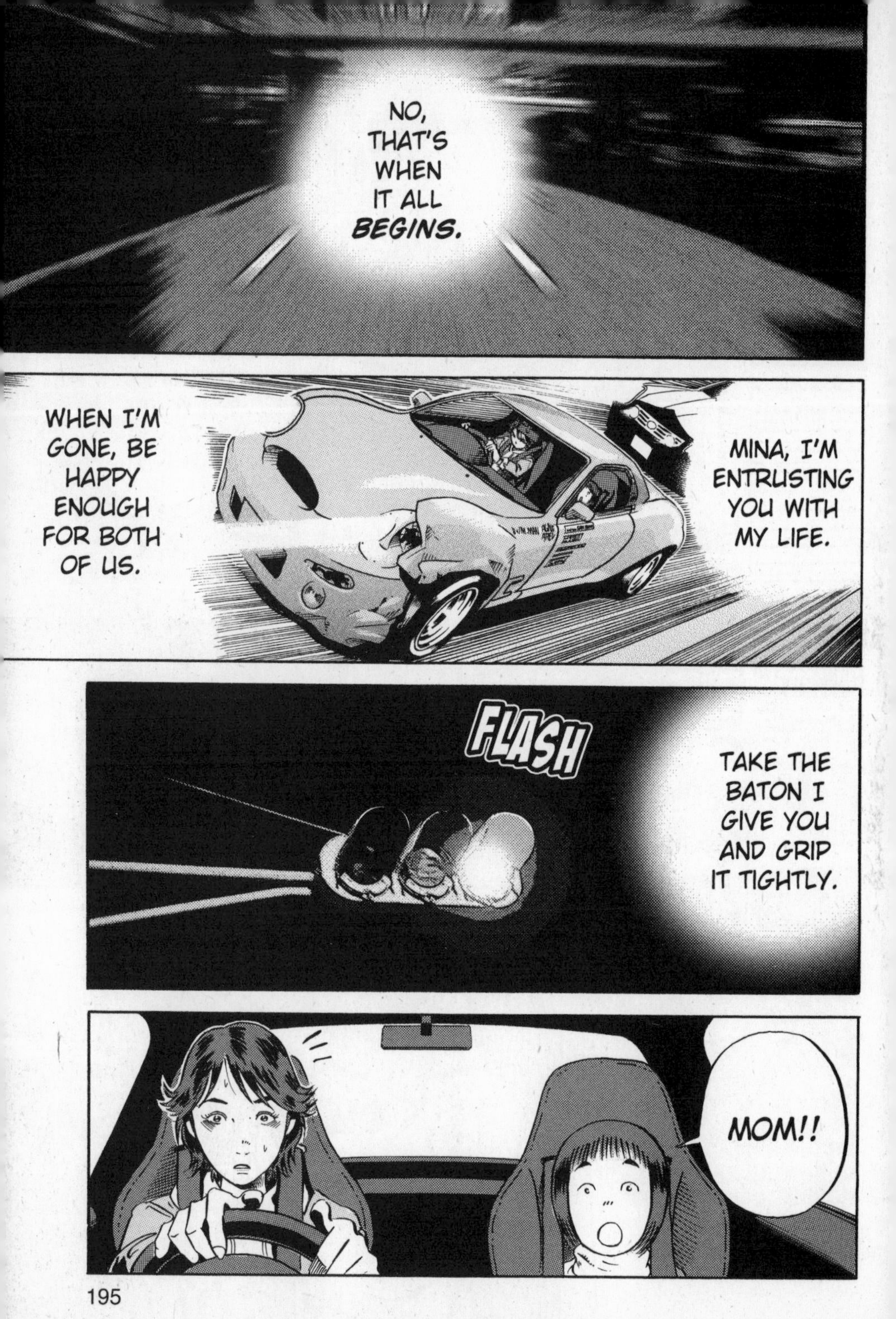
NO, THAT'S WHEN IT ALL BEGINS.
MINA, I'M ENTRUSTING YOU WITH MY LIFE.
WHEN I'M GONE, BE HAPPY ENOUGH FOR BOTH OF US.
TAKE THE BATON I GIVE YOU AND GRIP IT TIGHTLY.
FLASH
MOM!!

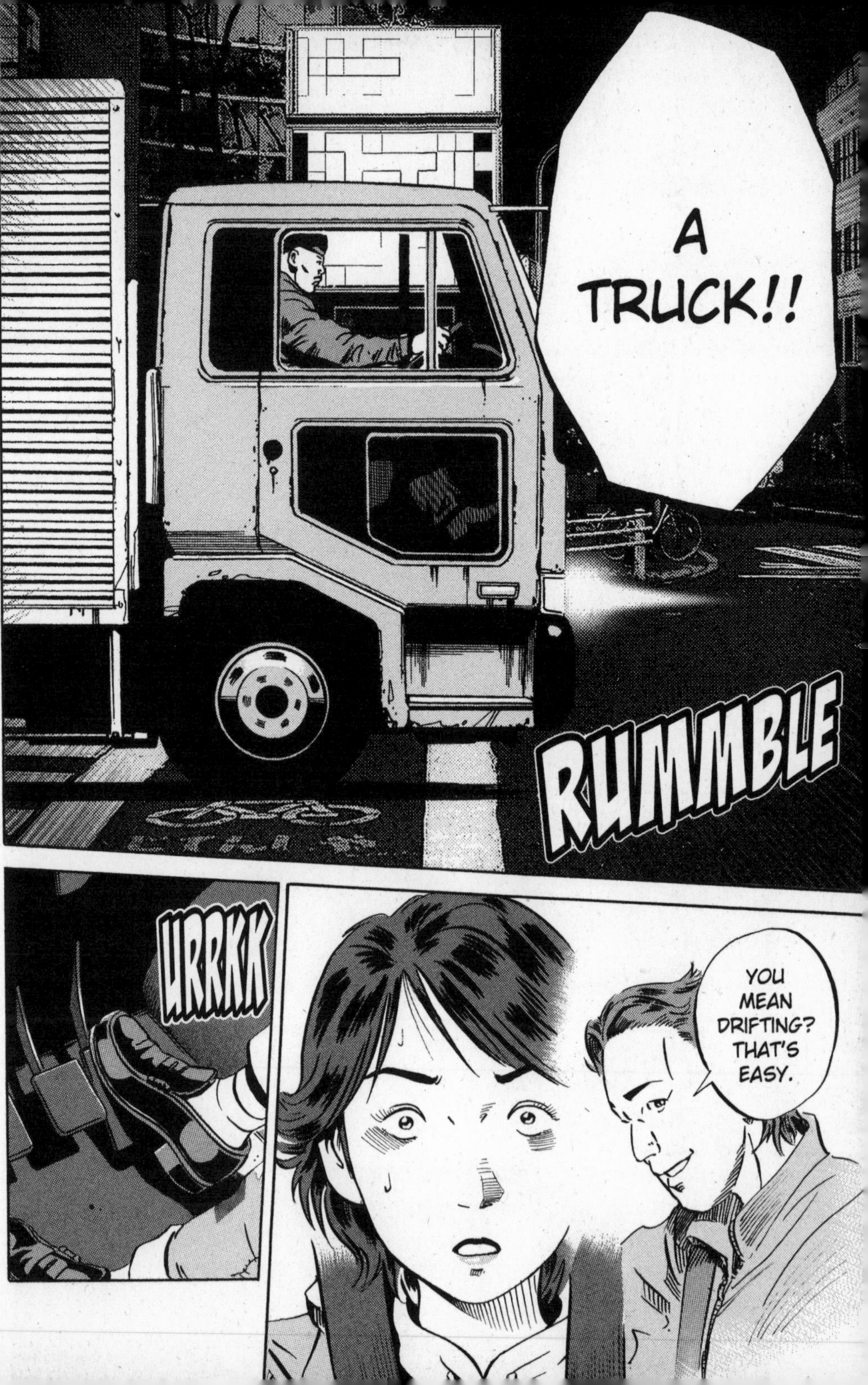
A TRUCK!!
RUMMBLE
YOU MEAN DRIFTING? THAT'S EASY.
URRKK

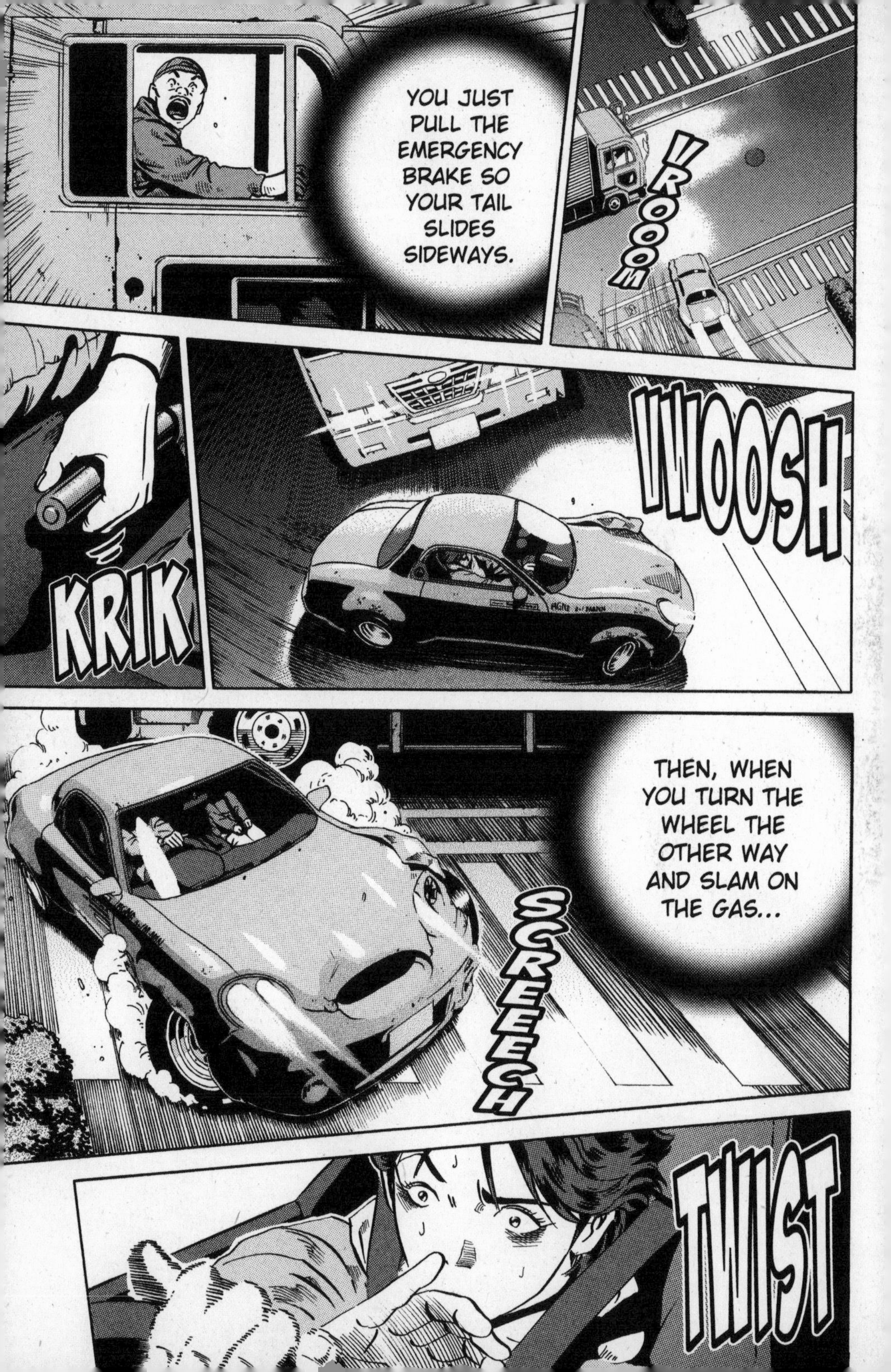
VROOOM
YOU JUST PULL THE EMERGENCY BRAKE SO YOUR TAIL SLIDES SIDEWAYS.
VWOOSH
KRIK
THEN, WHEN YOU TURN THE WHEEL THE OTHER WAY AND SLAM ON THE GAS...
SCREEECH
TWIST

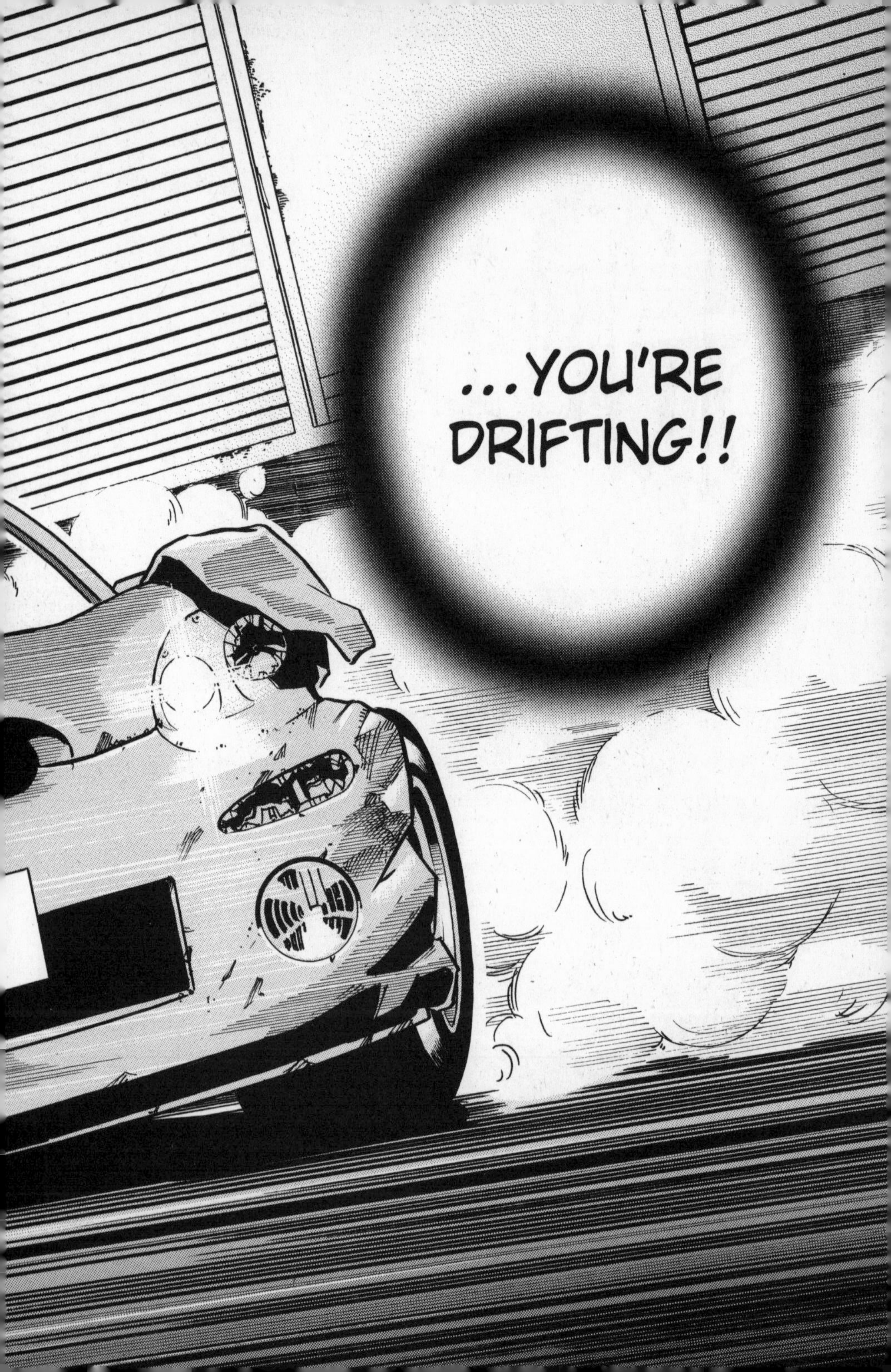
...YOU'RE DRIFTING!!

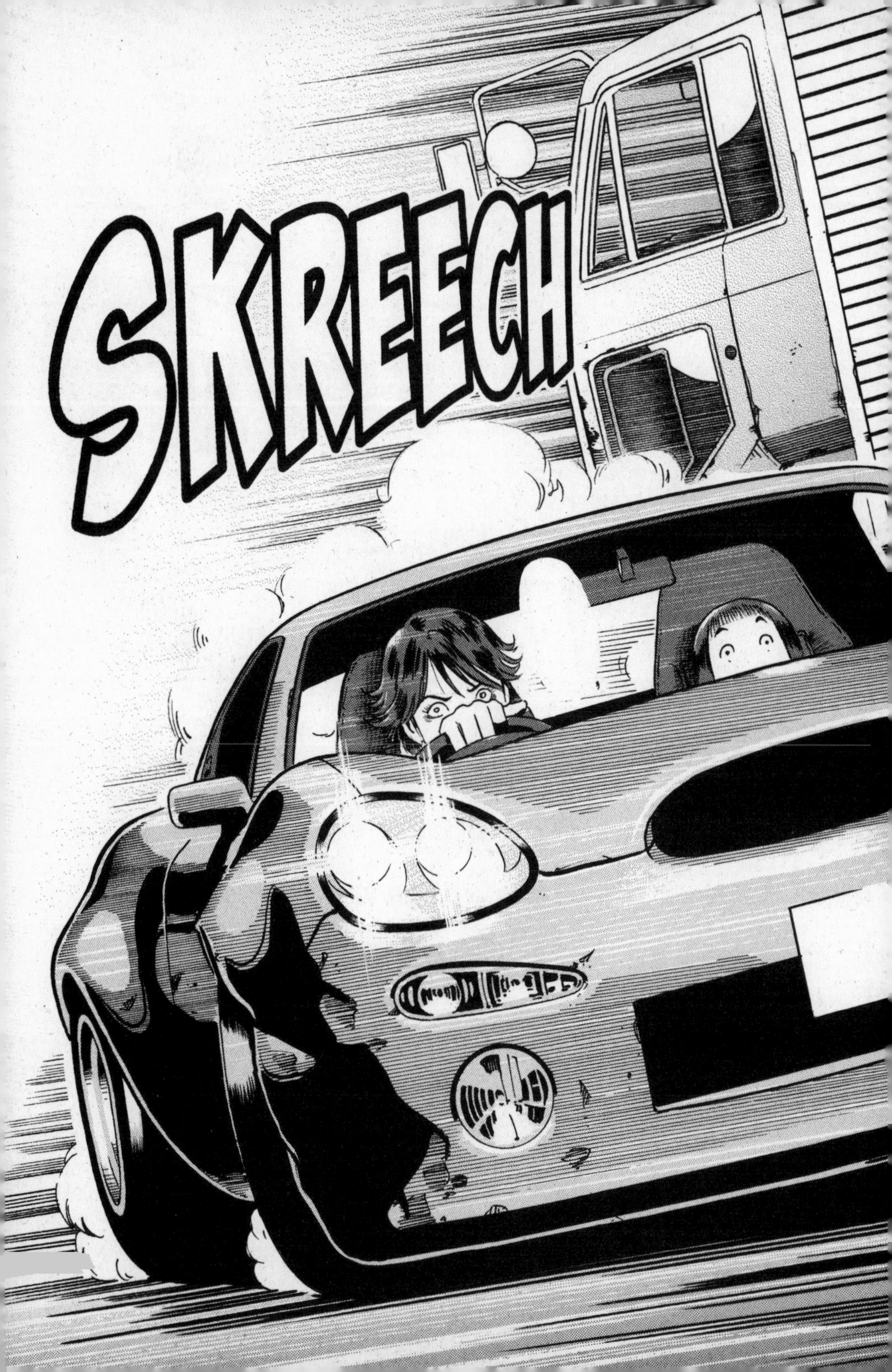
SKREECH

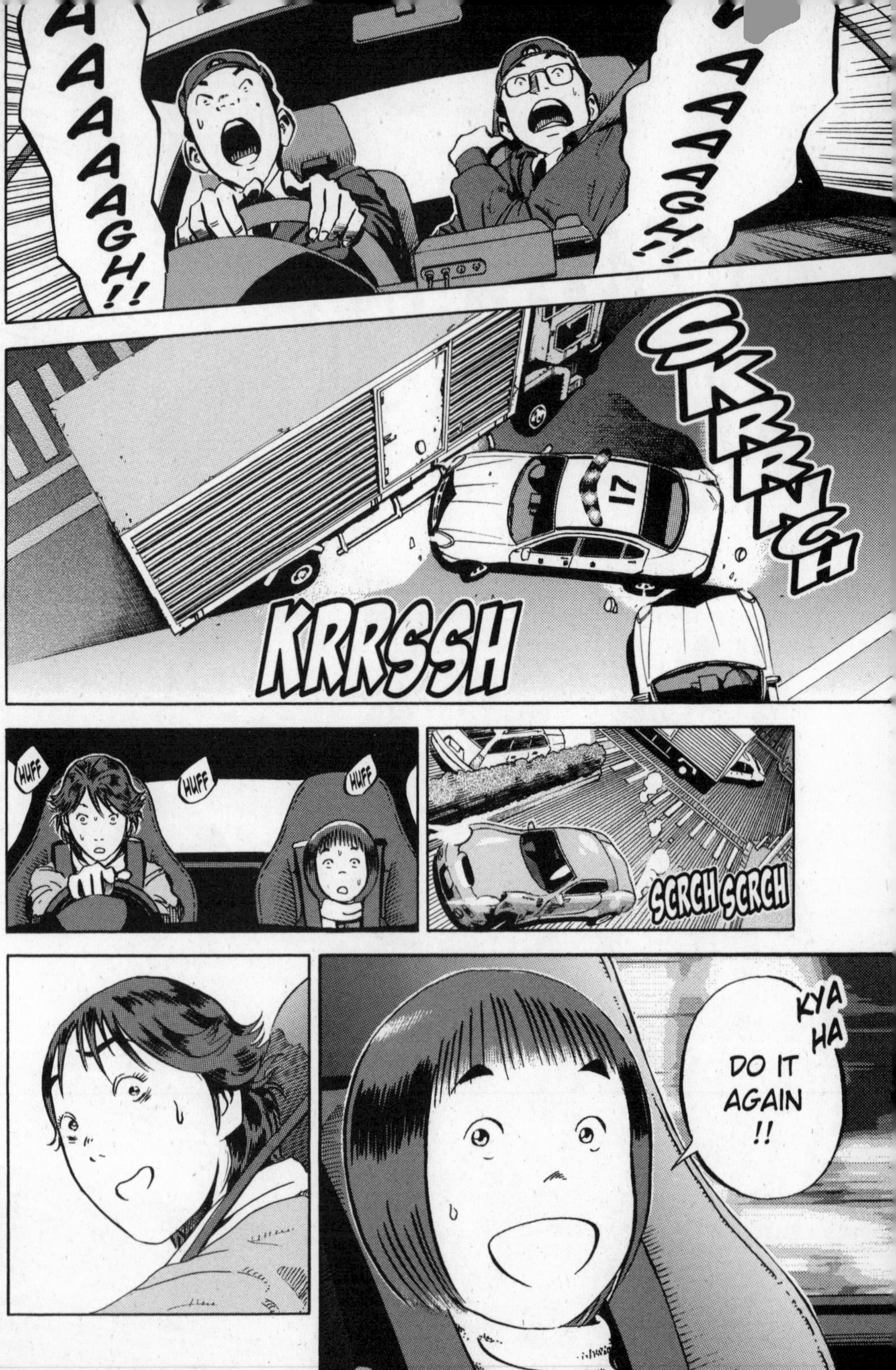
AAAAAAGH!!
AAAAAAGH!!
SKRRNCH
KRRSSH
SCRCH SCRCH
HUFF
HUFF
HUFF
KYA HA
DO IT AGAIN!!

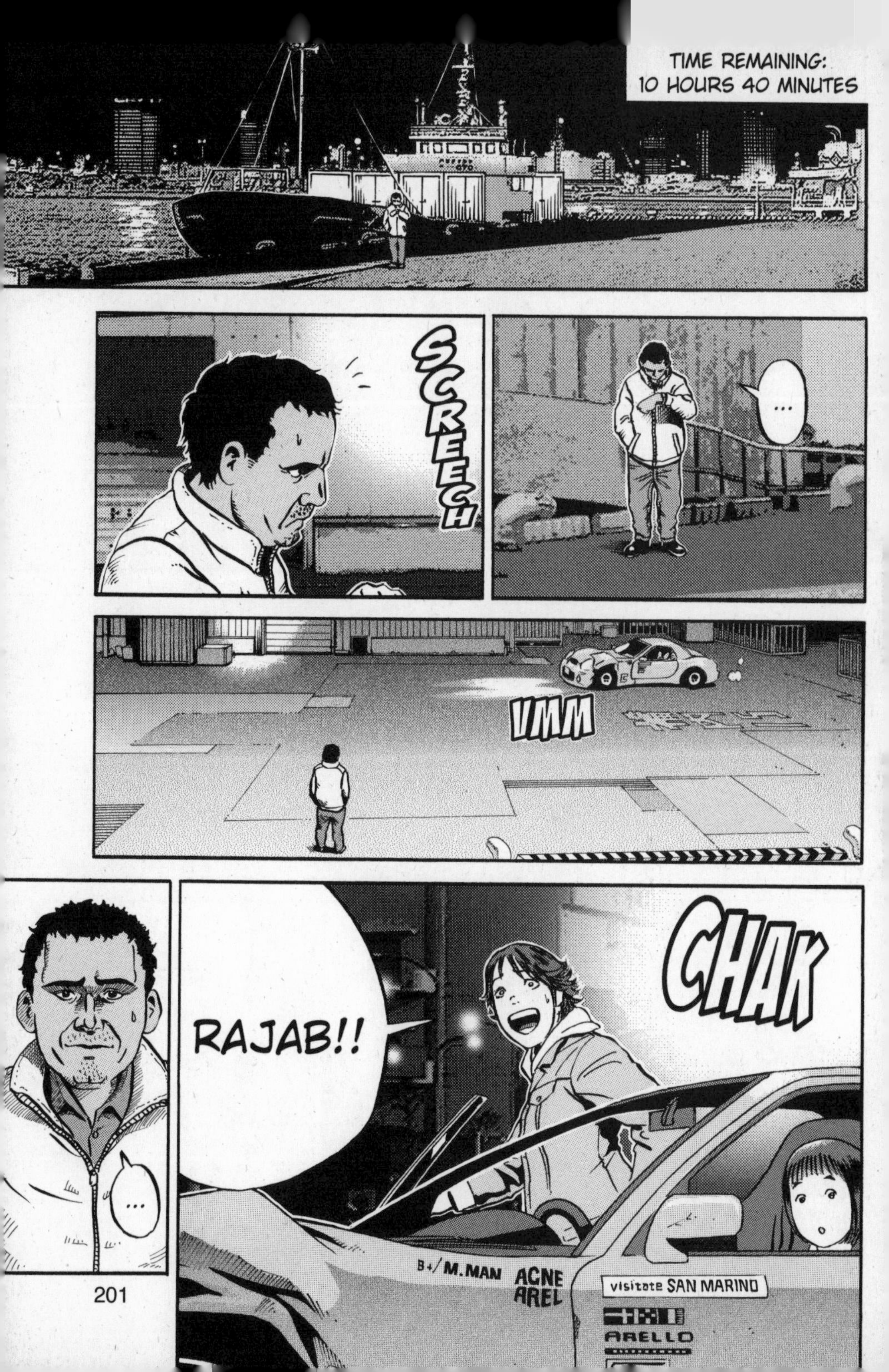
TIME REMAINING:
10 HOURS 40 MINUTES
...
SCREECH
VMM
CHAK
RAJAB!!
B+/M.MAN
ACNE
AREL
visitate SAN MARINO
ARELLO
...

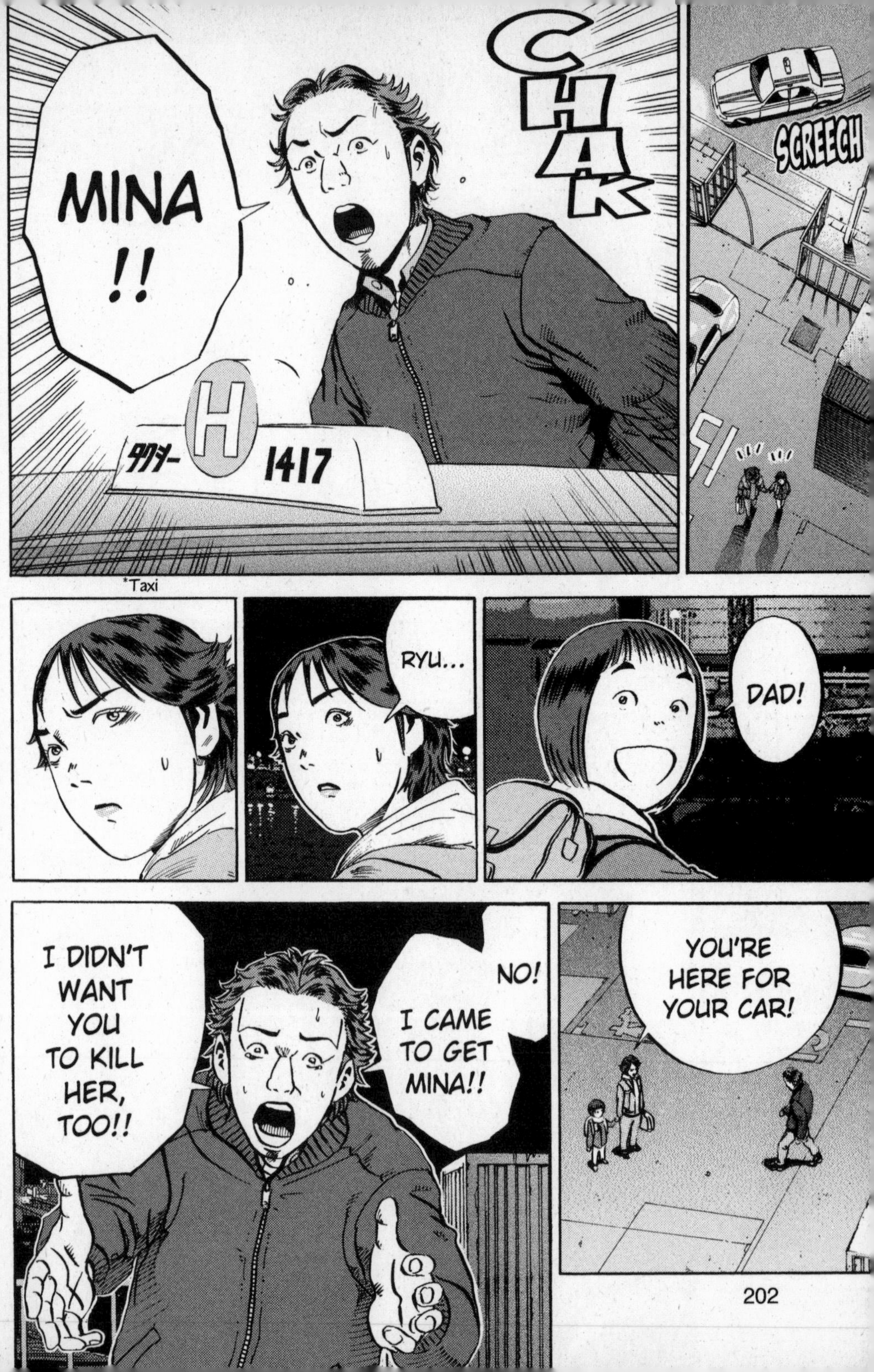
SCREECH
CHAK
MINA !!
タクシー 1417
*Taxi
DAD!
RYU...
YOU'RE HERE FOR YOUR CAR!
NO!
I CAME TO GET MINA!!
I DIDN'T WANT YOU TO KILL HER, TOO!!

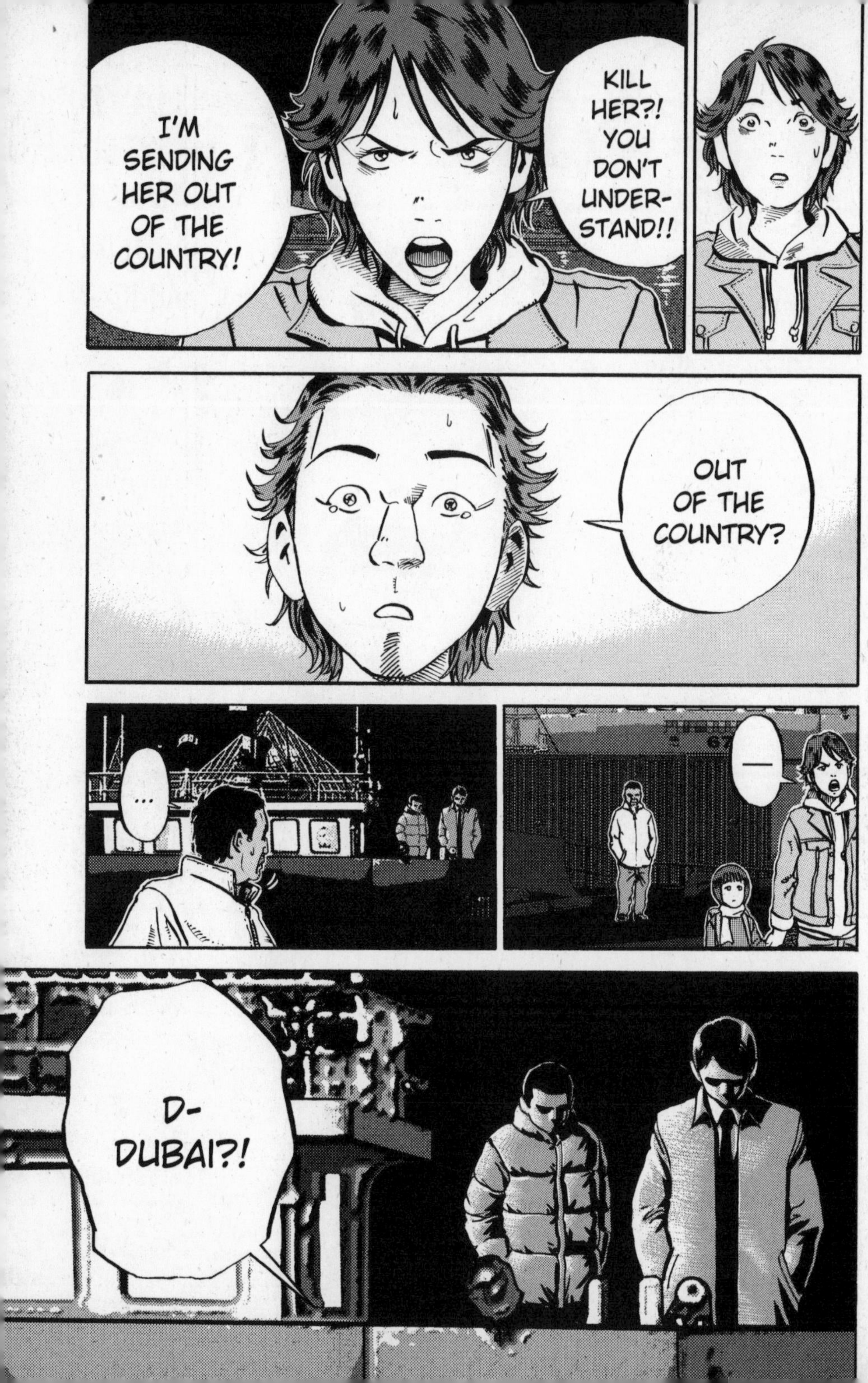
KILL HER?! YOU DON'T UNDER-STAND!!
I'M SENDING HER OUT OF THE COUNTRY!
OUT OF THE COUNTRY?
—
...
D-DUBAI?!

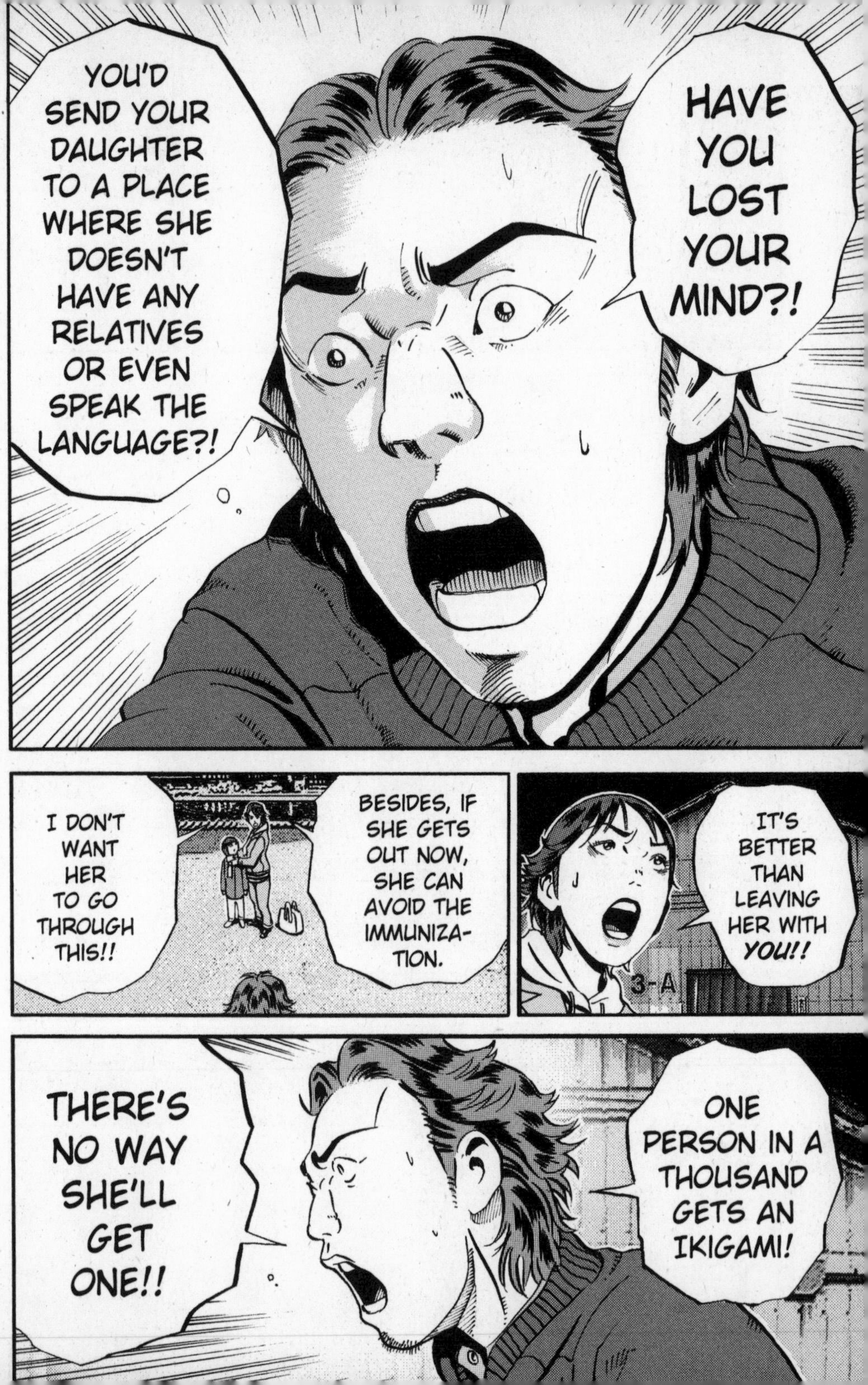
HAVE YOU LOST YOUR MIND?!
YOU'D SEND YOUR DAUGHTER TO A PLACE WHERE SHE DOESN'T HAVE ANY RELATIVES OR EVEN SPEAK THE LANGUAGE?!
IT'S BETTER THAN LEAVING HER WITH *YOU!!*
3-A
BESIDES, IF SHE GETS OUT NOW, SHE CAN AVOID THE IMMUNIZA-TION.
I DON'T WANT HER TO GO THROUGH THIS!!
ONE PERSON IN A THOUSAND GETS AN IKIGAMI!
THERE'S NO WAY SHE'LL GET ONE!!

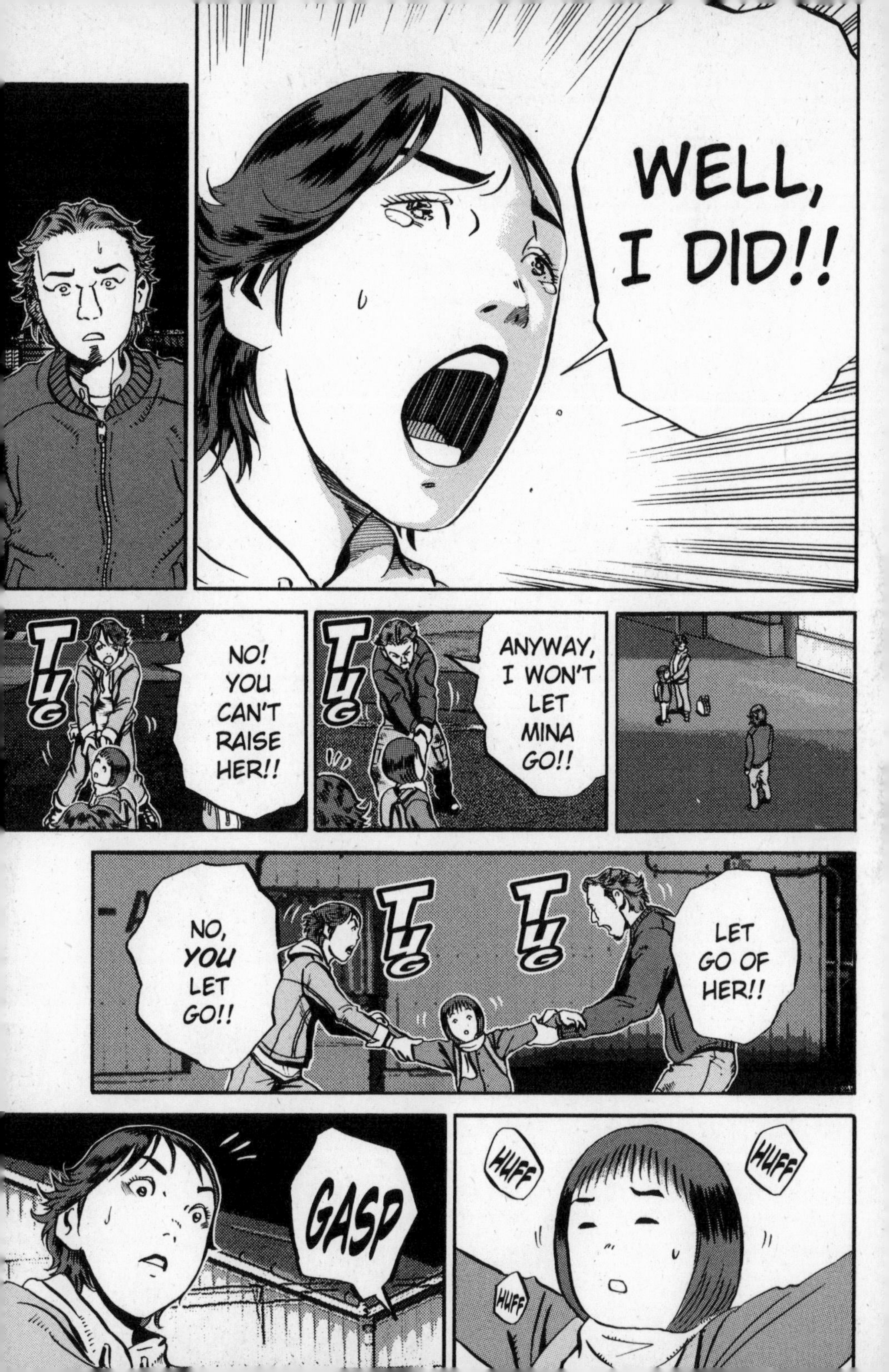
WELL, I DID!!
TUG
ANYWAY, I WON'T LET MINA GO!!
TUG
NO! YOU CAN'T RAISE HER!!
LET GO OF HER!!
TUG
TUG
NO, YOU LET GO!!
HUFF
HUFF
HUFF
GASP

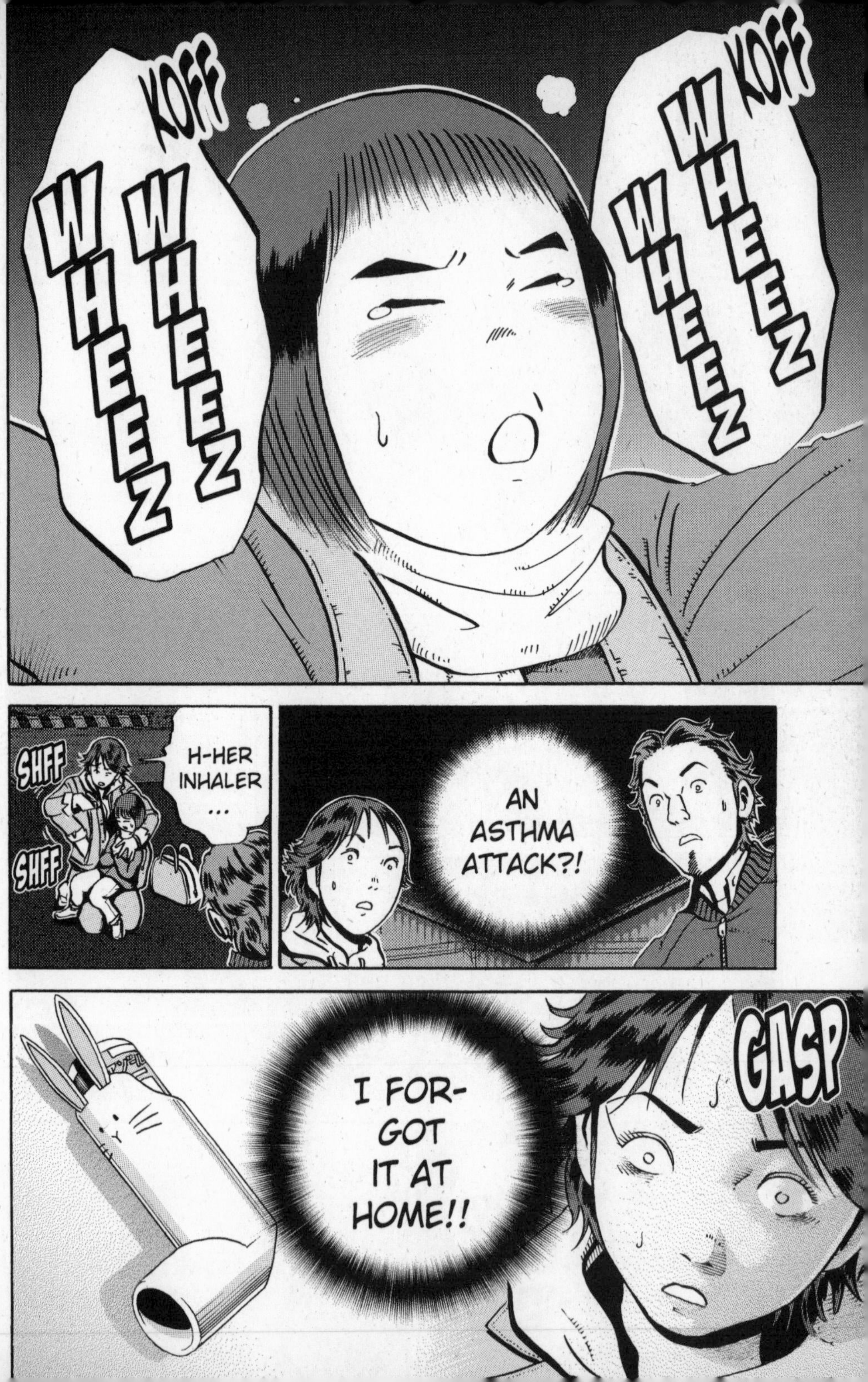
KOFF
WHEEZ
WHEEZ
KOFF
WHEEZ
WHEEZ
AN ASTHMA ATTACK?!
H-HER INHALER ...
SHFF
SHFF
GASP
I FOR-GOT IT AT HOME!!

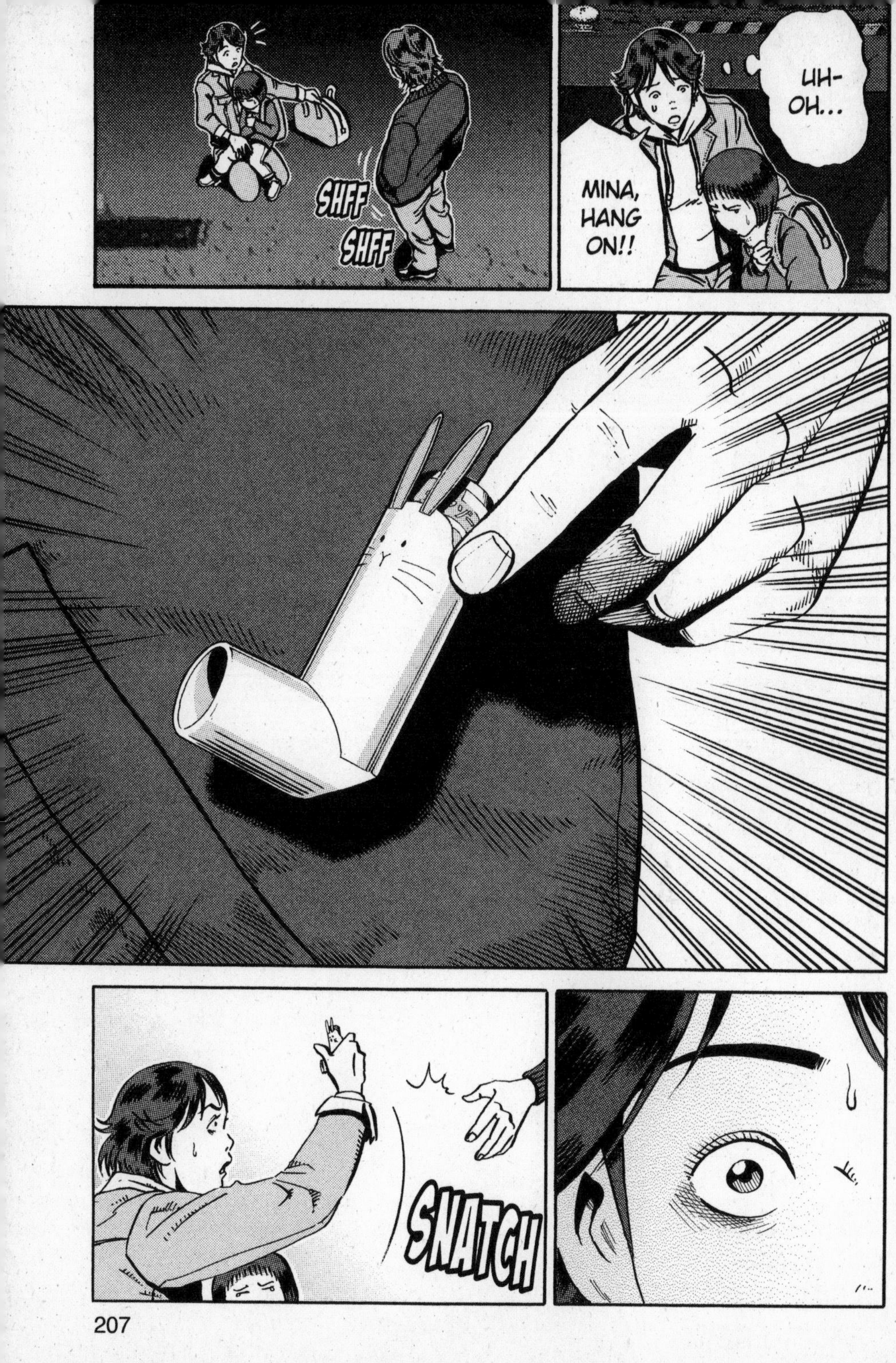
UH-OH...
MINA, HANG ON!!
SHFF
SHFF
SNATCH

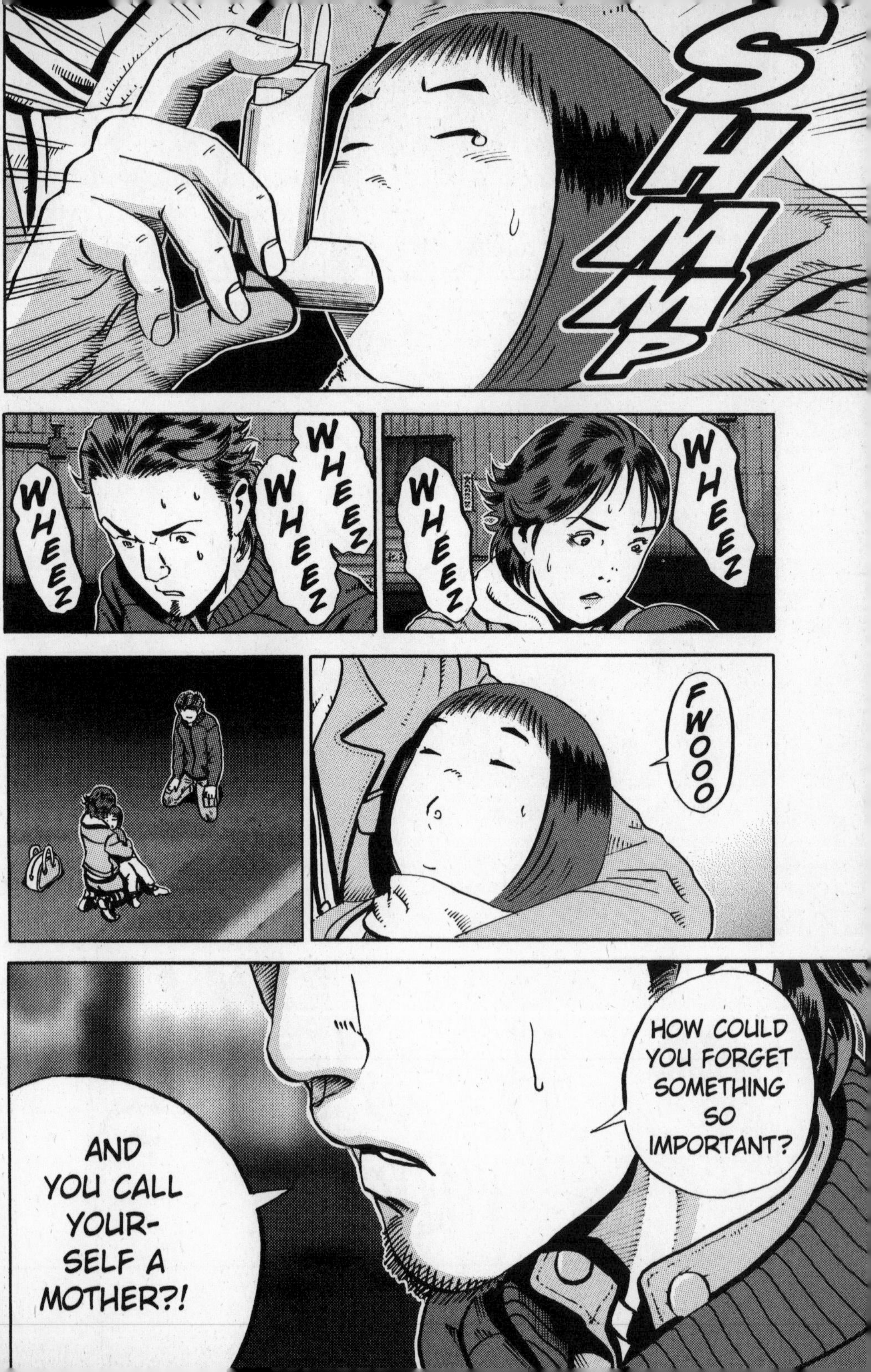
SHMMP
WHEEZ
WHEEZ
WHEEZ
WHEEZ
FWOOO
HOW COULD YOU FORGET SOMETHING SO IMPORTANT?
AND YOU CALL YOUR-SELF A MOTHER?!

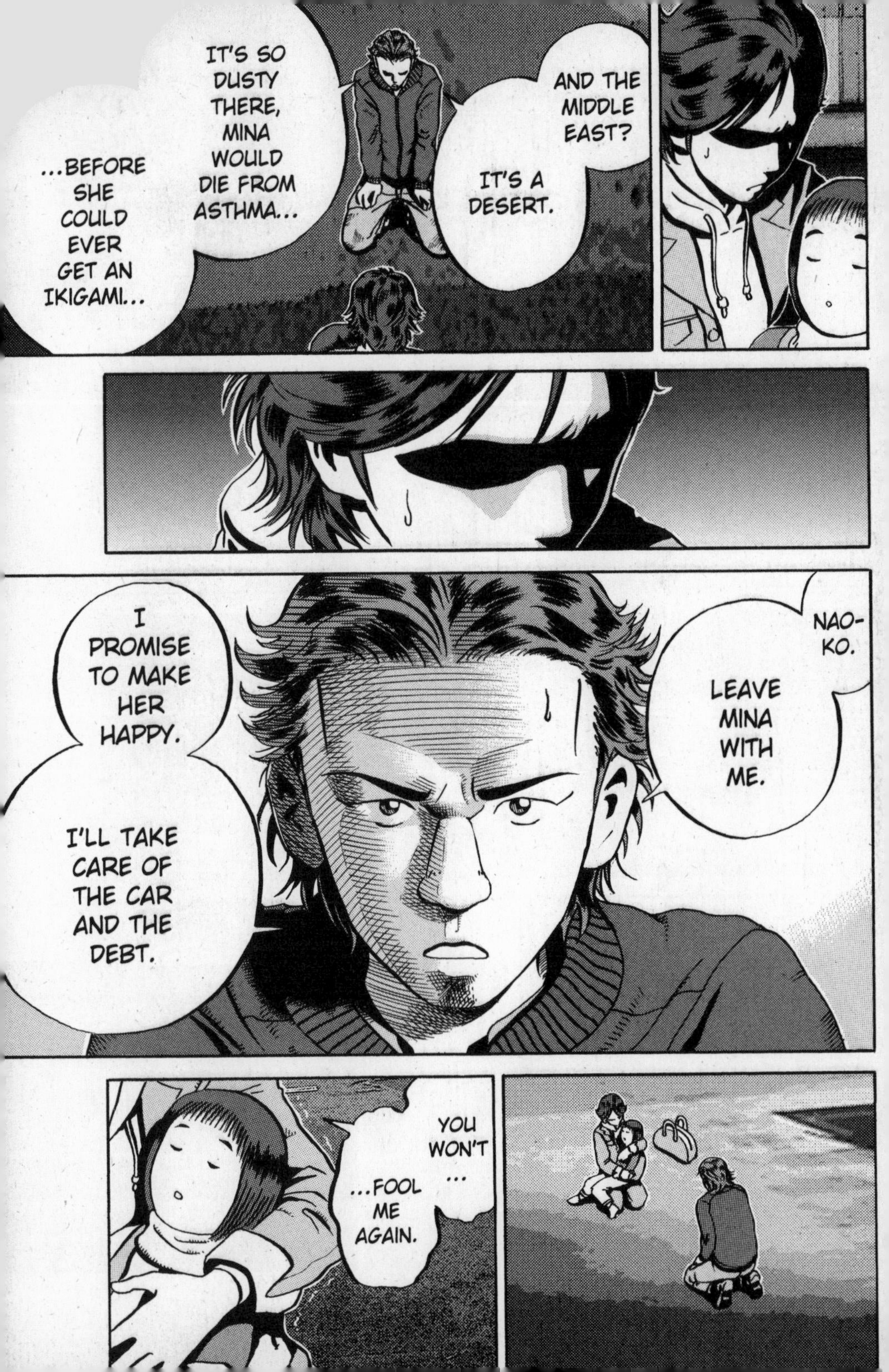
AND THE MIDDLE EAST?
IT'S A DESERT.
IT'S SO DUSTY THERE, MINA WOULD DIE FROM ASTHMA...
...BEFORE SHE COULD EVER GET AN IKIGAMI...
NAO-KO.
LEAVE MINA WITH ME.
I PROMISE TO MAKE HER HAPPY.
I'LL TAKE CARE OF THE CAR AND THE DEBT.
YOU WON'T ...
...FOOL ME AGAIN.

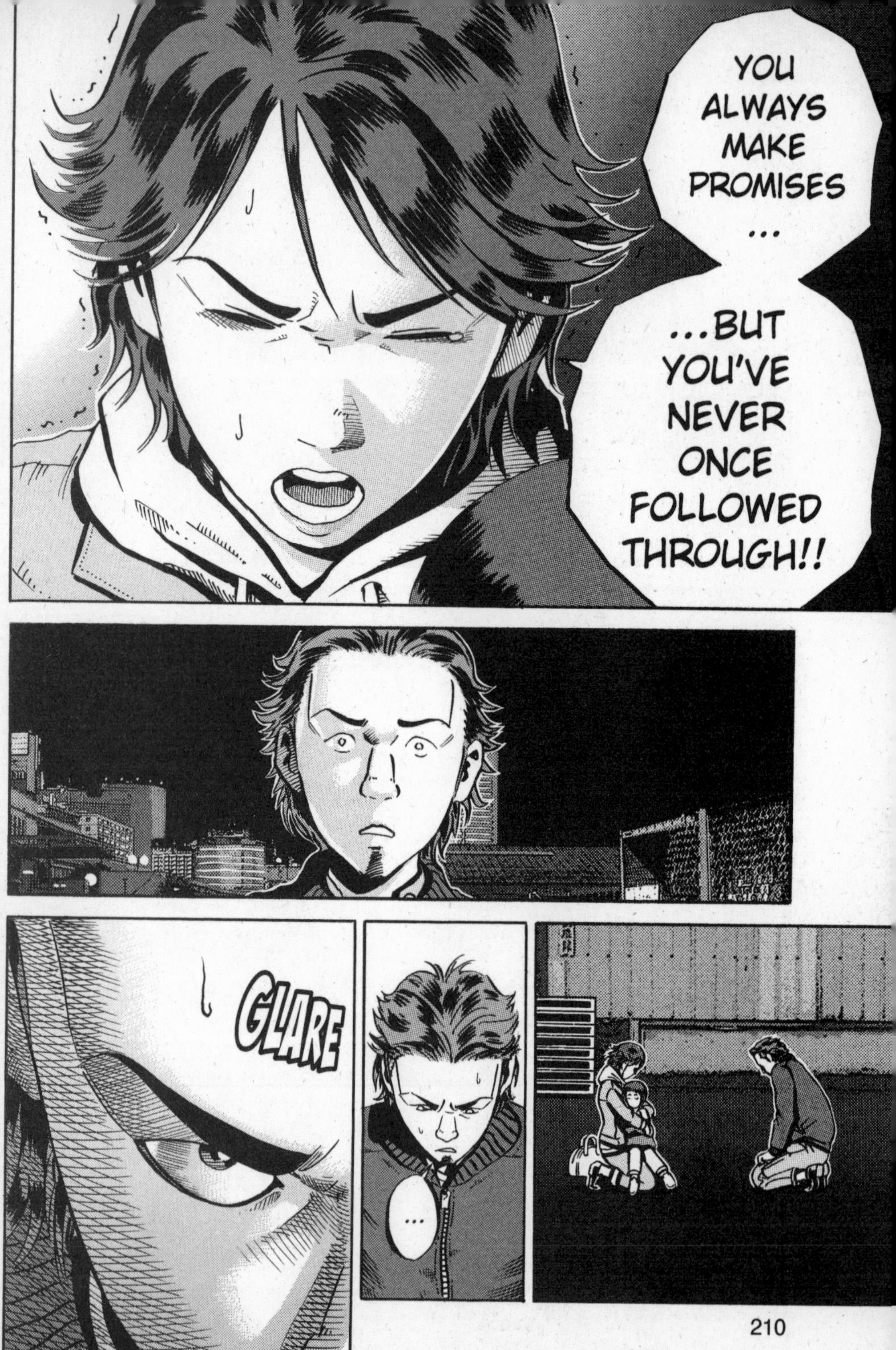
YOU ALWAYS MAKE PROMISES ...
...BUT YOU'VE NEVER ONCE FOLLOWED THROUGH!!
...
GLARE

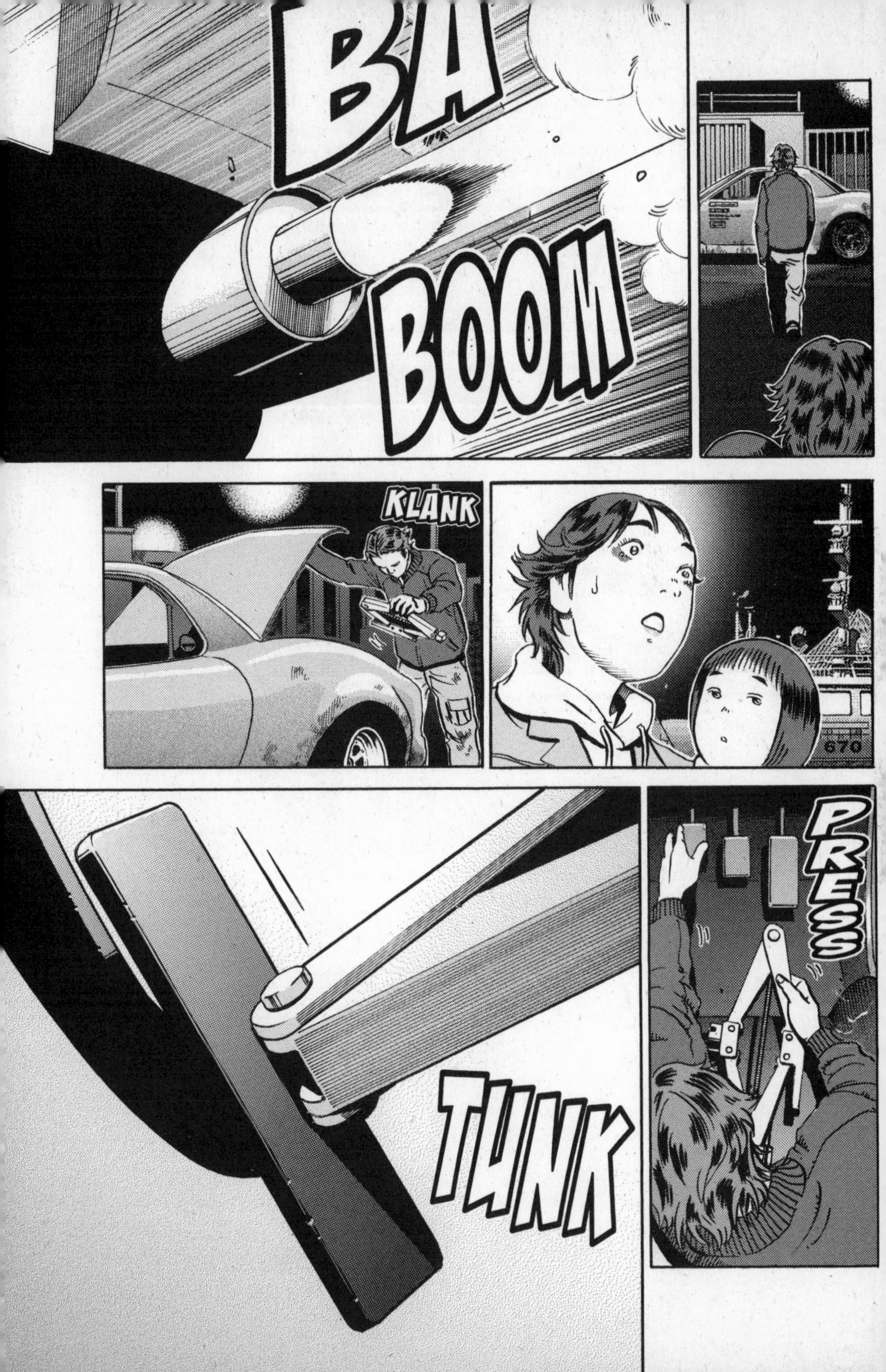
BA
BOOM
670
KLANK
PRESS
TUNK

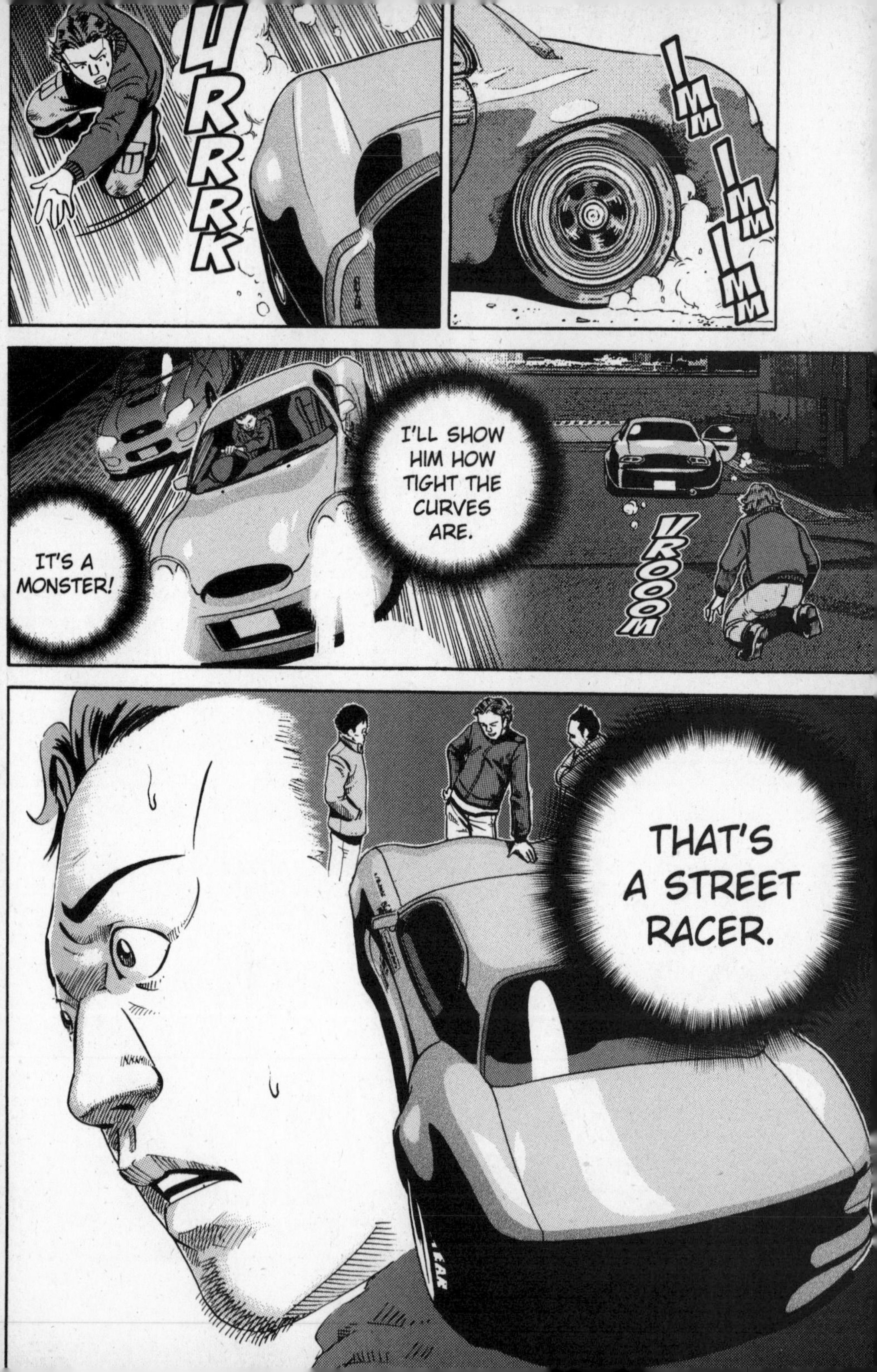
IMM IMM IMM
URRRK
I'LL SHOW HIM HOW TIGHT THE CURVES ARE.
VROOOM
IT'S A MONSTER!
THAT'S A STREET RACER.

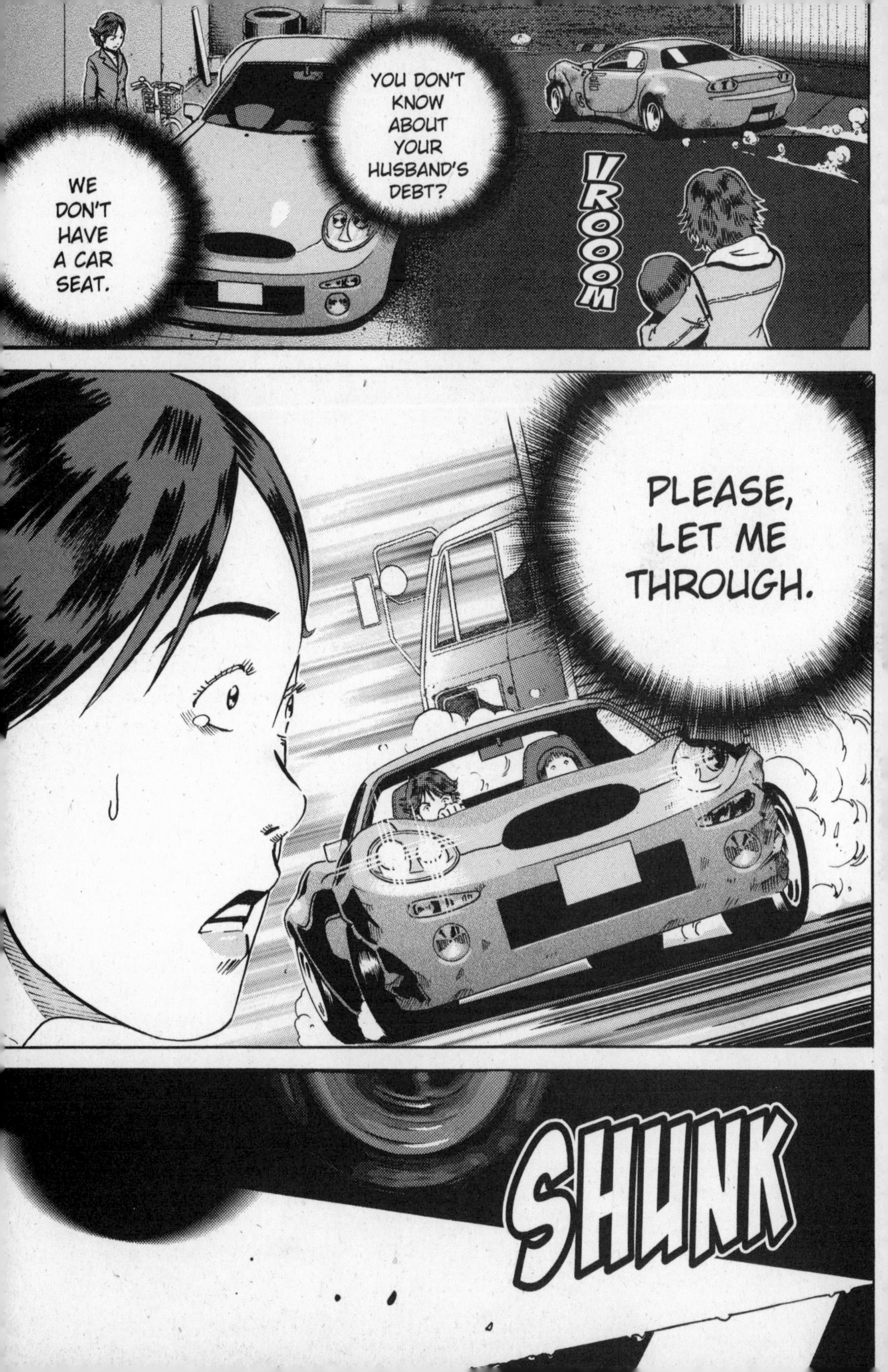
VROOOM
YOU DON'T KNOW ABOUT YOUR HUSBAND'S DEBT?
WE DON'T HAVE A CAR SEAT.
PLEASE, LET ME THROUGH.
SHUNK

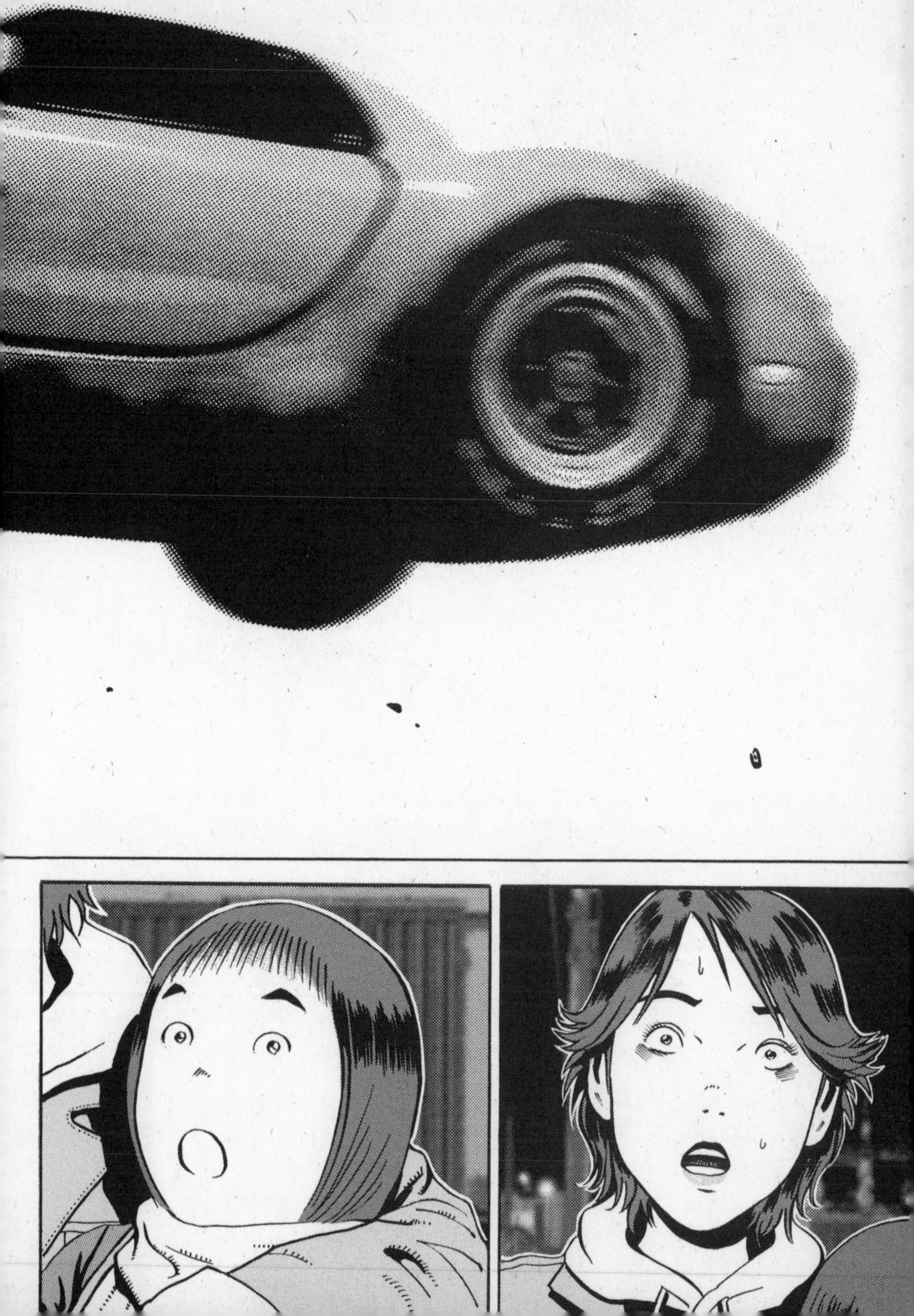

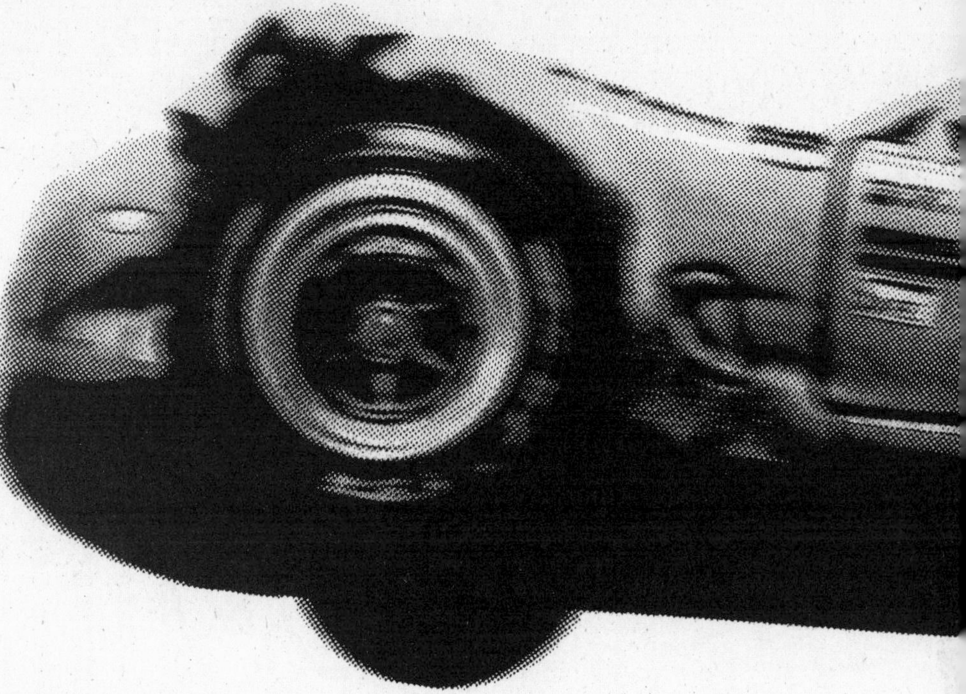

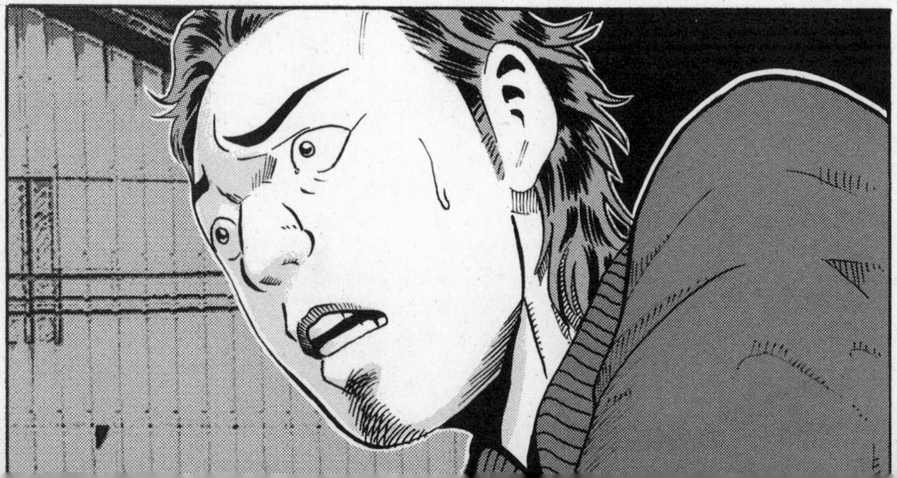

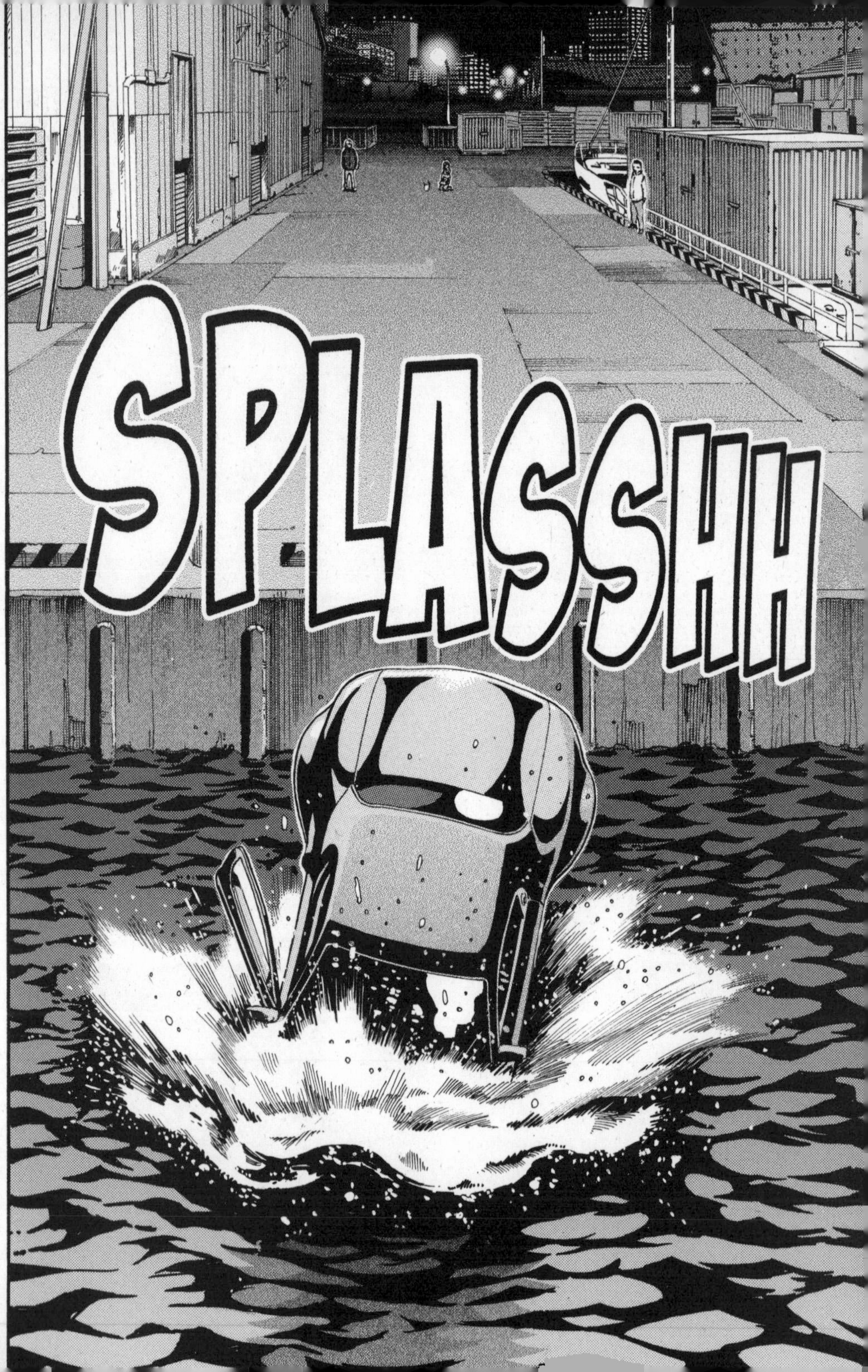
SPLASSHH

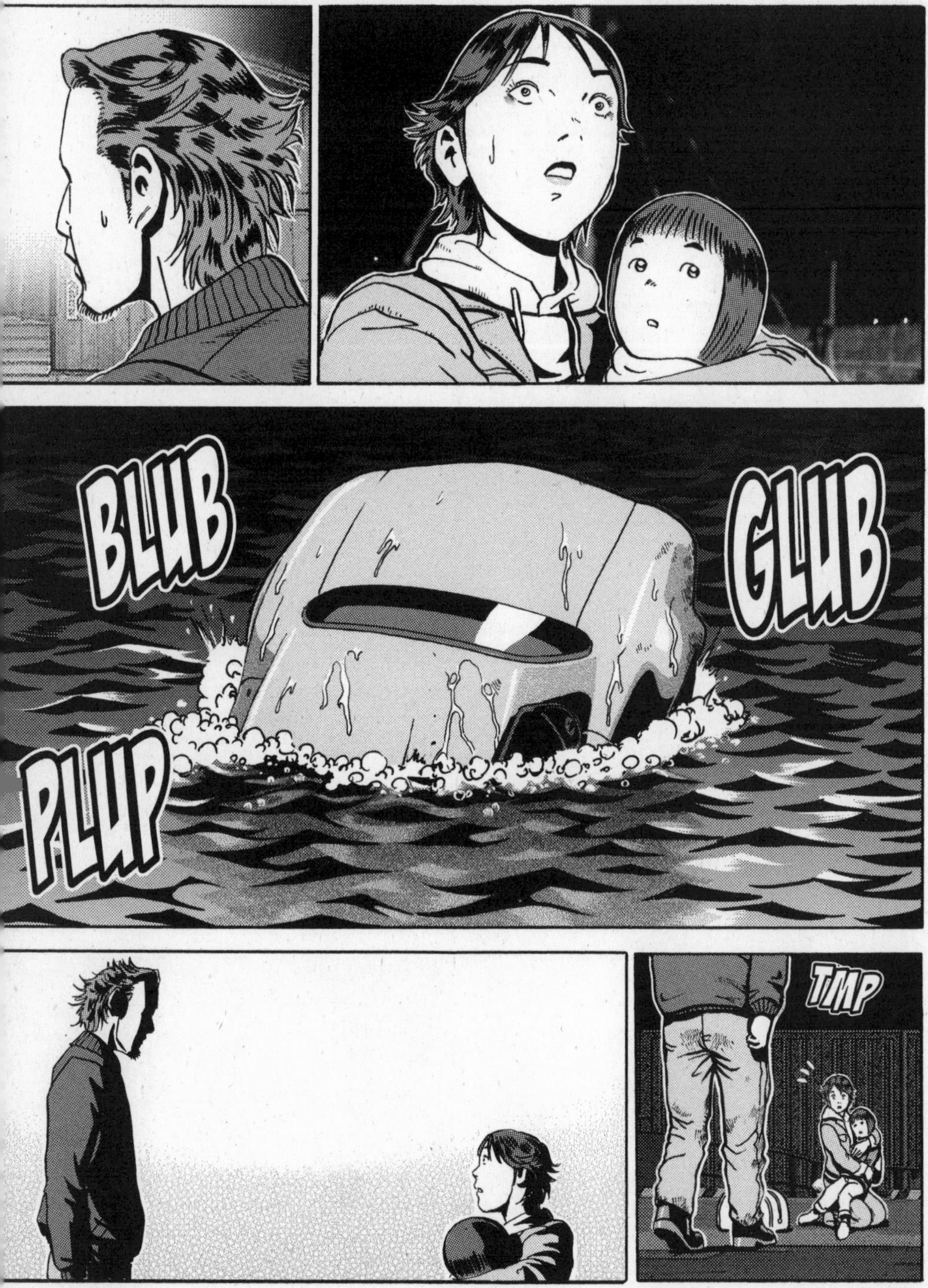
GLUB
BLUB
PLUP
TMP

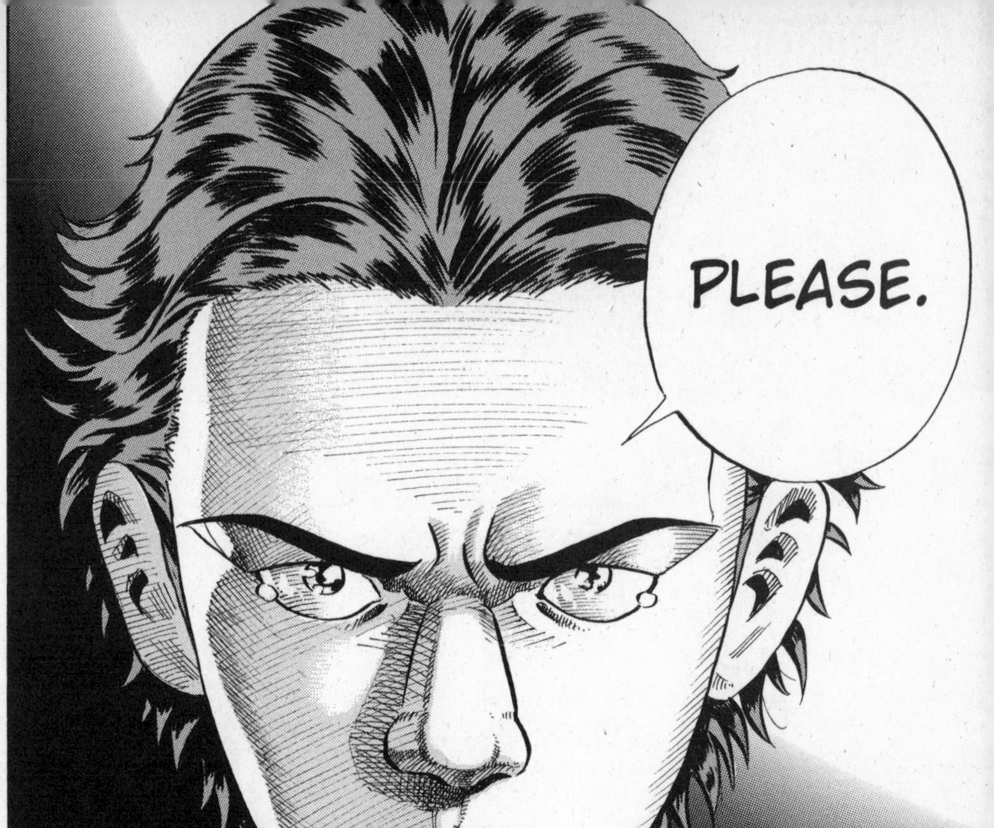
PLEASE.
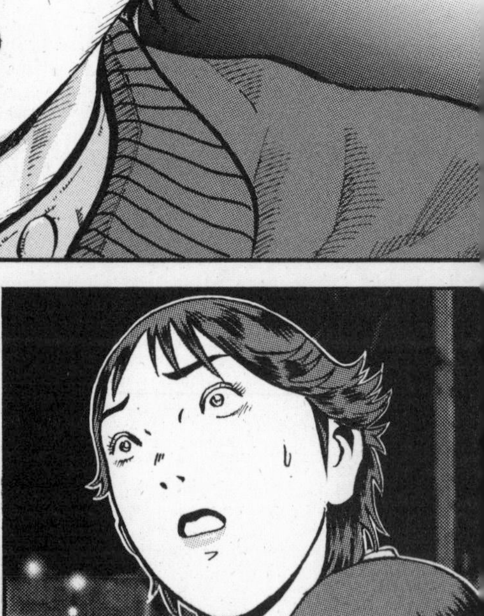
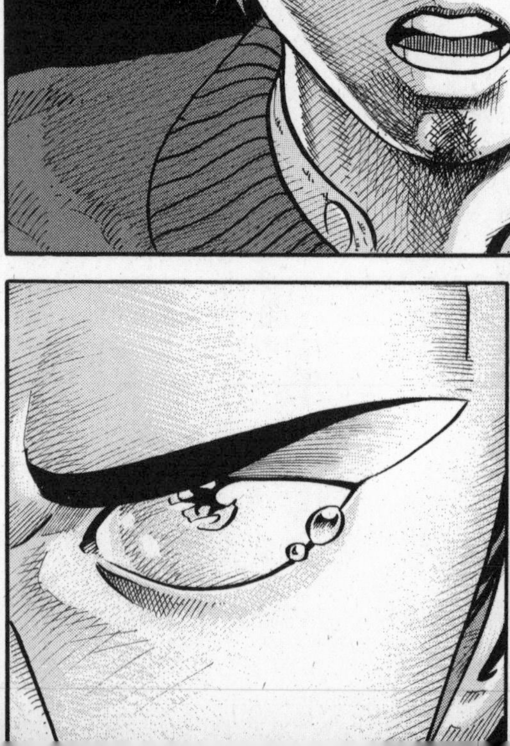

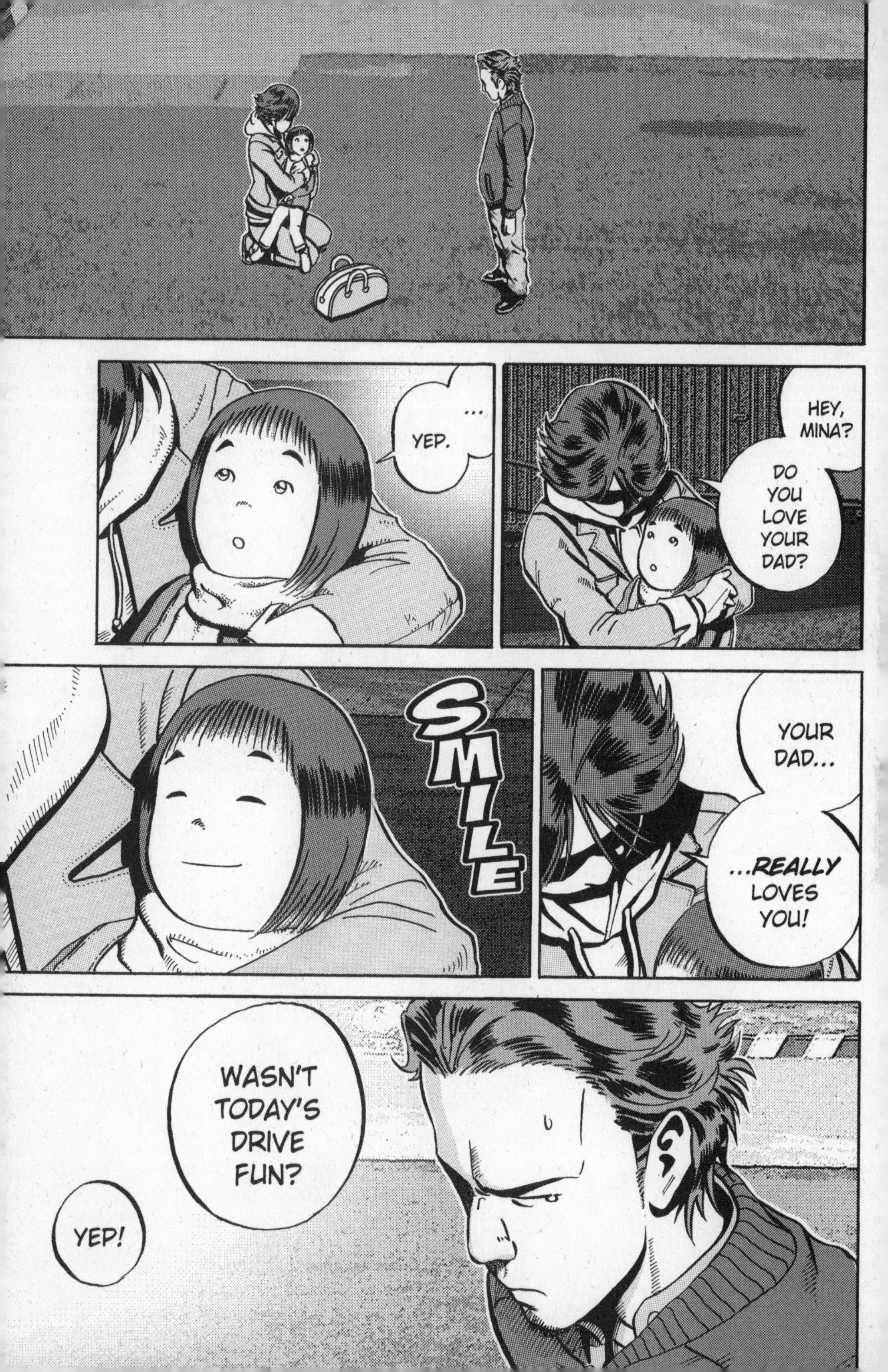
HEY, MINA?
DO YOU LOVE YOUR DAD?
... YEP.
YOUR DAD...
...*REALLY* LOVES YOU!
SMILE
WASN'T TODAY'S DRIVE FUN?
YEP!

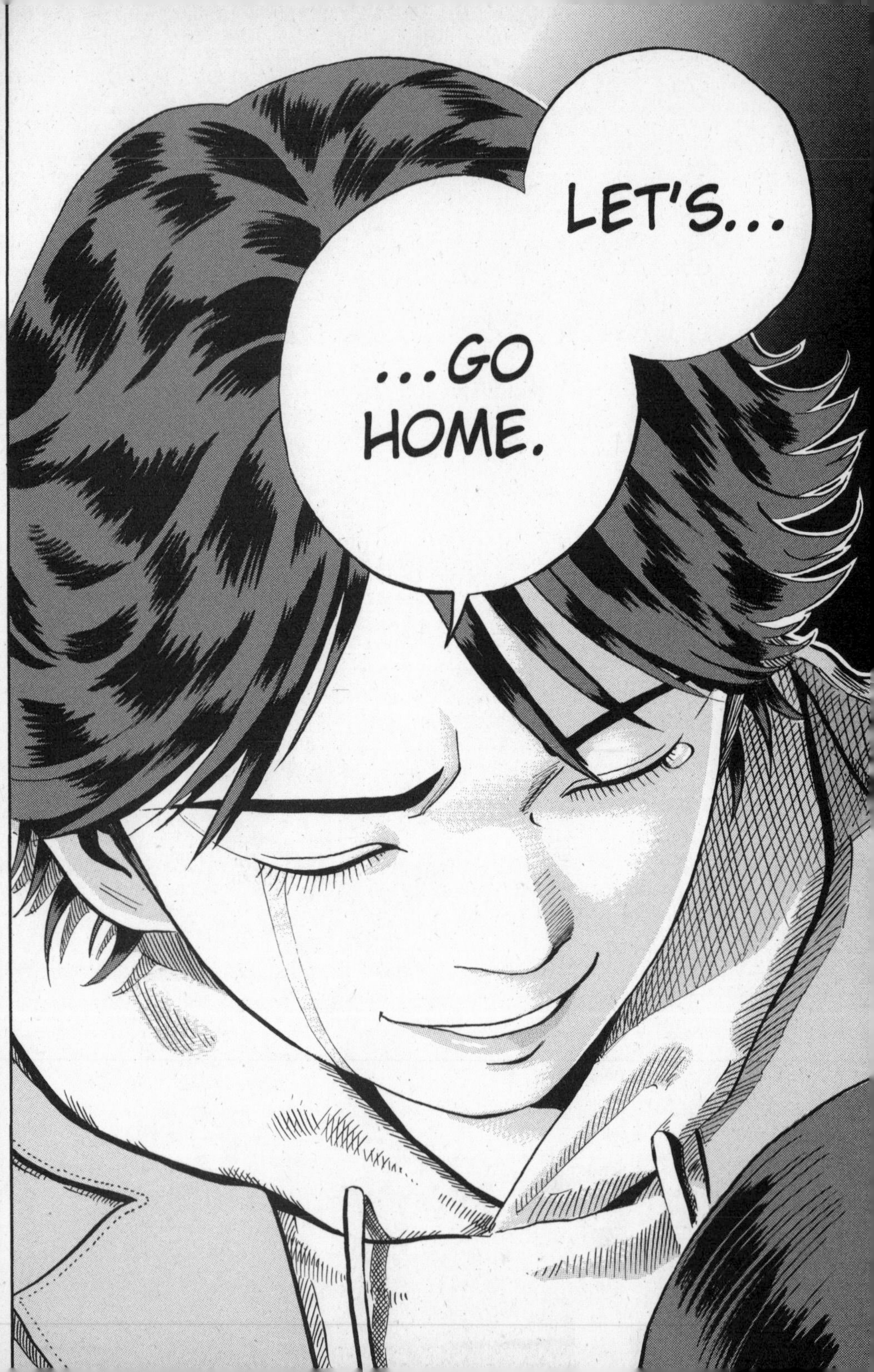
LET'S...
...GO HOME.

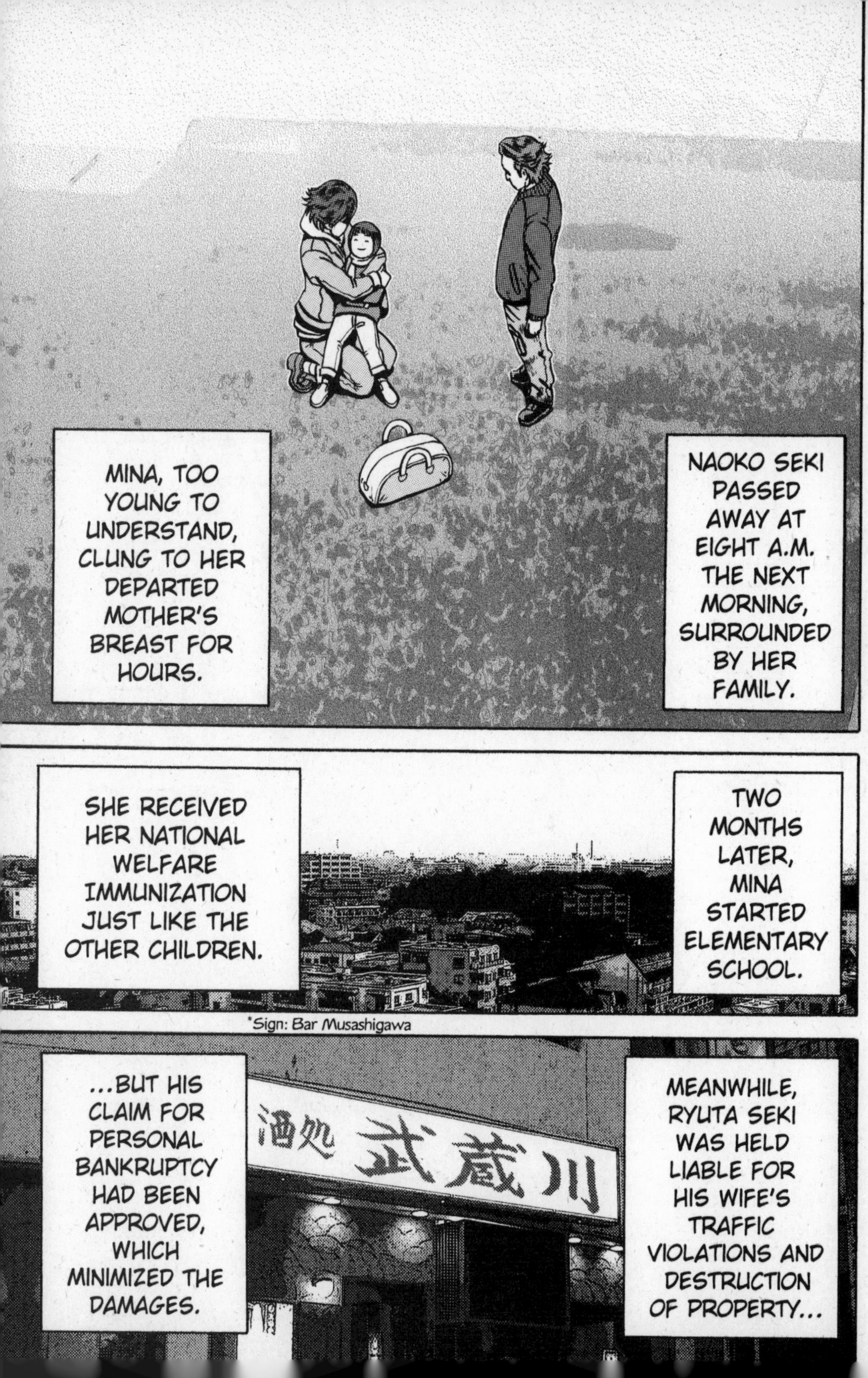
NAOKO SEKI PASSED AWAY AT EIGHT A.M. THE NEXT MORNING, SURROUNDED BY HER FAMILY.
MINA, TOO YOUNG TO UNDERSTAND, CLUNG TO HER DEPARTED MOTHER'S BREAST FOR HOURS.
TWO MONTHS LATER, MINA STARTED ELEMENTARY SCHOOL.
SHE RECEIVED HER NATIONAL WELFARE IMMUNIZATION JUST LIKE THE OTHER CHILDREN.
*Sign: Bar Musashigawa
MEANWHILE, RYUTA SEKI WAS HELD LIABLE FOR HIS WIFE'S TRAFFIC VIOLATIONS AND DESTRUCTION OF PROPERTY...
酒処 武蔵川
...BUT HIS CLAIM FOR PERSONAL BANKRUPTCY HAD BEEN APPROVED, WHICH MINIMIZED THE DAMAGES.

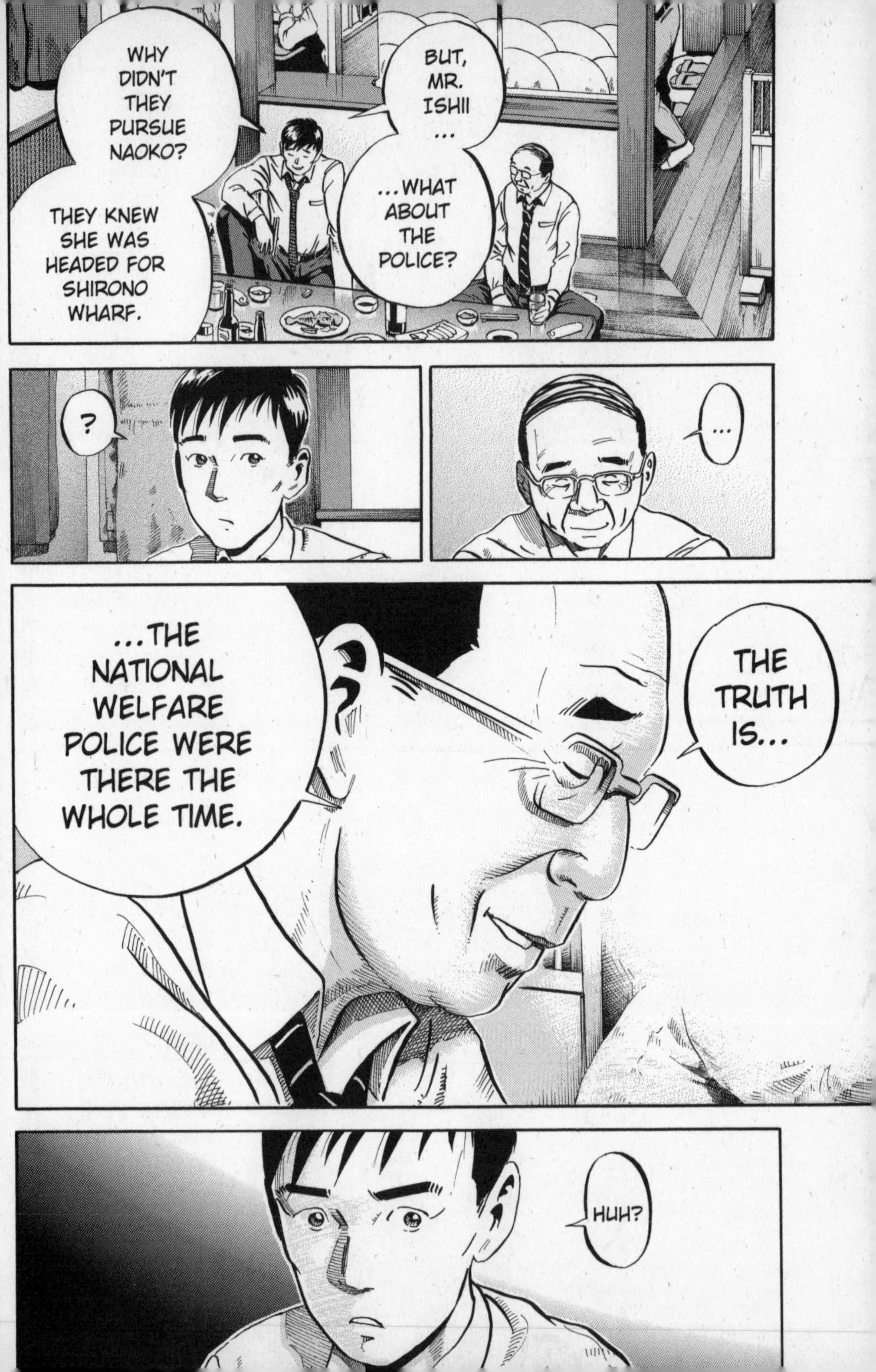
BUT, MR. ISHII...
...WHAT ABOUT THE POLICE?
WHY DIDN'T THEY PURSUE NAOKO?
THEY KNEW SHE WAS HEADED FOR SHIRONO WHARF.
...
?
THE TRUTH IS...
...THE NATIONAL WELFARE POLICE WERE THERE THE WHOLE TIME.
HUH?

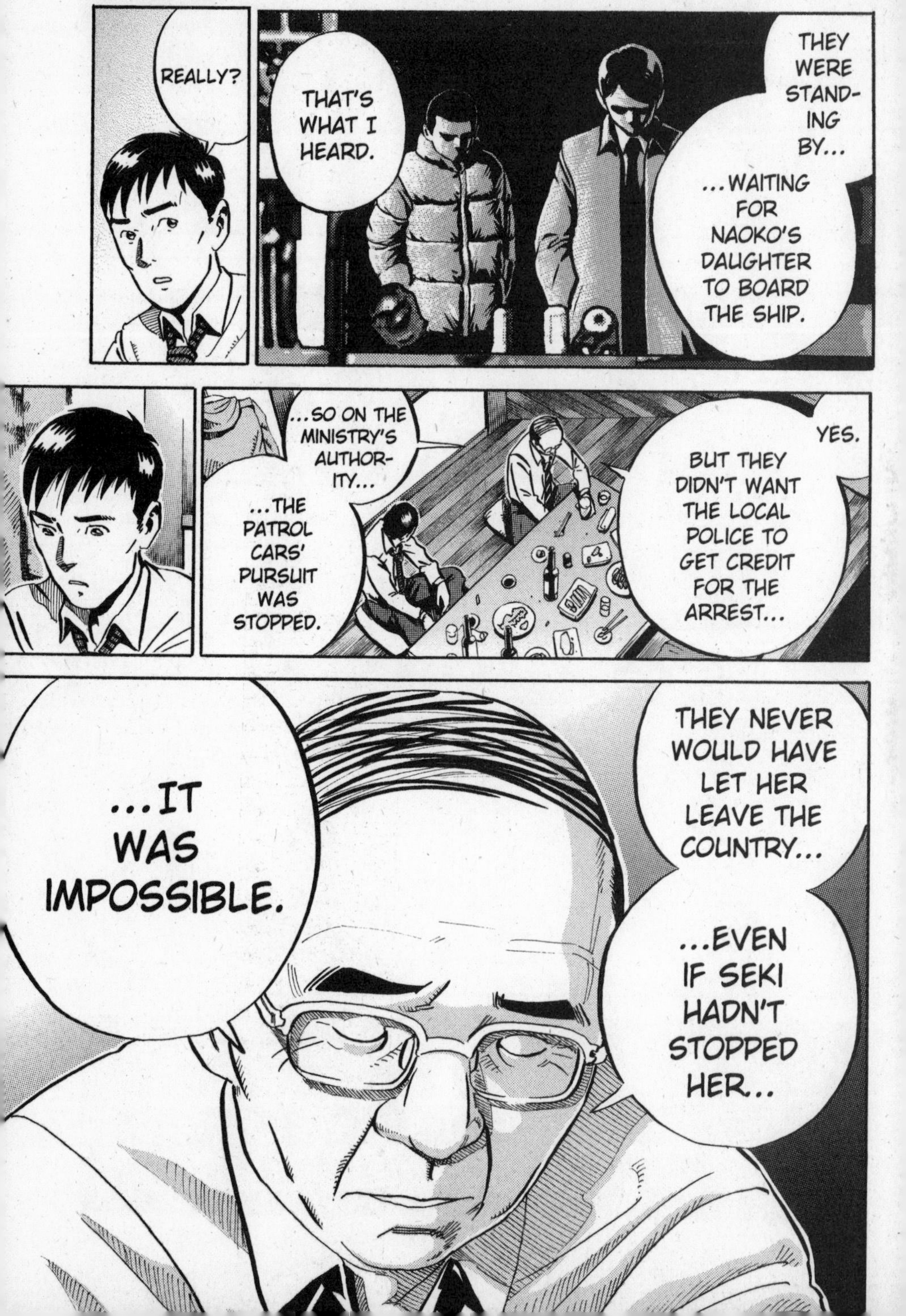
THEY WERE STANDING-ING BY...
...WAITING FOR NAOKO'S DAUGHTER TO BOARD THE SHIP.
THAT'S WHAT I HEARD.
REALLY?
YES.
BUT THEY DIDN'T WANT THE LOCAL POLICE TO GET CREDIT FOR THE ARREST...
...SO ON THE MINISTRY'S AUTHOR-ITY...
...THE PATROL CARS' PURSUIT WAS STOPPED.
THEY NEVER WOULD HAVE LET HER LEAVE THE COUNTRY...
...EVEN IF SEKI HADN'T STOPPED HER...
...IT WAS IMPOSSIBLE.

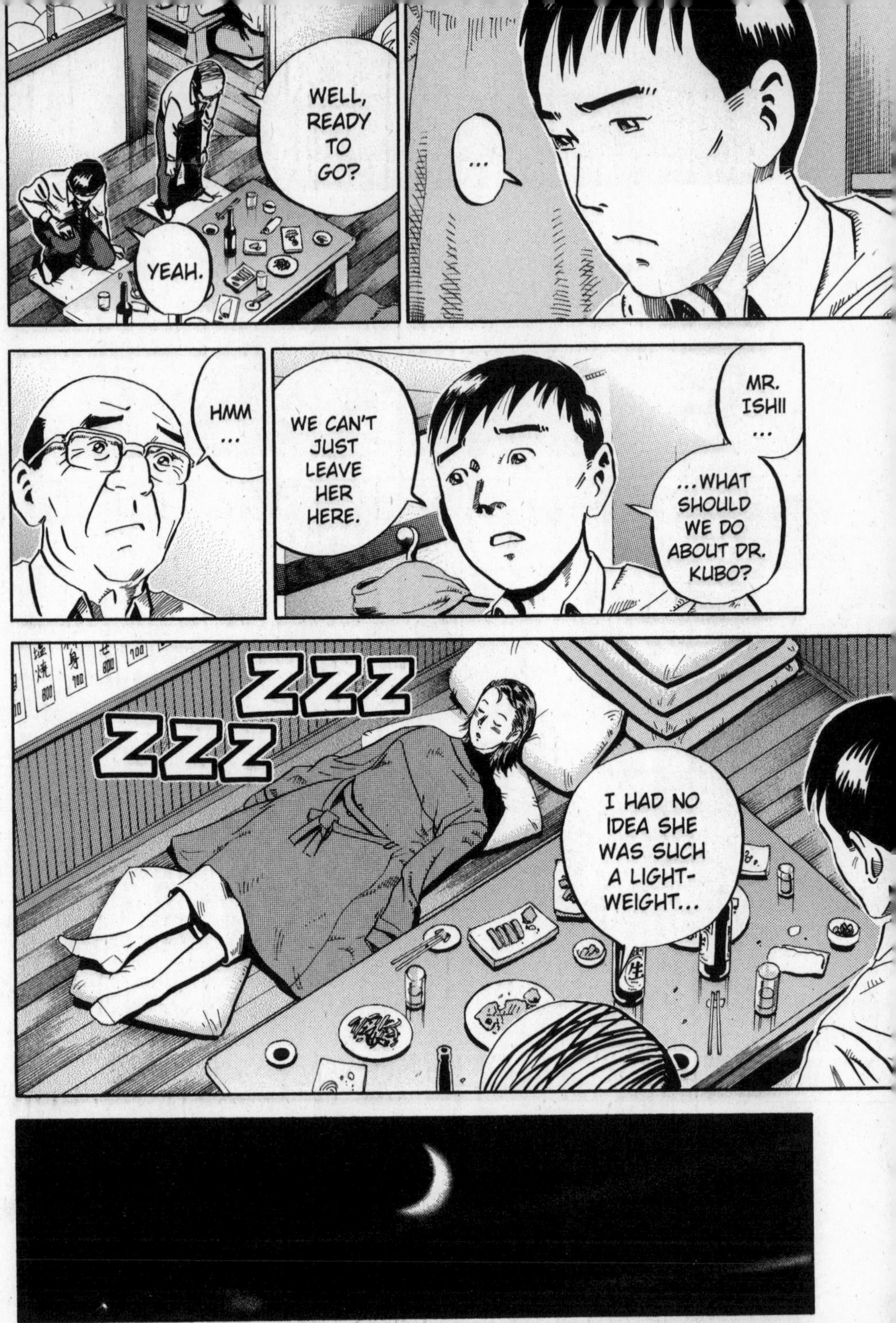
...
WELL, READY TO GO?
YEAH.
MR. ISHII ...
...WHAT SHOULD WE DO ABOUT DR. KUBO?
WE CAN'T JUST LEAVE HER HERE.
HMM ...
ZZZ
ZZZ
I HAD NO IDEA SHE WAS SUCH A LIGHT-WEIGHT...

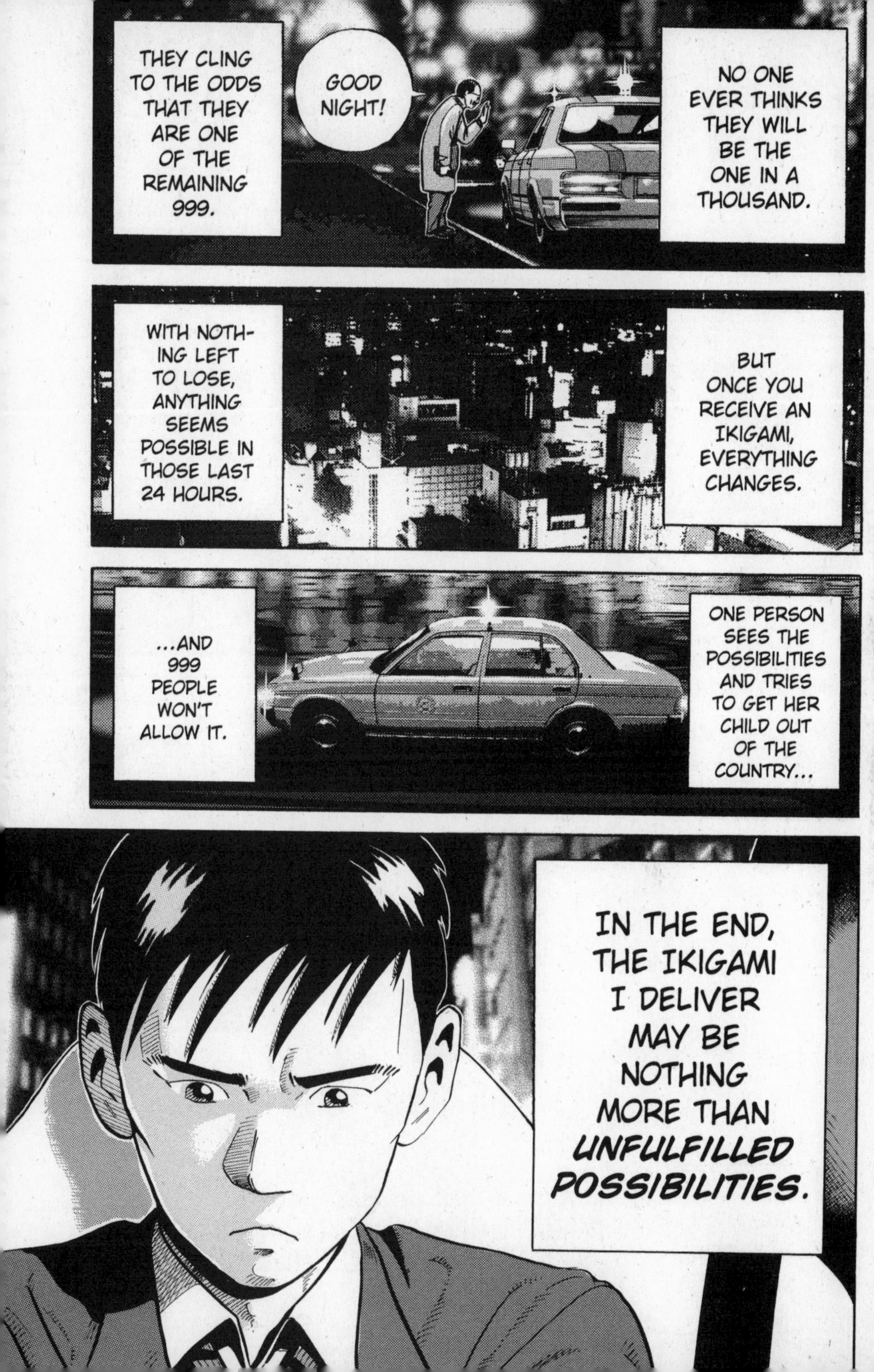
NO ONE EVER THINKS THEY WILL BE THE ONE IN A THOUSAND.
GOOD NIGHT!
THEY CLING TO THE ODDS THAT THEY ARE ONE OF THE REMAINING 999.
BUT ONCE YOU RECEIVE AN IKIGAMI, EVERYTHING CHANGES.
WITH NOTHING LEFT TO LOSE, ANYTHING SEEMS POSSIBLE IN THOSE LAST 24 HOURS.
ONE PERSON SEES THE POSSIBILITIES AND TRIES TO GET HER CHILD OUT OF THE COUNTRY...
...AND 999 PEOPLE WON'T ALLOW IT.
IN THE END, THE IKIGAMI I DELIVER MAY BE NOTHING MORE THAN *UNFULFILLED POSSIBILITIES*.

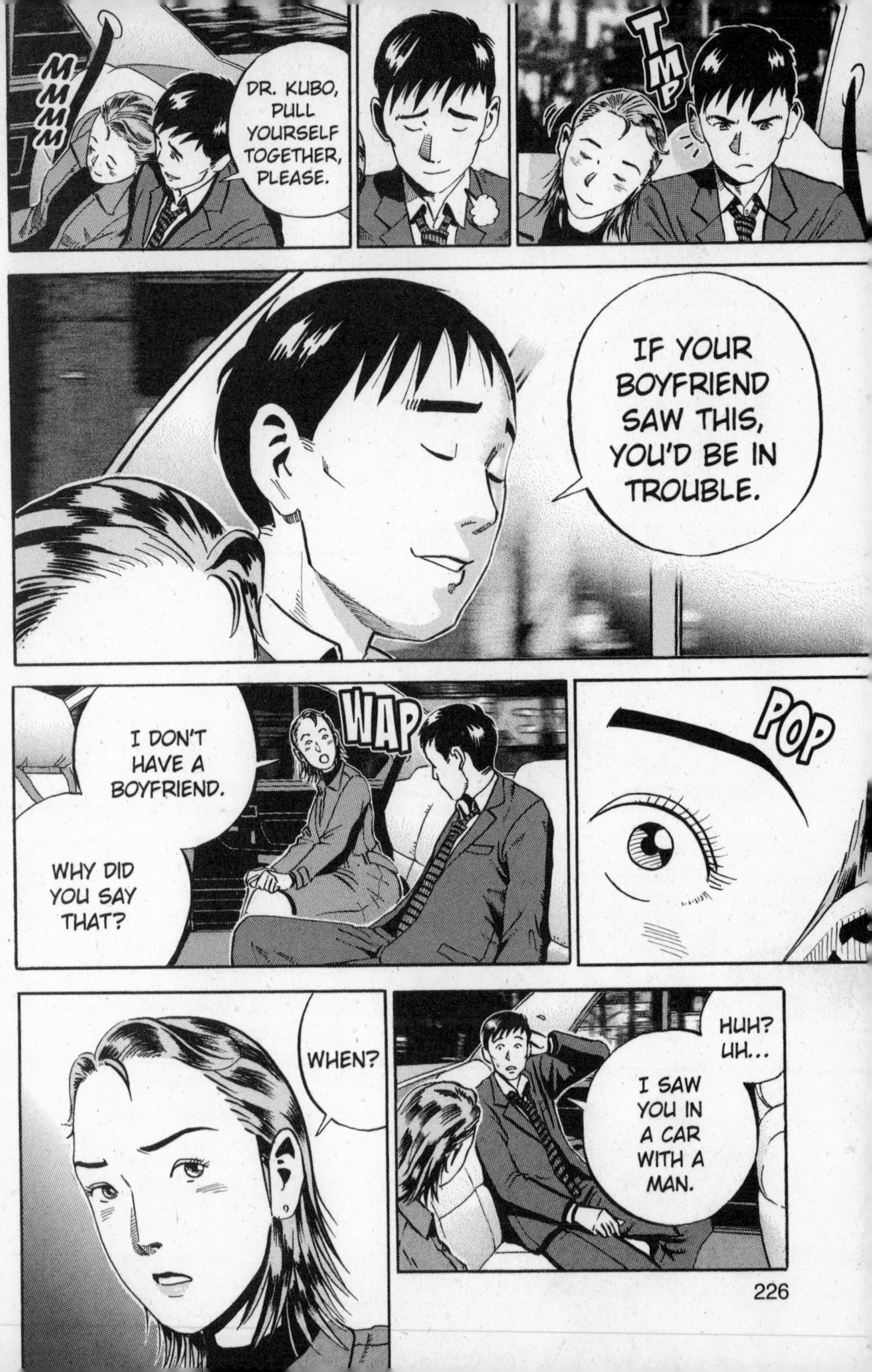
TMP
DR. KUBO, PULL YOURSELF TOGETHER, PLEASE.
MMMM
IF YOUR BOYFRIEND SAW THIS, YOU'D BE IN TROUBLE.
POP
WAP
I DON'T HAVE A BOYFRIEND.
WHY DID YOU SAY THAT?
HUH? UH...
I SAW YOU IN A CAR WITH A MAN.
WHEN?

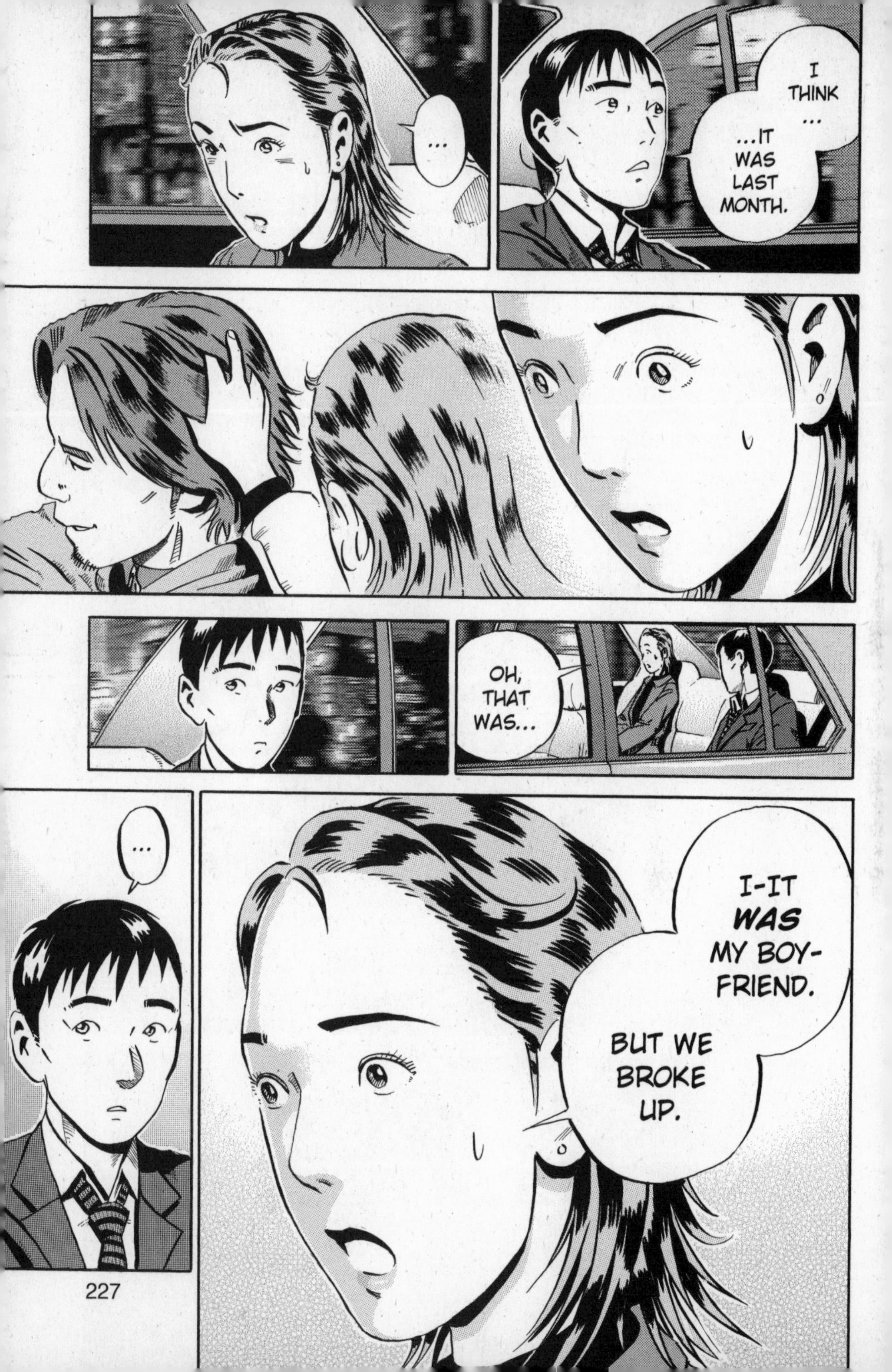
I THINK ...
...IT WAS LAST MONTH.
...
OH, THAT WAS...
I-IT ***WAS*** MY BOY-FRIEND.
BUT WE BROKE UP.
...

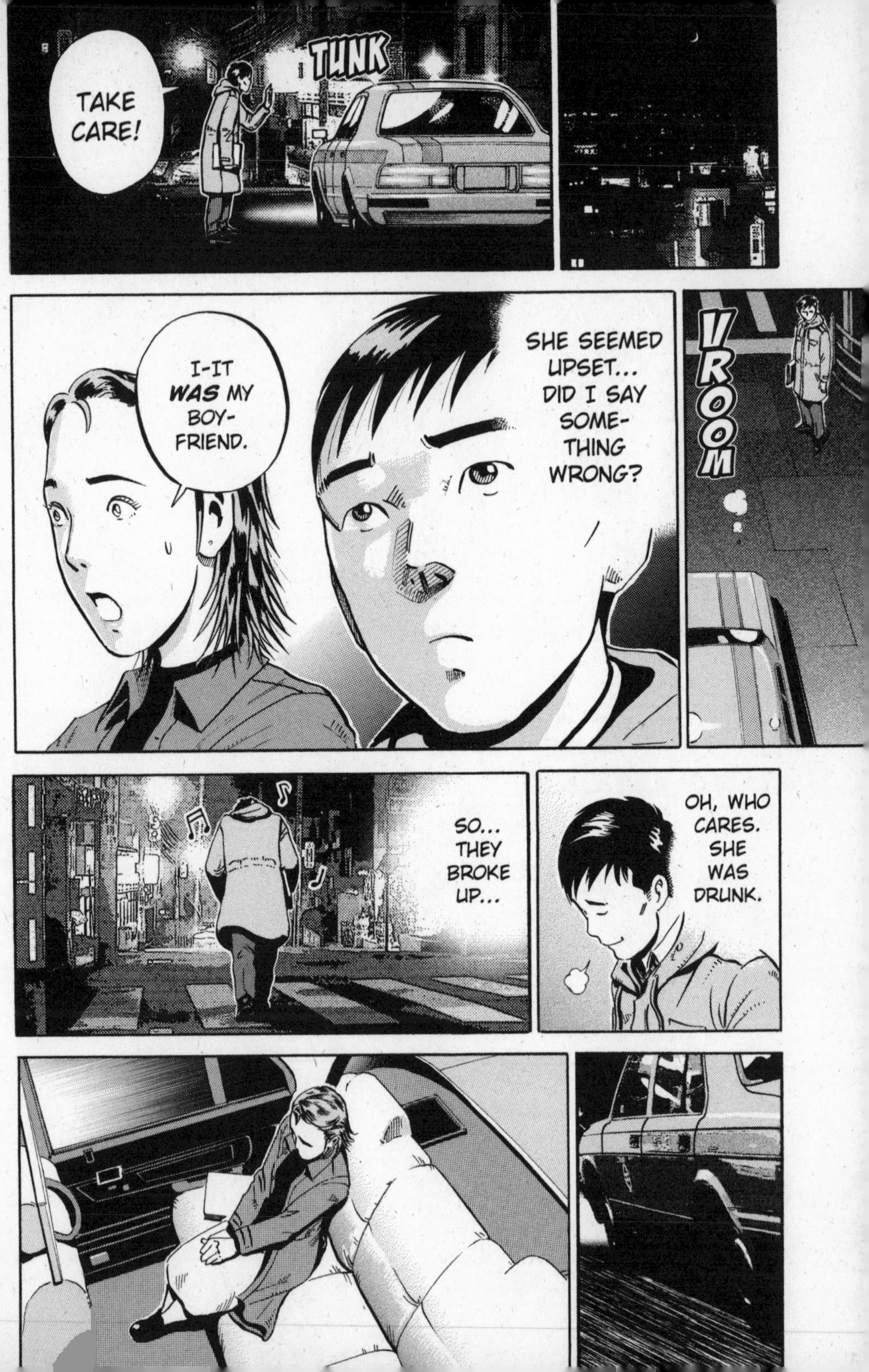
TUNK
TAKE CARE!
VROOM
SHE SEEMED UPSET... DID I SAY SOME-THING WRONG?
I-IT *WAS* MY BOY-FRIEND.
OH, WHO CARES. SHE WAS DRUNK.
SO... THEY BROKE UP...

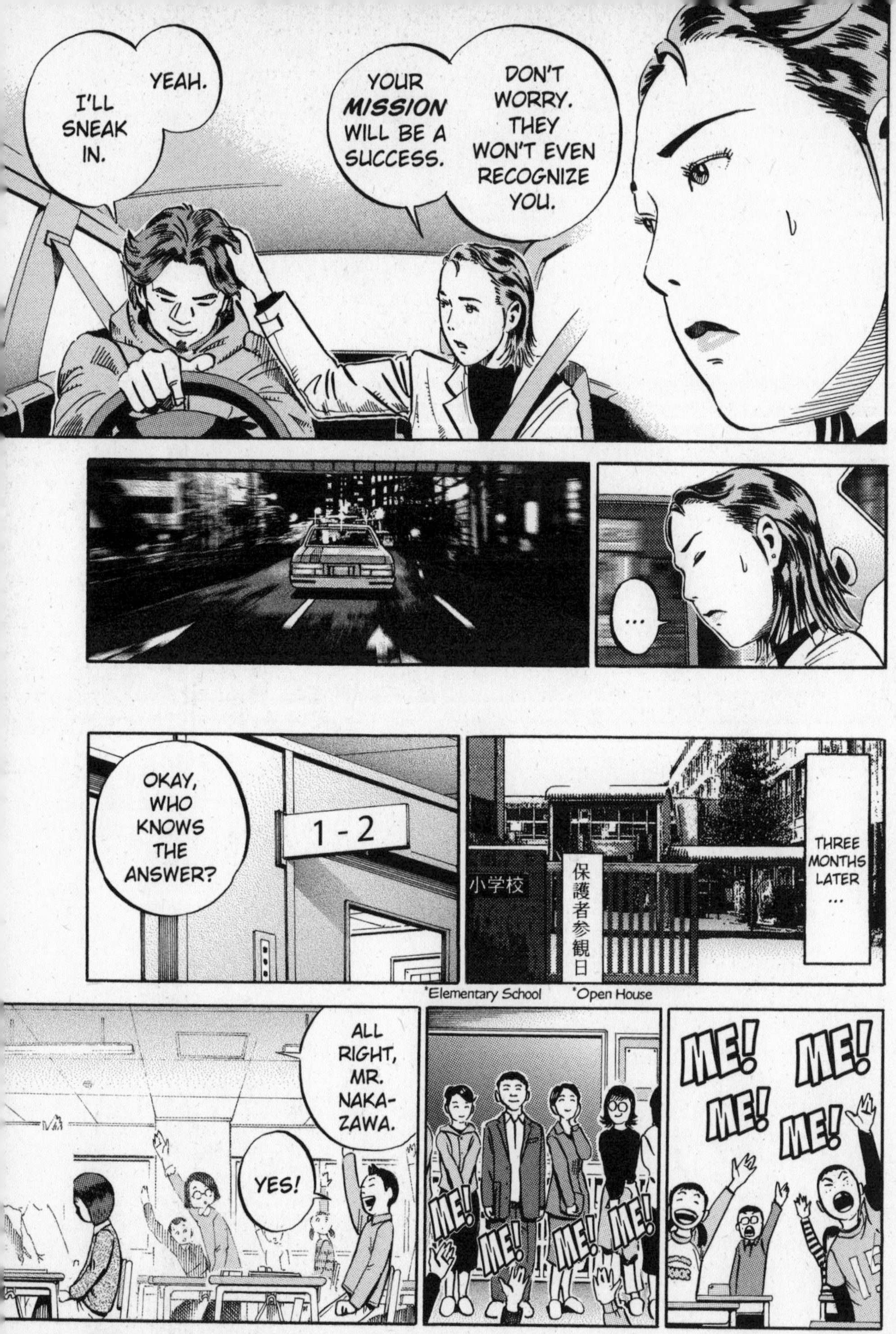
DON'T WORRY. THEY WON'T EVEN RECOGNIZE YOU.
YOUR *MISSION* WILL BE A SUCCESS.
YEAH.
I'LL SNEAK IN.
...
THREE MONTHS LATER ...
保護者参観日
小学校
1 - 2
OKAY, WHO KNOWS THE ANSWER?
*Elementary School
*Open House
ME!
ME!
ME!
ME!
ME!
ME!
ME!
ME!
ALL RIGHT, MR. NAKA-ZAWA.
YES!

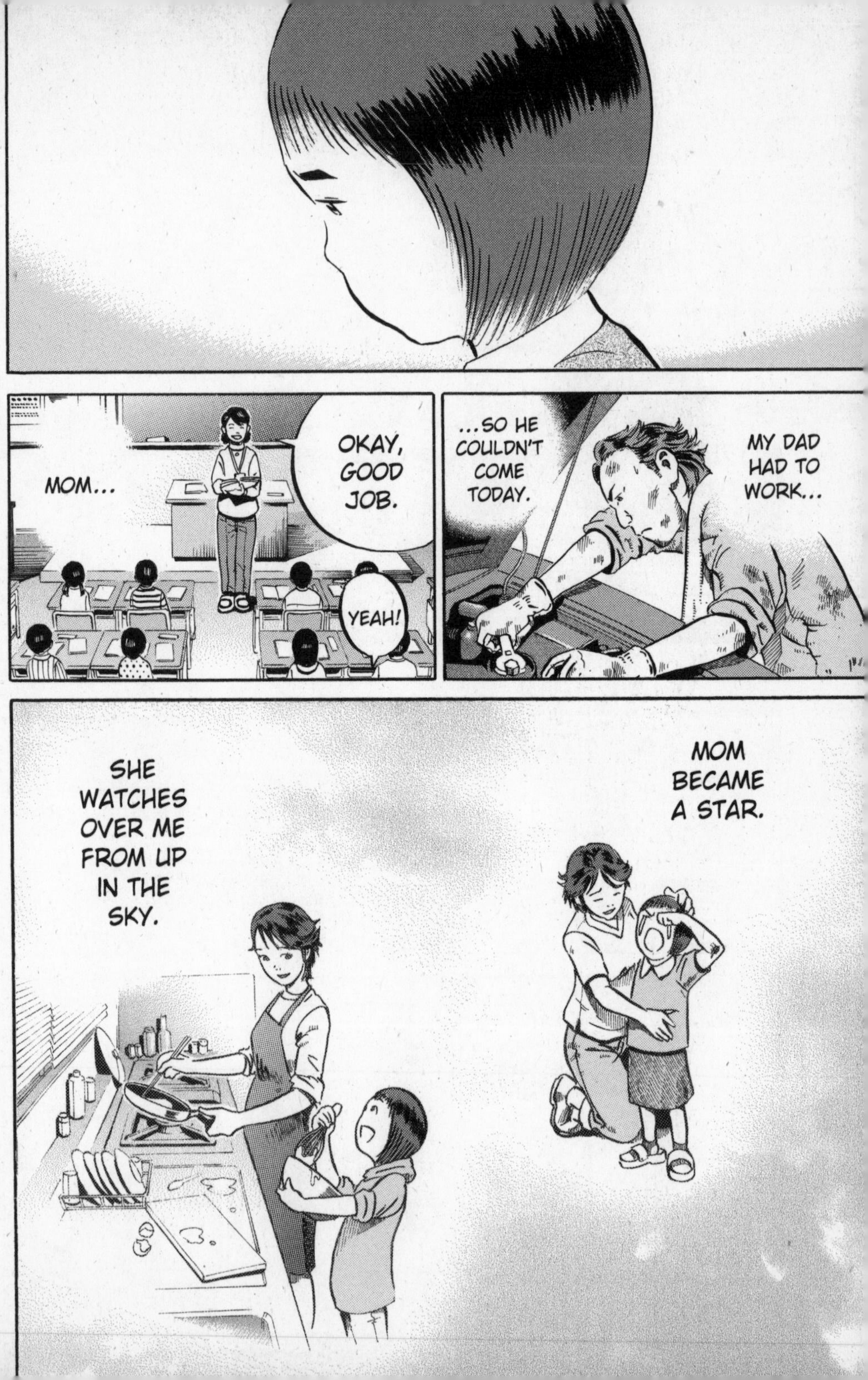
MY DAD HAD TO WORK...
...SO HE COULDN'T COME TODAY.
OKAY, GOOD JOB.
MOM...
YEAH!
MOM BECAME A STAR.
SHE WATCHES OVER ME FROM UP IN THE SKY.

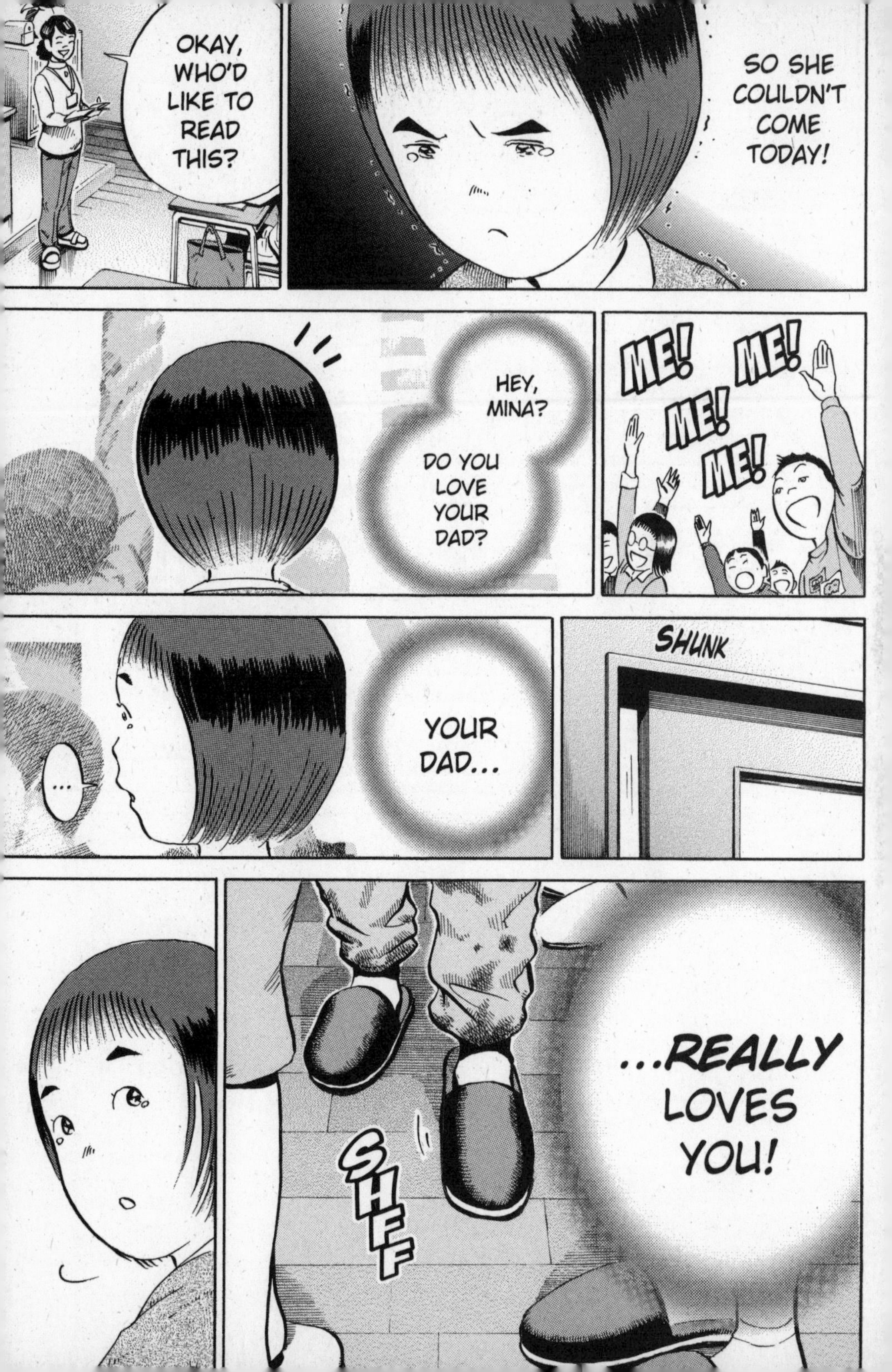
SO SHE COULDN'T COME TODAY!
OKAY, WHO'D LIKE TO READ THIS?
ME!
ME!
ME!
ME!
HEY, MINA?
DO YOU LOVE YOUR DAD?
SHUNK
YOUR DAD...
...
...REALLY LOVES YOU!
SHFF

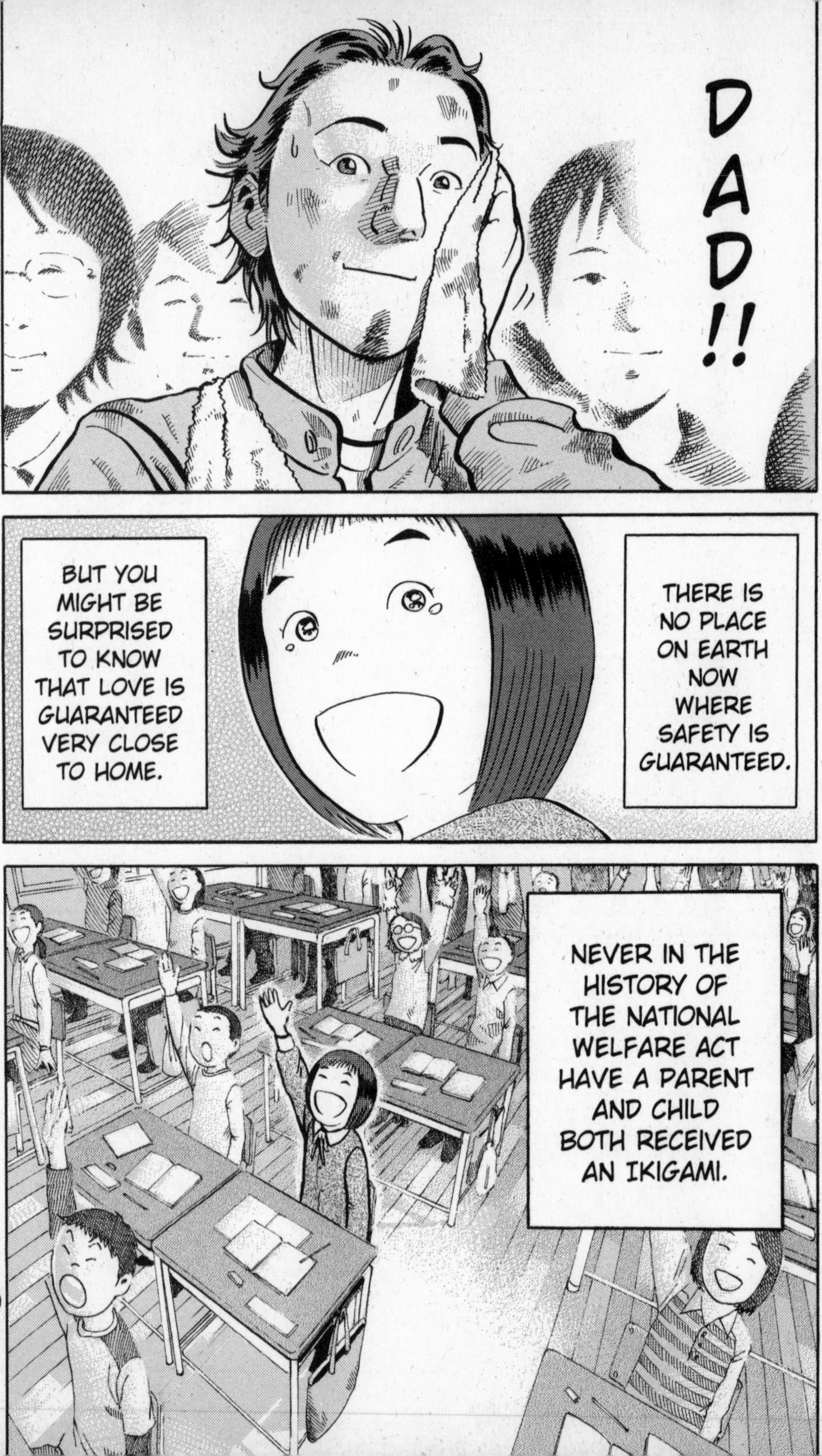
DAD!!
THERE IS NO PLACE ON EARTH NOW WHERE SAFETY IS GUARANTEED.
BUT YOU MIGHT BE SURPRISED TO KNOW THAT LOVE IS GUARANTEED VERY CLOSE TO HOME.
NEVER IN THE HISTORY OF THE NATIONAL WELFARE ACT HAVE A PARENT AND CHILD BOTH RECEIVED AN IKIGAMI.

Ikigami 4 / The End

ARE *YOU* NEXT?

IKIGAMI

THE ULTIMATE LIMIT

VOL. **5**

Featuring Episodes 9 *The Writing on the Wall* & 10 *Honor and Duty*!

Motoro Mase was born in Aichi in Japan
in 1969 and is also the artist of *Kyoichi*
and, with Keigo Higashino, *HEⱯDS*,
which, like *Ikigami*, was serialized in
Young Sunday. In 1998, Mase's *AREA*
was nominated for Shogakukan's 43rd
grand prize for a comic by a new artist.

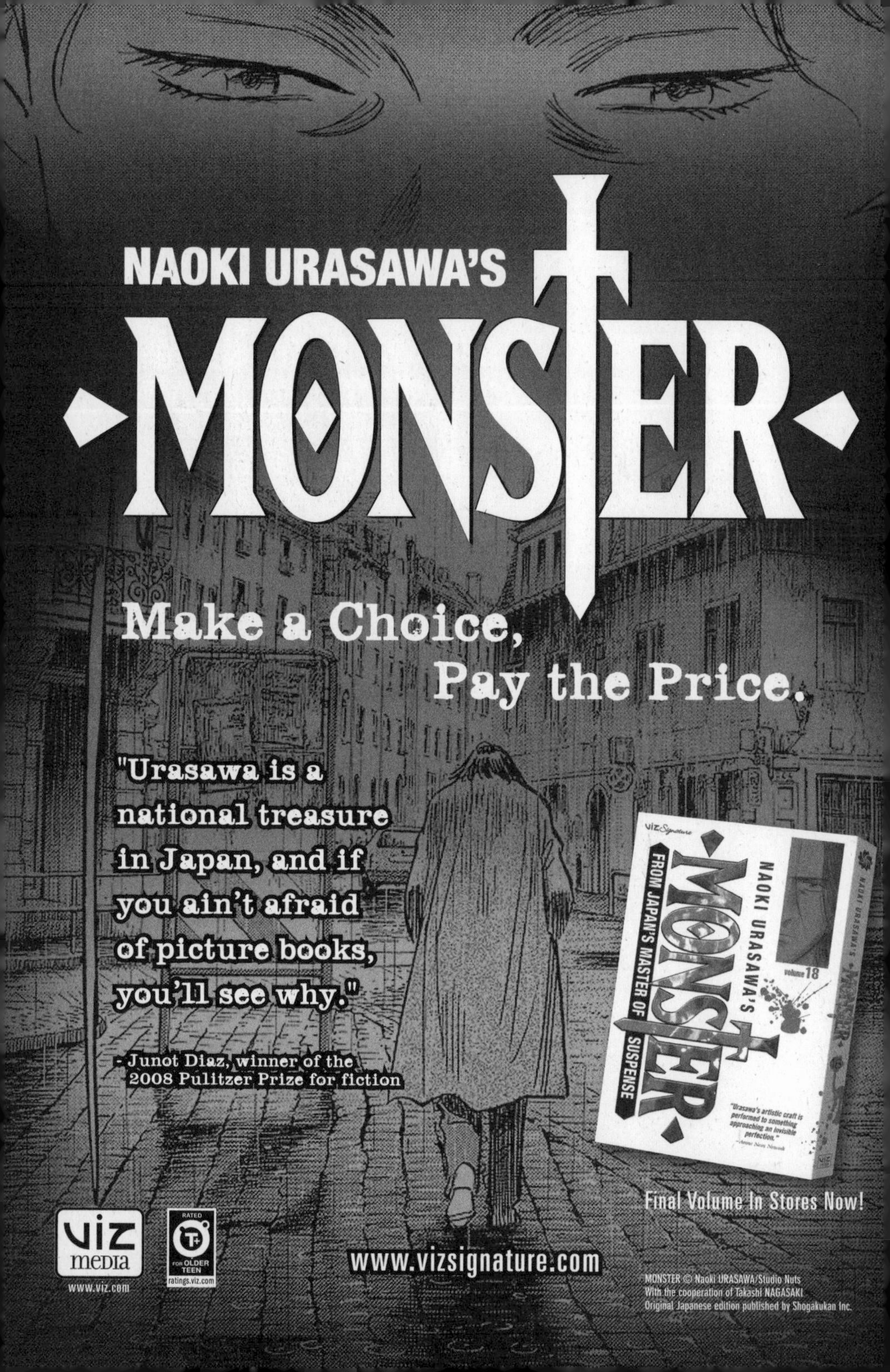
NAOKI URASAWA'S
MONSTER
Make a Choice,
Pay the Price.
"Urasawa is a national treasure in Japan, and if you ain't afraid of picture books, you'll see why."
- Junot Diaz, winner of the 2008 Pulitzer Prize for fiction
NAOKI URASAWA'S MONSTER
FROM JAPAN'S MASTER OF SUSPENSE
volume 18
"Urasawa's artistic craft is performed to something approaching an invisible perfection."
Final Volume In Stores Now!
VIZ MEDIA
www.viz.com
RATED T+ FOR OLDER TEEN
ratings.viz.com
www.vizsignature.com
MONSTER © Naoki URASAWA/Studio Nuts
With the cooperation of Takashi NAGASAKI
Original Japanese edition published by Shogakukan Inc.

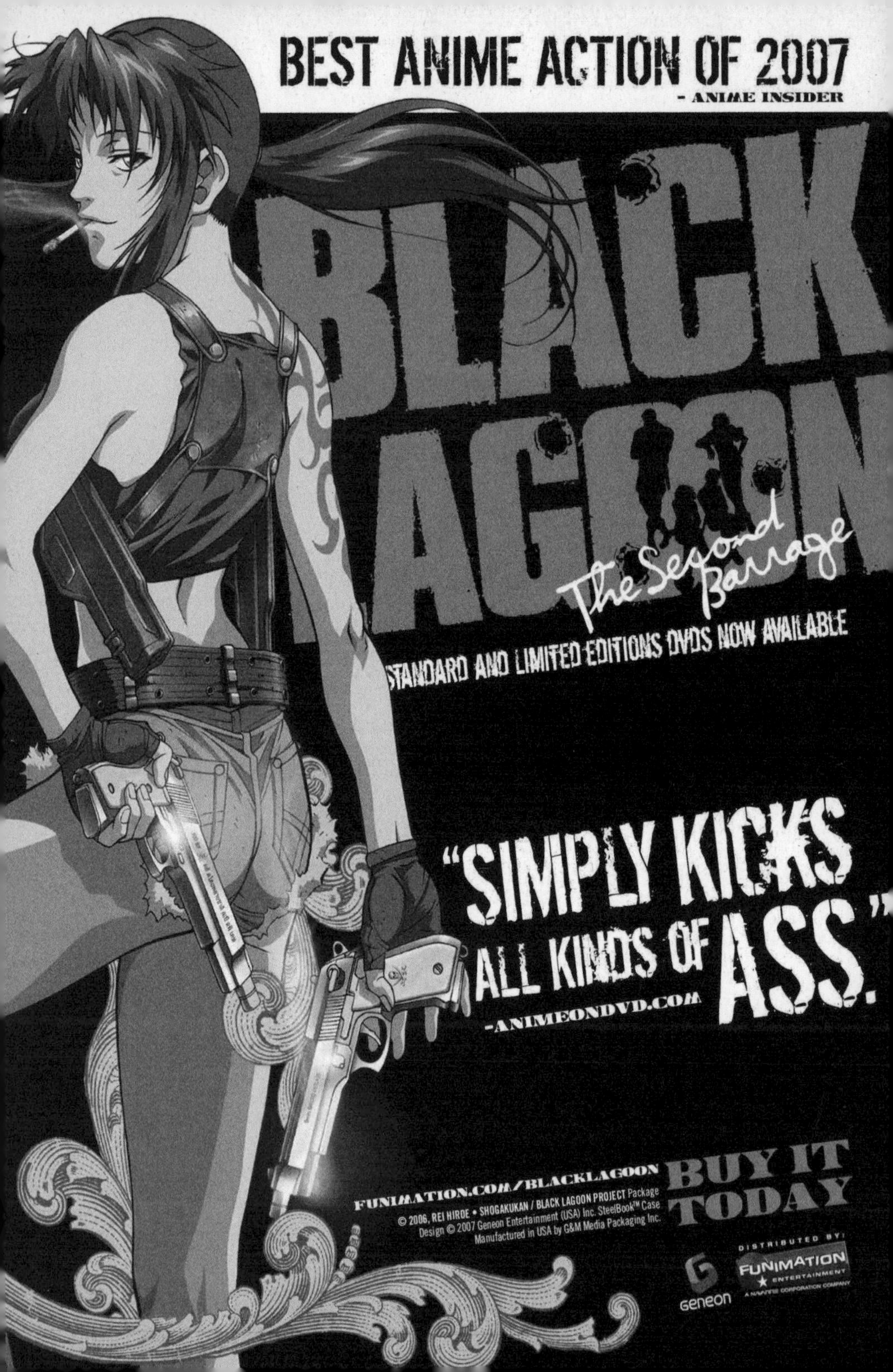
BEST ANIME ACTION OF 2007
- ANIME INSIDER
BLACK LAGOON
The Second Barrage
STANDARD AND LIMITED EDITIONS DVDS NOW AVAILABLE
"SIMPLY KICKS ALL KINDS OF ASS."
-ANIMEONDVD.COM
FUNIMATION.COM/BLACKLAGOON
BUY IT TODAY
© 2006, REI HIROE • SHOGAKUKAN / BLACK LAGOON PROJECT Package Design © 2007 Geneon Entertainment (USA) Inc. SteelBook™ Case Manufactured in USA by G&M Media Packaging Inc.
Geneon
DISTRIBUTED BY:
FUNIMATION ENTERTAINMENT
A NAVARRE CORPORATION COMPANY

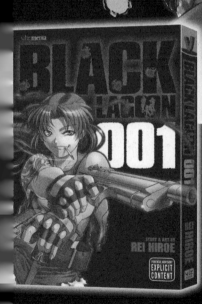

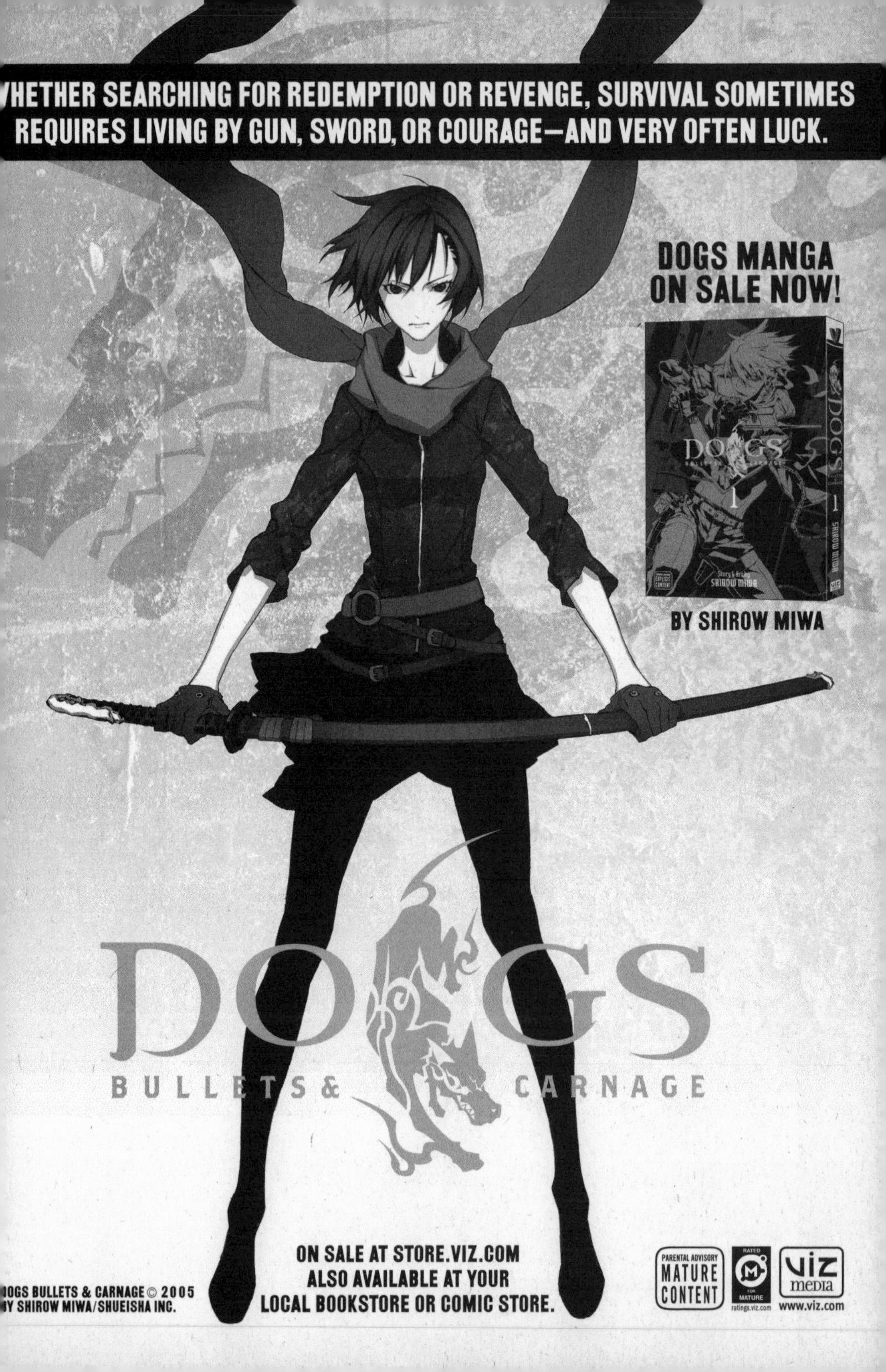
WHETHER SEARCHING FOR REDEMPTION OR REVENGE, SURVIVAL SOMETIMES REQUIRES LIVING BY GUN, SWORD, OR COURAGE—AND VERY OFTEN LUCK.
DOGS MANGA ON SALE NOW!
BY SHIROW MIWA
DOGS
BULLETS & CARNAGE
ON SALE AT STORE.VIZ.COM
ALSO AVAILABLE AT YOUR
LOCAL BOOKSTORE OR COMIC STORE.
DOGS BULLETS & CARNAGE © 2005
BY SHIROW MIWA/SHUEISHA INC.
PARENTAL ADVISORY
MATURE CONTENT
RATED M FOR MATURE
ratings.viz.com
VIZ media
www.viz.com

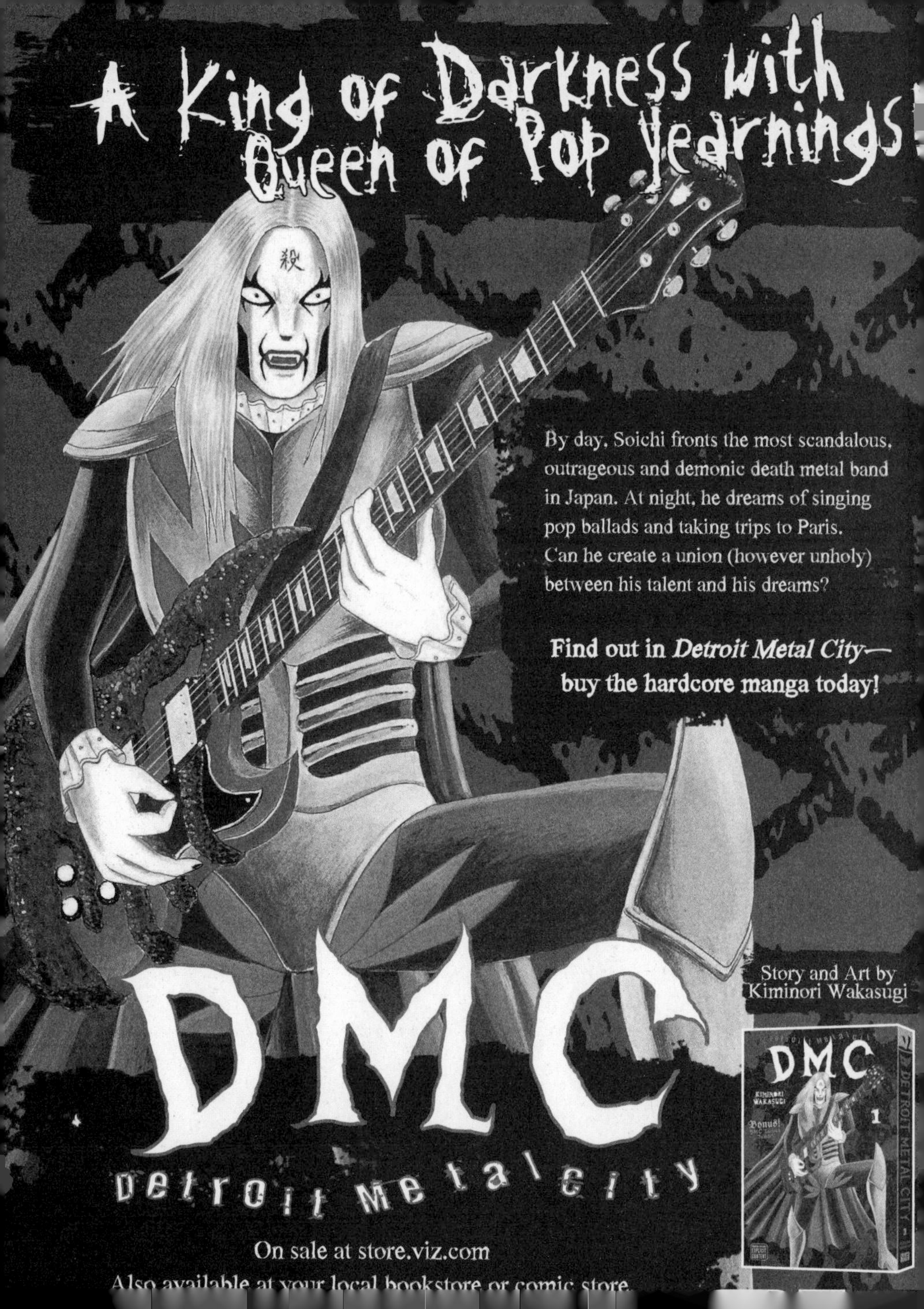
A King of Darkness with Queen of Pop Yearnings!
By day, Soichi fronts the most scandalous, outrageous and demonic death metal band in Japan. At night, he dreams of singing pop ballads and taking trips to Paris. Can he create a union (however unholy) between his talent and his dreams?
Find out in Detroit Metal City—buy the hardcore manga today!
Story and Art by Kiminori Wakasugi
DMC
Detroit Metal City
On sale at store.viz.com
Also available at your local bookstore or comic store.

LOVE MANGA?
LET US KNOW WHAT YOU THINK!

OUR MANGA SURVEY IS NOW
AVAILABLE ONLINE. PLEASE VISIT:
VIZ.COM/MANGASURVEY

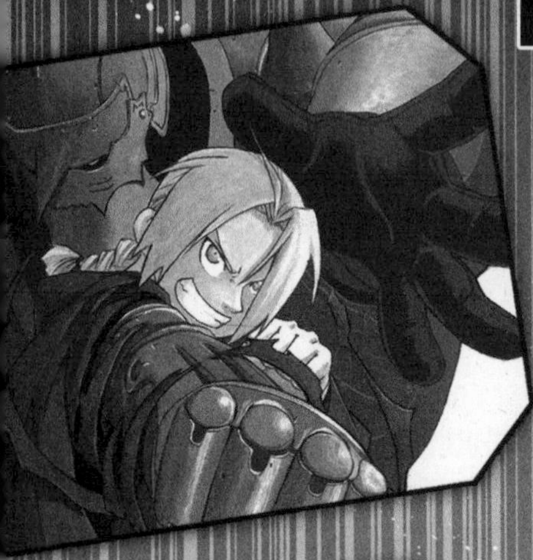
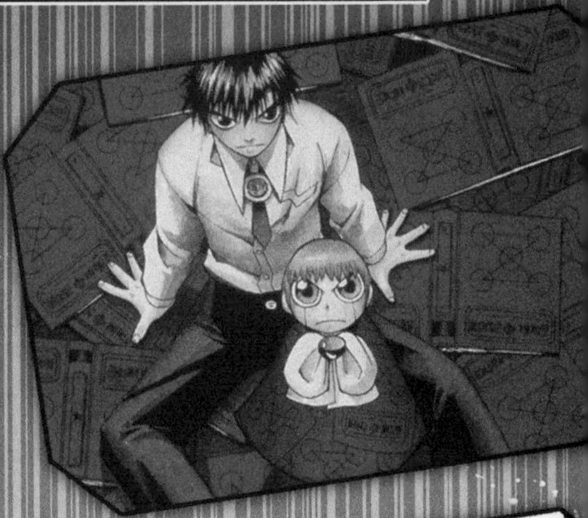
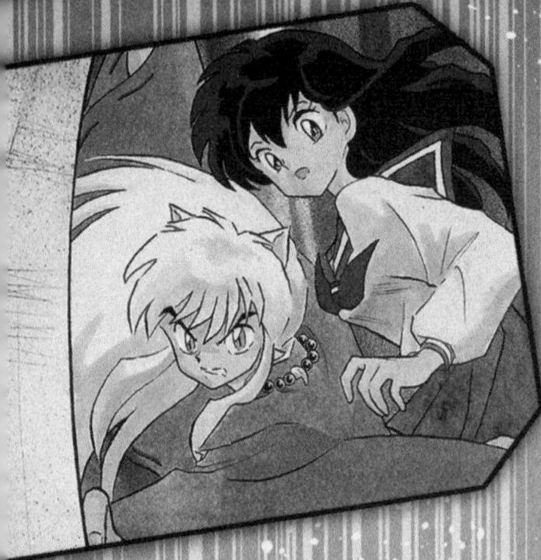
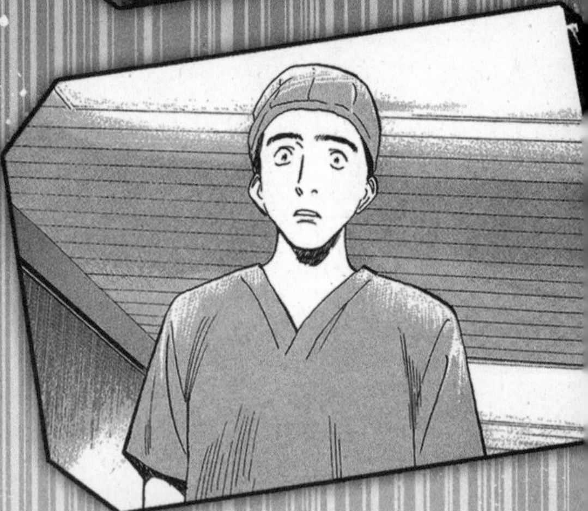

HELP US MAKE THE MANGA